BEYOND REALISM

'Robert Singer's *Beyond Realism: Naturalist Film in Theory and Practice* is a breathtakingly comprehensive and insightful investigation of naturalist themes in film. From Lumière *actualités* to the latest examples of international cinema, each chapter focuses on a separate facet of "naturalism's grinding tradition" and its themes of violence, degradation, disease, and the tension between the human spirit and naturalism's relentless assault on the body.'

Professor Donna M. Campbell, author of *Bitter Tastes: Literary Naturalism and Early Cinema in American Women's Writing*

'Robert Singer's *Beyond Realism: Naturalist Film in Theory and Practice* is a comprehensive guide to naturalistic film; Singer has been the leading global expert on this topic for many years. His book is a life's work. He is able to move from the dark corners and sharp bright angles of early film to similar naturalist concerns in cinema today: social struggle, poverty, homelessness, violence, injustice, the naturalistic body, psychological conflicts and many other features. It's an erudite but engaging read and a must for any naturalist or film student.'

Jeanne Campbell Reesman, Professor Emerita, University of Texas at San Antonio

'*Beyond Realism: Naturalist Film in Theory and Practice* is a treatise on naturalist themes and the moving image, a platform of continuous intertextual references. With this book, Singer takes us on a fascinating (inter)national journey of theories, genres and themes dedicated to the naturalist film, while also presenting a renewed vision of ourselves and our bodies as spectacles.'

José Duarte, Film Studies Professor at the School of Arts and Humanities, ULisboa.

BEYOND REALISM
Naturalist Film in Theory and Practice

Robert Singer

EDINBURGH
University Press

Edinburgh University Press is one of the leading university presses in the UK. We publish academic books and journals in our selected subject areas across the humanities and social sciences, combining cutting-edge scholarship with high editorial and production values to produce academic works of lasting importance. For more information visit our website: edinburghuniversitypress.com

© Robert Singer, 2024, 2025

Grateful acknowledgment is made to the sources listed in the List of Illustrations for permission to reproduce material previously published elsewhere. Every effort has been made to trace the copyright holders, but if any have been inadvertently overlooked, the publisher will be pleased to make the necessary arrangements at the first opportunity.

Edinburgh University Press Ltd
13 Infirmary Street
Edinburgh EH1 1LT

First published in hardback by Edinburgh University Press 2024

Typeset in 10/12.5 pt Sabon by
Cheshire Typesetting Ltd, Cuddington, Cheshire

A CIP record for this book is available from the British Library

ISBN 978 1 4744 2633 6 (hardback)
ISBN 978 1 4744 2634 3 (paperback)
ISBN 978 1 4744 2635 0 (webready PDF)
ISBN 978 1 4744 2636 7 (epub)

The right of Robert Singer to be identified as the author of this work has been asserted in accordance with the Copyright, Designs and Patents Act 1988, and the Copyright and Related Rights Regulations 2003 (SI No. 2498).

CONTENTS

List of Figures	viii
Acknowledgments	ix

1. Introduction — 1
   Qu'est-ce que le cinéma naturaliste? — 3
   Historical Spaces — 4
   Naturalist Threads — 7
   Chloé Zhao's Reclaimed West — 9

2. Naturalist Tropes — 13
   Experimental Advances — 13
   From Sea to Seen: Realism to Naturalism — 14
   Images in Motion — 20
   Fault Lines — 23
   'Roid Rage — 30
   Syphilis hereditaria tarda — 33

3. Operative Spaces — 43
   A Productive Species — 45
   Invisibility Observed — 48
   Factory Life — 52
   The Daily Exploited — 56
   Mining as Menace — 60

BEYOND REALISM

	More Invisible	67
	Bottles and Bipeds	71
4.	The Body Politic	79
	For Sale	79
	Covert Labor	82
	Grinding Streets	91
	Brothels/Factories	96
5.	Fleshy Imagery	106
	Sharp Blades	106
	Porcine Desire	108
	Abattoir	110
	Parts of the Whole	117
	The Morgue	124
	Broken Up	132
6.	Darwinian Disconnections	138
	Growth Signs	138
	Gene Pool	140
	Imperfect Beings	145
	Growing Up	150
	Family Portraits	155
	Almost Human	160
	Early Sightings	165
7.	Moreau Narratives	177
	Beastly Derivations	177
	Dark Hearts	179
	Lost Cities	181
	Isolationism	191
	Beyond Moreau	197
	Imprisonments	198
8.	Naturalist Comedy	211
	Painfully Funny	211
	Charlie's Labors	212
	Celebrating Idiots	215
	Bell Ringing	220
9.	A Joker's World	228
	Unreal City	228
	Clown Time	228
	Weighty Issues	230

Criminaloids	236
Disorders	239
Performing Artist	246
Coda	251
Index	255

FIGURES

1.1	André Antoine's *La Terre*	5
2.1	Jean Renoir's *La Bête humaine*	22
2.2	Roy Calnek's *Ten Nights in a Bar-Room*	24
2.3	Robert Aldrich's *What Ever Happened to Baby Jane?*	26
2.4	George Nichols' *Ghosts*	38
3.1	Ousmane Sembène's *Borom Sarret*	51
4.1	Wu Yonggang's *The Goddess*	87
5.1	Tobe Hooper's *Texas Chain Saw Massacre*	114
5.2	Charles Burnett's *Killer of Sheep*	115
6.1	Mervyn LeRoy's *The Bad Seed*	152
6.2	John S. Robertson's *Dr. Jekyll and Mr. Hyde*	167
7.1	Erle C. Kenton's *The Island of Lost Souls*	184
8.1	Jerry Lewis' *The Bellboy*	224
9.1	Raoul Walsh's *White Heat*	246

ACKNOWLEDGMENTS

I want to express my gratitude to those who have helped me to create this volume. This includes the inspirational gifts given to us by Erik Satie, the Lumière brothers, and Lisette Model, among others.

Many have played a vital role in the development of this volume, whether aware of this or not. Colleagues at the City University of New York, especially Joe Dauben, Jerry Carlson, Enid Stubin, and Frank Percaccio, all merit special expressions of gratitude. I also include the strong support from librarians across the City University of New York and others working at the New York Public Library at Lincoln Center and the 42nd Street branch, as well as the research facilities at the Museum of Modern Art and other cultural venues.

Courbet, Zola, Engels, and Darwin stimulate the naturalist world, and added to this list would be the works of Gerard Genette, Guy Debord, Roland Barthes, Mikhail Bakhtin, Raymond Williams, and especially Gilles Deleuze, all of whom made this volume possible. Eminent film scholars and critical thinkers have been a consistent intellectual resource, and great inspiration has been drawn from Ian Aitken, Julia Hallam, Margaret Marshment, Jose Van Dijck, Guy Standing, and many others.

I especially thank the Edinburgh University Press. Sam Johnson, the senior assistant editor, has been a wonderful person to work with over the past few years, and nothing would have been possible without the ongoing support of my publisher and dear friend, Gillian Leslie, a true guiding light.

Gary Rhodes, my great friend and colleague, has been a brilliant comet in whose light we all bathe—long may he illuminate the sky with his creativity and critical thinking. There's so much more to do . . .

And Diane Smith, to whom I dedicate this work and all else—nothing would have been possible without your insight, integrity, and intelligence. There is still "none like thee among the dancers."

My wish for my late parents to have seen this book remains an elusive thought.

1. INTRODUCTION

Todd Phillips' *Joker* (2019) is a film about profound male disillusionment, alienated, precariat labor, and urban survival in a predatory landscape and era, a film about the presence and release of a raging, masked human beast, a victim of unknown genetics and serial abuse. Like Joker's predecessor in another narrative of masks/unmasking, self-discovery, and its horrific consequences, Sophocles' *Oedipus Rex*, working-class Arthur Fleck/Joker (Joaquin Phoenix) does not know himself. His whole life has been a crippling lie; his drug-addicted mother adopted him and allowed him to be viciously abused. However, in the classical sense, Arthur Fleck is neither a tragic figure, nor is *Joker* a tragedy. Fleck's "destiny" is not supernaturally fated, but a product of compromised, degenerative mental health, childhood serial abuse, and class bias. This is the universe of naturalist cinema—gods need not apply.

Jose Luis Borges' *Manual de zoología fantástica/The Book of Imaginary Beings* (1957) presents a zoological survey of mythical beasts found in international folklore, including amorous, inebriated Centaurs, vile Harpies, and the enraged Valkyrie, "imaginary beings ... strange creatures conceived through time and space by the human imagination."[1] These fantastic specimens from international cultures are found in the literature of inspired inventiveness, and exist there alone. This study of naturalist cinema would add one more unique creature to the list, the human being of the modern and postmodern era, who is represented in an intertextually based cinematic canvas of historical, aesthetic, and narrative design. Borges suggests such a clinical shift: "Let us pass ... to the zoo whose denizens are not lions but sphinxes and griffons and centaurs. The population of this second zoo should exceed by far the population of the first, since a monster is no more than a combination of parts of real beings, and the possibilities of permutation border on the infinite."[2]

As Borges comments on the imaginary, supernatural dragon, "It is, so to speak, a necessary monster, not an ephemeral or accidental one,"[3] the human being is *the* essential creature, the strange animal inhabiting the naturalist narrative. Naturalist cinema, its intertextual precedents and ongoing formations, provides a close reading of the multifaceted, cinematic image of society, the mob-group, and one man or woman, under the microscopic, observable view of experience as it is lived.

Beyond Realism: Naturalist Film in Theory and Practice details Naturalism's role as a vital signifying presence in international film narrative. Naturalist cinema is defined as a broad aesthetic classification that demonstrates significant intertextual associations, principally with nineteenth-century art, scientific history, technology, and literature, and extending to the present era of the postmodern renewed formulations of society, selfhood(s), and identity. Selections drawn from select classic and contemporary international film and film theory will provide evidence of a templated, intermedial narrative at the core of the naturalist film, a film aesthetic emerging from the modern, largely Western realist tradition beginning in the mid-nineteenth century. As an intertextual nexus of aesthetic, clinical, and historical formation, like a DNA strand, naturalist cinema generates familiar tropes and interrelated narrative criteria.

Among the questions this study will respond to are the following: Is the naturalist film a genre, style, or movement? Are there formal, aesthetic considerations linking representative naturalist film narratives, more than a set of thematic similarities and stylistics that constitute the shot, sequence, and totality of the film in question? Is the naturalist film largely an adaptation of naturalist literature—for example, Émile Zola's novel *La Terre* (1887) adapted in the André Antoine production, *La Terre* (1921)?[4] Are there original naturalist films, not adaptations of pre-existing works like novels, containing naturalist narratives and images unique to and originating in the cinema? How does the naturalist film link intertextually with other artistic forms and interdisciplinary movements such as naturalist literature, painting, photography, philosophy, and science? Is the naturalist film an international and/or national product, as evidenced in select markets and histories? What role does the spectator assume in the shaping of the naturalist film experience, its taxonomy, and its narrative postulates?

From the earliest international silent film productions to the contemporary era of the computer generated "real," the naturalist film aesthetic has thrived and continues to do so, evolving from its determinist philosophical foundation, its quasi-scientific "experimental" methodology, its sources in realist art, literature, and other intermedial foundations into a narrative mode evident in film movements, genre, and forms. This introduction focuses on interrelated case studies of several seminal naturalist tropes to formulate thematic patterns that function like a dynamic genetic process across generic specificities. This chapter is followed by individual chapter analyses of select Auguste and Louis Lumière *actualités*—along with respective case studies—to establish each *actualité* as an evolving, symbolic presence in international naturalist cinema, and examine all their informative tropes and hypertexts. This volume concludes with a close, analytical reading of Phillips' *Joker* as naturalist narrative.

QU'EST-CE QUE LE CINÉMA NATURALISTE?

The naturalist film is predicated on two foundational, intersecting paradigms that configure as one ideological system in an overarching structural paradigm: the scientific and the social experimental narrative. Thomas S. Kuhn suggests the application of such a framework, a structural design that requires more than empirical research and the elaboration of universal constants, a scientific model with related theoretical applications: the conceptual paradigm. According to Kuhn, "In learning a paradigm the scientist acquires theory, methods, and standards together, usually in an inextricable mixture."[5] The clinically suggestive, scientific structures of thought informing Naturalism were enunciated by Naturalism's foundational figure, Émile Zola, in his most theoretical text, *Le Roman experimental/The Experimental Novel* (1880). In this work, Zola invoked the investigative model of experimental research and observation to delineate his narrative praxis, which is mostly an authorial pose, a presumed expository posture.

As Leonard Tancock notes, "one side of Zola burned with zeal for scientific truth at all costs, for a literature based on the laws of physiology, and direct observation of phenomena," which becomes the substance of an experimental process structuring the fictional.[6] But that suggests blank reproduction, "art in mere realism,"[7] a documentation rather than an artistically edifying experience. According to Tancock, "[Zola] was equally convinced that a purely scientific report of observed phenomena can never be art," which owes its value, its *raison d'etre*, to "modifications of objective truth made by the personality of the artist."[8] The ongoing dialectical process of the agencies of observation and temperament make the artistic product genuine, an experimental methodology. Zola was an active reader of scientific culture and inculcated progressive views, representative of his era, concerning *ideas* of heredity and determinism, within the body of his novels and theories.

This volume proposes a classificatory status upon Zola as a transdiscursive author of modern critical theory. Zola's *The Experimental Novel* processes

Realism's commitment to ideologically informative verisimilitude into naturalism's experimental field of analytical and theoretical narrative possibilities—incorporating socio-biological imperatives, indicated largely by Marx and Darwin, and a *conceptual* application of heredity—establishing an imminent presence and engaging tradition in multiple artistic and philosophical sets of discourse, especially cinema. Like Marx and Darwin, Zola's "signature" has a palimpsestic, foundational presence in international critical and artistic thought; his theories inform future aesthetic formations. Foucault defines this conceptual approach:

> One can be the author of a theory, tradition, or discipline in which other books and authors will in their turn find a place. These authors are in a position that I will call 'transdiscursive' . . . In the course of the nineteenth century, there appeared in Europe another, more uncommon, kind of author . . . we shall call those 'founders of discursivity.' They are unique in that they are not just the authors of their own works. They have produced something else: the possibilities and the rules for the foundation of other texts.[9]

The naturalist film in international cultures engages issues associated with race, gender, and especially, class-based social systems as a materialist, ongoing construct. As Clifford Geertz concludes, "Culture is not cults and customs, but the structures of meaning through which men give shape to their experience."[10] The socio-biological frame of reference knows neither borders, bodies, nor language barriers. However, it is not the documentary, therefore the "actual," scientific Darwinian model or socio-economic, humanist Marxist model that the naturalist film reproduces; the naturalist film narrative conceptualizes ideas, creative deductions, historical or contemporary "post" readings of Marx and Darwin, among others, to produce an amorphous template. This volume is a study in *applied* fundamental theories and will activate the aesthetic philosophies of relevant figures and sets of discourse to present the naturalist film narrative as a clarified idea with an overarching framework activated by recurring cinematic tropes and consistent with other naturalist intertexts. One illustrative selection focuses on age, poverty, and loneliness.

Historical Spaces

Entire shot sequences from André Antoine's *La Terre* might have been lifted from a Courbet canvas depicting life and work on a farm. Via the reality of illusion, *La Terre* exhibits a painterly Realism revealing a historical space and time that seem to the contemporary viewer to be as remote as the Zola novel of 1887. Antoine's naturalist adaptation possesses a quality of immediacy in

INTRODUCTION

its exploration of animal-like human violence, including murder, rape, and elder abuse, and the (un)endurable cycles of the routine and mechanical forms of a life of unremitting labor. In Zola's controversial novel, and Antoine's adaptation, the demanding and ever-present burdens of physical labor, with its rote practices, represents the stifling nature of the grinding routine experience. Painterly images of the idealized, romantic working world in the countryside are vitiated by images of darker human nature entrapped by economic and social forces.

Among other characters, *La Terre* focuses on the decline of the patriarchal figure, old Fouán (Armand Bour), the landowning father who prematurely parcels away his land to his ungrateful family. Fouán's position as head of the family, as landowner, and as a human being is compromised by this legal blunder. As long as he holds title to the farm and an annuity, his family is attentive to him; yet once the land and the annuity savings are removed, his value is lost. His age makes him dependent on others who basically view him as surplus life, one of the useless aging farmyard animals put down mercifully or just left to die. In one compelling sequence, set in long shot, the broken and disenfranchised Lear-like old Fouán walks toward the camera, into a close-up shot, in which aimlessness and loss of self are established by his vacuous stare into the space ahead, complementing the stark setting. This affect shot

Figure 1.1 André Antoine's *La Terre* (1921)

concretizes despair; like a wounded old bull wandering on a plain. A reduced Fouán stumbles to the end of his life as snow swirls around him. This shot sequence, nearly engulfing the aimless Fouán, refutes the depiction of reflective, romantic nature; in naturalist narratives, nature is empirically dispassionate.

Antoine's immersive images of Fouán's desultory wandering and anxiety recall the sensory impression of ominous spatial emptiness depicted in Courbet's *La Diligence dans la neige* (1860), a canvas—artist Edward Wakeford refers to it as a "tragic conception"[11]—depicting wintery entrapment in a snowscape featuring an overturned carriage, horses, dark clouds and forest, and struggling individuals. Produced four years after Antoine's *La Terre*, in Charlie Chaplin's snow-bound setting in *The Gold Rush* (1925), the tramp similarly trudges across a hostile frozen tundra in comical fashion as he combats and survives a near-overwhelming Alaskan landscape, full of snow and perilous distractions.

When the viewer watches any film, such as *La Terre*, sets of interpretive discourse, aligned with the immediate reception of the film narrative and all that it connotes, produce the resulting perspective-interpretation, recovered and reformed by the activated host consciousness. This is especially evident in the analytical and comparative discussion of the naturalist film narrative in its synchronic and diachronic positioning as an interdisciplinary practice that reveals a process of incessant production, as activated by intertextual memory. These film narratives are "controlled not by lexical coincidences but by a structural identity, the text and its intertext being variants of the same structure."[12] In the naturalist film paradigm, whether an escaped felon fleeing from the chain gang, an entrapped coal miner, exhausted push-cart worker, laboring laundress, or hallucinating alcoholic, individuals are not caricatures, miniatures, or microbes: they are human. These individuals, male, female, or children, remain susceptible to economic, social, and other ideological operations that either symbolically or literally "grind" them into naturalist nubs, but they are depicted as human beings, in which survival is calculated. This is a transformative and violent process, a phenomenon of material decline facilitated by an emerging eruptive catalyst, evident across media platforms, renewed by tropes of thematic discourse.

In David Chase's "Pilot" episode of the HBO gangster-melodrama *The Sopranos* (1999), after a rival gangster is murdered by his nephew in a butcher shop's backroom amid hanging meat carcasses and dripping cleavers, mobster Tony Soprano (James Gandolfini) sits in a psychiatrist's office in order to understand the source of his recent disabling blackout. While conversing, Soprano reveals disturbing recollections involving his parents' bickering, especially his mother's calculating attitude toward his father, "When he was alive, nothin. My dad was tough: he ran his own crew, a guy like that and my mother wore him down to a little nub, he was a squeaking little gerbil when he died." The image of Tony's father, a dangerous gangster reduced in stature by his allegedly carping wife into a small, helpless creature, a metaphorical "nub" of his former self, is unprecedented in the gangster genre but indicative of the dynamics of personal and social experience. Soprano later describes himself as a kind of diminished performer, as he confesses to his psychiatrist that he feels like a "sad clown," laughing on the outside and crying on the inside. The Soprano family, in its past and present incarnation, like other families and individuals, exhibits troubling interpersonal relationships and social crises in a naturalist context. The HBO network has been particularly instrumental in revitalizing aspects of the naturalist narrative on broadcast television. Productions such as *Oz* (1997–2003), *The Sopranos* (1999–2007), *The Wire* (2002–2008), *Deadwood* (2004–2006), and *Barry* (2018–2023) exhibit recurring naturalist themes and tropes.

The naturalist film's paradigmatic structure evolves along ideological lines as it situates the audience as active readers of the spectacle of the human in penetrating sociological and scientific models. Louis Althusser's conceptual interpellation describes the process by which ideology addresses the individual subject and suggests how systems of truth, knowledge, and the elements of the superstructure function and are perceived. This describes how the viewer establishes the images and illusion of coherence and narrative. The audience reacts to the ideological cues within a film, especially when the cues relate to individual psychology, however bizarre, and character identification. The moment of perception precedes the subject and involves the process of recognition of one's interaction with the ideological content of this moment. The audience functions as the interpreter of such phenomena, and as it is evident in the naturalist paradigmatic design, the narrative consistently foregrounds the interplay of genetics, environment, and the socio-historical milieu.

Naturalist Threads

In the introduction to *The Major Realist Film Theorists* (2016), Ian Aitken concludes how the ongoing discussion of film Realism is "*speculative* and explorative in character, and [his volume] aims to probe the issue of Realism from a number of perspectives to suggest new ways of considering classical realist film theory and encourage new pathways of research into the subject."[13] Likewise, *Beyond Realism: Naturalist Film in Theory and Practice* advances multiple experimental analyses as it posits a conjectural presence of naturalist cinema and examines international naturalist film narratives to illustrate the genetic linkage and design of the film aesthetic in an intermedial capacity as a signifying presence in the history of film narrative.

In naturalist film narrative, either the scientific or social paradigm may be dominant or these may simply coexist, but a naturalist film reveals either or both templates and, most significantly, suggests a structurally implicit cinematic anthropology that renders the human as spectacle, incorporating and invoking both post-Darwinian and post-Marxist principles as signifying practices. The scientific paradigm invokes the (mal)function of genetics and the effects of heredity, the metaphorical trope of the survival of the fittest, and related representations of experiment, observation, and conclusion. The neo-Marxist theoretical naturalist framework has its roots in Marx's earlier humanist writing rather than in his later economic and historical texts. Among the most significant contributions Marx made to the comprehension of the social and economic order of the modern world was examining the relationship of work and the worker to an experientially based, complex, and conditional alienation.

Julia Hallam and Margaret Marshment's *Realism and Popular Cinema* (2000) presents realist cinema and the naturalist aesthetic as historically and thematically interrelated, concluding that realist film is "the dominant form of representation in our culture . . . [and] is less a metaphysical problem than a contextual one . . . We need to see it as locally and historically specific."[14] Their goal is not, "to define realism as a mode of representation . . . [but rather] begin with a basic definition of realism as a mode of representation that, at the formal level, aims at verisimilitude (or mimesis),"[15] which leads to the narrative shift, the alteration in perspective to the secular from the supernatural and metaphysical. Hallam and Marshment consider realist film as the primary historical model of narrative exposition linked to naturalist cinema. Naturalist film narrative evolves from realist precepts into thematic, ideological, and formal considerations, an amorphous experimental-observational paradigm, linked to industrial, generic models, that exposes the unfiltered image. Hallam and Marshment cite Realism's "alliance [with] the notion of truth,"[16] which suggestively leads to the critical, theoretical manifestos espoused by Courbet and Zola.

Mark Seltzer concludes, "The naturalist aesthetic doctrines of determinism and degeneration systematically render explicit and reinforce these premises and the power-effects in them."[17] Arnold Hauser's comments on the naturalist aesthetic introduce the structural parameters of pre-cinematic Naturalism: "Naturalism is not a homogeneous, clear-cut conception of art, always based on the same idea of nature, but changes with times . . . one discovers a trait, a tendency in reality on which one would like to put more emphasis."[18] It is the "tendency in reality" of naturalist art, such as depicted in the canvases created by nineteenth-century realist artists Courbet and Millet, to represent the individual, group, and life in the modern world in ideologically imbued narratives that address the image-driven medium of cinema.

For the majority of art historians, Realism and Naturalism are linked by formalistic precepts, but Naturalism extends the range of subject and substance; it is a socially and politically suggestive positioning, aimed at representing social life particularly in engaged, critical perspectives, depicting what is not beautiful or classically heroic but instead, portraying the shockingly plain lives of the middle class in despair and/or the experiences of the working class.[19] Sarah Faunce states, "Realism was at best a minor mode, and at worst a dangerous one because of its potential capacity to undercut the powerful belief in art as that which should affect the viewer primarily through forms of idealized beauty and heroic actions," to which she adds, "The new territory Courbet claimed for his art was that of his own perceptions and existence, with all their rough edges . . . [this was] a major shift in the subjectivity of vision."[20] Arnold Hauser states: "Naturalism is not aimed at reality as a whole . . . but at social life in particular, that is, at the province of reality that has become specially important . . . the social consciousness of a generation."[21]

Naturalism was the essential art of a post-realist, speculative, experimental era, and remains an ongoing reactive-aesthetic praxis, a cohesive, cultural product of the contemporary world. In P. Adam Sitney's introduction to *The Avant-Garde Film* (1978), he describes the relationship between avant-garde film and its artistic predecessors: "The earliest impulses toward the establishment of an independent cinema arose from a desire to temporalize pictorial strategies by Cubist, Futurist, and Dadaist painters."[22] The naturalist film paradigm may be specifically linked with and is structurally evident in later avant-garde styles and movements such as Expressionism, New Objectivity, film noir, and neorealism. The naturalist paradigm demonstrably functions as an operational aesthetic within a broader, experimental narrative scheme that calls for a revaluation of traditional formalist representational strategies. The human spectacle reveals itself along structurally coherent narrative lines; in this sense, the naturalist film is an extension, a theoretical reappropriation. Therefore, the naturalist film is neither purely a film genre nor a film movement but demonstrably engages these taxonomies and industrial classifications, as the following examples of Chloé Zhao's films illustrate.

Chloé Zhao's Reclaimed West

Chloé Zhao's trilogy of reality-based films, *Songs My Brothers Taught Me* (2015), *The Rider* (2017), and *Nomadland* (2020), are minimalist, painterly studies of relegated individuals and families in arduous states of survival. Whether performing in the rodeo ring, surveying dusty roads leading to a run-down camp ground, waiting in the medical clinic for emergency procedures, working in a factory, or sitting in a lounge chair gazing upon an empty horizon, Zhao's characters live and labor under deleterious economic and social conditions. Zhao's films neither romanticize native-Americans and the working class nor wholly render them as victims. Zhao's three cited films participate in the discursive renewal of naturalist themes.

As noted by Hervé Mayer, Zhao's films exemplify a dynamic relationship between Realism and its aesthetic-ideological repositioning within the naturalist landscape:

> Realism, in Zhao's films, has a strong social dimension. Life in trailer parks surviving on low-paying jobs and smuggling, families turned dysfunctional by the toll of poverty and alcohol, social perspectives among the youth limited by their environment ... Camera positions that alternate distant and close shots, combined with shallow focus composition and a sustained use of racking focus to direct the gaze, construct a form of empathetic observation that serves to level social and cultural differences between viewers and characters.[23]

Zhao's contemporary, neorealist narratives are shot mostly in natural light, with low budgets, frequently use non-professional performers, and are produced with an emphasis on social themes depicting a struggle to survive as seasonal or precariat labor; these are studies in observed, subaltern culture. In Zhao's *Songs My Brothers Taught Me*, the desire to leave the reservation and escape from unfavorable economic conditions intrigues a native American youth who, despite multiple setbacks and widespread impediments such as alcohol, drugs, incarceration, and the unlikely reality of escape, survives within the proscriptive setting.

The Rider focuses on multiple characters, physically wounded young men suffering from labor-related incidents and a developmentally challenged young woman, and the impact disabilities have on survival in the beautiful yet inhospitable environment of the contemporary western states. In particular, a young rodeo rider, Brady Blackburn (Brady Jandreau), is a vulnerable, thoughtful young man with a steel plate in his head who must decide if he will pursue life in the factory, engage other forms of menial labor, or re-enter the extremely dangerous rodeo ring and face common, potentially crippling accidents. Unlike the lame horse shot to curtail its agony in *The Rider*, Brady's hospitalized brother, another rodeo rider, remains a permanently broken man. In his study "Neandertals, Early Modern Humans, and Rodeo Riders," Erik Trinkaus makes a startling comparison between professional riders at the rodeo—a high-intensity entertainment spectacle—and their genetically linked, archaic ancestors:

> [There is] a close relationship between the Neandertal pattern and that of serious traumatic injuries among North American rodeo (PRCA—Professional Rodeo Cowboys Association) athletes. Principally, both samples exhibited a disproportionate frequency of upper body (head and arm) injuries.[24]

The Rider examines contemporary cowboy culture and is neither pessimistic nor sentimental; characters, even when damaged, somehow survive. In *The Rider*, while Brady walks away from a final potentially fatal challenge in the rodeo ring, he goes back to a family and future, a limited circulus with vague economic or social prospects, but one of his own choosing. Unlike Mike Milo (Clint Eastwood), the cantankerous old rodeo rider who initially accepts menial forms of labor but then takes a dangerous across-the-border job in order to survive after recuperating from breaking his back and subsequent alcoholism in Clint Eastwood's *Cry Macho* (2021), Brady Blackburn considers other potential labor venues.

Zhao's *Nomadland* is a study of female aging, labor, and varieties of social interaction among those alone, but not necessarily lonely—just nomadic. The aptly named Fern (Frances McDormand), roots where and when desired. She is an aging widow living alone in a motorhome who travels across the western states taking occasional jobs to support herself because of the economic recession—"the gypsum mine closed"—like millions of other displaced workers who subsist on survival wages as members of the semi-skilled American working class. Unlike the workers exiting the factory in the Lumière brothers' *La sortie de l'usine Lumière à Lyon/Workers Exiting the Factory* (1895), in Zhao's *Nomadland*, the plant gates are closed, an ironic indication of economic progress. Zhao's frequent use of long and wide shots of the open, inviting natural settings such as the desert and South Dakota's Badland National Park function like a landscape painting, to contrast with the box-like, enclosed spaces of the factory and Fern's remote, confined family whom she visits for support.

Fern occasionally works in a factory, stores, and restaurants making enough money to survive in the picturesque landscape. Just as the aging and lonely Umberto, an eventually homeless pensioner adrift in postwar Rome hawking goods in Vittorio De Sica's neorealist, naturalist study of human expendability, *Umberto D.* (1952), the aging Fern must also scrape together enough capital to remain an independent woman. Both Umberto and Fern are classifiably obsolete. As De Sica's Umberto (Carlo Battisti) walks off into the impersonal urban void that describes his life in postwar Rome as a survivor, Fern spends time on the beach watching the waves crash and then drives off into uncharted space and time as her own person. De Sica and Chao's horizon shots of characters departing into an unknown distance belies the inevitability of cynical, totalizing closure. In the next chapter, select naturalist tropes demonstrate a vital, recurring presence in international film narrative.

Notes

1. Jose Luis Borges with Margarita Guerrero, *The Book of Imaginary Beings*, trans. Norman Thomas di Giovanni (New York: E. P. Dutton, 1978), 13.

2. Ibid, 16.
3. Ibid, 17.
4. All cited films are available as DVDs, on internet websites, or through private-archival collections, such as located at MOMA or the Anthology Film Archives (NYC). In addition, this volume is published in English to accommodate its readership but select quotations from rare source material will appear in the original language in the endnotes section. Unless noted, all translations are mine.
5. Thomas S. Kuhn, *The Structure of Scientific Revolutions*, second edition (Chicago: University of Chicago Press, 1970), 109.
6. Leonard W. Tancock, "Some Early Critical Work of Emile Zola: *Livres D'Aujourd'hui et de demain* (1866)," *Modern Language Review*, Vol. 42, No. 1 (January 1947), 46.
7. Ibid, 51.
8. Ibid, 46.
9. Michel Foucault, "What is an Author?" *Aesthetics, Method, and Epistemology*, ed. James D. Faubion, trans. Robert Hurley, Vol. 2 (New York: The New Press, 1998), 216–17.
10. Clifford Geertz, "The Politics of Meaning," in *The Interpretation of Cultures* (New York: Basic Books, 1973), 312.
11. Edward Wakefield, "Courbet's 'La Diligence dans la neige'," *Leonardo*, Vol. 12, No. 2 (Spring 1979), 154.
12. Michael Riffaterre, "Sémiotique intertextuelle," quoted in Mikhail Iampolski, *The Memory of Tiresias: Intertextuality and Film*, trans. Harsah Ram (Berkeley: University Press, 1995), 36.
13. Ian Aitken, "Introduction," *The Major Realist Film Theorists*, ed. Ian Aitken (Edinburgh: Edinburgh University Press, 2016), 7. Note: italics appear in the original.
14. Julia Hallam and Margaret Marshment, *Realism and Popular Cinema* (Manchester: University Press, 2000), x.
15. Ibid, XII.
16. Ibid, XIII.
17. Mark Seltzer, *Bodies and Machines* (London: Routledge, 1992), 43.
18. Arnold Hauser, *The Social History of Art*, vol. 4 (New York: Random House, 1957), 25.
19. Ibid, 26.
20. Sarah Faunce, *Courbet* (New York: Harry N. Abrams, 1993), 8.
21. Hauser, *Social History of Art*, 26.
22. P. Adams Sitney, "Introduction," *Avant-Garde Film*, ed. P. Adams Sitney (New York: New York University Press, 1978), x.
23. Hervé Mayer, "Neo Frontier Cinema: Rewriting the Frontier Narrative from the Margins in *Meek's Cutoff* (Kelly Reichardt, 2010), *Songs My Brothers Taught Me* (Chloé Zhao, 2015) and *The Rider* (Chloé Zhao, 2017)," *Miranda*, Vol. 18 (2019), 16.
24. Erik Trinkaus, "Neandertals, Early Modern Humans, and Rodeo Riders," *Journal of Archaeological Science*, Vol. 39, Issue 12 (December 2012), 3691.

2. NATURALIST TROPES

Experimental Advances

Before the celebration of the irrational and the subconscious in Dada, Surrealism, Expressionism and other styles and movements, Naturalism looked within, to the internal terrain of genetics and temperament, to provide a context for representing the human. Whether applying montage theory and the aesthetics of mob violence in Sergei Eisenstein's *Stachka/Strike* (1925), examining ubiquitous poverty and social decay in Luis Buñuel's surrealist documentary, *Las Hurdes/Land Without Bread* (1933), or floating across a sexualized, drug-saturated landscape in Gaspar Noé's *Enter the Void* (2009), the naturalist aesthetic participates frequently in avant-garde cinema's formalist-thematic intertextualities, with its experimental methodologies and defamiliarized subjects in states of crisis and decline, in which the spectacle of the human advances the uncertainty of identity and representation. There is a viable ongoing link, a "co-presence," among naturalist cinema and other experimental film aesthetics, such as Surrealism.

These recurring depictions illustrate Naturalism's crisis of experience in relationship to pervasive, material determinism, which is often misread as fatalism. Naturalism's "grinding tradition" reveals the individual as s/he experiences an impersonal yet controlling sense of environmentally discernable or biologically predisposed "fate" that is frequently a product of racial (mis)conception, class prohibition, and gender-based proscription within a given historical milieu.

These intermedial spectacles of decline invoke a literary, painterly, and theatrical mise-en-scène, or may be indicated by the signifying camera placement framing, to render a layered, affect shot; these compositional strategies directly invoke socio-biological causalities that are placed within recurring tropes of naturalist cinematic discourse. As Anton Kaes invokes the need for a revitalized and "radical interdisciplinarity"[1] in academic and critical research, he also concludes how "film has become a preferred locus for studying the various ways in which 'many cultures' enter into a dialogue and separate realms of knowledge compete with each other."[2] Naturalist cinema theorizes an amorphous film paradigm, a working aesthetic. Representative tropes of signifying discourse in naturalist cinema are evident in adapted or original screenplays from the silent to the contemporary era. As Darwin speculated that life begins in water, so too will this volume, and then proceed to solid land, full of struggling specimens.

From Sea to Seen: Realism to Naturalism

In a letter written in 1871 by Charles Darwin to the British botanist, Joseph Dalton Hooker, Darwin expressed his belief that a relationship existed between the foundational stages of life and bodies of water:

> It is often said that all the conditions for the first production of a living organism are now present, which could ever have been present.—But if (& oh what a big if) we could conceive in some warm little pond with all sorts of ammonia & phosphoric salts,—light, heat, electricity &c present, that a protein compound was chemically formed, ready to undergo still more complex changes, at the present day such matter would be instantly devoured, or absorbed, which would not have been the case before living creatures were formed.[3]

In the clinical study, "Molecules, Water, and Radiant Energy: New Clues for the Origin of Life," the research team examined the complex origin of life as it evolved on earth and, nearly restating Darwin, conclude, "water [is] at the center of life, which serves in turn to make clear why life is not possible in the absence of water. Life almost certainly originated (or, is originating) in water, and life cannot go on without water."[4] Darwin's watery "living creatures," in various stages of biological configuration and social interaction within an observed environment, reveal a past leading to a formative present that indicates a setting for naturalist narratives. Whether above or below the surface of any watery body, each may function as physical site of purposeful motion—a generative "field of play"—for the observed subject in a floating zoo, viewed on canvas or projected on screen.

Courbet's seascape, *Stormy Sea* (1869), a painting of vast, energized nature is a severe, realist study of eruptive natural motion. As if anticipating a split-screen frame composition in a film, Courbet's seascape divides into halves, with the top portion of the canvas featuring a tinted white bluish cloud covering and the bottom portion of the canvas depicting, in a muted color palette of brown, blue, and gray tones, waves of water crashing onto the rocks.

In the Lumière brothers *actualité* production, *Baignade en mer/Swimming in the Sea* (aka) *The Sea* (1895), a group of boys repeatedly jump from an extended plank into the flowing sea—a study of motion in motion—set within a fixed, medium shot. Todd McGowan notes the achievement of the Lumière brothers cinematic Realism, especially *Swimming in the Sea*, and observes how the film "focuses on the transience and contingency of existence."[5] The Lumière film frame celebrates exuberant moments of real or imagined childhood-past for the observer. Other images of released masculine freedom are depicted in American Ashcan artist George Bellows' urban landscape painting, *Forty-two Kids* (1907), in which groups of boys jump from a pier, using it as a diving board, to momentarily escape from clothing and concrete, while filmmaker Rudy Burkhardt's city symphony, *Under the Brooklyn Bridge* (1953), an avant-garde, black and white documentary film, records and observes in a realistic collage, interrelated images of urban life and boys swimming. Franziska Heller notes the historical presence of water imagery in cinema:

> The fascination with water started . . . in the 1890s during which time the filming of waves breaking on the shore caught the interest of pioneers exploring the possibilities to recreate rhythmic impressions of the world with moving images . . . Water and its concept of movement is seen as comparable to the relation between moving images and the viewer. The most important aspect is the fact that within these forms of movement the traditional, 'logical' categories of time and space—and thus comprehensible meaning—do not apply. They become relational . . . Water is fabulously filmic.[6]

Another "fabulously filmic" *actualité* produced in 1895, Birt Acres' *Rough Sea at Dover*, documents running water rendered in real space and time, a study of nature in motion. Acres documents a self-contained subject in two settings in two distinct stationary medium shots of the coursing sea, as if actualizing the flowing energy of a seascape painting as a recomposed narrative in a technological medium. The first setting is a view of water repeatedly crashing against a pier, while the second setting reveals water floating, presumably from the seashore, in a riverbank with a tree foregrounded in the frame, adding compositional perspective to the turbulence. Claude Monet's seascape painting *A Stormy Sea* (1884), a densely layered image of primitive nature rendered from a seashore perspective, likewise overwhelms the canvas. Monet's painting registers a sense of powerful motion, as indifferent, flowing energy engulfs the observer in shades of colliding blue and white strokes. Monet's explosive, open space seascape is a study in the movement—swirls and dashes—of framed natural chaos breaking on the barely visible shore.

Both the Lumière brothers' *Swimming in the Sea* and Acres' *Rough Sea at Dover* are studies of a motion-filled watery setting, running for one minute, depicting a presence of energy-as-subject, which attracts the observer to the frame. Bodies of water and other dynamic naturalist settings conditioned by regulatory realism reveal the human struggling to survive in the presence of catalytic, grinding external agencies in a filmic, Darwinian context. In Winslow Homer's *Gulf Stream* (1899),[7] a lone Black male figure adrift on a small, broken-down boat with few discernable provisions, no rudder, and a waterspout forming in the background of the frame in a shark-infested and unstable sea, appears oblivious to a potential rescue boat in the background of the frame. Although Homer's painting depicts one man's isolation and effort to survive, a sense of peril and hopeful endurance qualifies the observer's reaction. In a writerly manner, *we* create the threatened man's fulfilling fiction in a naturalist context, one of survival or death.

Whether the engaged, scrutinized subject is besieged, thriving, or simply surviving, the naturalist film seascape and landscape inherently function as contextual, affective settings. From the microscope's slide to the shoreline of the beach, the swimming pool and beyond, the seascape and landscape settings in naturalist film narratives reveal and sustain depths of layered, visual textualities. In naturalist cinema, space and time are relational as the human, an engaged specimen, is a study in observed and explicated motion.

In a conclusive image of failed life, the suburbanite "Neddy" Merrill (Burt Lancaster) lies prostate, a shivering broken male, in Frank Perry's *The Swimmer* (1968), the adaptation of John Cheever's eponymous short story (1964). Perry's *The Swimmer* illustrates Realism's segue into Naturalism's grinding tradition as the once-wealthy Merrill is reduced to accommodating crowds at a public bathing site, where he must first wash his feet before entering the teeming pool. Perry's film invokes images of middle-aged Merrill's public, class-based humiliation and personal decline as a process of disillusionment and collapse, like witnessing a microbe fade once a membrane is pierced. According to Franziska Heller, Perry's swimmer traverses "through the posh backyard pools of his Connecticut neighborhood—only to find in the end, as an allegory of his own decaying life, his own home locked and abandoned."[8] Perry's powerful, concluding shots—the image of a ruined, exhausted male lost before an empty, eerie home—recalls Colin Hunter's seascape painting, *The Naturalist* (1878), in which a lone male figure lies across jagged rocks as a rough sea flows in the background; Hunter's romantic frame juxtaposes male immobility with environmental mobility in contemplative contrast.

Read along with Frank Perry's film narrative of one man's decline, Lucrecia Martel's broader investigation of disaffected social class in *La Ciénaga/The Swamp* (2001) begins with a preponderance of close-up shots of alcohol poured into glasses and a zoo-like exhibition of unattractive, disaffected human grotesqueries sitting around an unclean swimming pool, smoking and consuming food, with little to do except observe and ignore each other. Martel frames isolated parts of the body—arms, upper torsos, heads—rather than full body shots to suggest disembodied presence in a soundscape composed of people murmuring, thunder, dogs barking, chairs pushed across concrete, and glasses filled with ice cubes, until a glass is dropped and cracked. Martel's film cross cuts from three interrelated local settings: the swimming pool, boys hunting in the nearby woods to locate an entrapped cow in the muddy swamp, and children aimlessly lounging in bed and bothering each other. Martel's opening shot sequence reveals gendered, racial privilege in stages of personal decline. According to Jennie Irene Daniels, the film is a study of social classes in crises: "Lucrecia Martel's *La Ciénaga* delves less into the lives of the lower classes, instead demonstrating the decadence of the Argentine provincial agricultural oligarchy through the lives of two families ... *La Ciénaga* introduces family members and domestic servants through scenes of their daily lives."[9] Daniels notes that in *La Ciénaga* physical decay is a marker of social identity frequently based on age: "the middle-aged characters are overweight, but their unhealthiness is still more striking since they often are wearing bathing suits. In an early scene, close-ups of bare, thick waists and loose, wrinkled skin decry a lack of self-care."[10] *La Ciénaga*'s "neorealism"[11] is a study of boredom and waste sites, with a lack of swimming by anybody at the pool despite its symbolic centrality.

Tank Cleaner (2021), Parvinder Singh Wraich's Hindi-language melodrama of soap, sweat, and survival, seemingly contradicts Darwin's supposition that life begins in water. *Tank Cleaner* features a semi-skilled laborer, Monti (Money Sabharwal), who works at several jobs in contemporary India and is assigned to clean out the interior of rooftop water tanks in various housing developments; in Wraich's film, Monti nearly drowns while entrapped in a visually claustrophobic vat-container. Like Arthur Fleck, Monti is a hard-luck figure with little social standing. Monti owes money to several people, including loan sharks, so his semi-skilled labor is physically demanding, incessant, and frequently humiliating, as he is reminded by his bosses that he is replaceable. In one sequence, while waiting tables at an outdoor restaurant, Monti has liquid thrown into his face by a dissatisfied customer, but this vicious act hardly solicits a reaction from other diners. Monti is barely visible to the public and seemingly nameless; he is the "cleaner" who exists like the Lumière brothers' unseen women wringing out clothes in *Laveuses sur la rivière/Washerwomen on the River* (1897). Until he is trapped inside a water vat, Monti works exhaustively throughout *Tank Cleaner*, and Wraich's close-up and medium shots consistently reveal a realistic, sweaty struggle to survive as well as to impress a young woman and her family from a higher class.

Monti travels across town like Vittorio DeSica's frustrated day laborer Antonio (Lamberto Maggiorani) in *Ladri di biciclette/The Bicycle Thief* (1948), as both men peddle across avenues to drone-like employment. *Tank Cleaner* recalls the economic and personal anxieties of the cart-driver in Ousmane Sembène's *Borom Sarret* (1963), in which the frustrated man is known simply as "the driver." Multiple aerial shots in *Tank Cleaner* highlight the impersonal, near-invisibility of the day laborer, as the city is a vast space in which a person may be lost while in full view of others. From one apartment complex to the other, such as those areas depicted in Matty Rich's *Straight Out of Brooklyn* (1991) and the "Casa" episode of David Riker's *La Ciudad* (1998), Monti, the tank cleaner, works and nearly dies in an uninviting, lonely space.

In a naturalist context, working-class Monti is a floating microbe, a barely visible specimen in water on a slide under the microscope. Late in the narrative, in an extreme close-up shot, Monti gasps for oxygen as water rises in the tank, with his head barely above the surface, but his will to live sustains him. The worker's light stick, which illuminates the inside of the tank to reveal dirt and germs, now reveals Monti. Monti's face exhibits anxiety and exhaustion, mirroring his sustained struggle to survive. Monti is perceived by the audience as an image of human entrapment. In *Tank Cleaner*, Monti barely keeps "his head above water," both economically and literally. In a naturalist reading of *Tank Cleaner*, Wraich's commercial melodrama depicts the class-based struggle to survive in a contemporary urban setting.

As it involves naturalist cinema, Raymond Williams' "cultural hypotheses"[12] suggest numerous recurring naturalist tropes set within a specific milieu in which a socio-biological circulus reveals literal catalytic agencies of destabilization—an essential naturalist *derangement*—frequently linked to the reckless consumption of alcohol, legal and illegal drugs, expressions of sexual desire, class and labor discontent, or bio-genetic malfunctions that surface without restriction. These "structures of feeling"[13] are revealed in artistic movements and cultures.

In *The Experimental Novel*, Zola refers to a "vital [biological] circulus"[14] that energizes life, and then suggests a prescient comparison with sociologically based fiction:

> There is in this a social or organic [medical] solidarity, which keeps up a perpetual movement, until the *derangement* or cessation of the action has broken the equilibrium . . . the problem of the experimentalist . . . [is]

seizing the initial phenomenon. The social circulus is identical with the vital circulus; in society, as in human beings, a solidarity exists which unites the different members and the different organisms in such a way that if one organ becomes rotten many others are tainted ... When we experiment on a dangerous wound which poisons society, we proceed in the same way as the experimentalist doctor; we try to find the simple initial cause in order to reach the complex causes of which the action is the result.[15]

In the naturalist film narrative, emplotment involves indexical tropes—a pointing to the subject—experiencing the alienating, violent, and entangling world, manifest within a circulus that reveals the core naturalist derangement. These are narratives of individual and social malfunction, a debilitating, literal presence, such as labor- or family-related conflicts involving economics, interpersonal relations, or one of individual, biological origins, such as a genetic predisposition toward feeblemindedness, a deformed bodily appearance, alcoholic degeneration. These dysfunctions—derangements—are viewed as vertical ruptures of the horizontal, narrative flow of space and time—"*le moment naturalist*"—and represent discernable, affective causalities. In this study, the cited film stills signify a dynamic naturalist moment, as theme and form collaboratively fulfill the aesthetic as presence. The derangement, whether in the form of lust, atavistic reversion, or crippling economic setback, is more than a singular effect; it signals a conditional alteration, a restructuring of dynamics in the narrative, as if a new bacterium were introduced into a pre-existing bacterial colony on a slide under the microscope, causing irreparable damage. In *The Origin of Species* (1859), Darwin makes a compelling analogy with the Zola's conceptual derangement:

In looking at Nature, it is most necessary to keep the foregoing considerations always in mind—never to forget that every single organic being may be said to be striving to the utmost to increase in numbers; that each lives by a struggle at some period of its life; that heavy destruction inevitably falls either on the young or old, during each generation or at recurrent intervals. Lighten any check, mitigate the destruction ever so little, and the number of the species will almost instantaneously increase to any amount.[16]

The derangement is the presence and moment of realization of the social-personal flaw, loss, failure, mistake, as it emerges, the paradigmatic affective moment, *the verb*, of the naturalist experience. The naturalist derangement, a conceptual variation on Barthes' penetrating *punctum*, engages and interrupts critical perceptions of alleged normalcy. In naturalist film narratives, the derangement may be the presence of a life-altering irritant, a psychological malfunction, or a repressed, impactful energy exposed. The catalytic agency of destabilization is often linked to class, racial, and gender-based concerns, such as labor-related issues and familial, sexual discontent. A familiar source narrative, Zola's *La Bête humaine* (1890) and select film adaptations will illustrate the range and relevance of the naturalist derangement.

Images in Motion

Whether cleverly contrived or impulsively irrational in origin, violent murder is a common manifestation of the naturalist derangement, an act of fulfillment. Zola's *La Bête humaine* features the troubled, physically ill railroad worker Jacques Lantier, who compulsively assaults Flore, a desired acquaintance, and later murders his lover, Séverine. Jacques' atavistic arousal-violence exemplifies Zola's status as a theorist, but not as a clinician of modern culture. As a direct descendant from Zola's fictional Rougon-Macquart family line, Jacques possesses the genetically based "default" structure, a critical concept recurring in naturalist film narrative. Jacques Lantier contains a submerged beast within, which, as it is affected by catalytic agencies in the environment such as the deleterious effects of alcohol and sexual arousal, solicit his subhuman violent behavior. Jacques and subsequent cinematic representations of the conceptual *Bête humaine*, regardless of race, class, or gender, exhibit variations of what Gilles Deleuze describes as "petite hérédité," the *particulars* of the atavistic reversion, such as a corruptive predisposition to alcoholism and the uncontrolled release of violent inclinations, as well as lead to the clinically expansive, rupturing inheritance of genetically based enervation: "grande hérédité."[17] In a symbolic sense, the "petite" is a component, an indicative presence of the greater "grande." Jacques is an *imagined* product of blemished genetics, a descendant of a tainted biological lineage.

Jean Renoir's *La Bête humaine* (1938) engages and documents the pathological self and ensuing panic involving violent ruptures of identity and inherited illness. Renoir's depiction of Zola's skilled railroad worker, Jacques Lantier (Jean Gabin), reveals the presence of the submerged Darwinian beast and illustrates that "the dark side of naturalism is Renoir's true heritage from Zola."[18] Renoir's consistently realistic mise-en-scène, as denoted by the expressive lighting and set design, wide and medium shots of trains, tracks, men and women working in the historical setting of France in 1938, documents the social milieu and the experiences of principle characters. Daniel Pick refers to Zola's selection of the railroad as a structural trope in his novel, and this could also be applied to Renoir's adaptation: "The train which forms the continuing motif ... focuses that obsession with communication, circulation, destination. The railway is implicitly linked to Zola's narrative project [and Renoir's adaptation], the body and the lineage of heredity."[19] The film, like its literary predecessor, suggests a series of "interlocking transgressions."[20] Of special importance in Renoir's set design is the strategic placement of mirrors, which suggests a surface context revealing a latent, darker metonymical context. In *La Bête humaine*, reflections in mirrors are associated with and indicate repressed Jekyll/Hyde-like identities and capacities, an "other" side of oneself, a familiar trope in naturalist film narrative.

Renoir's *La Bête humaine* exemplifies the binary relationship between Realism and naturalist aesthetics and its pathologies. In this adaptation, Renoir's shot composition produces climactic framing in which space and time literally meld, creating moments of essential naturalist imagery. Renoir's medium close-up shot of two potential lovers embracing close by the train tracks, in which cable poles and electric wires in the background of the frame suggestively *emerge* from Jacques' head, indicates his "charged" murderous impulses aroused by Flore's (Blanchette Brunoy) surrender to his initially rebuffed sexual advances. He nearly strangles her after kissing her. The shot cuts to a close-up of the "other" Jacques, the beast, enraged and aroused. The overhead power wiring, a symbolic sign of spatialized circuitry, disassembles in Jacques' brain. As the shot cuts to a two-shot of the hunter and his ensnared prey, at the top of the frame a speeding train functions as an auditory and visual interruption and reconnection (rewiring) back to his social, non-primal self. His snarling grimace dissolves, and as he turns away, Jacques exits the frame. Jacques' interior self was essentially exteriorized, rendered as visual signage of the conflicted, entrapped beast.[21] This shot sequence depicts the naturalist image-as-spectacle.

E. Paul Gauthier has clarified the relationship between Zola's referencing of naturalist physiognomy with Darwinian atavism, which is effectively rendered by Renoir:

> *La Bête humaine* marks Zola's return to extensive use of physiognomic theories and intensified exploitation of man-animal resemblances ... Zola must have relied in part on Darwin for his notion that man is but an animal more developed and ennobled, as exemplified in *La Bête humaine*.[22]

Along with its scientific and literary intertextualities, this shot-image exists in the moment of the cinematic frame. Jacques, Renoir's atavistic individual, eventually succumbs to the effects of deleterious genetic impulses mediated by the alcohol-besotted working-class environment. In *La Bête humaine*, when Jacques refers to "pain behind the ears" and states that he is "paying for his ancestors," the expression of resigned sadness in his face recalls a strong yet

BEYOND REALISM

Figure 2.1 Jean Renoir's *La Bête humaine* (1938)

confined animal. The cage exists but remains indiscernible; Renoir's *La Bête humaine* is a study of naturalist pathology in determinist time-space.

Both Flore and Séverine (Simone Simon) facilitate Jacques' encroaching entrapment. When Séverine, the other woman in Jacques' life, is murdered by him, Jacques' atavistic demeanor wholly emerges. As the adulterous lovers wait and contrive to murder Roubaud (Fernand Ledoux), her husband, Jacques, becoming aroused and troubled by the thrill of an impending kill, embraces and kisses Séverine. Renoir's close-up shot reveals that as Jacques opens his eyes, these are the eyes of a hunter, not a lover. Renoir's shot composition, set in realistically shaded boudoir lighting, exposes the sexual and murderous impulses beginning to overwhelm Jacques. Although Séverine flees, she is caught by the stranger in her bedroom. He begins to fight, strangle, and then stab at her as she screams. Séverine's history of sexual brutalization, including incest and rape, and her subsequent adultery serve as destructive catalytic agencies that lead to reckless impulses and Jacques' homicidal response. For Séverine's murder sequence, Renoir's medium shot frames the doorway into the bedroom and settles on the bed, which is momentarily empty; the audience witnesses the assault. Séverine is violently sacrificed to Jacques' frenzied impulses. Jacques and Séverine's naturalist pathologies have a dual structural function; everyone is damaged within, and damaging to others. In an audio and visual segue, the soundtrack and camera cut to the music of a nearby public dance hall, full of singing and merriment. The song, entitled "Ninette's little heart," functions as a form of ironic juxtaposition to the corresponding set of nearby sadistic circumstances. As local working-class people have their fun, unknowingly, another victim is claimed. As the camera cuts back to the now deceased Séverine, moving initially from a synecdochical shot of her limp hand, up her body, and finally settling on the head, her eyes remain open yet lifeless, having seen the unleashed Jacques for the first and last time.

As this diegetic music continues off screen, Jacques exits from the bedroom, knife in hand. Renoir's camera follows Jacques within the frame and settles on his reflected image in the mirror. The audience, along with Jacques, sees his other, brutish side reflected and revealed. Jacques executes a rapid double take into the mirror and gazes upon his reflection, as his vision penetrates the surface Realism into a naturalist vision of Lombrosian implications. "In *La Bête humaine*, the mirrors reflect a constant turning inward ... an inability ... to be free of the [bestial] self."[23] He leaves the crime scene and wanders aimlessly along the railroad tracks, as the tracks contain him like a set of enclosing genetic markers, the strands of a stained life. When Jacques is later working on the train, he cries out "I can't go on," and leaps to his death; this is a mercy killing in the form of a suicide. His body, like an animal smashed on the side of a road, remains peacefully broken. As the product of blemished genetics, a tainted biological lineage established in prior literary narratives, Renoir's atavistic Jacques is one of Naturalism's seminal figures: the trope of the wounded man.

Fault Lines

As another essential recurring conceptual derangement, alcoholism is an indicative malfunction, and this core precept is evident in naturalist cinema from the silent to contemporary era in both adapted or original screenplays, frequently linked with familiar generic, industrial formula.

In Douglas Jerrold's celebrated melodrama, *Fifteen Years of a Drunkard's Life* (1828), Vernon, the alcoholic protagonist, experiences personal and social humiliation and decline from his former life of wealth and fine clothing, to the rags of a raging alcoholic, which leads to consequential acts of violence. Though at times, Vernon reveals a level of self-awareness that might seemingly forestall his conditional deterioration: "Oh, drunkenness! Thou smiling demon, that raises us from out ourselves to sink us 'neath the worm," and later exclaims, "The drunkard has no son, no wife, no friend; with one frantic grasp he tears from his heart all ties of blood and honor. Oh! that I had ne'er been born—ne'er had life to crawl a wretched outcast, hateful to the world, loathsome to myself. But no, I must not reflect—'tis horror."[24] Vernon *becomes* an alcoholic.

The presence of melodramatic, generic tropes as enunciated in Jerrold's play are redeployed in naturalist cinema; the undermining of the family as a coherent unit, collateral issues of domestic abuse, estrangement from work, and frequent violent acts are the products of alcoholism, a destabilizing agency of decline. Roy Calnek's *Ten Nights in a Bar-Room* (1926), based on T. S. Arthur's eponymous temperance novel (1854) and more specifically, William W. Pratt's stage melodrama *Ten Nights in a Bar-Room* (1858), depicts the rise–fall–rise narrative of Joe Morgan (Charles Gilpin), who states, "I have lived to see and suffer all the evils that cling around a drunkard's home."[25] Calnek's naturalist adaptation of *Ten Nights in a Bar-Room* is a silent film with a uniquely racial context. The cast features several African-American performers, including Charles Gilpin, who according to Donald Bogle, was a "legendary black stage actor,"[26] and Bogle has referred to Calnek's film as "remarkable."[27] Although there are multiple film adaptations of *Ten Nights in a Bar-Room*, the depiction of a Black middle-class family in conflict is historically noteworthy.

Calnek's framing sequence in *Ten Nights in a Bar-Room* initiates this naturalist narrative of alcoholic despair and consequential violence. During a brawl in a saloon, a little girl is killed by a whiskey bottle that strikes her head as she attempts to lure her father away from the site. After this melodramatic sequence, Calnek's tripartite cross-cutting links the space and time of her

Figure 2.2 Roy Calnek's *Ten Nights in a Bar-Room* (1926)

father's furious acts of revenge, leading to a form of middle-class redemption. This extended sequence includes framing from a high angle an enraged lynch-like mob, a medium shot of a burning home hiding a villain, and location shots of a father chasing the murderer through the woods, across a river in small boats. This sequence effectively communicates tension, violence, and resolution in a unique narrative of *nearly* conclusive male decline.

In Mike Figgis' *Leaving Las Vegas* (1996), the alcoholic screenwriter Ben Sanderson (Nicolas Cage) literally drinks himself to his premature death while in the company of a sympathetic prostitute/sex worker, surrounded by a garish, sleepless urban landscape. Sanderson's downward spiral, from a once-prosperous career into a lonely hotel room surrounded by empty bottles of consumed alcohol, lead to his self-pitying decline. Sanderson is an observed example of failed masculinity, alcoholism, and degeneration—a sinking, unredeemed male—representing Naturalism's grinding process, in which a nub of his former self, like gangster Tony Soprano's father, remains.

Wojciech J. Has' *Petla/The Noose* (1958) is a stylish, grimy study of male decline documenting the final day in the life of a chronic alcoholic, Kuba Kowalski (Gustaw Holoubek). Although Kuba makes an effort to stop his compulsive drinking, his isolation and continued wandering about the streets of postwar Krakow lead him to bars and fellow drunkards; there is no escape from the proscriptive circulus. According to Piotr Kryczka, Kuba's alcoholism was a familiar form of social pathology occurring in postwar Poland:

> Alcoholism is ... the Number One problem in Poland. Ours is a society in which drinking has been a time-honored custom. It has become so much part of the custom and culture that in many circles even excessive drinking is tolerated.[28]

Kryczka notes that during this era, "most suicides in Poland are committed by men."[29] *Petla* documents Kuba's worsening suicide narrative in tense real time leading from his apartment and traversing throughout a neo-expressionist black and white working-class setting in which he returns to a pressing, desolate life. Kuba gets into fights, abandoned in an alley, and finally elects to end his perennial wretchedness, alone and dangling from a rope. *Leaving Las Vegas* reveals Sanderson drinking himself to death in a compromised state of pitiful awareness, whereas Kuba's self-grinding down is drearily inescapable, revealing a naturalist specimen under the lens.

Guru Dutt's *Pyassa/The Thirsty One* (1957), set in postwar, independent India, examines the consequential relationship between the Urdu poet-alcoholic Vijay (Guru Dutt), and the sympathetic prostitute Gulabo (Waheeda Rehman), who meet by chance and establish a bond. Vijay's impossible desire for another woman from higher society, his dream of publication, and his increasing alcohol consumption lead to stages of relentless despair. According to Nasreen Munni Kabir, "In *Pyassa*, Guru Dutt shows how well he understood the subtlety of emotions,"[30] as Vijay's decline and eventual salvation—naturalist inflected films do not always end in death and damnation—is abetted by Dutt's frequent use of atmospheric lighting, close-ups, plot twists, and the use of musical interludes suggesting inner states of emotional and personal expression. Carrie Messenger notes,

> one of the unusual features of Guru Dutt's cinematic style, whether the film succeeded or failed at the box-office, is a literal gaze, the regular use of unusually large close-ups. Guru Dutt's use of black and white is gorgeous; light is almost a character in his films.[31]

Dutt's dynamic camera placement and framing are evident in *Pyassa*. At one point, given Vijay's irrational behavior and excessive drinking, he is sent to an asylum where he will fearfully react and expressly desire to leave. Dutt's asylum shot sequence recalls Billy Wilder's *The Lost Weekend* (1945), during the alcoholic novelist Don Birnam's (Ray Milland) hospitalization, where he experiences fantastic delusions, as well as the vicious, seemingly demented alcoholic "Baby Jane" (Bette Davis) serving her handicapped sister, Blanche (Joan Crawford), a parakeet and a dead rat on a plate as a meal, and later wandering on the beach in kabuki-like makeup and clownish clothing in Robert Aldrich's *What Ever Happened to Baby Jane?* (1962). Fear and anxiety inform entrapment.

Figure 2.3 Robert Aldrich's *What Ever Happened to Baby Jane?* (1962)

In *Pyassa*, Dutt's atmospheric lighting and camera framing are visually prominent during the near-suicide train track accident shot sequence in which a despondent Vijay gives a shivering homeless man a coat, but the homeless man is mistaken for Vijay after he is accidentally killed while pursuing Vijay across the tracks; except for the coat, the mangled body cannot be identified. Vijay is presumed dead, yet Gulabo pursues a quest for his public recognition, and Vijay becomes a posthumously revered poet. Some of the most appealing shot sequences in *Pyassa* involve the traditional Indian cinema's fantasy-musical interludes in which character and conflict are revealed through song-and-dance spectacle. In *Pyassa*, these performances are otherworldly moments of romantic, personal revelation. Similarly, in Hector Babenco's *Ironweed* (1987), the alcoholic Helen (Meryl Streep) launches into a performance of a song, "He's Me Pal," in a fantasy interlude, a recalled memory, set in a Depression-era saloon in which Helen, a former professional singer, reverts to her one-time attractive, talented self. She sings a glorious rendition of the song to the acclaim of the patrons in the bar; once the performance ends, the fantasy collapses into reality to reveal that she was barely noticed by the audience, despite some polite applause, and she looks worn out from her chronic alcoholism. These musical fantasy interludes provide a cinematic space and time, a calculated, fantastic interruption of the real world that situates moments of expansive counter realities, imaginary placements within naturalist narratives.

Rainer Werner Fassbinder's *Händler der vier Jahreszeiten/The Merchant of Four Seasons* (1972) depicts the decaying life of Hans Epp, an alcoholic push-cart fruit seller, as he is revealed in a state of inexorable decline. Fassbinder's use of deep-focus shots, depicting the home, the street, the bar, and other sites, produces a realist, balanced perspective. Hans, haunted by memories, remains a creature of the reactive and bleak present, with a future circumscribed by the weight and sounds of a push cart in the city: "Even the sound-track reflects the movie's predominant negative tone by having a constant, whispering background of automobiles and street noise: the mechanized city is always some-where behind the action."[32] Hans is an extension of the push cart, an urban presence. Fassbinder's spatial-distancing shots, set through windows or in front of mirrors, suggest framing perspectives of stages in Hans' crisis of decline.

Hans Epp (Hans Hirschmüller), an observed spectacle ruined by alcoholism, trudges across the paved streets with a push cart, weighed down with besotted memories of replayed personal failures of his own making. Epp's depressing struggle incorporates his own debilitating impulses as well as external social forces, especially his judgmental family of in-laws. As if describing Hans' ceaseless suffering, Engels observes that alcohol is readily available for the alienated working class, despite its detrimental effects:

> All possible temptations, all allurements combine to bring the workers to drunkenness. Liquor is almost their only source of pleasure, and all things conspire to make it accessible to them. The working-man comes from his work tired, exhausted, finds his home comfortless, damp, dirty, repulsive; he has urgent need of recreation ... Drunkenness has here ceased to be a vice, for which the vicious can be held responsible; it becomes a phenomenon, the necessary inevitable effect of certain conditions upon an object possessed of no volition in relation to those conditions.[33]

Middle-aged Hans Epp, in a conclusive suicidal act, drinks himself to death in a frenzy of alcohol shots as he sits among his friends in a saloon. According to George Lellis, Hans Epp is "a clinical case study"[34] of Naturalism's grinding forces abetted by alcoholic consumption. *The Merchant of Four Seasons* chronicles domestic crisis linked to earlier naturalist film melodramas in which alcoholism, abusive behavior, sexual betrayal, and class tensions are elemental precepts. The audience is positioned to read Fassbinder's revisionist melodrama as a study in failure, as Hans is worn down to a nub of his former self. As Hans consumes alcohol, it consumes him.

Fassbinder's reading of Douglas Sirk's melodramas from the 1950s has been well documented, but there is another industrial reference: D. W. Griffith. In early productions such as *What Drink Did* (1909), *A Drunkard's Reformation* (1909), and *The Struggle* (1931), "the saloon and alcohol consumption are represented as major threats to home and hearth, functioning as environmental catalysts, [n]aturalist 'derangements,' for male-moral degeneration."[35] In D. W. Griffith's dark fairy tale, *Broken Blossoms* (1919), Lucy (Lillian Gish), a lonely young woman, experiences an intense level of torment caused primarily by impoverished living conditions and her father, a brutish, besotted variation of *La Bête humaine*. According to Robert Lang, D. W. Griffith's melodrama demonstrates "the failure of femininity in dealing with the world."[36] Wandering about the physical and human decay surrounding her, nearly ethereal in her gentle loneliness, while evading violence from her abusive, near-alcoholic father, the boxer known as Battling Burrows (Donald Crisp), Lucy is Griffith's melodramatic heroine struggling to survive in a battle of the emotionally abandoned in an implacably sordid environment.

According to Sandy Flitterman-Lewis, in *Broken Blossoms*:

> it is the figure of Lillian Gish's heroine-victim that serves to unify ... the melodramatic mode: the spectacle of female suffering crystallizes in the melodramatic mainstays of violence and sexuality... and binds the theatrical and the cinematic into one singularly compelling form.[37]

In Griffith's naturalist narrative of suffering and loss set in London's Limehouse district, a run-down site of violence, drugs, prostitution, and poverty amid the misery of turn-of-the-century social debris, Lucy can barely survive.

Griffith deploys the familiar rhetoric of naturalist narrative when describing Burrows as "an abysmal brute ... a gorilla of the jungles,"[38] and in Griffith's first shot of Burrows, the audience witnesses his alcohol consumption. Griffith places this family in established naturalist sites: the impoverished home, boxing ring, and seedy bar-room. As if entrapped in an abusive domestic relationship, Lucy is not only an abused teenager, but also an abused woman, substitute wife. Perhaps the most infamous and harrowing shot sequence in *Broken Blossoms* is the claustrophobic closet sequence. Drunk with rage and quite plausibly in a fit of sexual jealousy over Lucy's innocent friendship with an Asian man, Burrows breaks down the door of a closet in order to finally beat his daughter to death. In a series of close-up shot–reverse shots, Burrow's enraged face is juxtaposed with Lucy's terrified, affective expressions of silent screams. As the camera cuts between entrapped, closeted Lucy—her face is a study in hysteria—her father breaks down the door in near-psychotic rage—a study in male hysteria—as he ensnares his prey for the last time. This is her final beating.

In Freud's essay "The Relation of the Poet to Daydreaming" (1908), he states that "happy people never make phantasies, only unsatisfied ones. Unsatisfied wishes are the driving power behind phantasies [which] improve on unsatisfactory reality."[39] "Phantasies" cannot save Lucy, Griffith's broken blossom. She could not survive in the ceaselessly hostile environment with her enraged father and no viable means of escape.

Fassbinder's naturalist melodrama also demonstrates a historical linkage with Griffith in its production design; there are two *Griffithesque* tableau vivant shots in *The Merchant of Four Seasons*. As Hans is no longer drunk but visibly unsettled and desperate, he goes to retrieve his wife and child and advances toward them, but they stand behind the protective formation of a clutching group of in-laws. Each family member holds the next in a line of resistance; the dynamic is alternately humorous and pathetic, but it is successful, for it deters Hans. The theatrical pose renders a "naturalist moment" of cohesion. In a later shot sequence, set in the saloon, Hans has collapsed dead on the table as the other revelers sit passively around him with shot glasses in the foreground of the frame; it is the moment of Hans' self-destructive fulfillment, and Fassbinder's tableau shot solidifies the process of decline. Hans' death is met with an overwhelming, ironic silence.

'ROID RAGE

Nicholas Ray's postwar melodrama *Bigger Than Life* (1956) is a study in the deflation and near demise of teacher Ed Avery (James Mason), an educated postwar middle-class male who is taking the cure, the newly marketed wonder drug cortisone, for his illness. Ray's wide screen technicolor production, composed in realistically framed medium and close-up shots, exposes the deleterious consequential effects of *legal* drug abuse. The film refutes the promise of the "miraculous" new consumer product and salvation. *Bigger Than Life* may be viewed as an intergeneric blending of the melodramatic and the horrific in its critique of a drug-addled society and as a study of male decline into the Hyde-like posturing of an enraged, violent predator. James Mason's performance as a sympathetic man, loving father, husband, and schoolteacher feverishly shifts into an incensed and uncontrollable male threatening the American family, as he becomes a menacing, failed exception to the industrial myths associated with pharmaceutical progress and the consuming patient. In the name of research development, legal drugs frequently produce frayed results. In *Bigger Than Life*, Adrian Danks notes, "[how] its almost architectural and spatially confining use of the cinemascope frame, and how it circulates, places, and over-signifies objects, is indeed extraordinary."[40] *Bigger Than Life* explores critically relevant medical and social issues—a record of experimental near-failure—as it observes unforeseen side-effects. In his home, Avery is as frightening as a caged, angry beast in the zoo.

Michaël R. Roskam's crime drama, *Rundskop/Bullhead* (2011), set in Belgium's "cattle country," focuses on the grim life and experiences of the oddly sympathetic criminal, Jacky (Matthias Schoenaerts), a "steroid monster" working in a corrupt syndicate. Like the tainted, chemically enhanced beef he markets across Belgium, Jacky is a tainted man; as a child, he was savagely attacked and his testicles were literally smashed with a rock in an act of brutish juvenile cruelty. As an adult, Jacky takes hormone shots to enhance his impressively fit body—an external sign of masculinity masking his terrible disfigurement—and he is a very aggressive black marketeer. When alone, he throws punches into the air against invisible opponents, like Jake LaMotta (Robert De Niro) in *Raging Bull*, whose self-loathing inspires him to act out against his ghosts. Whether in a brothel or with interested female companions, Jacky does not fully function, but he acts. In one late shot sequence, immersed in steroid rage, Jacky shoots at the police, gets shot as a result, and in a close-up shot, he is fully exposed, like a slab of raw beef served on a plate.

Darren Aronofsky's *The Wrestler* (2008), an entertainment spectacle of protracted male decline, focuses on drugs, sports, a broken family, and the survival strategies of fringe people. *The Wrestler* details the daily humiliations of an aging, near-famous wrestler, a slight myth, whose life is subject to economic erasure due to unstable employment. The film begins with a retrospective view of photographic images of the wrestler's recent past life, a popular culture, fantasy image of male power in profile. In the present moment, ranging from a strip bar he frequents, to the parked van where he lives, to a grocery store where he slices meat as a part-time butcher/counter-worker, to a third-rate wrestling ring after shooting up steroids to sustain him physically, "Randy, the ram," is no more; he is a forgotten poster left hanging in a room, similar to the poster hanging on his van's wall covering holes and gaps in time. The crowd no longer roars as it did a few decades ago to see him fight; while occasionally supportive, they frequently mock him as he enters small arenas for pick-up money, coming from staged fights. When out of the local wrestling ring, Randy (Mickey Rourke) works at odd jobs while longing for a final opportunity at elusive fame, attention, respectability, and as the nearly broken Terry Malloy states in Elia Kazan's *On The Waterfront* (1954), some "class." Randy has nothing of substance left except elusive recollections; he is the spectacle of a bruised, drugged, mostly forgotten man who at one point is literally stapled together to prevent further bleeding. Randy tells his uncaring daughter, "I'm an old broken down piece of meat."

At this late stage of his career, Randy resembles "Mountain" Louis Rivera (Anthony Quinn), the damaged former boxer belatedly transformed into a racialized and pathetic costumed wrestler—the howling native American—in Ralph Nelson's *Requiem For a Heavyweight* (1962), as well as "Stoker" (Robert Ryan), the betrayed aging boxer in Robert Wise's noir narrative *The Set-Up* (1949). Stoker is nearly ruined by mobsters who fail to corrupt his one last fight and who lose money on their fixed bet. Wise's diegetic human and musical sound effects and chronological sequencing of events compose a naturalist study in exploited, battered male decline.[41] Randy, "Mountain," and "Stoker" face medical calamities should they continue in their preferred careers inside the ring, but the humiliation of performance-failure, even death, does not deter them.

Laurent Cantet's *Entre les murs/Between the Walls* (2008), released the same year as *The Wrestler*, features emotionally and occasionally physically contentious encounters between opposing semi-friendly foes in the enclosed space and time of a classroom. Cantet's film suggests fighting without "fighting." *Between the Walls* is a blending of fictionalized, reality-based daily experiences with extensive sequences of sharp dramatic focus that observe a young male teacher, François (François Bégaudeau), moving cautiously in an enclosed (ring) classroom set in a contemporary Parisian working-class neighborhood junior high school in which groups of mostly immigrant fourteen- and fifteen-year-old students wrestle with their hapless teacher over the specifics of mundane knowledge. When the nearly exhausted, frustrated teacher—the true "other" in this narrative of others—in a moment of predictable pique, erupts and labels two especially uncooperative female students as "skanks"—a slang expression for women of low moral esteem, and one occasionally used to signal prostitutes—the class turns on him, and as the teacher is exposed as fallible and imperfect, the students symbolically win a round in the uneven match of willful pugilism. Cantet's film employs long takes in realistic settings with local dialect spoken by non-professional actors in this neorealist experiment detailing the battering and humiliation of a skilled laborer as well as revealing the pervasive sense of stratified hopelessness, infused with dreamy illogic, that his students will likely experience in their future. Regardless of encountering repetitive facts and fracas, the spent teacher inevitably returns to the ring-classroom to engage new opponents.

In *The Wrestler*, Randy's increasing addiction to steroids and its ability to prop him up for another round in the ring is filling—and killing—him with false bravado. To enhance whatever professional opportunities may be available to him, Randy meets with a drug dealer in the gym and purchases powerful steroids. Randy believes that he needs steroids, but his body is evidently in decay due to past abuse and natural aging. With the promise of an anniversary match that recalls, potentially re-enacts, his most famous wrestling bout, Randy attempts to reverse his physical decline. Even a heart attack does not stop his re-entry into the sport-labor that exploited him for years. Aronofsky's camera positioning frames Randy in multiple traveling shots from behind, with occasional facial close-ups. Aronofsky's emphasis is on displaying the worn, near-broken body of a non-green Hulk figure, as if Randy were becoming a freak. As Randy is no longer a prime physical specimen, he tries to get work loading and unloading crates and working part time at a meat counter.

Aronofsky's medium, close-up, and over-the-shoulder combination of handheld and set shots of Randy working in a blue-collar position behind the meat counter in a local grocery store reveals the mundane routines associated with food preparation: slicing, cutting, weighing, and making sales. Like Martin Scorsese's Bête humaine, Jake LaMotta/"Raging Bull," Randy stares into the mirror as he puts on his work clothes in a manner recalling a fighter preparing for a bout, but this formless wardrobe indicates symbolic, humiliating decline. As Randy walks through the store to the meat counter, in his mind, he concurrently approaches the wrestling ring as he hears the crowd chant in unison, indicating the lingering effects, the presence of injections and altercations. After he is exposed and humiliated by a customer, Randy loses his self-control and irrationally slams his thumb into the slicer, with blood gushing all over, followed by the screams of the shocked shoppers. After trashing the counter and the aisles and harassing the customers, Randy exits, disrobing from his work clothes. As long as steroids prop him up, for Randy there is only the ring. At his last match, Randy reveals himself to the audience: a brutalized spectacle. Aronofsky's protracted medium shot of Randy hovering precariously on the ropes is the conclusive identity marker of a looming, drug-addled body, signifying that Randy was a wrestler and not a discounted meat carcass.

Syphilis Hereditaria Tarda

In 1898, Eugene S. Talbot's analysis of social degeneracy erroneously concludes, "There are very good reasons for believing that the race is becoming immune to syphilis, and that this disease will disappear."[42] According to Jackie Stacey, the hereditary-based illness appears as one of the nineteenth century's recurring signs linked with the "genetic imaginary": a fantasy landscape generated by images, icons, scenarios, and discoveries, the genetic imaginary cuts across science, the cinema, and popular culture. Particular narrative and visual formations recur and mutate, borrowing and extending familiar tropes and motifs and inventing new associations and transpositions.[43] Stacey classifies the "genetic imaginary [as] an organization of cultural fantasies ... the imaginary refers to the fears and desires organizing a particular repertoire of fantasies that have a deeper, often indirect, set of cultural investments and associations," to which she adds, "genetic discourse has proliferated multiple metaphors through which the gene has been produced as imaginable, knowable, and tangible."[44] Henrik Ibsen's study of a bourgeoise family and inherited causalities, the naturalist drama *Gengangere/Ghosts* (1881), documents a series of clinically sound, emplotted melodramatic disasters as the final-stage syphilitic Oswald Alving asks his mother to give him, "The sun.—The sun."[45] Oswald's body and brain will imminently cease to function, leading to inevitable death in the final stages of an inherited venereal disease contracted from his father. As Oswald sits motionless in his chair, the biological-familial "ghosts" appear, not as supernatural presence, but in pathological space and time as inherited, genetic imperatives. In *Ghosts*, Oswald is a naturalist case study of bodily decline.

The imperfect gene and related notions of heredity function as deconstructing agencies, metaphorical landscapes of the individual or family, with the body as fluid setting. Expressions of biological illness become spaces linked to the Deleuzian imaginary, part of the naturalist schema. Daniel Gerould and Oscar Méténier observe the relationship between these codes and their presence in naturalist narratives: "The Naturalists in the theater insisted on direct observation, research, and documentation; precise notation of fact; and objectivity of technique. They applied to drama the discoveries and methods of nineteenth-century science, particularly those of experimental medicine, to produce authentic case histories and clinical studies."[46]

In *Ghosts* and subsequent naturalist narratives, the human body contains not only the seeds and metaphorical blueprint of life but also microbes of destruction—the affective agencies of declining mortality—such as the germs and genes involved with venereal diseases, birth defects, inherited feeble-mindedness, and other deleterious inherited illnesses. The conceptual gene and notions of heredity are biologically implicit—*not* supernatural—conceptual designs suggesting "fate" as a field of play in naturalist narrative. In 1903, Martin Schütze observed the socio-biological imperatives prominently informing *Ghosts*: "Fate in the consistent naturalistic drama is not a directing benign providence, nor some transcendental reason . . . but a dumb, blank mechanical power, senseless and purposeless . . . To the naturalist, man is a midge setting forth into the limitless void."[47] The horrific presence of inherited venereal disease—the invisible derangement—traceably destroys Oswald in multiple narrative formations.

As noted by theatrical and film director André Antoine, "I have read *Ghosts*. It is like nothing in our theatre; a study of heredity, the third act of which has the somber grandeur of a Greek tragedy."[48] The modern era of the socio-biological supplants the classic era of tragedy. In 1890, *Les Revenants/Ghosts* was staged by Antoine in the fourth season for the Théâtre Libre. In Antoine's diary, he wrote: "We played *Ghosts* last night. I believe that it made a profound impression; in the last scenes, a veritable anguish gripped the assembly . . . I found myself shaking, unnerved, and incapable of regaining my self-control for some time."[49]

In Edvard Munch's *Oswald's Collapse* (1920), a lithograph illustration printed in black on beige paper depicting Oswald's terminal remaining moments, the prostrate body of Oswald's dispirited mother clings to the chair containing what is left of her son. Munch's studies of Ibsen's crumpling bourgeoise family in crises were the product of a commissioned theatrical collaboration; "In 1906–07 he [Munch] fulfilled his most exacting literary commission, which was to design sets for the productions of *Ghosts* . . . at Max Reinhardt's Kammerspieltheater."[50] According to Carla Lathe, this Munch–Reinhardt collaboration institutes malfunctioning heredity as a recurring trope in naturalist narratives—the genetic mystique—within the spatial and temporal design of the home: "Reinhardt asked Munch to decorate an upstairs reception room with a frieze and to design sets for the performance of Ibsen's *Ghosts* . . . The enclosed space on the stage demonstrates a confined state of mind."[51] The Alving home, a spatialized metaphor, is the confining, claustrophobic objective correlative of Oswald's dissolving mind, as the experimental narrative produces an experimental set design. The same nuanced setting is evident in George Nichols' unsettling adaptation of Ibsen's naturalist melodrama *Ghosts* (1915).

With screen intertitles such as "the first sign of the inherited taint . . . the clutching hand of heredity [and] locomotor ataxia," Nichols' *Ghosts* examines a family and individual's decline. Oswald (Henry B. Walthall) is doomed by inherited biological factors not of supernatural origin. Oswald suffers from a highly visible and documented illness affecting mental and bodily control. According to James Goodwin, in the late nineteenth century, the emerging art of medical photography documented multiple examples of genetic and social diseases: "In the 1880s Muybridge compiled an extensive, systematic photographic record of the movements of different human body types, a few of which could have been rendered easily as grotesques."[52] Goodwin concludes that Muybridge's *Animal Locomotion: An Electro-Photographic Investigation of Consecutive Phases of Animal Movements, 1872–1885* (1887), presents motion study images of scientifically relevant, clinical data:

> One volume . . . documents Abnormal Movements of male and female subjects, both nude and semi-nude. The physical conditions and disorders among these patients . . . include locomotor ataxia . . . the images effectively avoid overtones of the grotesque, which typically involve distorted, reflexive appearances.[53]

Muybridge's historical photographs are signifying records of various maladies; these images objectively depict the body in decline. For the viewer, Muybridge's photographs of infirm people defamiliarize the bodily familiar; the images fascinate, while frequently repulsing the observer. Muybridge's photographic images feature a series of pictures-in-motion; in particular, one series features a nude man suffering from "locomotor ataxia," the degeneration of the spinal cord, a likely product of venereal disease. However, as Stacey declares, "the gene is not an object that can be readily identified in a photograph,"[54] and in Muybridge's images, it is unknown whether the subject of the photograph contracted the disease or it is a consequence of heredity.

Locomotor ataxia, a disfiguring (now curable) illness, is linked with progressive stages of venereal disease and significantly associated with the theme of the "body in decline" naturalist narrative given its medical and moral linkage. The link between cause and effect fueled research and speculation in the nineteenth and early twentieth centuries: "For a long time, the etiology of this disease remained unknown. The link between syphilis and tabes dorsalis was gradually established in the second half of the 19th century, mainly based on epidemiological observations."[55] Tatu and Bogousslavsky review the historical record: "The relationship between tabes dorsalis and syphilis progressively emerged toward the end of the 19th century in a medical world beset by the notions of predisposition and heredity."[56] In 1911, *The American Journal of Nursing* published "Locomotor Ataxia Joe: A Human Document Founded on Facts," which chronicles a nurse's case study of a deceased patient as a victim of locomotor ataxia. According to his nurse, former day laborer Joe Brown, a released prison inmate and hospital patient, was overwhelmed by chronic circumstances. Joe Brown is described as nearly crippled at the spinal cord, incapable of walking steadily, and with poor vision. In *Ghosts*, Oswald belongs to a privileged social class yet suffers from locomotor ataxia, the same inherited disease as Brown, who is described by his nurse in compelling language: "Joe Brown stood before the desk of the supervising nurse in one of the New York city hospitals ... His disease was an incurable one of locomotor ataxia, and ... a hopeless case ... There was a haunted look in his downcast eyes."[57] These anecdotal and medical publications, along with photographs, theatrical productions, and film, provide multiple representations of defective heredity, genetic malfunctions, and the resulting body as naturalist spectacle, largely commencing with Ibsen's *Ghosts* and its hypertextual narratives.

Like Dr. Jekyll's peering into the microscope at living organisms in the opening shot sequence of John S. Robertson's *Dr. Jekyll and Mr. Hyde* (1920), something unseen is now detected: "Before the discovery of the Treponema pallidum bacterium in 1905, the affirmation of the syphilitic etiology of tabes dorsalis could be regarded as the first demonstration of the power of careful observational studies for the advancement of medical knowledge."[58] Naturalism accesses visibility for both germ and its product—the sick individual—evolving into speculative narratives. These naturalist narratives involve tropes associated with class, race, and sexuality, developed in plots involving promiscuity, troubled marriage, and most significantly, the unknown yet considerable power of theoretical heredity, from evolution to degeneration.

In Nichols' *Ghosts*, Henry B. Walthall plays two roles—the senior, corrupting Mr. Alving and Oswald, his corrupted son—as the linkage between the males is visually and genetically situated in the passing of fatal illness from the former to the latter. In Nichols' study of heredity and inevitability, alcohol is consumed, prior debaucheries are referenced, incest is nearly committed, venereal disease is present, and the peaceful normalcy of the more privileged social class is subject to ruination. Nichols depicts Oswald's descent into madness and death as a protracted, grinding process, the end-product of his biological fate. According to nineteenth-century medical researcher Alfred Fournier, "Paternal influence ... [is] liable to exercise itself ... by inherent degeneration of the germ, which reveals itself subsequently under very diversified morbid forms."[59] It is common for naturalist narratives to incorporate the notion that "a syphilitic father can, by virtue of a syphilis still recent and active, be eminently prejudicial to his children."[60] Therefore, marriage would inevitably be "cursed" in a biological, non-supernatural sense. In *Ghosts*, the solemnity of a wedding service between unknowing brother and sister is revealed as potential entrapment, another aspect of an inherited curse. In multiple naturalist film narratives, an ill-fated wedding sequence, its "before and after" denotes consequential sexual coupling involving venereal disease.

Eugène Brieux's corrosive drama about the syphilitic and ignorant society, *Les Avariés/The Damaged* (1901),[61] was the subject of multiple film adaptations. Edgar G. Ulmer's *Damaged Lives* (1933) features a young, privileged couple who grapple with the issue of an errant man's—Don Bradley's (Lyman Williams)—reckless pre-marital affair, his resulting venereal disease, and a consequential pregnancy. According to Christopher Justice, *Damaged Lives*, with its extended shot sequence in a medical clinic featuring a bevy of scientific horrors, including patients with the bodily signage of locomotor ataxia linked to the individual's moral as well as physical decline, may be categorized as a "sex hygiene film."[62] Justice notes that "as the doctor opens each room, a new spectacle is exposed to produce shock and teach Bradley a lesson."[63] Ulmer's controversial misery exhibition also contains one suicide, one attempted suicide, extensive prevarication, and alcohol consumption. These intimidating images serve a dual function, denoting clinical authenticity and serving as a dreadful admonition to the Depression-era audience.

In a notable shot sequence from another adaptation of Eugène Brieux's drama, Phil Stone's *Forbidden Desire*, aka *Marriage Forbidden* & *Damaged Goods* (1937), the afflicted young male George Dupont (Douglas Walton) peers into a microscope at hordes of swimming bacilli—just as Dr. Jekyll did some years earlier—as one infectious specimen beholds another. Like Ulmer's Don Bradley, Stone's Dupont picks up a "loose woman" at a party while both are drunk. Their illicit intercourse leads to his damaged condition. Stone's adaptation unfolds as a series of revealed bad news, and Dupont's illness is eventually revealed to the perplexed family.

In *Ghosts*, Nichols establishes the encroaching space and time of Oswald's demise inside the home as a pathetic dynamic between Oswald and his emotionally collapsing mother (Mary Alden). Oswald's loss of bodily control, his directionless mutterings, and the inevitable physical collapse situated within the parlor serve as the fulfillment of his crippling heredity. Like a grim patient in a hospital experiencing the final stages of physical degeneration, Oswald expires as a broken naturalist spectacle brought about by debilitating inherited biological sources. Nichols' closing shot, the close-up of a deceased, nearly grinning face of Oswald lying on his side, technically renders a terrifying irony that a staging of Ibsen's drama could not. Nichols' ghastly, final shot of Oswald appears like an Andres Serrano morgue photograph.[64]

In Akira Kurosawa's postwar study of conscience and crisis, *Shizukanaru kettô/The Quiet Duel* (1949), as a young unmarried doctor (Toshirô Mifune) prepares for surgery, he accidentally cuts his finger on an unclean scalpel, thus infecting himself with the blood of a syphilitic male patient. Kurosawa's film, featuring long-shot sequences in realistic settings, confronts social issues including poverty, abstinence, illegitimacy, debilitating infections, and the passing of contaminated genetic material. As rain falls

Figure 2.4 George Nichols' *Ghosts* (1915)

outside the medical clinic serving the local population, the doctor's personal visions of marital bliss are confounded. The "quiet duel" is fought within the doctor's distressed mind and otherwise healthy body. In one tranquil sequence, photographs in an album recall recent history, the visible past of a once-promising relationship between the doctor and his fiancée. But there is neither a future nor potential recreation of these images; the doctor breaks off this engagement without providing an explanation, thus agonizingly accepting his celibacy until medically cured. Kurosawa features a working-class couple as a study in contrast with the doctor and his conflicted intended: the original infected, dishonest male patient and his soon-to-be pregnant, unknowing wife. According to clinician Alfred Fournier, this is a form of biological determinism:

> What is more deplorable than to give a virtuous young woman the pox as a wedding present! This infected couple will engender children that will, inevitably, either die almost as soon as they are conceived, or be born with the father's disease. And what more hideous for a young household than the pox in the cradle![65]

The death of a deformed premature baby occurs off screen, and in a final irony, after his wife leaves him, the syphilitic patient blames the doctor for destroying his family.

Josh Trank's *Capone* (2020) is a gangster-syphilis narrative focusing on the final weeks in the life of fabled, infamous American Al Capone (Tom Hardy). According to Stephen C. Bousquet,

> In the last week of Capone's life, amid reports of his deteriorating health, a ghoulish death watch commenced on the street outside the Palm Island estate. Newsmen gathered outside the compound reported a parade of dark, sinister-looking limousines, many with Illinois license plates."[66]

Trank's naturalist narrative represents the final phase of Capone's waning life, a study of the disintegrating male. Bousquet notes that "While Capone was imprisoned at Alcatraz, the syphilis in his body began to attack his brain, and in 1938 prison doctors declared him a mental patient."[67] *Capone* is not a film about prior criminal intrigues; Trank's sick man—like Oswald in the final stages of his life, haunted by ghosts and microbes—weaves in and out of reality as his consciousness disappears among the living. Trank's Thanksgiving dinner table shot sequence especially reveals Capone's violent decline to his family. As Capone, Tom Hardy portrays a frequently raging, defecating, wounded male beast, subject to real or imagined ghost-like products of his guilt. As a fascinating, repellent spectacle, Capone is the subject of ongoing surveillance by his family, reporters, clinicians, and the public. Trank's disturbing bio-pic utilizes various medium and close-up shots and low lighting, followed by streams of silence, to establish a grim, inescapable sense of space and time. As microbial linkage and deleterious biological conditions indicate, Nichols' *Ghosts*, Kurosawa's *The Quiet Duel*, and Trank's *Capone* are naturalist narratives of decline.

Notes

1. Anton Kaes, "German Cultural History and the Study of Film: Ten Theses and a Postscript," *New German Critique*, No. 65 (Spring–Summer 1995), 48.
2. Ibid, 56.
3. This excerpt from Darwin's correspondence, accessed June 4, 2023, may be located in its entirety at https://www.darwinproject.ac.uk/letter/?docId=letters/DCP-LETT-7471.xml&query=february%201%2C%201871#DCP-BIBL-7703. Accessed August 31, 2023.
4. Gerald H. Pollack, Xavier Figueroa, and Qing Zhao, "Molecules, Water, and Radiant Energy: New Clues for the Origin of Life," *International Journal of Molecular Sciences*, Vol. 10 (2009), 1427.
5. Todd McGowan, "Atemporality amid Lumière Temporality," *Empedocles: European Journal for the Philosophy of Communication*, Vol. 5, Nos 1 & 2 (2015), 61.

6. Franziska Heller, "Water and Film: Fluidity of Time and Space and its Somatic Perception," *WIREs Water*, 5:e1315. See https://doi.org/10.1002/wat2.1315 (2018), 1, 3. Accessed June 4, 2023.
7. Winslow Homer reworked this painting in 1906 to include the presence of the larger ship in the background.
8. Heller, "Water," 10.
9. Jennie Irene Daniels, "Elite in Crisis: The Marginalized as a Site of Resistance in *La ciénaga* and *Coronación*," *Delaware Review of Latin American Studies*, Vol. 14, No. 1 (August 31, 2013), 3.
10. Ibid, 3.
11. Ibid, 3.
12. Raymond Williams, *Marxism and Literature* (New York: Oxford University Press, 1997), 132–3.
13. Raymond Williams and Michael Orrom, *Preface to Film* (London: Film Drama Limited, 1954), 21–2.
14. Émile Zola, *The Experimental Novel and Other Essays*, trans. Belle M. Sherman (New York: Cassell Publishing Company, 1898), 27.
15. Ibid, 27–8. Note: the italics are mine.
16. *Darwin*, second edition, ed. Philip Appleman (New York: Norton, 1970), 53.
17. Gilles Deleuze, "Introduction," *Oeuvres complètes*, VI, in *La Bête humaine*, by Émile Zola, ed. Henri Mitterand (Paris, Cercle du Livre Précieux, 1967), 14.
18. Leo Braudy, *Jean Renoir—The World of His Films* (New York: Doubleday, 1972), 51.
19. Daniel Pick, *Faces of Degeneration* (New York: Cambridge University Press, 1993), 84.
20. Ibid, 84.
21. John Anzalone disparagingly refers to Jacques' expository speech as this dramatic highpoint of the film as "the least convincing moment in an otherwise brilliantly composed and photographed sequence," in his article "Sound/Tracks: Zola, Renoir and *La Bête humaine*", *French Review*, Vol. 62, No. 4 (March 1989), 584. This author does not agree.
22. E. Paul Gauthier, "New Light on Zola and Physiognomy," *PMLA*, Vol. 75, No. 3 (June 1960), 300–7.
23. Braudy, *Renoir*, 90.
24. Douglas Jerrold, *Fifteen Years of a Drunkard's Life* (1828) (New York: Happy Hours Company, n.d.), 14, 33.
25. William A. Pratt, *Ten Nights in a Bar-Room: A Drama in Five Acts* (New York: Harold Roorbach Publishing, 1875), 39.
26. Donald Bogle, *Toms, Coons, Mulattoes, Mammies, & Bucks: An Interpretive History of Blacks in American Films* (New York: Bantam Books, 1974), 142.
27. Ibid, 147.
28. Piotr Kryczka, "Some Phenomena of Social Pathology in Poland," *Polish Sociological Bulletin*, No. 42 (1978), 102.
29. Ibid, 107.
30. Nasreen Munni Kabir, *Guru Dutt: A Life in Cinema* (Oxford: Oxford University Press, 2004), 87.
31. Carrie Messenger, "Poetry and Image in Guru Dutt's *Pyassa*," in *Verse, Voice, and Vision: Poetry and the Cinema*, ed. Marlisa Santos (Lanham, MD: Scarecrow Press, 2013), 63.
32. George Lellis, "Retreat from Romanticism: Two Films from the Seventies," *Film Quarterly*, Vol. 28, No. 4 (Summer 1975), 20.
33. Frederick Engels, *The Condition of the Working Class in England* (1892), (London: Panther Books, 1974), 133–4.

34. Lellis, "Retreat," 19.
35. Diane Smith and Robert Singer, "A Drunkard's Representation: The Appropriation of Naturalism in D. W. Griffith's Biograph Film," *Griffithiana*, No. 65 (Pordenone, 1999), 111. Note: *What Drink Did* was released two months after *A Drunkard's Reformation*.
36. Robert Lang, *American Film Melodrama* (Princeton: University Press, 1989), 62.
37. Sandy Flitterman-Lewis, "The Blossom and the Bole: Narrative and Visual Spectacle in Early Film Melodrama," *Cinema Journal*, Vol. 33, No. 3 (Spring 1994), 5.
38. Karl Brown, *Adventures with D. W. Griffith* (New York: Da Capo Press), 241.
39. Sigmund Freud, "The Relation of the Poet to Daydreaming," in *Character and Culture*, ed. Philip Rieff (New York: Collier Books, 1963), 37.
40. Adrian Danks, "'God was wrong': Nicholas Ray's *Bigger Than Life*," *Senses of Cinema*, Issue 50, March 2009, www.sensesofcinema.com/2009/cteq/bigger-than-life/. Accessed June 6, 2023.
41. Weegee, the famed photographer, plays the ringside announcer in Wise's film.
42. Eugene S. Talbot, *Degeneracy: Its Causes, Signs, and Results* (1898), (New York: Garland, 1984), 129.
43. Jackie Stacey, *The Cinematic Life of the Gene* (Durham, NC: Duke University Press, 2010), 69.
44. Ibid, 10–11.
45. Henrik Ibsen, *Ghosts*, trans. William Archer. See https://www.gutenberg.org/files/8121/8121-h/8121-h.htm. Accessed June 6, 2023.
46. Daniel Gerould and Oscar Méténier, "Oscar Méténier and 'Comédie Rosse': From the Théâtre Libre to the Grand Guignol," *Drama Review*, Vol. 28, No. 1 (Spring 1984), 15–16.
47. Martin Schütze, "The Services of Naturalism to Life and Literature," *Sewanee Review*, Vol. 11, No. 4 (October 1903), 436–7.
48. André Antoine, *Memories of the Théâtre-Libre*, ed. H. D. Albright, trans. Marvin Carlson (Miami, Florida: University of Miami Press, 1964), 123.
49. Ibid, 183.
50. Carla Lathe, "Edvard Munch's Dramatic Images 1892–1909," *Journal of the Warburg and Courtauld Institutes*, Vol. 46 (1983), 193.
51. Ibid, 202–3.
52. James Goodwin, *Modern American Grotesque: Literature and Photography* (Columbus: Ohio State University, 2009), 22.
53. Ibid, 28–9.
54. Stacey, *Cinematic Life*, 4.
55. L. Tatu and J. Bogousslavsky, "Tabes Dorsalis in the 19th Century: The Golden Age of Progressive Locomotor Ataxia," *Revue Neurologique*, Vol. 177 (2021), 377. See https://www.sciencedirect.com/journal/revue-neurologique. Accessed June 6, 2023.
56. Ibid, 380.
57. Marjorie Alice Watt, "Locomotor Ataxia Joe: A Human Document Founded on Facts," *American Journal of Nursing*, Vol. 12, No. 3 (December 1911), 209–10.
58. Tatu and Bogousslavsky, "Tabes Dorsalis," 381.
59. Alfred Fournier, *Syphilis and Marriage*, trans. P. Albert Morrow (New York: D. Appleton, 1882), 46.
60. Ibid, 32.
61. The title has also been translated as "damaged goods."
62. Christopher Justice, "Edgar G. Ulmer: The Godfather of Sexploitation?," in *Edgar G. Ulmer: Detour on Poverty Row*, ed. Gary D. Rhodes (Lanham, MD: Lexington Books, 2008), 27.

63. Ibid, 37.
64. See https://andresserrano.org/series/the-morgue. Accessed June 6, 2023.
65. Fournier, *Syphilis*, 5.
66. Stephen C. Bousquet, "The Gangster in Our Midst: Al Capone in South Florida, 1930–1947," *Florida Historical Quarterly*, Vol. 76, No. 3 (Winter 1998), 308.
67. Ibid, 307.

3. OPERATIVE SPACES

One recurring precept of naturalist cinema is that it documents the lives of non-idealized, unexceptional people, frequently at work or within the family structure. In some of the earliest productions of international film culture, the Lumière brothers and other pioneering filmmakers depict indexical non-fictional enactments, *actualités*, along with "cinema of attraction"[1] narratives of spectacular visual experiences. These *actualités* are a fundamental and ongoing aesthetic presence, a symbolic-precedent DNA strand in naturalist cinema—the "building block" of Realism—which reformulates footage exhibiting the space and time of the naturalist moment as it enters narrative formation. Megan Minarich links these *actualités* to an earlier photographic tradition that encounters and reveals the world, and concludes:

> Insofar as subjects of Lumière films exemplify the quotidian ... parents feeding a baby, workers exiting a factory—this direct engagement with the subject (or engagement as direct as something mediated can be) suggests that a degree of realism inheres in their transition from picture to moving picture. The camera, which remains stationary instead of jumping between shots, denotes a singularity of perspective much like that of the objective observer. Mise-en-scène enhances the realism of such films. In *Exiting the Factory*, we find an intensely realist subject situated firmly in a domestic space, as these are not just actors pretending to exit

a French factory, but the Lumières' own employees exiting the brothers' own factory.[2]

Actualités augment realism. According to Anthony R. Guneratne, in select Lumière films, space and time appear interconnected via the visual mechanics of movement: "What gives these early films a documentary quality ... is the Lumières' consciousness of the way in which the presence of their camera shaped the reality being filmed, a consciousness in the process of formation and therefore all the more revealing."[3]

In the following chapters, a close reading of several Lumière *actualités* suggests that international film traditions related to generic and industrial practices later surface as tropes endemic to the naturalist film aesthetic, like a shifting symbolic genetic line flowing from the past to the present. A non-chronological reading of five Lumière brothers films: *La sortie de l'usine Lumière à Lyon/Workers Leaving the Lumière Factory* (1895),[4] *Laveuses sur la rivière/Washerwomen on the River* (1897), *Charcuterie mécanique/The Mechanical Butcher* (1896), *Repas de bébé/A Baby's Meal* (1895), and *Démolition d'un mur/Demolition of a Wall* (1896), and other significant silent narratives fundamentally capture footage of the everyday, experienced routines of life and establish a theoretical entry point to suggest the nascent presence of the naturalist aesthetic in film narrative. Although not identified as *actualité*, the Lumière brothers' *The Mechanical Butcher* is a parody of labor- and work-related practices endemic to naturalist cinema, a comical extrapolation of themes and familiar tropes.

These Lumière brothers' films are consequential narratives: four films, a series of observed labor-related motions, quantifications of the real, are set within the world of work, while the fourth film is set in the home. These brief narratives from the earliest era of silent film production—exiting the worksite, wrecking a wall, grinding meat, scrubbing clothes, and feeding a baby—establish tropes endemic to the international naturalist film aesthetic linked to Realism's precepts of verisimilitude. These films are a series of observed motions, performative platforms from which the naturalist aesthetic, as conceptualized in film narrative, might be rearticulated in more complex industrial and experimental variations. Susana Viegas discusses the technical presentation of Realism in these *actualités*: "The Lumière Brothers ... sought the realism of the fixed single-shot equivalent to the spatiotemporal continuity of our everyday natural perception,"[5] then focuses on the specificities of each narrative and concludes:

> The Lumières' films were then seen as a reproduction of life as it is while, by contrast, Méliès' films [in historical contrast]were seen as a manipulation and creation of a wholly other, eccentric, reality. Thus, *La sortie de l'usine Lumière à Lyon/Workers Leaving the Lumière Factory* (1895)

takes us to real life and to the way that we naturally perceive it. In this case, it takes us to the naïve pretension of representing reality as it is and as we would perceive it.[6]

Naturalism, as an aesthetic formation emanating from Realism, renders acts of substantive "pretension": this is a critical informing conceptual premise. In relationship to the "real" of the *actualités*, naturalist cinema advances the ideological and mimetic propensities of realism, generating within the film frame a site of interpretive, experimental observation, whether inside the living room, bedroom, or outside the factory, office building, and other labor-related physical venues, such as the brothel, prison, and coal mine. Realism's space and time are dynamically contextualized within the motion and the frame of naturalist cinema.

A Productive Species

One of the first films ever produced involved a factory and workers in a routine common to the modern world of labor: exiting from the worksite. The Lumière brothers' *La sortie de l'usine Lumière à Lyon/Workers Leaving a Factory* (1895) is a one-reel film shot in three extant versions, in which unidentified men, women, horses, carriages, and bicycles flow from two factory exits toward the foreground of the frame, and then all proceed outside a demarcating gate, beyond the frame, into turn-of-the-century Lyon and the imagination of the observer. Minarich notes that *Workers Leaving a Factory* fundamentally exhibits a "surface/depth dialectic"—movement without narrative—to which she adds: "the lack of a plot propelled by causal relationships ... [and the film's] non-narrativity helps fuel fragmentation by disabling the viewers' ability to identify with characters."[7] This is a film with subjects. *Workers Leaving a Factory* is a "realist text ... For the Lumières, the realism of the film and the realism of its subject are paramount,"[8] yet the notion of narrative closure—a readerly sensibility—is indeterminate.

Todd McGowan comments, "If the film ... *Employees Leaving the Lumière Factory* (1895) does not show what happens to the workers who leave the Lumière factory, the film nonetheless allows us to imagine a future in which we might acquire that knowledge."[9] This film invites a writerly open-endedness, in which the viewer's interpretive response extends the initial attraction and impression of the images into a substantive presence, complete with a corresponding metaphysic beyond the immediacy of the frame, leading, according to Haroun Farocki, to a glimpse into prefaced Realism:

> In the Lumière film of 1895, it is possible to discover that the workers were assembled behind the gates and surged out at the camera operator's

command. Before the film direction stepped in to condense the subject, it was the industrial order which synchronised the lives of these assembled individuals. They were released from this regulation at a particular point in time, contained in the process by the factory gates as within a frame ... In the opening sequence of this first film, the cinema's basic stylistic principle is already present. Its signs and meanings are not put into the world, they arise from the real. In the cinema it is as if the world itself wanted to tell us something.[10]

In this brief, enacted film, a swirling spectacle of compliant bodies in motion, many aware of the performative aspect of their energized departure, is a study in the movement of the prepared "real." The strutting, impulsive dogs traversing the frame are a playful, eruptive presence. Pao-Chen Tang notes how the dogs affect a painterly perspective: "This symmetry, however, is tempered throughout by a natural randomness as the dogs walk freely in and out of the two frames."[11] For the viewer, the effect of the workers' recorded exiting strategy is a vital kinetic presence, a familiar spectacle of modern life. For these workers, life outside the frame is to be imagined, but life and labor inside the factory are not in evidence, only moments of ambulatory departure. Their identities remain unknown, invisible beyond the recollected immediacy of the image. According to Farocki, this *actualité* initiates cinema's foray into images of modern labor. There are naturalist implications to this cinematic, historical linkage:

> The first camera in the history of cinema was pointed at a factory, but a century later it can be said that film is seldom drawn to the factory and even repelled by it. Films about work or workers have not emerged as one of the main film genres, and the space in front of the factory has remained on the sidelines. Most narrative films take place in that part of life where work has been left behind.[12]

According to Keith B. Wagner, *Workers Leaving the Lumière Factory* may be viewed critically in a more specific, socio-political context:

> The Lumiere brothers' *The Workers Leaving the Factory* (1895) was one cue to the barrenness that modernity held for those of the French working classes; in such images we see the pronounced drudgery of work that underpinned much turn-of-the-century urbanization in Lyon, France. A memorable but contested moment in film history for its dramatic compositional arrangement of men filing out of the bowels of their father's factory, which acted as a new type of cinematic vision. Construed in this way, *The Workers Leaving the Factory* was an actuality film in which the experience of their subjugation became a mode of observation.[13]

The Lumière's seminal glimpse into industry and people energizes the stillness of the painting and photograph into a visual, mobile image. Sara Nadal-Melsió notes:

> For a long time considered the first film ever shot, the Lumière brothers' footage stands as a glimpse of the promises of a medium that the filmmakers, and factory owners, as well as their ostensible subjects, the factory workers, seemed to be equally in awe of. Thus, the relationship between cinema and the factory is foundational in a very literal sense . . . The mise-en-scène, the contingencies of the weather and the appearance of the only non-worker, a dog, rapidly become the focus of the spectator's gaze as it searches for the singular in the repetitive. Thus, it is the reproductive qualities of film, which can be read as a substitute for those of the factory, that force the spectator's attention to turn to the disruptions and deviancies that resist the obedient flow of the workers as they exit the building.[14]

Nadal-Melsió also comments that "The film [*Workers Leaving the Lumière Factory*] does not in fact document the exiting of the workers into their everyday lives outside the factory but rather the imposition of the repetitive rhythms of capitalist labor onto that everyday life." She concludes, "Capitalism's temporal abstractions [are] inscribed in the gestures of the working body . . . capitalism in film is depicted as a work force of bodies consumed as images. The protocols of the factory film were therefore established as early as 1895."[15] The Lumière brothers' films contain a narrative propensity, generating fields of interpretive discourse, a suggestive "forward motion" beyond the initial documented realism of the *actualité* toward a naturalist context involving literal and symbolic acts; in the films depicting the modern world of labor, work is a process in which the worker is also product—frequently, a raw spectacle of disaffection.

According to Elizabeth Cowie, "Work is a process, a physical activity in time and space. Cinema, as a medium of representation, for the first time captured this process of work as motion, that is, as the transfer and transformation of energy into movement and action."[16] The factory, the laborers, and the related spectacle of human and machine in motion are a dominant aspect of naturalist film narrative. As Cowie concludes, "Work must not only be signified as such but also be contextually placed and qualitatively defined."[17] Ensuing film narratives documenting modern labor go inside the factory with the workers; what begins with an exit from a bicycle factory functions as hypertextual invocation to narratives of the assembly line, the meatpacking factory, and other industrial sites.

Workers Leaving the Lumière Factory thus stimulates a meditative reaction. There are many forms of commerce and business practices, some illegal, that occur inside and outside building and gates, and the assembly line, a critical feature of modern industrial standards, assumes a significant role in the cinematic motion of labor. As Nadal-Melsió notes:

> Because cameras were not allowed inside factories, footage of workers at the assembly line was, until the emergence of the militant factory film in the late 1960s, extremely rare. Partly because of this, the imaginary of the factory continued to be mediated for a long time through a very small number of cinematic images that, although fictional, acquired an unexpected mimetic density.[18]

The Lumière brothers' *Workers Leaving the Lumière Factory* provides a theoretical entry point in naturalist film for depicting laborers in multiple settings, ranging from narratives of the pathetic, to the dramatic and the humorous. From the assembly line, the mining site, the brothel, and beyond, in other relevant, experimentally consequential venues, the observed yet invisible human at work invokes naturalist analyses.

Invisibility Observed

Ashcan artist George Luks' *Street Scene: Hester Street* (1905), a dynamic urban landscape of social and ethnic groups in motion, depicts non-idealized moments of marketplace commerce on the streets of New York City, complete with push carts and locals hawking consumer products. Two years earlier, a similar flow of people and images were visualized in Alfred C. Abadie's *Move On* (1903),[19] an *actualité* as cited by Charles Musser:

> The Edison Manufacturing Company resumed production activities in the United States in late April, 1903 ... By this time, the Edison Manufacturing Company had three cameramen: Edwin Porter, Alfred C. Abadie, and James Blair Smith ... [Later,] Abadie subsequently devoted most of his efforts to making news films and actualities.[20]

Move On is a brief, unstructured observed series of moments, an *actualité* filmed in the urban setting of Manhattan's celebrated Lower East Side, depicting a minute-plus of motion on a street with people, police, trains, and push carts. Abadie's narrative foray into ethnic representation captures passing moments of turn-of-the century life and commerce. In the center of the frame, in a mostly static medium shot, social and business activity is recorded in depth, like an eyewitness watching street life. Abadie's camera then pans slightly from left to right; on the left side of the frame there are push carts and people, while on the right, an open space indicates an area for pedestrian and vehicular traffic. Starting from the background of the frame, aggressive police activity moves forward as pushcart vendors are urged to "move on" and out of the picture. Remaining in the background are images of passing overhead trains, people, and storefronts. Although accents, street life, and other historical markers may have changed—even what the push cart looks like—the socio-economic function of the push cart has not changed for the working class.

In 1913, J. W. Sullivan pondered, "What are the circumstances essential to the success of the push-cart business? What will the masses lose through the extinction of the ambulant pushcart man?"[21] In the modern urban environment, commerce and business relations are not only about constructing skyscrapers and market speculation; the building and commerce might be portable, even with wheels, and the market might stock oranges, not bonds. Sullivan's concern about any theoretical extinction involving the urban push cart was unfounded, but the question of a vendor's success remains, as it involves personal and professional issues. Ramin Bahrani's *Man Push Cart* (2005) is a film about an immigrant laborer's loneliness, and loss as he toils daily, mostly unnoticed, with his push cart; Pakistani refugee Ahmad (Ahmad Razvi), the merchant of crullers, may be read as a case study in naturalist declension.

In Clarence Brown's *The Goose Woman* (1925), the former opera singer Marie de Nardi's (Louise Dresser) career abruptly ends with the birth of an illegitimate son, resulting in the loss of stature and acclaim. She is reduced to hearing herself perform on a recording disk; likewise, Ahmad, once a popular recording artist in his native country, abandons his career after his son dies unexpectedly, thus losing his voice except when played on audiotapes like a retrieved memory. Ahmad daily faces the public, voicelessly vending to strangers, in his struggle for survival.

Engels concludes, "Happy are such of the 'surplus' [laborers] as can obtain a push cart and go about with it. Happier still those to whom it is vouchsafed to possess an ass in addition to the cart."[22] Bahrani's extended opening shot sequence of Ahmad's pre-dawn daily preparatory labor runs over seven minutes, revealing the grinding routine and its long hours, as he begins to sell fast food from an enclosed mobile cart, a technological advancement from the earlier days of urban street peddling. Bahrani's documentary-like images are an abstract mixture of close-up and medium shots, shifting in and out of focus, creating transitory impressions, recalling Scorsese's in motion, point-of-view shots from the driver's window in *Taxi Driver* (1976). Bahrani's urban images are enhanced by the natural sounds of Manhattan's streets at night, with passing expressions of local slang and dialogue, followed by realistic moments of brief exchange and commerce.

Ahmad, who lives by the strength of his back and willpower, is largely an invisible man, passed by people daily thousands of times, until he serves them fast food. Ahmad's day begins at night and ends later in the day; at one point, on an exhausted Ahmad's way to his empty home, he falls asleep on the subway. Like many immigrants, Ahmad works in Manhattan but lives in the historically déclassé borough of Brooklyn. According to Polina Kroik, this is a realistic change of venue, indicating class and economic prerogative:

> Bahrani captures the déclassé geography of the city by following Ahmad on his arduous route to and from the push-cart garage, as he pushes the heavy cart through traffic, and as he later makes his way back to his apartment in Brooklyn. By doing so, Bahrani differentiates the landscape of middle-class consumption (the abstract space of exchange) from the city as it is experienced by its working-class residents.[23]

Bahrani documents the circumscribed, troubled life and arduous physical labor of a contemporary worker by unraveling the tragic circumstances, "the fall," that is Ahmad's existential narrative. His push cart functions like a symbolic coal mine; as miners trudge to work to shovel coal, Ahmad's anonymous walk across the urban landscape with a portable, enclosing pit is as stultifying. In one shot, as Ahmad serves a customer from the push cart's window, establishing a frame within a frame, his hands represent the invisible whole man, functioning as synecdochic presence. Although Polina Kroik notes that, "In *Man Push Cart*, Ahmad is likened to Sisyphus, forever pushing his cart up a Manhattan hill,"[24] Ahmad may alternatively be viewed as a struggling, emotionally wounded man, one of a thousand nameless laborers.

Ousmane Sembène's *Borom Sarret/The Wagoner* (1963) is a short Senegalese film documenting the frustrating experiences of a working-class man (Ly Abdoulay) whose horse-driven cart/taxi/hearse labors between two parts of a bifurcated, yet singular setting: the "native quarters" of impoverished Dakar, old Africa, where payment for his service is infrequent, and the modernized spaces of apartment houses and countless automobiles in urbanized Dakar, new Africa, in which his service is not welcome. *Borom Sarret* is a film about motion, both mechanical and human, that barely goes anywhere without consequential economic or class-related conflict, as the wagoner winds up eventually leading his exhausted horse back to his wife and child. Sembène's film begins with a prayer but ends with a whimper; the wagoner repeatedly fails to get paid by those he serves, yet he serves. In medium, neorealist compositional framing, a traveling camera documents stalls of local commerce, the people and living quarters of old Africa, and then tony neighborhoods where the wagoner and his family will likely never live. Amadou T. Fofana refers to Sembène's narrative as "the chronicle of a typical day in the life of an ordinary post-independence Senegalese worker living in the outskirts of Dakar, trying to earn a living by carrying loads around in his cart."²⁵ Fofana notes a contentious socio-economic subtext functioning in *Borom Sarret*:

> an institutionalized and rationalized kind of discrimination and exploitation seems to reinforce and perpetuate the gap between the elite and the masses. There exists a clear divide between quarters for the poor and those for the elite, and a severe restriction of movement on the part of the masses who live in populous and disorderly neighborhoods.²⁶

In a startling close-up shot signifying demeaning power relations in the modern, urban "plateau" area, after the wagoner is cheated out of his due payment by a well-dressed African, Sembène positions the wagoner kneeling before the policeman who took his cart and now purposefully stands upon a fallen medal while the wagoner waits, posed in a troubling, near-begging image, for the policeman to lift his leg. According to Andrea Dahlberg, after the wagoner informs his wife about his failure to raise money for his daily labor, in a suggestively troubling conclusion, she leaves the immediate run-down area, "the unspoken implication is that she is prostituting

Figure 3.1 Ousmane Sembène's *Borom Sarret* (1963)

herself to feed her family."²⁷ By refusing to valorize poverty and labor as well as demonstrating an entrenched racial, class, and geographic divide, Sembène's study of privation, work and the family in post-colonial Africa is a naturalist film.

Kiran Rao's *Dhobi Ghat/Mumbai Diaries* (2010) examines class stratification, manual labor, and gender relations in location shots set in Mumbai. "Dhobi" is Hindi for washerman; Munna (Prateik Babbar) is portrayed as a hard-working, honest laundryman who delivers clean clothing to clients, one of whom is an educated, attractive woman of an upper class. Although she is attracted to him, Munna's attraction to this woman is unlikely to blossom into a relationship as he is inordinately self-conscious of his night-time job as a rat catcher working the sordid back alleys, clubbing rats. In one shot sequence, Munna is revealed as the neighborhood rat catcher by the woman as she unknowingly takes his picture and exposes Munna's secret vocation. She exposes him as he exposes rats. Rao's unglamorous setting, primarily portrayed in medium and close-up shot sequences of women and men washing clothing for clients recalls Lumière's *Laveuses sur la rivière* (1897); both films present precariat invisibility laboring in a modern city.

Factory Life

In Robert Koehler's painting of labor discontent, *The Strike* (1886), restless workers in the foreground of the frame emerge from the factory engaged in tense conversation with the likely owner of the factory to the left of the frame, while buildings in the background remain obscured in smoky perspective. These workers are not working, but exiting. Koehler's image of labor discord, created a year after Zola's *Germinal* (1885), a naturalist novel depicting the impoverished lives of miners and their consequential strike, documents a moment of aggressive near-confrontation on Koehler's politicized canvas.

Gerhart Hauptmann's historically based naturalist drama *Die Weber/The Weavers* (1892) focuses on the troubled lives of skilled Silesian laborers facing obsolescence at the textile mill during the Industrial Revolution and their subsequent rebellion leading to crushing results. One considerable feature of Hauptmann's drama and its adaptation by Friedrich Zelnik in *Die Weber/The Weavers* (1927) is its de-emphasis on the heroic individual and its greater focus on the mob in accelerating moments of class discontent, leading to a crushed rebellion. As noted by Martin Esslin, "*The Weavers* has no hero; its principal character is the mass of Silesian weavers ... [A] multi-focal snapshot technique makes the playwright concentrate on a single static segment of time."²⁸ Graphic artist Kaethe Kollowitz's woodcut-print series, an interpretive study of *The Weavers*, reproduces the naturalist cycle of poverty, rebellion, and defeat of the Silesian workers. Kollowitz's "Etching-Leaf 4-March of *The*

Weavers" (1897) reveals particularly vividly the furious, wearied workers inevitably heading toward their own destruction. Zelnik's film structures the inevitable grinding process of hordes of trade-trained workers as a flow of oppressive energies.

John Baxter's *Love on the Dole* (1941) an adaptation of Walter Greenwood's novel, documents the lives of an unemployed (previously working at a local factory and mine) working-class British family during the Depression in Hanky Park, 1930. Baxter's film provides a timely, grim reading of those socially dispossessed by class barriers, especially as they affect gender/sexuality, labor, subsistence employment, and survival in prewar Britain. In a film rich with local dialect and anachronistic slang, *Love on the Dole* is an intergeneric blending of melodramatic conventions—a critical emphasis is placed on the "fall from grace" narrative of the family's attractive daughter Sally (Deborah Kerr), who becomes a bookie's mistress so that they can survive, and the political film narrative examining class discontent. According to Caroline Levine, "the film's bleakly realist style suggested that Britons were allowed access to difficult truths and so lived in an open society."[29] Levine notes the film's imperfections while recognizing that it remains an interesting work:

> Compared to Hollywood movies of the same period, *Love on the Dole* has a low-budget look and a number of clumsy shots. All outdoor scenes happen against obviously painted sets, and there are remarkably few point-of-view shots, which makes it difficult to identify strongly with the characters. The film's bleak view of living conditions in working-class England is interspersed with stock footage of huge, churning machines and groaning factories.[30]

In Karel Reisz's study of alienated labor, adultery, and precision lathe turning, *Saturday Night and Sunday Morning* (1961), skilled working-class laborer Arthur Seaton (Albert Finney) is introduced in narrative voice-over and later depicted as a brooding statement of male disaffection in a postwar factory setting. Reisz's opening shot functions like a photograph documenting the space and time of a postwar factory; the establishing shot, in right panning motion, will lead to Arthur, in close-up and side angle framing, working at a machine. Arthur's descriptive voice-over registers discontent and self-awareness of other workers' lives; Reisz cuts from and juxtaposes close-up shots of laboring hands, a synecdochic constant, to working machinery. Although Arthur does not work on an assembly line, he is an integral part of the assemblage process; the line may be invisible, but the labor and its products are directed in the same conclusive direction as such machinery would indicate.

Unlike Chaplin's ballet-like motion on the assembly line in *Modern Times* (1936), Arthur is not graceful but possesses a genuine skill set as he labors under impersonal conditions, basically repeating the same task every day. Siegfried Giedion concludes that "The symptom of full mechanization is the assembly line, wherein the entire factory is consolidated into a synchronous organism."[31] In this sense, Arthur is the preferred worker compared with Chaplin's distracted, asynchronous worker. Although György Lukács declines to categorize Chaplin's *Modern Times* as a naturalist narrative, the depiction of Chaplin's drone-like labor, impoverished living conditions, implacable surveillance by management and the police, and a workers' strike do suggest a naturalist reading of personal and social class-based discontent. Giedion states, "its [the assembly line's] ultimate goal is to mold the manufactory into a single tool wherein all the phases of production, all the machines, become one great unit,"[32] which is humorously contradicted by Chaplin's persona; he is an eruptive presence. *Modern Times*, despite romanticized heteronormative relations and implausible closure, offers a credible surface view of impersonal working-class experience. As a disposable factory worker, Chaplin's character barely relates to his fellow workers: he seems playfully absent though dutiful, does not control his assigned task, and is out of touch with the product he makes. Ian Aitken examines Lukács' criticism of Naturalism in relationship to film form and content, specifically commenting on *Modern Times*:

> Lukács believed some allowances could be made for the inauspicious position which nineteenth-century naturalist writers found themselves in; he did not believe that any similar allowance could be made for the continued existence of a naturalist approach after 1900, when the growth of what he refers to as 'the new humanist movement' (Marxism and other forms of socialism) made it possible once more to envision and represent social reality as a totality . . . a film such as *Modern Times* 'must not be referred to as naturalist.'[33]

Modern Times is not a Depression-era documentary film probing the depths of class stratification; Chaplin utilizes humor and social satire, when he is forced to eat a meal by a malfunctioning machine, and the visually absurd, when ingested by a malfunctioning machine, to focalize core naturalist tropes. Engels notes that "The consequences of improvement in machinery under our present social conditions are, for the working-man, solely injurious and often in the highest degree oppressive."[34] These consequences are ripe for satire; the celebrated "Chaplin ingested by machine technology" shot sequence is a surreal-naturalist image: the worker as a meal, as the consumer is consumed. In this shot sequence, Chaplin, the flawed worker, obfuscates popular notions of mechanization and progress. According to Christopher Falzon, *Modern Times* is a study in labor and dehumanization, confirming Chaplin's comedic naturalist narrative as a prime example of the exploited and déclassé on the factory site:

Where workers are not simply replaced, they now have to conform to the requirements of the machinery. The speed and rhythm of their work is subordinated to that of the machine. Thus, workers have effectively been reduced to an appendage of the machine ... It is this dehumanization of the modern industrial worker that is the target of the first part of *Modern Times*.[35]

Contrary to Lukács' ideologically inflected appraisal of *Modern Times*, like Reisz's *Saturday Night and Sunday Morning*, these are films with pronounced naturalist capacities, testing and confirming a presence, favoring observational "empirical 'description' over a rendering of the social totality."[36] Naturalism's "insistence on immediate reality"[37] theoretically functions as a gateway to intertextual, contemplative practices rather than anachronistic humanist-ideological agendas. In *Saturday Night and Sunday Morning*, Arthur's voice-over reveals contemplative alienation from his labor and fellow workers; he defines himself as resistant to the normalization of routines and the mundane drudgery of life outside the factory in compelling naturalist terminology. Arthur states, "don't let the bastards ground you down," as a work ethic and life motto; he concludes, referring to older workers, that "they got ground down," and comments on his own existence: "I'd like to see anybody try to grind me down." Reisz's film, shot in black and white, a visual correlative for the immediate social setting, is a study in the grinding process and resultant nub theory signifying consequential entrapment.

For nearly two minutes, in multiple medium shots appearing like a traditional documentary revealing work and workers, Reisz's camera traverses the bicycle factory on a typical late afternoon. Within minutes, the workers are released from the factory and exit, some literally fleeing, as if discharged from imprisonment. B. F. Taylor notes the moment of release from the factory for these workers:

> The film cuts to a view of the factory from outside. The camera is positioned high above the ground and this position allows us to watch the workers leave. Men and women enter the frame from various points and slowly the frame begins to fill. The interest in this moment can be found in the direction taken by the workers, all moving in the same direction at the same time. This journey from work to home, like the one they make in reverse, from home to work, becomes a metaphor for the rigidity and repetition that governs their lives. In addition, this daily routine is characterised by a uniformity of direction, a linearity that is specific to a life structured in this way.[38]

As Arthur hastily flees on a bicycle—recalling Lumière's exit strategy—the other workers exit from the factory taking various routes while the opening credits roll. In *Saturday Night and Sunday Morning*, Reisz artfully contrasts Arthur Seaton's two lives: unhappy worker and outraged, predatory male; the former wears a mask while the latter removes his, at least for forty-eight hours, while away from his place in the factory.

The Daily Exploited

Vu du Pont/A View from the Bridge (1962), Sidney Lumet's adaptation of Arthur Miller's urban drama *A View from the Bridge* (1955), remains a critically neglected transnational naturalist film production that examines the betrayal of the code of the streets as it involves illegal aliens in a postwar setting. Lumet's low-budget film was shot in black and white on location at the docks and factory shipyard in Red Hook, Brooklyn, at that time a pre-gentrified, seedy area full of old apartment houses and gritty streets, with Lumet's interior settings shot in a French film studio. *A View from the Bridge* is a narrative of the working class, a formative study of unstable, undocumented, semi-skilled laborers and tropes endemic to naturalist cinema: raging male behavior, repressed-expressive sexualities, a near-claustrophobic sense of entrapment, and failed personal and social aspirations.

Omertà is the Southern Italian code of silence negating the cooperation with any and all authorities. In Lumet's adaptation, violating this unwritten code leads to humiliating exposure and the downfall of longshoreman Eddie Carbone (Raf Vallone), a man who does not know himself. As a result of his intense sexual jealousy and near-incestuous desire, Eddie "rats out" Marco and Rodolpho, his wife's two "off the boat" cousins who entered the city illegally and live with them in a cramped apartment. Waves of repressed sexual desire for his nubile niece undermine Eddie, who, like Miller's lost Brooklyn salesman Willy Loman, had the wrong dreams. *A View from the Bridge* is not only a film about a working-class laborer. Eddie's heterosexual rage—a previously submerged, private, and then public spectacle—levels the false accusation of homosexuality against Rodolpho, a perceived rival. According to Frank R. Cunningham, "In ... *A View from the Bridge* ... Lumet treats themes of fragmented identity,"[39] centering upon an uncontrollable, destabilizing sexual tension set to explode inside the apartment, and then on the streets.

Lumet's combination of close-up and tight shots of a triangulated family in decline, enacted in a claustrophobic set design in the kitchen, the living room, and the bedroom, creates a dynamic sense of soiled tension. Cunningham notes, "Through suggestive use of in-depth compositions and camera placements, Lumet here establishes the different emotional planes occupied by Eddie's subliminal conceptions of Catherine (Carol Lawrence) and of his wife Beatrice (Maureen Stapleton)."[40] Along with its examination of class and labor, as it reveals the decline of a violent, unsettled man and his family, *A View From the Bridge* intentionally documents the intersection between a flawed legal system and the undocumented inside and outside of the worksite.

Béla Tarr's non-linear, documentary-like narrative *Panelkapcsolat/The Prefab People* (1982) is a naturalist film examining the lives of a family nominally surviving in postwar, industrialized Hungary. In a series of claustrophobic medium close-up and reverse shots, set in protracted sequences, Tarr depicts tedious, combative life in an unattractive housing project as it is experienced in a cramped apartment and focuses on people entrapped in a dissolving marriage to reveal "the banal, desperate unhappiness of his working-class Budapest protagonists."[41] Alcohol and passionless sexual relations seemingly sustain the couple (Judit Pogány and Róbert Koltai). The husband receives the offer of a job away from their confined living quarters and his thankless job, but he elects to remain. As the film concludes, the couple purchase a new washing machine, a sign of material progress, as if to cleanse their unhappy past away. Jared Rapfogel notes that, in Tarr's *The Prefab People*, a study of grinding interpersonal relations between unexceptional people unhappily employed, "the relationship is a fraught, over-burdened one, with the struggle to subsist eating away at the emotional foundation of a marriage".[42]

David Riker's *La Ciudad/The City* (1998), an episodic narrative about the lives of immigrant workers, class, language barriers, and racial discontent, expands upon the theme of undocumented physical labor:

> Although a film like *La Ciudad* (1998) demonstrates that there is an underside to life in New York, it is a narrative of immigrant 'others' and represents, in a weave of social (neo) realism and magical romanticism, the experiences of exploited workers, women, and non-whites. These people are Ralph Ellison's new 'invisible' men and women, who mostly live in ghettos or housing projects if they are not homeless. They do dishes and clean gardens but disappear from respectable Manhattan at night, back to the South Bronx, Jersey—and to Brooklyn.[43]

In the first of four episodes, "Ladrillos/Bricks," Riker establishes naturalist themes involving the lives of undocumented migrants as they salvage the remains of a broken city in a former industrial, factory area that exists outside of progressive urban space and time; to the unnamed man who hires and exploits them, each migrant is useful human detritus. According to Laura Hapke, "Riker as a filmmaker concentrates on long-held shots of the faces of laborers and shoots footage using actual workers who volunteered to act in his film in ways that would mirror their actual work."[44] Hapke notes that "Riker aims his camera in a way that locates them in the workplace and pauses to take in their expressions, their sorrows."[45] Riker's *La Ciudad*, a complex blending of neorealism's low-budget black and white photography, on-site setting, and mostly non-professional immigrant actors speaking the Spanish language is also a documentary-like narrative of politically committed subject matter with a touch of romanticized messaging.

La Ciudad is a study in contemporary precariat labor. Sociologist Guy Standing examines the improbable status of contemporary, politically invisible laborers and their unestablished position in international socio-economic culture: "The precariat is a class-in-the-making . . . their labour is insecure and unstable . . . it relies almost entirely on money wages, usually experiencing fluctuations and never having income security . . . the precariat is exposed to chronic uncertainty."[46] Living and laboring under conditions augmenting Marx's conceptual alienation, the Latino men in "Bricks" survive day-to-day, exhausted, in search of a life they can see but not safely inhabit, yet they are not wholly demoralized. Jefferson Cowie notes how in the "harsh grey cinematography of *La Ciudad*, the framing of the characters amidst barren urban landscapes"[47] creates a bleak visual correlative for the film's overall thematic preoccupation concerning the urban immigrants' experience, especially for the initial episode: "'Bricks' begins with throngs of workers at a hiring corner competing to be selected by anonymous Anglo bosses. . . . [T]he only thing worse than being exploited in the day-labor market is not being exploited."[48] These worn laborers, speaking Spanish and slight, imperfect English, do hear each other, but nobody hears them, whether they demand a promised fair wage, seek information about the location of their worksite, or even request medical assistance for an injured worker. Hapke states, "Riker's mise-en-scène of liquor stores, lottery ticket booths, bodegas, and sidewalk debris is reminiscent of the wartorn [sic] vistas of Rossellini's *Open City* [1945] and Fellini's *La Strada* [1954]."[49]

In "Bricks," men literally stand on a street corner waiting for a van's occupant to solicit their non-unionized day labor collecting fallen bricks. Unlike workers, recycled bricks have value: "the production of bricks with its relatively high-energy input may be regarded as an investment for the future. Brickwork can survive for centuries without maintenance costs worth mentioning, giving the original environmental burden a long payback time."[50] Riker's camera placement frames the imploring faces of the exploited, in medium and close-up shots, on typical neighborhood streets and in the van's window—a frame within a frame—engulfed by the cacophonous mix of voices and street noise. Riker's *La Ciudad* is a film indicating a silenced presence, the invisibility of the day laborer. African-American artist Charles White's Depression-era realist canvas of expressive labor discontent, *Four Workers* (1940), depicts in frontal, cropped perspective the purposefully unattractive images of the non-idealized masculinity of workers in revolt. White's desaturated color schema complements the visual reception of rising, energetic sensations; the viewer intuits anticipatory movement arousing the formerly invisible.

In *La Promesse/The Promise* (1996), the Dardenne brothers examine the repetitive dehumanization of the disenfranchised immigrant in a sordid urban environment. *The Promise* is a naturalist narrative of exploited and undocumented illegal aliens arriving from several nations who are smuggled into the country and work as menial laborers for basic survival pay. These immigrants live surreptitiously in the seedy section of a Belgian city in a ramshackle boarding house where they are supplied with falsified documentation. As directed by Luc and Jean-Pierre Dardenne, *The Promise* frames a father (Roger) and son (Igor) portrait in multiple two-shots in a hand-held, "nervous" style, linking them visually and biologically as interrelated images. Eventually, each immigrant must pay off a debt to Roger, the smuggler-landlord. While working for Roger (Olivier Gourmet), Amidou (Rasmané Ouédraogo), an invisible African laborer, is accidentally killed falling from a construction platform, but he has managed to ask Igor (Jérémie Renier) to take care of his soon-to-arrive African wife and son. The promise, made to an undocumented and exploited dying man, is kept by the nearly corrupted son of a criminal in a credibly conciliatory moment.

As a documentary study in semi-skilled labor and worker invisibility, Juan Carlos Rulfo's *En el hoyo/In the Pit* (2005), focuses on the daily experiences of indistinguishable male and female laborers working on a Mexican highway construction site. The film is shot without Eisenstein-inspired low-angle shots that glamorize labor and laborer. *In the Pit* is a naturalist narrative of survival depicting the lives of the primary developers of Mexico City's roads and freeways. The freeway is the situational locus; the men and women who work there are exposed to natural elements such as relentless heat and rain, as well as to problems created by careless drivers and unforeseen yet preventable serious site accidents. In Rulfo's opening shot sequence, the camera is placed directly above a hole in the ground in which a worker is dangerously trapped. He is illuminated by a flashlight, emanating from a surface source beyond his reach, illustrating why the workers utter the word "hell" most often to describe their working conditions and the quality of their lives. This introductory sequence focusing on a life sunk into a pit sets the tone of the working conditions. After hours, the workers freely consume alcohol and playfully humiliate each other with threats directed against their masculinity; these shots effectively engage the viewer and contrast their down time with their impersonal labor.

Instead of workers plowing and planting in the earth, *In the Pit* reveals workers digging up asphalt with shovels and power tools into what is left of the earth, laboring day and night like an exposed colony of worker ants. As *In the Pit* traces the development of the next freeway, multiple shots document hands and bodies shaking from endless drilling, backs bending with each thrust of the shovel, and figures climbing into and out of the pit, performing like machines frequently without machinery. Rulfo alternates his shots of real-time labor with multiple sped-up motion shot sequences at the construction location. The laborers, passing automobiles and industrial machinery, are dizzily processed in a flurry of motion. These additional shot sequences, framed in wide-angle composition, reveal the city and its endless traffic as a spectacle in motion, creating near-impressionist rhythms of floating, colorful light appearing like blood passing through the veins and arteries of a great beast, through the asphalt heart that keeps beating.

As Rulfo's *In the Pit* examines the hazardous lives of semi-skilled Mexican laborers, Adrián Caetano's study of class, labor, and mindless violence, *Bolivia* (2001), a black and white naturalist narrative, examines the relentless spiraling downward, the unwarranted misfortune, of Freddy (Freddy Flores), an undocumented immigrant precariat laborer working in a seedy café frequented by unfriendly locals in contemporary Argentina. According to Amanda Holmes, "the café as mnemonic site. ... serves to question, confront and challenge feelings of identity and connection to community. Caetano's film offers a critique of the nostalgia surrounding the institution of the café for its inability to include new immigrants."[51] Caetano's *Bolivia* depicts a Bolivian national as the victim of poverty and abuse by the local police, and an unthinkable act of prejudicial violence. At a critical moment in *Bolivia*, there is a drive-by shooting fueled by a perceived insult, the product of near-deranged nationalistic rage, leading to Freddy's death like a swatted fly on a windowsill. Despite his efforts, Freddy cannot escape his own superfluousness in an ever-shrinking global economy that grinds the individual down into a nub.

Mining as Menace

René Girard concludes that "Violence too long held in check will overflow its bounds ... The slightest outbreak of violence can bring about a catastrophic escalation."[52] In naturalist cinema, the human animal's ability to reason and recollect frequently leads to reaction and revolt at the worksite in defiance of social order and logic. In discernible manifestations, violence is frequently a conditional product of socio-biological origin; whether a silent, controlled cry or one at incorrigible, ferocious decibels, the human is heard: disturbed, wounded, or combative. American filmmaker Barbara Koppel's documentary about the lives and escalating struggles of coal miners in rural Kentucky in the 1970s, *Harlan County, USA* (1976), begins with a darkly lit shot of a miner preparing and setting off a precise explosion in the mine. He shouts three times, "fire in the hole," and then throws the igniting switch; these are foreshadowing images. Kopple's historical narrative, a study in abusive power relations, focuses on the nearly forgotten, invisible, socially entrapped lives of coal miners and their suffering families, the struggle against corrupt elements in their own union, and the campaign to win a stronger contract from an unconcerned, elusive corporation. Kopple documents the history of a violent labor strike.

The strike and its historical-fictional permutations have an immutable presence in naturalist film narratives of divisive labor relations, the beleaguered working class, and, like a recurring genetic marker, the strike initiates acts of eruptive violence as stark realities. Zola's revolutionary anarchist Souvarine, in *Germinal* (1885), advocates a predatory "religion of destruction."[53] Souvarine's ideological pose is nihilistic. In a conversation about labor struggle, Souvarine comments, "Don't talk to me about evolution. Raise fires in the four corners of cities, mow people down, wipe everything out, and when nothing whatever is left of this rotten world perhaps a better one will spring up,"[54] later concluding, "The real hero is the murderer, for he is the avenger of the people, the revolutionary in action."[55] Souvarine calls for a violent reordering of the social order as he sees the working-class society of miners as sleeping brutish beasts. Aristotle's *History of Animals* provides observations about animal life and behavior that draw intriguing comparisons with human nature:

> Some animals utter a loud cry, some are silent, and others have a voice, which in some cases may be expressed by a word, in others it cannot . . . Man is the only animal capable of reasoning, though many others possess the faculty of memory and instruction in common with him. No other animal but man has the power of recollection.[56]

Naturalist narratives examine dehumanizing labor, which yields diagnostic volatilities challenging the very status of the human, for the human and animal may be made to labor for survival in some form of reductive existence. In *Germinal*, Zola describes one child laborer:

> this child . . . with his pointed muzzle, green eyes, long ears, resembled some degenerate with the instinctive intelligence and craftiness of a savage, gradually reverting to man's animal origins. The pit had made him what he was, and the pit had finished the job by breaking his legs.[57]

Zola adds compelling images of uncaged, animal-like frenzied behavior during the strike at the mine: "And indeed rage, hunger, and two months of suffering, and then this wild stampede through the pits, had lengthened the placid features of the Montsou miners into something resembling the jaws of wild beasts."[58] Naturalism's animal imagery conflates with and comments upon the human condition under siege from resurfacing external sources, like a repressed gene advances a disease. The human animal is a dynamic product of comingling factors of biological or socio-historical origin, particularly evident in families and individuals in cinematic narratives of the working class in crises.

Ferdinand Zecca's *Au Pays Noir/Tragedy in a Coal Mine* (1905),[59] an adaptation of Zola's *Germinal* (1885), features in a series of interlinked tableau settings the naturalist declension from a struggling working-class family's home into the hazardous mining site and the resulting unforeseen misery. Inside the mine there is an accidental explosion followed by flooding and death. *Au Pays Noir* documents the generational succession of calamitous labor-related, grim determinism; Zecca's final shot reveals, lying in a Christ-like pose, the near-invisible dead. Richard Abel notes that Zecca was considered a director of "realist dramas,"[60] and *Au Pays Noir*'s realistic compositional qualities overcome theatrical staging, producing a noteworthy impression of deep staging-depth. Zecca's two pan shots traversing the frame from right to left display work as a field of action, something to be experienced, not just described. Zecca's alluring perspective of manual labor and the chaos generated by a mining disaster's eruptive lighting and framing vividly portray an essential naturalist trope: the human as a laboring, imperiled creature.

Au Pays Noir begins with a notable medium close-up, side-angle claustrophobic image of a toiling miner, lying on his back on top of rocks on the floor of a cave, hammering and chipping at stone. This prefatory compositional framing, a paratextual image of stultifying manual labor, establishes the anticipated flow of fatalistic imagery, the "before the story/after the story" of entrapped working miners. This image not only introduces *Au Pays Noir* but functions as an indicative naturalist sign as stultifying as genetic encoding. Zecca's documentary-like image of this miner functions like the later image of the horse dragging tonnage of rock and coal in the mine: this is life, as lived.

Friedrich Engels concludes about industrial workers: "they were comfortable in their silent vegetation . . . in truth, they were not human beings; they were merely toiling machines in the service of the few aristocrats who had guided history down to that time."[61] Zecca's *Au Pays Noir* indicates class divisions—there are workers, families, supervisors, local citizens, and upper management—and portrays the lives of labor's "toiling machines" via contrasting set designs of the home and the mineshaft. Zecca's depth of framing in medium shots and pans across the frame achieves a realistic staging, complemented by the appearance of farm animals, streets, homes, the mine, and especially by the presence of a working horse wearing blinders, ironically commenting on the men who lead it around the mine. Along with the miners, there are multiple images of women and children laboring in supportive capacities, like a family enterprise mirroring and ultimately subverting earlier shot sequences of transient domesticity. In these shot sequences, Zecca contextualizes notions of a symbolic socio-biological determinism, class struggle, and labor conflict. In the final sequence of *Au Pays Noir*, as the surviving miner-father uncharacteristically rages and mourns over the body of his dead son, capital has lost another worker, a clichéd sacrificial lamb to the slaughter, as workers, like the laborers in Robert Frost's "Out, Out" (1916): "And they, since they/Were not the one dead, turned to their affairs," to prepare for tomorrow's shift, and then the next day's schedule.

Unlike shots of laboring miners in Zecca's film, in Paul Thomas Anderson's *There Will Be Blood* (2007) Daniel Plainview, one of the most fascinating of naturalist beasts, full of murderous rage and intelligence, rises beyond social and class expectations. Based on Upton Sinclair's novel *Oil!* (1927), Anderson's naturalist critique of unabated capitalism, set at the very end of the nineteenth century, features the dreadful male, Plainview (Daniel Day-Lewis), initially portrayed as a working miner. Anderson's introductory medium close-up, side-angle shot sequence is a near copy of Zecca's opening shot of the miner's laborious work experience; men silently, invisibly work underground on their backs and labor like human shovels, fracturing the earth. Prior to any dialogue spoken between characters, Anderson's opening shot sequence of Plainview in various stages of mining runs nearly six minutes, broken only by occasional soundtrack music, the noise of the natural world, and the din of tools and machinery.

Peter Hitchcock notes how in the opening segment of Anderson's adaptation, "There is no dialogue, just Day-Lewis shot against an impressive Western landscape ... [the film depicts] the stripped-down moral universe that sees Americanness as primarily an effect of individual characterisation."[62] Anderson's narrative fully displays American "rugged individualism" and its discontents. Plainview's rise as a tycoon and personal decline—his erratic, excessive violence and caged isolation compromising his presence—is a unique blending of a reimagined historical era of gilded opportunism. As Plainview discovers that oil prospecting is the natural site for his ruthless disposition to take root and flourish, *There Will be Blood* ends as it begins, in silence.

Plainview is a predatory naturalist beast. *There Will be Blood* is a naturalist film narrative that re-examines the myths associated with the historical milieu of corrosive, emerging wealth, class, and labor practices at the turn of the nineteenth century in America. Anderson's film differs from Zecca's film in specific plot points: the focus in the former is on the deterioration of a single predatory individual, corrupt and corrupting, with a disposable family, whereas Zecca's film, while far briefer in running time, focuses on a representative family, another generation of symbolically genetically marked laborers. In *Au Pays Noir*, Zecca portrays people entrapped in a family line by circumstances they inherit and do not control. This family is essentially "fated" to go back to work in the mines. Plainview eschews the myths of family—literally ignoring or destroying it—in the nihilistic present. Toward the end of *There Will be Blood*, in ape-like fury, Plainview savagely clubs to death a perceived enemy with a bowling pin, like the conquering beast's assault on a less intelligent human ancestor in Stanley Kubrick's *2001: A Space Odyssey* (1968). This violent act literally delights Plainview, who glares and smiles at his victim during the assault, perhaps intuiting how the butler will later clean up the mess.

The linked naturalist imagery between human-animals engaged in symbolic crises is starkly evident in Eisenstein's film *Stachka/Strike* (1925), in which lumpenproletariat-strikebreakers emerge from mole-like holes in the ground and from discarded machinery—surplus people in surplus technology—located in a remote junkyard, and the labor specific ("owl-observer") agents for the state shadow and spy on striking workers. The most indicative naturalist imagery in *Strike* involves the later montage sequence in which strikers are viciously assaulted by the police, intercut with shots of cattle being slaughtered. As Joy Newton concluded, "In the film *Strike* he [Eisenstein] intercuts scenes of the butchery of animals in an abattoir unto the massacre of the strikers, a symbol to place the idea of indiscriminate slaughter with visual concreteness into the mind of the spectator."[63] Eisenstein's ironic juxtaposition of images creates indelible perceptions of mindless carnage.

In Yang Li's film adaptation, *Mang jing/Blind Shaft* (2003), set in the bowels of the earth of contemporary China's mining camps, two criminals (Li Yixiang and Wang Shuangbao) disguised as workers discover how easily crime can succeed. In *Blind Shaft*, the mining camp and remote environment support a vicious social order, including murderers, prostitutes, pimps, indifferent-hostile bosses, and the pathetically innocent, in a confined space. In his discussion of *Blind Shaft*, Ban Wang comments upon the relationship between forms of alienated labor and brutish, impersonal sexual commodity exchanges, notable naturalist markers:

> The two miners have sex [with prostitutes] as if they were eating an insipid meal . . . Sexual life becomes animalistic, indeed more debased than animal life . . . The transactions in the brothel are a mirror image of the way coalmines operate: like the miners, the prostitutes are nothing but a means of money-making.[64]

Wang notes that *Blind Shaft* opens in a shot sequence recalling the overall gloomy, mute atmosphere of *Au Pays Noir* and *Harlan County USA*, in which workers' silence expresses the dehumanizing, numbing routine associated with their daily labor:

> The opening of the film's narrative gives a striking example: under a leaden sky in the early morning, shivering in chilly winds and sharing a cigarette to warm up, the ghostly miners emerge out of the low cave

dwellings and, in eerie silence, file in to the company office in order to go down the shaft.[65]

In *Blind Shaft,* the two murderers are uninteresting and survive by the near-limitless supply of desperate, fringe laborers. The murderers contrive to befriend a victim—generally, a clueless, out-of-work male—and in exchange for securing them work in the mine, one criminal pretends to be a relative of the unknowing victim as information is given to the company. After the victim is murdered in what appears to be a mining-related accident, the insurance policy is paid to the next of kin, one of the murderers. This criminals' assembly line leads to death and capital.

At one point, the murderers identify an impressionable younger man and initiate their illicit scheme; however, one of the criminals unexpectedly feels a sense of responsibility toward the youth, mentioning that he is concerned about ending the youth's family line if he were murdered, a symbolic biological referencing. As if to assuage guilt, in two humorous shot sequences, the murderers take the young man to a brothel for an introductory sexual experience and then celebrate this experience over cheap alcohol, as if ritualistically preparing him for an oncoming sacrifice. A similar chain of events occurred in Hal Ashby's *The Last Detail* (1974), in which two military police take a young, awkward sailor about to go to prison for experiences involving beer and a brothel.

Whether set in a factory, coal mine, or at various sites of menial work, naturalist cinema consistently depicts narratives of survival and exploitation: the laboring human beast. Richard Ladkani and Kief Davidson's *The Devil's Miner* (2005) records the contemporary exploitation of children working extensive hours underground in the Bolivian silver mines of Cerro Rico. The documentary narrative focuses primarily on the circumscribed life and labor of fourteen-year-old Basilio and his family, barely surviving in the mountainous region. Upon entering the mine, despite the pervasive presence of Catholicism, the fate of both old and young miners is supposedly determined by statues and offerings to their totemic "tío/uncle," in the form of several devil figures. As if entering Dante's portal into the punitive chthonic region and accepting one's fate, the miners believe the heavenly supernatural outside of the mine stops at the entrance. To assist with the miners' labor, alcohol and coca leaves chewed by workers of all ages provide a numbing, drugged experience. Images of extensive work in the mine, in medium and close-up shots, document both skilled and unskilled adults and children toiling silently inside "the mountain that eats men." Painted satanic images on the walls of the cave with miners' offerings placed below recall primitive cave paintings, and the underground, maze-like tunnels call to mind the deep, dangerous trenches in Kubrick's *Paths of Glory* (1957), from which few escape intact.

In Zecca's *Au Pays Noir*, mining is a precarious vocation involving several generations of a family; in *The Devil's Miner*, children barely experience childhood as the lure of a slight education and meager capital for their labor sustains them and their families. *The Devil's Miner* graphically exposes falling rocks, cave-ins, mining cars running off track, poisonous gas, and explosions, in which children like Basilio are in imminent range of catastrophic danger. Debra A. Castillo notes, "From the sixty hours of material they shot, the filmmakers stitched together a story about the precarious existence of these miners, who are proud of their work, although they know it is terrible and deadly," to which she conclusively adds: "Basilio had already been working in the mines for four years . . . [he] serves as a synecdoche of an exploitative system of labor."[66] In its darkly realistic view of treacherous labor practices, *The Devil's Miner* is a troubling naturalist narrative that documents the skilled and unskilled labor of indigenous people who have little opportunity for survival, except for a daily return to the mine, in which children are welcome.

Erich von Stroheim's majestic, albeit truncated, *Greed* (1924) seeks dramatic closure with an exhausted, violent McTeague (Gibson Gowland) sweltering under the desert's fulgent sun, handcuffed to a corpse, anticipating his own slow, futile death. Lea Jacobs has discussed the "radical nature of von Stroheim's experiment, its especially virulent anti-sentimental tendencies,"[67] as a major contribution to American naturalist cinema. McTeague's illusions of wealth and escape from his past will briefly fade in remoteness. In Laurent Salgues' narrative of exploitation, precariat labor, and isolation, *Rêves de poussière/Dreams of Dust* (2006), Mocktar Dicko (Makena Diop), a Nigerien peasant, leaves stultifying poverty and unpleasant memories back home as he mines for gold dust under a scorching, relentless West African sun. Salgues' long silences and extended shot sequences, framed in close-up and medium shots, visualize this unhealthy environment and the workers' drone-like, nearly endless labor. *Dreams of Dust* repeatedly portrays Mocktar and other laborers as they toil for gold dust that they cannot own in documentary-like images. At this worksite, accidents frequently occur as the workers endlessly pound the dirt; ironically, each worker is symbolically ground down while moving like silent pistons keeping the machinery functional. The workers' debilitating chains are invisible yet palpable; cheap alcohol and pills temporarily alleviate their loneliness and sense of distrust of each other. As one laborer enters a deep mining hole in the ground, it appears like a voluntary entry into a grave. Eventually, Mocktar walks off into the dry sea that is the desert, heading home to an unknown future, but still living.

MORE INVISIBLE

Women of all ages work and survive in visible and invisible capacities. In 1896, the Lumière brothers produced *Laveuses sur la rivière/Washerwomen by the River*, an *actualité* revealing unseen and uncelebrated women laboring and moving the world by their unrewarded labor. *Washerwomen by the River* renders the working world visible in the fleeting perception of a familiar daily phenomenon: the cleaning of clothes. Susana Viegas notes that the Lumière brothers produced several types of narratives, among them *Washerwomen by the River*, which "provided historiographical evidence [of] ordinary people's unimportant familiar and social events."[68] With a running time of less than a minute, in an unmediated single wide shot, *Washerwomen by the River* documents the near-ritualistic laundering efforts of a group of nine unidentified women kneeling at the edge of a river's edge in the city, while the world above watches and moves along on its own schedule. Honoré Daumier's painting *La Blanchisseuse/The Laundress* (1863), read cinematically as a medium two-shot documenting a moment of unembellished realism, features a bent-over and exhausted washerwoman carrying a load of laundry trudging along with her child. His canvas provides a close-up look at anonymous labor in its subdued palette of an obscured city. Like the Lumière brothers' *Washerwomen by the River*, Daumier's canvas is a framed perspective of an unidealized image common to the working world and naturalist aesthetic.

Aritha van Herk suggests that the washing of laundry, a frequently anonymous form of labor, was a gendered reality in the working world: "the refreshment of clothing has generally been the province of women. Because of this [historical] delegation, laundry interrogates the value of women's work,"[69] to which she adds:

> laundry's significance to a critical and discursive world impels a number of questions about . . . domestic paradigms . . . What kind of work and text is privileged, as opposed to the work and text that is marginalized? How is the credible determined and then documented?[70]

However ignored by society or difficult conditions may be for these washerwomen, naturalist cinema establishes a platform for clinical observation of unromanticized labor.

Washerwomen by the River's framing reveals gendered precariat labor in an urban setting; the film depicts spatial relations of painterly proportions. The bottom layer of the multi-layered, horizontally structured frame suggests floating, impressionist reflections of nine women kneeling and laboring above the riverbank. Each woman is handling and/or washing clothing. Directly above the women are semi-protective shades and storage spaces for the clothing;

above this area of the riverbank are the sidewalk and a moving city in fulfilling perspective. There are three men standing to the right of the frame in front of fencing, watching these women at work; behind the men, the frame reveals housing, streets, and in the far background, passing pedestrian and vehicular traffic obliviously moves along in both directions. These are indicative images of a now remote era. Although there is no close-up shot of any of the laboring nine women in *Washerwomen by the River*, the *actualité* depicts a landscape of uncelebrated naturalist moments.

In the novel *L'Assommoir* (1877), Zola's laundress-heroine, Gervaise Macquart is granted a measure of social visibility as she labors as a washerwoman to eventually start her own laundry business, but these efforts cannot be sustained, as she suffers extreme states of personal and social deterioration: poverty, debt, domestic abuse, and eventually, alcoholism. Like Flaubert's Emma Bovary, Zola's Gervaise envisioned and later evokes in her solitude a different conception of her life when she was younger; like laundry, dreams become soiled in real space and time. In Flaubert's realist narrative, *Madame Bovary* (1856), during a late, reflective moment of her life, Emma Bovary, the unhappily married and entrapped woman, while sitting alone on a bench, recalls her experiences attending Catholic school and observing its associated rituals. This is Emma's illusory respite, an escape from inevitable social and economic disaster. The Deleuzian past functions like an imagined strand of invoked, recalled moments that affect the inescapable present.

Such an educed moment is experienced in William Busnach and Octave Gastineau's stage version of Zola's novel, *L'Assommoir: Drame en cinq actes et neuf tableaux* (1881), as Gervaise recalls her youth during a moment of unguarded conversation while arduously laboring as a washerwoman:

> 'Yes, yes, laundress, at ten. Eight years ago. We were going to the river . . . Ah! it was prettier than here . . . There was a corner under the trees, with clear water flowing . . . (she stops laboring.) The water is hard in Paris.'[71]

As one of Naturalism's case studies in decline, Gervaise experiences a series of distressing personal losses that lead to the bar and to the streets, becoming a public spectacle of worsening failure. These personal failures occur outside the laundromat and bar, yet remain linked to dysfunctional labor and related issues.

Barbara Loden's *Wanda* (1971) is an achievement in naturalist cinema. According to Anna Backman Rogers, "At once both a road movie and a heist film, [*Wanda*] is also neither of these things in any 'major' sense. Rather, Loden uses genre subversively in order to indict specific American values through a woman's perspective."[72] *Wanda,* a low-budget 16 mm production shot on location in the coal region and small towns of Pennsylvania and Connecticut, is a case study of a woman's decline into a naturalist image of a drinking and smoking nub. Wanda (Barbara Loden) initially appears in the film like a worn-out woman in an Edvard Munch sleep painting. Outside Wanda's current (temporary) residence, unpaved, gravel streets and box-like factories in an unattractive landscape inform her life as one of the imminent lost in lonely America. She abandons her family, gets embarrassingly fired from her factory job, drifts in and out of her working-class community, and seems to lose herself in Loden's narrative of ever-encroaching aloneness, as Wanda achieves near invisibility. Rogers notes:

> The ethical import of *Wanda* lies in this aesthetics of denial, of the margin, its exploration of the underside, its use of slowness, its persistent use of counter-images and in-between-images and its invocation of crisis ... [amidst] the ravaged faces of its Appalachian coal field inhabitants ... *Wanda* dares to suggest that, for many, the life into which one is born is inherently damaged and damaging and that not all experience is equally valuable.[73]

Long shots and extensive periods of silence create the sensory impression of serial emptiness that frequently cuts photographs of sites associated with images from a lurid magazine: bedrooms, bars, courtrooms, and lonely roads. According to Rogers, in the beginning of *Wanda*, "Establishing shot: the camera pans slowly and steadily to screen left revealing incrementally a barren and undifferentiated landscape of coal banks dominated by shades of brown, grey, and black."[74] A pervasive sense of stark, class-based realism begins with the opening location shots in the working-class coal mining section of forgotten Pennsylvania, with malls, buses, road signs, and unpaved roads as common sites. Wanda is an unanchored remnant of what is left of her failed life, evident throughout her survival struggle and especially during the courtroom sequence, when she basically leaves her family, and when she is fired at work as she discovers that she is "too slow" to fit into the factory schema.

Wanda is a directionless mass of ambulatory rage directed inwardly and outwardly. She is repeatedly mistreated by men who use her for fast company and unromantic, unattractive sex; even Mr. Dennis (Michael Higgins), her doomed lover–bank robber "male friend," has trouble figuring out how to work with and respond to her. She even fails as a petty criminal, which leads to the death of Mr. Dennis. As Wanda wanders the street, enters a mall, peers into windows, and generally has nowhere to go, a sense of fatalistic urgency increases with every misstep she takes. Loden features a shot sequence in which Wanda runs out after being sexually assaulted and nearly raped in the woods, fleeing like a frightened feral creature in an aimless direction. Men do not define her as much as briefly accompany her in any direction. Bars and cigarettes are constants in her life, to which guns are a later addition. Eventually, one sympathetic woman finds Wanda alone, outside a motel area, and she invites Wanda to a party. Wanda, a nearly broken, isolated presence, eats, drinks, and smokes amid a crowd of patrons in a bar. Rogers concludes:

> She assumes the form of ghost-flesh, a figure who lives out her life permanently in spaces that are designed specifically for the transitory, fleeting, and liminal moments of life (motels, roadside cafes, shopping malls). She is fundamentally a woman who cannot gain purchase on any space a decentred, displaced, and nebulous adumbration of a person.[75]

Guilty or not, unsure about the nightmare ahead, Josef K. wakes up in *Der Prozess/The Trial* (1925) into a spiraling landscape. Like K., Wanda is implicated in her own nightmarish landscape of jagged gravel and disturbing faces. In a movement from Loden's cinematic frame into a photographic, near-painterly image of class and gender displacement, Wanda is freeze-framed in a medium close-up protracted shot, in the proximate portraiture of an invisible subject. As Wanda sits alone in a saloon with strangers, her suffering, motionless presence is a stunning naturalist image.

In the Dardenne brothers' film *Rosetta* (1999), a narrative of precariat labor and compromised childhood, seventeen-year-old Rosetta (Émilie Dequenne) lives a post-scavenger subsistence life in a trailer camp with her alcoholic mother, who is not above making herself sexually available for liquor or related living expenses. The trailer camp as naturalist setting appears in Chloé Zhao's *Nomadland* (2020), the site where the lost may be found. Although Rosetta constantly fights with her mother, deprivation unites them in this survival narrative of a drifting family. In *Rosetta*, the Dardenne brothers' long, unmediated sequences feature over-the-shoulder close-up and medium hand-held shots to capture the frenetic, enclosed space and time of a troubled, post-feral, silent young woman. In Patty Jenkins' *Monster* (2003), the young, brutalized Aileen Wuornos is abandoned to live in the woods; in *Rosetta*, the young Rosetta seems to emerge from the woods like an uncontrollable, predatory yet vulnerable creature. She hides pairs of shoes in a drainage pipe, like territorial markers, and enters the trailer camp underneath wires as if to conceal herself while desperately looking for work and struggling to survive; even while working, she is barely surviving. She is frequently seen running across highways and frantically misreading or ignoring social cues during her encounters with other people.

The Dardenne brothers' location shots are realistically unglamorous; in *Rosetta*, the audience witnesses blue-collar people working in unceremonious, invisible positions. While Louis Lumière's *Workers Leaving a Factory* displays workers cheerfully exiting the factory gates, in the Dardenne brothers' opening shot sequence, Rosetta is frantically running inside a factory, on its staircases and across hallways, to confront her boss. Janice Morgan considers this a "form of pure motion, a kinesthetic force. We do not view Rosetta, we intercept her, like a moving target at close range."[76] Rosetta has been fired but cannot accept the loss of her job. As noted by Eun-Jee Park, "The opening sequence of *Rosetta* has the feel of a battlefield."[77] Given her combative reaction, Rosetta is consequently escorted from the factory. Always searching for employment, Rosetta secures but loses these low-wage jobs in an economy and labor pool that bypasses her.

In another thoughtless act with later, personal ramifications, Rosetta plots to replace and then betrays Riquet, a young man who attempts to befriend her, and he loses his job. At this employment site, a local food stand similar to Bahrani's *Man Push Cart*, Rosetta cooks, cleans, makes change, and operates the mini-business, but this too fails to help her survive. The Dardenne brothers document emerging cracks in Rosetta's life when she collapses from exhaustion carrying a heavy gas cannister, and haltingly allows Riquet to assist. According to Morgan, this is a positive gesture:

> This final look at Riquet (and at us) signals the hope that she is now ready to renegotiate the boundaries between herself and the rest of the world, doing so consciously and by choice, rather than standing guard over the lines that had been drawn for her by chance and circumstance.[78]

Rather than commit suicide or go off alone into the woods, Rosetta might survive in a less hostile world, if she could also find stable work.

Bottles and Bipeds

Chinonye Chukwu's *Clemency* (2019) is the narrative of a working woman's alienating labor experiences and personal decline. In this prison "death-house" drama, in which an African-American woman, Bernadine Williams (Alfre Woodard), portrays the duty-bound, conflicted warden, the melodrama and related film genres reveal a shift in power and gender relations. However much *Clemency* is a traditional tale of a doomed male prisoner, the issue of clemency involves both the prisoner and his keeper, the warden, who drinks to cope and deaden the psychological effects of her labor. Warden Williams is as insufferably entrapped as her condemned prisoner by her stultifying and depersonalized middle-class existence—the specifics of her demanding, disagreeable job—as she responds to official orders leading to excessively cruel, guignolish, chemically based execution procedures. Her symbolic imprisonment also involves her drifting marriage and the ensuing small talk it generates at the dinner table, in which her husband refers to her as living like "a fragment." Chukwu's stylized multiple-shot sequences set in a darkly lit bar emphasize the loneliness and spatial distancing that Williams feels from others, temporarily ameliorated by alcohol. Like the figure of a deflated, worn woman drinking absinthe in Edgar Degas' *L'Absinthe* (1875–6), Warden Williams sits in a dark section of a bar as the camera dollies back to reveal her troubled image of imbibing loss. Whether in the bar, her home, or the prison, Williams is distant.

Chukwu's use of natural sounds—closing iron gates, footsteps, buzzers, and ringing phones—and her extensive use of medium framing and close-ups, reversal shots—contribute to the encroaching, isolating conversational silences. Chukwu's narrative gaps in dialogue between characters render thoughtful spaces for the interpellated viewer, conditioned for traditional revelations of innocence and a last-minute rescue. These silences inevitably lead to a nearly minute-long exit from the execution sequence, featuring the warden leaving the area to traverse the prison corridors and passages until she pauses to breathe, literally swallowing an atmospheric load of angst-filled air. In a final gasp, in a close-up affect expressing dread, the shot reveals the realization of her ugly labor and its near-routine ordinariness on her face. In Robert Wise's bio-pic prison narrative *I Want to Live!* (1958), in documentary-like, naturalist detail, convicted murderer-prostitute Barbara Graham (Susan Hayward) is led from the prison cell on death row into the gas chamber. As Wise records the final moments of Graham's life, the enclosed prison space and circumscribed time of her death emphasize Graham's ghastly expiration, the audience acting as witness to the proceedings. In *Clemency*, the narrative focus is on the survivor—the warden—as she experiences a mixture of self-doubt and self-disgust. This is the final, observed face of a woman at work.

In *Clemency*, a rehearsed execution is conducted to ensure later successful application after a nearly botched effort, which features a surrogate White male substituting for the prisoner-elect. This shot sequence presents something horrific as realistic, orderly, and clinical. In *Clemency*, a voice registers the "time of death" after the actual execution of a questionably culpable man; in Chukwu's unsentimental naturalist film narrative, the warden is diminished, a wounded, alcoholically inclined by-product of legalized violence, perhaps hoping to become invisible.

While awaiting imminent execution for the multiple homicides of middle-aged, White male clients, the very visible sex worker Aileen Wuornos, who claimed to have acted repeatedly in self-defense, was quoted in a letter stating: "Even on death row, I still have sins."[79] What are the sins of Aileen Wuornos? Patty Jenkins' film *Monster* recreates the incipient fall and continued decline of the unemployable Aileen Wuornos, from victim to victimizer, all the way to her execution in the death chamber. Jenkins' bio-pic presents a vivid, protracted analysis of multiple crimes committed by Wuornos (Charlize Theron), a woman frequently subjected to festering environmental causalities throughout her life. Wuornos is a focalizing, naturalist presence—a working prostitute and murderer—in the mythos of the female serial killer. Jenkins' multiple shots of Wuornos' expressive, bloated face in close-up produce a mask-like, haunting image, a disembodied part of the whole, a spectacle of disaster. Nick Broomfield's complementary documentaries, *Aileen Wuornos: The Selling of a Serial Killer* (1992) and *Aileen: Life and Death of a Serial Killer* (2003), are narratives of observational decline that present serial killer pathology in a frenetic, revelatory manner involving marketing strategies, personal betrayals, and the volcanic spectacle of Wuornos.

In *Psychiatric Times*, Harvey Roy Greenburg concludes:

> Wuornos' past reads like the history of a Jerry Springer guest. She was born in a seedy Detroit suburb. Her mother ran out on her and a brother early on; her father, a convicted child molester, would later kill himself in prison. The children were sent to 'Kallikak' grandparents, who enthusiastically continued the daily round of brutal abuse, physical and perhaps sexual.[80]

Wuornos is a life-long study in human disposability, a betrayed, lonely, repeatedly beaten lesbian whose violence committed against multiple male clients led to her inevitable sanctioned demise. In Leonard Kastle's *The Honeymoon Killers* (1970), based on a series of documented events in postwar America, serial-killer nurse Martha Beck (Shirley Stoler) goes about murdering patients for money and to please her lover–fellow serial killer. Like Wuornos, Beck defensively claimed to have been sexually violated, beaten, and used by men. The grainy, black and white low-budget naturalistic compositional style complements the seediness of the unprincipled principles.

As a young woman, Wuornos was a working prostitute by the age of thirteen. Later, she was a mostly unemployed woman who found a place among the seedy atmosphere of freeway Florida, with its bars, motels, convenience stores, and assorted varieties of dangerous, imbibed, or drugged humanity. Wuornos never successfully establishes herself with a routine form of traditional labor and employment, remaining a fringe person; in a humiliating shot sequence in a bank, Wuornos, applying for work there, fails to get beyond the initial interview.

In Jenkins' *Monster*, Aileen Wuornos is an unredeemed created by-product throughout most of her life. She is not wholly categorized as the product of a *Zolaesque* "tainted line," although her father was an incarcerated schizophrenic child molester who committed suicide, and her mother was sixteen years old at the time of Wuornos' birth in 1956. After her mother abandoned

Wuornos to live with her alcoholic grandparents, Wuornos suffered repeated incestuous relations and was eventually impregnated, only to be forced to surrender the child. Wuornos had to live in the surrounding, rural wooded area once thrown out of her home; this is the blueprint planning of an angry, abandoned monster-in-the-making, unprepared for the real world of work.

Wuornos is a broken, fermenting product trying to survive in the working world. Wuornos' adult life is marked by her overall, pre-murderous social invisibility and class-based, near-impoverished living conditions. Jenkin's *Monster* features a realistic survey of Florida's semi-rural/semi-suburban déclassé hell as the landscape containing Wuornos as she spins out of control. Bryan McCann notes that Jenkins' film "asked its viewers to consider the kind of world that produces an Aileen Wuornos."[81] Perhaps "Our Frankenstein, Ourselves" suggests a clue, as Wuornos responds to past and immediate instances of social and personal cruelty. She is portrayed as a raging patchwork of conflicting selves—the violent, the emotionally starved, and the victimized—a Floridian Frankenstein as complex monster, which is prominently exhibited on her emotive face. In Jenkins' film, the road, the home, and the courtroom are framing sites in which Wuornos' life de-escalates. While Wuornos murders seven men within the space of a year, the lethal injection terminating her life on death row is both horrifying and seemingly inevitable, the perverse fulfillment of a life not chosen.

After an introductory prologue, Jenkins reveals Wuornos sitting underneath a Florida interstate road bridge in the pouring rain: unemployable and increasingly angry. The voice-over provides a contextual perspective; these "before" shots and verbal insights into Wuornos' life are flashback recreations of a sordid, lonely past unfolding into the present; roads, bars, cheap hotels, and generally, a vision of run-down, seedy Florida—a netherworld that few tourists wish to experience. In films such as Patty Jenkins' *Monster*, Barry Jenkin's *Moonlight* (2016) and Sean Baker's *The Florida Project* (2017), the "Florida of the imagination," rendered on billboards, television commercials, and radio spots, yields to a less fantastic image of sunlit venues and rum cocktails. *Monster* reveals the Florida of personal failure. Wuornos' immediate environment functions in a deleterious capacity as it, along with her pathologically self-destructive behavior, grinds her down into a spectacle of misery with a complementary, wrathful attitude, except when it involves her lesbian lover, who ultimately betrays Wuornos in the courtroom. Everybody betrays Wuornos. Her bloated, contorted face reveals present and past anxieties—pain and anger—surfacing like lethal gases poisoning the immediate atmosphere.

In Jenkins' extreme close-up shot, Theron-as-Wuornos is a confrontational, bloated image of smoking rage that leaps from the frame. Her gorgon-like stare overwhelms itself, as if about to explode, while she dangles a cigarette like a symbolic hunter's rifle. Jenkin's shot composition suggests the Deleuzian affect image, a conceptual block of space and time from which, in this case, one endures and experiences the inscribed rage in Theron's face, now read as an indexical sign pointing to her internalized horrors.[82] She is a wounded woman. The actual posted mug shot of Aileen Wuornos is unsettling; while appearing worn and bloated, Wuornos' stark gaze outwards unsettles the observer. Even after her execution, Wuornos still intimidates.

In Lav Diaz's naturalist narrative of needless female suffering and fringe people, *Ang babaeng humayo/The Woman Who Left* (2016), after returning to her home in the Philippines following thirty years' imprisonment for a crime she did not commit, the aging, nondescript ex-schoolteacher Horacia (Charo Santos-Concio) cannot restore her stolen life or fully envision a future without some form of retribution against her male accuser. Her teaching career is reduced to tutoring female inmates during her prison stay. In a protracted series of experiences, Horacia encounters prostitutes, alcoholics, semi-skilled laborers, and assorted marginalized people while befriended by a transvestite prostitute who later plots revenge on her behalf. Diaz's prolonged opening shot sequence of women working on the prison ground recalls Millet's *The Gleaners* (1857) canvas depicting laborious toil in the field. Diaz's narrative gradually reveals Horacia's self-awareness of her victimhood and its consequences, to simultaneously expose her anguished resolve and great empathy over measured shot sequences. According to Tiago de Luca, "slowness" is a demarcated compositional aesthetic: "slow cinema elicits a heightened awareness of the viewing situation ... slow time makes cinema visible, turning the film auditorium into a phenomenological space in which a collectively shared experience of time is brought to light for reflection."[83] Diaz's neorealistic, low-budget, black and white location filming and use of multiple non-professional performers, utilizes long takes and medium shots to establish a naturalist milieu in a semi-urban, run-down, yet meditative setting.

Notes

1. Tom Gunning, "The Cinema of Attraction[s]: Early Film, Its Spectator and the Avant-Garde," *Wide Angle*, Vol. 8, Nos 3–4 (Fall, 1986), 63–70.
2. Megan Minarich, "Arnold Bennett's Moving Pictures: Early Filmic Vision in Anna of the Five Towns," *Studies in the Novel*, Vol. 51, No. 3 (Fall, 2019), 374.
3. Anthony R. Guneratne, "The Birth of a New Realism: Photography, Painting and the Advent of Documentary Cinema," *Film History*, Vol. 10, No. 2 (1998), 180–1.
4. This film has been translated into different titles, and there are three distinct versions of the film. The following website links them together: https://www.youtube.com/watch?v=DEQeIRLxaM4. Accessed May 30, 2023.
5. Susana Viegas, "Gilles Deleuze and Early Cinema: The Modernity of the Emancipated Time," *Early Popular Visual Culture*, Vol. 14, No. 3 (2016), 238. Note: the Lumière film is also frequently entitled *La sortie de l'usine Lumière à Lyon/Workers Leaving the Lumière Factory*.
6. Ibid, 239.

7. Minarich, "Arnold," 375–6.
8. Ibid, 374.
9. Todd McGowan, "Atemporality amid Lumière Temporality," *Empedocles: European Journal for the Philosophy of Communication*, Vol. 5, Nos 1 & 2 (2015), 61.
10. Harun Farocki, "Workers Leaving the Factory," in *Harun Farocki: Working on the Sight-Lines*, ed. Thomas Elsaesser (Amsterdam: Amsterdam University Press, 2004), 239, 243.
11. Pao-Chen Tang, "Of Dogs and Hot Dogs: Distractions in Early Cinema," *Early Popular Visual Culture*, Vol. 15, No. 1 (2017), 46.
12. Farocki, "Workers," 238.
13. Keith B. Wagner, "Historicizing Labor Cinema: Recovering Class and Lost Work on Screen," *Labor History*, Vol. 55, No. 3 (2014), 316.
14. Sara Nadal-Melsió, "A Work Force of Images: Militancy as Historical Experience in Joaquim Jordà's *Numax presenta*," *Journal of Spanish Cultural Studies*, Vol. 18, No. 4 (2017), 414.
15. Ibid, 414.
16. Elizabeth Cowie, *Recording Reality, Desiring the Real* (Minneapolis: University of Minnesota Press, 2011), 61.
17. Ibid, 63.
18. Nadal-Melsió, "Work Force," 414.
19. This eighty-six-second film, accessed May 29, 2023, may be viewed at https://www.youtube.com/watch?v=D0kbB2kbQls.
20. Charles Musser, *The Emergence of Cinema: The American Screen to 1907*, Vol. 1 (Berkeley: University of California Press, 1990), 347.
21. J. W. Sullivan, *Markets for the People: The Consumers Part* (New York: Macmillan Company, 1913), 68.
22. Frederick Engels, *The Condition of the Working-Class in England* (1892), (London: Panther Books, 1974), 118.
23. Polina Kroik, "Neoliberal Labour in Ramin Bahrani's Films: Uneven Development, Entrepreneurial Governmentality, and Political Resistance," *Canadian Review of American Studies*, Vol. 46, No. 2 (Summer 2016), 229.
24. Ibid, 233.
25. Amadou T. Fofana, "Sembène's '*Borom Sarret*': A Griot's Narrative," *Literature/Film Quarterly*, Vol. 39, No. 4 (2011), 260.
26. Ibid, 263.
27. Andrea Dahlberg, "On the Fortieth Anniversary of *Borom Sarret*, on Ousmane Sembene's 1963 Film," *Film-Philosophy*, 7.1 (June 2003), n.p. See www.euppublishing.com/film. Accessed May 23, 2023.
28. Martin Esslin, "Naturalism in Context," *Drama Review*, Vol. 13, No. 2 (Winter 1968), 74.
29. Caroline Levine, "Propaganda for Democracy: The Curious Case of *Love on the Dole*," *Journal of British Studies*, Vol. 45, No. 4 (October 2006), 851.
30. Ibid, 849.
31. Siegfried Giedion, *Mechanization Takes Command* (New York: Norton, 1948), 5.
32. Ibid, 77.
33. Ian Aitken, *Lukácsian Film Theory and Cinema: A Study of Georg Lukács' Writings on Film, 1913–71* (Manchester: Manchester University Press, 2012), 55, 98.
34. Engels, *Condition*, 167–8.
35. Christopher Falzon, *Philosophy Goes to the Movies: An Introduction to Philosophy* (New York: Routledge, 2002), 164–5.

36. Aitken, *Lukácsian*, 55.
37. Ibid, 56.
38. B. F. Taylor and Susan Williams, *The British New Wave: A Certain Tendency?* (Manchester: Manchester University Press, 2006), 132–3.
39. Frank R. Cunningham, *Sidney Lumet: Film and Literary Vision* (Lexington: University Press of Kentucky, 2001), 24–5.
40. Ibid, 52.
41. Jared Rapfogel, "Reviewed Work(s): *Family Nest* by Béla Tarr; *The Outsider* by Béla Tarr; *The Prefab People* by Béla Tarr," *Cinéaste*, Vol. 31, No. 2 (Spring 2006), 64.
42. Ibid, 63.
43. Robert Singer, "'What Grows in the Hood?' Projects, People and the Contemporary Brooklyn Film," in *The Brooklyn Film: Essays in the History of Filmmaking*, eds John B. Manbeck and Robert Singer (Jefferson, NC: McFarland Press, 2002), 53.
44. Laura Hapke, *Sweatshop: The History of an American Idea* (New Jersey: Rutgers University Press, 2004), 102.
45. Ibid, 102.
46. Guy Standing, "The Precariat and Class Struggle," *RCCS Annual Review*, No. 7 (2015), 5–6.
47. Jefferson Cowie, "*La Ciudad (The City)*," *Journal of American History*, Vol. 87, No. 3 (2000), 1170.
48. Ibid, 1169.
49. Hapke, *Sweatshop*, 102.
50. Anne Sigrid Nordby, Bjørn Berge, Finn Hakonsen, and Anne Grete Hestnes, "Criteria for Salvageability: The Reuse of Bricks," *Building Research and Information*, Vol. 37, No. 1 (2009), 56, 59. Note: Italics in the original.
51. Amanda Holmes, "Filming the Buenos Aires Café: Memory and Community in *Bolivia* and *Bor, El Chino*," *Arizona Journal of Hispanic Cultural Studies*, Vol. 20 (2016), 257.
52. René Girard, *Violence and the Sacred*, trans. Patrick Gregory (Baltimore, MD: Johns Hopkins University Press, 1997), 30.
53. Émile Zola, *Germinal*, trans. Leonard Tancock (London: Penguin Books, 1974), 236.
54. Ibid, 144.
55. Ibid, 236.
56. *Aristotle's History of Animals*, trans. Richard Cresswell (London: George Bell & Sons, 1883), 5–6.
57. Zola, *Germinal*, 265.
58. Ibid, 334.
59. This film was co-directed by Lucien Nonguet. For additional information, see Diane Smith and Robert Singer's "Les origines du film américain sur la grève dans les mines de charbon," in *Zola et le texte naturaliste en Europe et aux Amériques* (Lewiston, NY: Edwin Mellen Press, 2007).
60. Richard Abel, "In the Belly of the Beast: The Early Years of Pathé-Frères," *Film History*, Vol. 5, No. 4 (December 1993), 366.
61. Engels, *Condition*, 39.
62. Peter Hitchcock, "Oil in an American Imaginary (Report)," *New Formations*, No. 69 (2010), 9.
63. Joy Newton, "Zola and Eisenstein," *French Review*, No. 2 (Winter 1971), 109.
64. Ban Wang, "Of Humans and Nature in Documentary: The Logic of Capital in *West of the Tracks* and *Blind Shaft*," in *Chinese Ecocinema: In the Age of Environmental*

Challenge, eds Sheldon H. Lu and Jiayan Mi (Hong Kong: Hong Kong University Press, 2009), 168.
65. Ibid, 167.
66. Debra A. Castillo, "Bad Education," *Latin American Literary Review*, Vol. 44, No. 87 (2017), 46–7.
67. Lea Jacobs, *The Decline of Sentiment* (Berkeley: University of California Press, 2008), 27.
68. Susana Viegas, "Gilles Deleuze and Early Cinema: The Modernity of the Emancipated Time," *Early Popular Visual Culture*, Vol. 14, No. 3 (2016), 238.
69. Aritha van Herk, "Invisibled Laundry," *Signs*, Vol. 27, No. 3 (Spring 2002), 894.
70. Ibid, 898–9.
71. William Busnach and Octave Gastineau, *L'Assommoir: Drame en cinq actes et neuf tableaux* (Paris: G. Charpentier, 1881), 57.
72. Anna Backman Rogers, *Still Life: Notes on Barbara Loden's Wanda (1970)* (California: Punctum Books, 2021), 21. Available at https://punctumbooks.com. Accessed April 22, 2023.
73. Ibid, 28–34.
74. Ibid, 65.
75. Ibid, 57.
76. Janice Morgan, "The Social Realism of Body Language in 'Rosetta,'" *French Review*, Vol. 81, No. 6 (May, 2008), 1188.
77. Eun-Jee Park, "The Politics of Friendship and Paternity: The Dardenne Brothers' *Rosetta*," *Studies in French Cinema*, Vol. 12, No. 2 (2012), 140.
78. Morgan, "Social Realism," 1194.
79. "Personal Letter," *Dear Dawn: Aileen Wuornos in Her Own Words*, eds Lisa Kester and Daphne Gottlieb (Berkeley, CA: Soft Skull, 2012), 53.
80. Harvey Roy Greenberg, "Roadkill," *Psychiatric Times*, Vol. 21, Issue 6 (2004), 1.
81. Bryan J. McCann, "Entering the Darkness: Rhetorics of Transformation and Gendered Violence in Patty Jenkins's *Monster*," *Women's Studies in Communication*, Vol. 37 (2014), 2.
82. See Chapter 6 in Gilles Deleuze, *Cinema 1: The Movement-Image*, trans. Hugh Tomlinson and Barbara Habberjam (Minnesota: University of Minnesota Press, 1986).
83. Tiago de Luca, "Slow Time, Visible Cinema: Duration, Experience, and Spectatorship," *Cinema Journal*, Vol. 56, No. 1 (Fall 2016), 23–42.

4. THE BODY POLITIC

For Sale

In a naturalist context, as it involves merchandise, product placement, customer relations, and the sale itself, sex is work: an issue for modern labor studies and marketing.

According to information listed in the *Sears Roebuck Catalogue* (1897), "we have spared neither time nor money to care for our customers' every want ... they can buy their goods at wholesale prices ... our facilities for handling merchandise on a very large scale ... are unexcelled."[1] Whether in search of tea, cough syrup, pocket watches, shotguns, men's suits, or ladies' shoes, for a price, the object of desire was available. The marketing strategy of evolving modern corporate and small business America, as well as across the globe, consistently mentions service, credibility of product, and customer satisfaction. Marketing, especially when directed toward a select audience, creates the desire to experience and to consume a product as its goal. In James White's *Fifth Avenue, New York* (1897) in a medium set shot with slight pan movement, hordes of well-dressed people amble in and out of the frame on the street of this famous urban site, known for its shopping, churches, and signs of class-based wealth. Ironically, invisibly, in the same city and era, subaltern cultures were thriving significantly; everything is purchasable, including flesh.

A Gentleman's Companion (1870), a retrieved information guide/historical document, provided overwhelmingly male visitors to New York City detailed information about securing the best brothels, "establishments," and their local addresses across Manhattan. This pamphlet describes locations and sex workers in a rating-like system of first-, second-, and third-class services; for example, the pamphlet notes an especially appealing site with "bewitching smiles of fairy-like creatures who devote themselves to the services of Cupid and are unrivalled by any of the fine ladies who walk Broadway,"[2] as well as a brothel that is "frequented only by the fagends of the community,"[3] and also a brothel "patronized by roughs and rowdies who turn their shirts wrong side out when the other side is dirty."[4] The pamphlet includes several images of "calling cards,"[5] featuring the names and addresses of preferred locations as well as descriptions of the sex workers. One establishment notably kept a physician on call.[6] At the back of the pamphlet, multiple graphic advertisements for "Dr. Groves' Marriage Guide," "French Imported Male Safes,"[7] and other sex-related items and instructional manuals are featured. Sex is an advertised modern service industry, a pleasure factory with workers and clients.

John Girdner's *Newyorkitis* (1901), a prescient volume examining modern urban culture and its anxieties, presents a local man's experiences surviving in a seemingly dangerous setting:

> I am acquainted with a man who has lived for twenty-five years within the limits of that section of the city known as the Tenderloin, which is, by the way, a favorite resort of *Newyorkitic* vice-hunters ... He says that brothels, gambling-houses, and pool-rooms have never cost him anything in a pecuniary way, nor have they ever degraded him morally, for the simple reason that he never enters these resorts ... He says that no man is obliged to enter such resorts unless he wishes to do so.[8]

Not all Girdner's immediate society refrained from supposed perilous encounters and many did seek such "degraded" experiences. As noted by the crusading journalist William Thomas Stead in 1898, "In the Tenderloin there were a great number of disorderly houses, which were resorts for the criminals of the whole country, who came there to meet prostitutes."[9] As Judith R. Walkowitz notes a century later, "Historians certainly need to pay closer attention to the emotional and cultural lives of sex workers than we have done previously."[10] The prostitute, as s/he is linked with paintings, photographs, and literary narratives of the "fallen woman/man"—a corrupted and corrupting sex worker as sympathetic or predatory individual—is reappropriated in naturalist cinema as a gender-specific–metamorphic purchased product, an alluring, sexually commodified representation, a reconfiguration of the laboring body in states of precarious survival and decline, frequently indicating manifestations of the wound trope. In particular, the spectatorial position assumed by the film viewer varyingly invokes three specific interpellated positionings informing the prostitute trope: the requisite (male–female-metamorphic) prostitute/sex worker, the worksite/brothel and particulars of the milieu, and the engaged clientele. The prostitute labors and survives under the domineering cloak of invisibility, even walking the streets or in brothel settings, as the narrative produces momentary visibility.

The prostitute disrupts normative associations with home and identity while remaining mostly unseen, invisible; for sale or not, the prostitute is a sexual outlaw. In naturalist films set in a brothel or documenting the lives of prostitutes of all sexual identities, violence is an ongoing negative presence, whether physically and/or psychologically manifest, leading to the wound-as-trope. The act of prostitution—the selling of self by self or by others—raises issues involving exploitative labor and economics, power relations, criminology, and notions of fundamental, abnormal psychology. The prostitute is frequently portrayed as either/both victim or/and victimizer, a mysterious, seductive spectacle of engaging, transgressive behavior, an eruptive desired taboo, to be gazed upon in states of labor-performance in a respective era and location. Naturalist cinema observes the unseen prostitute—a product to be purchased and the conditions of the purchase—in multiple international cultures.

Whether set in the infamous "red-light" tenderloin district of San Francisco or, more likely, New York City, James H. White's *Tenderloin at Night* (1899) is one of the earliest films to depict a gathering of likely prostitutes and corrupt male patrons in a bar in which a sedative-like drug is administered into the drink of an unaware male patron. In *Tenderloin at Night*, it is the women who attract attention, as they rise, dance, and are visibly involved with documented intrigue. Russell Campbell notes that:

> the depiction of female prostitution generally ... is predominantly attributable to the working of the male imagination, modified by the requirement for a certain verisimilitude—the cinema being first and foremost a realist medium—and by the conceptual framework of patriarchal ideology.[11]

In *Tenderloin at Night*, White's interpretive positioning of cinematic Realism is credibly linked to cultural assumptions about the dangerous night life of taboo urban locations and dangerous women. Campbell confirms these suppositions as he states that White's film "clearly identifies its three prostitute characters, sitting gaudily dressed in a bar-room, and locates them within a criminal milieu,"[12] to reinforce the notion that the women are sexual distractions to enable the robbery.

Framed in a stationary medium shot, *Tenderloin at Night* documents an ongoing crime as the well-dressed women work in cahoots with lowlifes to rob the unaware man; the use of knock-out drugs was a common means of committing robbery or even of entrapping women for the white-slave bordello market, as suggested in Raoul Walsh's bio-pic of a turn-of-the-century New York gangster, *Regeneration* (1915). In Walsh's film, as a young, unaware woman (Anna Q. Nilsson) is poised to lift a doctored drink for consumption, it is knocked out of her hand. The crime victim in White's film is not as lucky as Walsh's heroine, as he is visibly robbed by the gleeful women and the men before reawakening. The waiter and the police are presented as either complicit or clueless. However abbreviated the narrative, White's seminal film contains or suggests several critical indicators of interrelated naturalist tropes: the prostitutes, criminal intrigue and corruption, alcohol and drugs, and the unseen, quotidian worksite, the brothel.

Covert Labor

George Frederic Watts' grimly realistic rendering of the presumptive suicide of a female prostitute, *Found Drowned* (c. 1848–50) is a portrait of the prostrate corpse of an anonymous young woman, with the lower half of her body still submerged in the River Thames. The upper torso of the woman is bathed in light and set underneath the Waterloo Bridge, the site of suffering featured in Robert E. Sherwood's World War One naturalist drama *Waterloo Bridge* (1930), in which Myra Deauville, the chorus girl who succumbs to prostitution in order to survive, finds a measure of happiness but is later killed unceremoniously at that site.[13] As if anticipating a cinematic rack focus shot, Watts' composition foregrounds in focus the woman's lifeless body and sets the murky river and a dark, urban background in out-of-focus contrast. As the Reverend C. Maurice Davies concluded, the suicide or murder of female prostitutes, especially by the River Thames, was a common occurrence in Victorian England: "One of the first girls to whom I spoke had just made the 'great experiment' of a leap . . . She had been rescued from the water and taken to prison, where she was kept for seven days."[14]

Moving from the mud-puddle to a dank river, in Stephen Crane's *Maggie: A Girl of the Streets* (1893), the abused and betrayed prostitute Maggie Johnson, an impoverished New York City streetwalker from the Bowery, dies a lonely death as a murder victim drowning in the river.[15] Crane's painterly description of the event is gruesome and compelling:

> When almost to the river the girl saw a great figure. On going forward she perceived it to be a huge fat man in torn and greasy garments. . . . His whole body gently quivered and shook like that of a dead jelly fish. Chuckling and leering, he followed the girl of the crimson legions . . . At their feet the river appeared a deathly black hue.[16]

As she was barely surviving as a streetwalker, Maggie's death is a product of betrayal and indifference; the filthy river affords closure. Georges Lampin's *Crime et Châtiment/Crime and Punishment* (1956) features a derivation of Maggie's wretched fate. René Brunel (Robert Hossein) is a brooding, impoverished postwar Gallic reconception of Dostoyevsky's Raskolnikov. To raise capital in order to thwart his sister's loveless marriage to Antoine Monestier, an older, obese, and unattractive shopkeeper who is perversely attracted to young women, René murders an elderly pawnbroker but later confesses his crime after some cajoling from the angelic, victimized prostitute, Lili (Marina Vlady), enmeshed in her own mud-puddle of survival. In a shot sequence set at a riverbank, a frustrated Antoine Monestier (Bernard Blier), in the unexpected company of working Lili, shoots himself and falls at the edge of the river. Unlike Maggie's fatal descent into the river, Monestier's death reverses Crane's lonely fate in the client–prostitute naturalist dynamic.

French-Moroccan Nabil Ayouch's *Zin li Fik/Much Loved* (2015) is a naturalist narrative observing the intersecting lives of four female prostitutes living in Morocco. Ayouch's study of marginalized people and the desire for capital features transvestites, a lonely child selling candy, and parties full of abusive men, but the central focus is the escapist fantasies of the women. While on the beach, overlooking the ocean, the women gaze upon the sea and imagine the lives they might live elsewhere, or might have lived in the past leading up to the perilous present. *Much Loved* concludes with shots of the sea, an expansive, diverting site. For the young prostitutes in *Much Loved*, the sea is a source of relief; however, respite is a rare occurrence in the life of the prostitute.

Jean-Luc Godard's *Vivre sa vie/My Life to Live* (1962) is composed of sequential documentary-like tableaux—a dozen separate slides to be examined on a microscope—as each segment focuses on the limited space and time of a doomed, observed specimen, the former housewife and mother, Nana (Anna Karina). *Vivre sa vie* is a realistic portrayal of a working prostitute in Paris. As she remains an alienated, atypical figure, Nana consistently but unsuccessfully attempts to live her life on her own terms. According to Russell Campbell, "deploying documentary techniques ... Godard's *Vivre sa vie* ... incorporated a voice-over narration offering facts and statistics on contemporary prostitution in Paris."[17] This narration provides the audience with an external, discursive framing of how Nana is perceived by others, but this information may be juxtaposed with Nana's perceptive intelligence and refined expression of alienation from immediate society as she rejects marriage, motherhood, and more brutish forms of male dominance. Nana may be viewed as an intellectually estranged prostitute. She reads and thinks—therefore, she is more than a reductive social problem. In *Vivre sa vie*, Godard documents the life of an exploited, intelligent, uncaged woman in search of another life.

Godard's under-the-credits images of Nana suggest the close-up framing from a wanted poster, as most prostitutes are visualized as social outlaws. From the first tableau sequence, in which faces remain unseen unless momentarily glimpsed in mirrors, while Nana and her husband argue in a restaurant, until the last tableau, in which Nana is used as a human shield during a botched shootout between rival gangsters during which she is killed and left in the gutter, not a river, Nana leads a troubled life.

Godard's *Nana* also clearly alludes to the actress—prostitute in Zola's eponymous naturalist novel, *Nana* (1880), and her rise-and-fall narrative. According to Peter Mathews, "the narrative resonance between Godard's film and Zola's novel is unmistakable."[18] Mathews concludes:

> By borrowing the dispassionate outlook of the scientific mind, naturalism would, in a sense, bring its readers to a grittier, less compromised view of everyday life. Godard frequently imports this style in *Vivre sa Vie*. Godard generally excludes sexual images from *Vivre sa Vie*, making the reality of Nana's prostitution extend beyond eroticism into the more profound reaches of her being. Devoid of physical actions, prostitution acts purely as a signifier of the paradoxical interplay between intimacy and alienation.[19]

In Godard's "paradoxical interplay," the process of decline unfolds. Nana is seen working in a record store, watching a film, bantering with the police, being picked up near a cheap hotel-brothel, meeting a friend, servicing someone in her role as a hooker, talking with an attractive but dishonest pimp, discussing business practices, dancing in a poolroom, back at work on the streets, or even engaging in philosophical discussion with an older man she casually meets. Campbell notes, "the philosophizing prostitute ... is a character construct that violates realist convention and defies any attempt at classification ... Nana becomes a complex, enigmatic figure ... who quickly exceeds any archetypal delimitation placed upon her."[20] Compared with Daniel Duval's attractive young woman, Marie (Miou-Miou), who is regularly abused by her pimp and clients in the post-Godardian entry into the prostitution film narrative also set in France, *La dérobade/Memoirs of a French Whore* (1979), Nana is a more complex, reactive figure.

It is noteworthy that late in the film, Godard references Poe's short story "The Oval Portrait" (1842) about a woman-model who dies from neglect after unendurably posing for her thoughtless husband. As Godard's Nana is framed by the camera, her betrayal by the men in her life leads to an unexpectedly swift, violent death. Like Crane's Maggie, Nana is another body to be claimed for the morgue, a site of conclusive, anonymous resolution.

In Fritz Lang's noir naturalist narrative *Scarlet Street* (1945), an attractive "actress" Kitty (Joan Bennett), living in New York City along with her sleazy, abusive boyfriend, fleeces money from an unattractive, unhappy older male who paints extraordinary canvases, mostly in secret from his disapproving, harridan wife. In one shot sequence, the dejected Chris Cross (Edward G. Robinson) washes the evening's dishes at the sink and turns around to his complaining wife wearing an apron, an image of domesticity, but he is holding a knife, a weapon of resistance, that he points at her; Lang's ironic medium shot expresses Chris' conflicting impulses.

Chris is hopelessly smitten with Kitty, his tainted, forbidden muse, and foolishly attributes his creative work to her in order to secure her wealth and for her to survive, while her pimp-like boyfriend continues the deception for his gain. Upon the discovery of his betrayal and humiliation, Chris murders Kitty with an ice pick. This crime leads to her boyfriend's wrongful arrest and execution for her murder while simultaneously prompting Chris' decline into a wandering nub of his former self, haunted by guilt and anxiety. At the end of *Scarlet Street*, Chris traverses the streets like a ruined, scorned man and, in a final moment of ironic closure, stares at one of his paintings in an art store window—his portrait of Kitty—selling for a large sum of money. Her falsely attributed self-portrait is a final moment of mockery. Chris Cross exemplifies film Naturalism's grinding tradition; he is an observed case study in humiliation and failure, like the wronged, wounded figure "he" in Victor Sjöström's *He Who Get Slapped* (1924).

In G. W. Pabst's *Tagebuch einer Verlorenen/Diary of a Lost Girl* (1929), the adaptation of Margarete Böhme's eponymous novel of 1905, Thymian (Louise Brooks) is the central figure in a corrosive narrative of lost illusions. Pabst deploys long camera pans and horizontal movements within multiple shot sequences as the audience witnesses Thymian's deterioration—she is a rape victim, impregnated, and abandoned by her family—from the respectable daughter of a middle-class family to serving as an inmate in a reformatory. She devolves into a woman wandering on the streets of the unemployed and eventually, she finds work in a brothel. Pabst's naturalist narrative is less about New Objectivity's social reformism and more plausibly about debauchery, brutality, and eroticism as depicted in a determinist-based series of social and economic declensions. Thymian is a struggling specimen.

After Thymian is forced to leave her home and the reformatory, the seduction shot sequence in the Weimar-era brothel reveals the forced degradation that she and thousands of other women experience. Her body, her face, her identity become a spectacle of exhausted resignation. She becomes what she was not, a pushed more than a fallen woman. After wandering around the streets of the city looking for her friend, who unbeknownst to her is already a working prostitute, Thymian arrives at a brothel, one of hundreds in Weimar-era Germany. The audience reluctantly yet voyeuristically enters the brothel to witness Thymian's predictable decline. After consuming champagne and changing her dress into something alluring, Thymian begins to dance around in the company of others, until she succumbs to fatigue and falls into the arms of her first trick in the new trade. As Thymian awakens the next day, the elderly female proprietress-pimp and another prostitute enter the bedroom to offer psychological relief and earned capital. Thymian suffers throughout the film from sexual psychological violence and persistent social indifference, and she loses her child. As Heidi Schlüpmann notes, "In *Dairy of a Lost Girl*, the objective moral world is transformed into a subjective sadistic voyeurism."[21] Despite Pabst's parody of Hollywood "happy endings," in which Thymian is implausibly rescued by a redeeming older male, Thymian's public and personal deterioration is a naturalist decline narrative.

In Wu Yonggang's *Shen nu/The Goddess* (1934), at a critical point in this melodramatic narrative of relentless personal and social decline, the "Goddess," (Ruan Lingyu) a working prostitute-mother, exhibits a fake-forced smile, which recalls the distressing simulated grin of Lucy in Griffith's *Broken Blossoms* (1919), before another powerful, abusive male. When the audience is introduced to this young working mother, who remains nameless in a silent film, she is already a fallen figure. The goddess's work as a streetwalker, depicted in shots of her sauntering across Shanghai streets and alleys at night, signals that the process of decline had already begun before the film, as a pre-textual social marker. According to Timothy J. Gilfoyle, in pre-revolutionary China: "courtesans were never depicted as exemplifying the seamy or furtive side of Shanghai ... courtesans were both powerful and subordinated actors, public figures with their own social networks."[22] Yonggang's afflicted goddess is a struggling and abused mother. She is a survivor but subordinated and judged by external agencies. The goddess and her child are unwelcome and scorned, as she discovers during a typical presentation at her child's school.

According to Miriam Hansen,

> the woman played by Ruan Lingyu in the famous film *Goddess* works as a prostitute to support her illegitimate child and give him an education, but that does not make her a fallen woman for the filmic narration, only in the eyes of a hypocritical schoolboard; nor is she simply a maternal saint.[23]

In *The Goddess*, the intolerant school board represents a pre-revolutionary, bourgeois value system. The "Goddess" is never part of the larger circle of mothers, who identify her as perennial outsider. In the school talent show sequence, mothers of the other children sit together to watch their children perform; however, when these mothers comment cruelly on the goddess's child and his mother's job, her nearly dissolving face, in an affective medium close-up shot, reveals the anguish of her present life and their anxious future. Yonggang's shot of mocking faces and whispering, unheard voices produces psychological wounds framing the space and time of shameful public degradation.

Yonggang's melodrama of female suffering, in which a prostitute-mother cannot transcend the socially proscriptive agencies of her immediate environment, reveals how and why she succumbs to the violence and continual control of a gangster-pimp, who serves as recurring negative presence. She tries to escape but there is nowhere to go. She also suffers at the hands of the middle-class society that ignores her and finds her child to be morally unfit to go to school. These are devastating judgments. Although there is no social space for her, her child may potentially escape from these structural inhibitions because a kindly older teacher—like the parody of a family she could never have—adopts him while she is in jail for the justifiable murder of her former pimp. For the crime of defending herself and her child, for the crime of working as a prostitute in order to survive, and for the crime of being a disposable human, the goddess is removed from visible space and time. She remains in jail, guilty of no longer being innocent, just invisible, voiceless, and nameless.

In the opening framing, flashback shot sequence in Teuvo Tulio's *Sellaisena kuin sinä minut halusit/The Way You Wanted Me* (1944), a woman easily

Figure 4.1 Wu Yonggang's *The Goddess* (1934)

identifiable as a prostitute works along the dockside areas and is summoned to climb the stairs for her services. Tulio's close-up shot captures a moment in the life of a woman's spent narrative-in-progress in a mysterious space and time: "In terms of atmosphere and imagery ... *The Way You Wanted Me* comes closest to poetic realism."[24] Tulio then cuts to a dissolve shot, the "before" of the prostitute's narrative. The shot initiates images of flower-picking in an idyllic field to commence the naturalist processing of her sequenced decay.

The Way You Wanted Me is a case study of a seduced young woman's degeneration from innocent maiden—an unsalvaged Gretchen figure without Faust's glowing magic, only Mephisthophelean, calculated misfortune—devolving from farm girl to working-class domestic, and finally to street-walking prostitute. Along with an unexpected pregnancy and a series of misfortunate events, Maija (Marie-Louise Fock) winds up working the docks at night, like Crane's destitute Maggie. Tulio's Maija is initially seduced by the lure of the city as well as the amorous intentions of her lover, a sailor entrapped by his family and its animosity toward her and her family. After one night of passion, the two lovers are discovered, but he fails to speak up on her behalf. She leaves him and her home behind for a refreshed future that never occurs. After a series of mishaps, usually involving the wrong man, her pregnancy signals a lack of viable career and social opportunities as well as her prospective, troubled future; Tulio's shots of Maija's meandering about, her failed work, and her personal relationships lead to inevitable decline. *The Way You Wanted Me* is a melodrama infused with moments of neglect and abuse. Maija struggles to survive but experiences the grinding naturalist design imposed upon her life; nothing legitimate works for her. Even Maija's illegitimate child is nearly killed by an automobile as she discovers who and what her mother is at a party of drunken revelers, and then flees into traffic. In *The Way You Wanted Me*, the concluding shots return to the dockside, Maija's present worksite, as she climbs the stairs into familiar darkness.

In Keren Yedaya's *Or (My Treasure)* (2004), a study of mother–daughter working-class prostitutes set in a déclassé section of Tel Aviv, Or (Dana Ivgy), a seventeen-year-old high school student acts to salvage what is left of her abused and exhausted mother, Ruthie (Ronit Elkabetz), a spent streetwalker. In a series of sequential stages of naturalist decline, Or succumbs to her own inevitable career. Yedaya presents Or's decline not as a matter of tainted genetics but as a result of pressing economic issues; Or is an attractive young woman and the streets are full of anxious male clients. Throughout the film, Ruthie, Or's mother services an assortment of low life men and can barely sustain the physical and emotional mistreatment that she continually experiences. At one point, Or unexpectedly walks in to witness her mother and an old client copulating in the apartment. Or and Ruthie live in a cramped, unattractive walk-up apartment and can barely pay the rent on time, which leads later to a repulsive exchange between the landlord and Or, as she services him in an awkward moment of resignation.

Or works at first as a dishwasher, collects empty bottles, and initially attends but abandons school. She rejects the prospect of romantic love from a gentle neighbor at the behest of the boy's mother and Ruthie. Or later discovers the immediate cash incentives of marketing herself as a call girl in a factory-like escort service, a "step up" from streetwalker. Although shot in color, Yedaya's series of long takes, medium-framed two-shots, and location setting suggests a revised neorealist narrative. The street scenes revealing Ruthie trolling the streets recall images of Pier Paul Pasolini's laboring, weary *Mamma Roma* (1962) as "Mamma" (Anna Magnani) engages in conversation while traversing the streets of a dark city in search of clientele, while her son pursues the life of petty street criminal, which thwarts his mother's survival strategy, as will Or complicate life for her mother.

In one late shot sequence, Or and a fellow sex worker are sent by the brothel manager to a bachelor party in a house full of boisterous, mostly besotted young men. Yedaya does not feature the images of sexual performance that are likely to ensue. For Or and her friend, the imminent scenario with these men is potentially dangerous, a crime scene in the making. This sequence potentially evokes the humiliating rape spectacle performance between two sex workers in Darren Aronofsky's *Requiem for a Dream* (2000), in which both women simultaneously sodomize each other as a group of cheering men watch them, throwing money at their bodies. In *Or (My Treasure)*, moments before the event occurs upstairs, Yedaya's final shot frames Or in medium close-up, alone in the room, as she turns her head cautiously and settles her gaze directly on the viewer, a movement of face-to-face. Like Antoine (Jean-Pierre Léaud), the lonely lost child on the beach escaping from his life in François Truffaut's *Les Quatre Cents Coups/The 400 Blows* (1959), Or returns a tense gaze to viewers, implicating them in the narrative, as she anticipates coming events in her troubled life, from performance to payment, working on or off the streets.

Situated outside of a major urban venue during the postwar era of American surface normalcy, Sam Fuller's *The Naked Kiss* (1964) is set in typical small-town USA. In Fuller's naturalist narrative detailing a few years in the life of a troubled, intelligent prostitute, manicured lawns, attractive homes, and mid-size buildings symmetrically order the landscape that excludes her presence. *The Naked Kiss* exposes sexual sordidness behind doors enclosing alleged class respectability. An analogous narrative, Joseph Sarno's study of deception, costume parties, and sexual intrigue, *Sin in the Suburbs* (1964) takes place in a suburban setting. The covert sexual escapades of several frustrated individuals, identifiable as middle-class housewives and an assortment of dreary males, are centered in the home, which lapses from a sanctuary with unattractive furniture and unappealing clothing to an orgiastic, free-for-all status, identifiably occurring in the nascent phase of the "wife-swapping," and "swinging" 1960s. The men and women in Sarno's *Sin in the Suburbs* are not professional prostitutes or pimps, only unhappy middle-class people desirous of unencumbered sexual expression who hide behind the refineries of class and its prerogatives. Eric Schaefer notes that "*Sin in the Surburbs*, and other exploitation films, demand to be carefully situated in a specific time and place in order to fully reveal their historical and cultural value."[25] In both *The Naked Kiss* and *Sin in the Suburbs*, the home, neither a brothel nor a prostitute's familiar workspace, is the morally deconstructed site of postwar sexual intrigue for its occupants.

Like Sarno's exploitation narrative, Fuller's *The Naked Kiss* presents a subversive, microcosmic view of ugly America in the town of Grantville, with its seedy bars, corrupt police, and despicable perverts, not far from another small town with traditional brothel service functioning as a tolerated, tainted presence. As noted by Grant Tracey, "[Fuller's] film takes us to Grantville, a town with picket fences and fresh-cut lawns . . . [the film] is shocking gritty, and at times surreal."[26] *The Naked Kiss* is a black and white, visually stunning, low-budget noirish narrative of violent, gendered decline, however much its "saccharine sentimentality"[27] accesses the escapist fantasy for Kelly (Constance Towers), an unsettled prostitute in search of her rejuvenated self, as she exclaims in a moment of self-awareness, "I'm a broken down piece of machinery."

In a remarkable pre-credit opening sequence, shot from the point of view of Kelly's corrupt pimp-victim, Fuller's decentered, moving camera frames stylized violence in both close-up and medium shots, as Kelly attacks and compulsively beats him. This sequence includes the shocking effect of a wig sliding from her head to reveal her baldness, as Kelly's head was shaved by her pimp after she was drugged as a form of male control–punishment. In the prostitutes' naturalist film narratives, women frequently receive cuts and disfigurements—facial markings—as acts of ownership or retribution, which now include a humiliating head-shaving. After Kelly beats him into unconsciousness, she takes only her earned money and leaves, but she pauses to rip up her photograph, one image among his stable of workers, as a final act of her defiance. Fuller then cuts to Kelly, as she peers into the mirror-camera, as the audience witnesses her in close-up recomposing herself, applying makeup and her wig, preparing a "face to meet the faces" as she contrives to re-enter the world while directly implicating the audience in her prior and pending narrative.

Set two years later in the anonymous space of Grantville, with a career selling champagne, Kelly exits from a bus but is instantly noticed by a predatory, relatively corrupt local policeman, for whom she plies her former trade. After the encounter, he suggests that she find familiar work outside of town. While Pier Paolo Pasolini's prostitute "Mamma Roma" leaves her contemptuous pimp and resettles in a housing project in search of a better life for herself and her son, laboring as a stallholder in a market in a respectable form of employment, her decline is inevitably linked to an inescapable past and environmental causalities. As noted by Campbell, "[Mamma Roma] must bear the weight of the world on her shoulders ... the prostitute here cannot shake the guilt that clings to her."[28] This pronouncement is applicable for Fuller's Kelly; in *The Naked Kiss*, Kelly re-strategizes her life and finds employment in a local hospital working with handicapped children, where she does a noteworthy job, but like a surfacing, viral presence, the past erupts into the present. Even after Kelly has a nasty encounter with a brothel madam in a nearby town in order to save a young woman working in the brothel, she manages things until conditions worsen in the form of men entering her life.

In *The Naked Kiss*, respectable people are the most dangerous; a naked kiss indicates a lifeless, cold exchange between people, an empty moment revealing the insubstantial, a present void. Kelly meets a wealthy and socially connected man who is attracted to her but for the wrong reasons. After a courtship, including watching his home movies of a trip to Venice, quotes from Lord Byron, and champagne consumed with music in the background, they make plans for marriage. Kelly discovers that he is not really a thoughtful, attractive benefactor but a child molester who sees her as equally "abnormal." As she walks in on his (off-screen) molestation of a young girl, Kelly strikes and kills him. Fuller's shot of the motionless child in medium close-up is realistically horrifying. Although Kelly is arrested for the crime of murder, and the child disappears, Kelly is eventually cleared of all charges after the child later reappears. Regardless, Kelly elects to disappear once the legal situation is clarified, and again tries to salvage her life elsewhere.

Grinding Streets

Naturalist cinema depicting the lives of sex workers features multiple examples of the straight, gay and/or transitional male prostitute/sex worker and his/their frequently problematic narrative.

Roger Richebé's *Gibier de potence/Gigilo* (1951) confirms that good looks and a firm male frame are assault weapons as well as self-destructive agencies in naturalist film narrative. Richebé's film begins with the adult Marceau (Georges Marchal), who was raised in a Catholic orphanage and was a former prisoner of war, returning to Paris as a troubled, exceptionally attractive man, who inevitably returns to work at his trade as male escort–sex worker for older, lonely women. Richebé's *Giglio* presents Marceau in a series of flashback voice-overs and chronicles Marceau's failed attempts to fit in anywhere, whether at finding legitimate work, including his brief effort as an assistant butcher who has relations with the butcher's wife, for which he is locked inside the meat locker to cool off, and later, as he is approached by Madame Alice (Arletty) initially to pose as a nude male model for a series of nature-related photographs. Madame Alice owns and operates a lingerie store—a magnet for older women with capital—and functions as both a scheming friend and Marceau's platonic pimp while arranging his career as reluctant escort.

In *Gigilo*, although Marceau is successful, he is uncomfortable with his exploitative career and becomes involved emotionally with a client, despite the difficulties this represents as a loss of capital. As Madame Alice mockingly rejects Marceau's desire to leave the escort's life behind him, a fight ensues in which, in the home of a wealthy targeted family, she shoots at him but misses. As he pushes her away in an act of self-defense, she falls and fractures her skull, dying instantly. Although Marceau is guilty of not being innocent, as he remains behind and confesses all to the woman he desired, their joint escape from his past indiscretions cannot be realized. Marceau is a doleful naturalist specimen: his working-class origin and illicit career collaboratively engulf him and lead to the police. Marceau does not fade; he is ground into a formerly attractive nub.

In a film examining the life of a (part-time) male prostitute, economic survival, and conflicted sexuality, John Turturro's comedy-drama *Fading Gigolo* (2014) is set largely in the exotic, patriarchal culture of the Hasidic community of Williamsburg in contemporary Brooklyn. This is an enclosed social circulus predicated on the observance of strict religious beliefs and ritual customs, with proscriptive rules for both men and women, especially involving sexual relations. Turturro's narrative features identifiable New York City streets and crossings, local people, traditional businesses, and the confluence of public social and religious-based events, visualized in outdoor location shots as well as indoor settings, with conventional furniture, clothing, and religious objects, to constitute a sense of visual normalcy. This penned setting creates a realistic backdrop for comedic and romantic relations to infuse with naturalist precepts involving forbidden sexuality and labor amid blossoming, taboo personal relations. Turturro's performance as Fioravante, the gentle bookstore worker and part-time prostitute who is set up for appointments by Murray (Woody Allen), the bookstore owner-pimp in need of cash to remain in business in a city in which book stores are disappearing, chronicles the experiences and mores of unexceptional working-class people. Religious people and their culture are not fetish or ridiculed subjects. Turturro's film avoids industrial clichés along with excessive romantic and comedic flourishes, as unexceptional individuals experience measures of personal and economic conflict.

In the history of lost, incomplete, or censored narratives, Stephen Crane's novel *Flowers of Asphalt* (1894) is rumored to have focused on the life of a male prostitute in late nineteenth-century New York City's subaltern culture. Nothing is assuredly known about the novel except the legends associated with its absence. In an act of experimental renewal, avant-garde filmmaker Gregory Markopoulos' *Flowers of Asphalt* (1951)[29] appropriates the title from Crane's missing novel, and in Markopoulos' seven-minute production, he designs an associative, dream-like flow that visually defamiliarizes the space and time of domestic realities into a series of interrelated motions, frames of homoerotic desire, indicating escapist sexual identities.

Wiktor Grodecki's *Mandragora* (1997) graphically depicts an attractive young urban street hustler, Marek (Miroslav Caslavka), barely surviving in the gay underworld of lonely Prague, without the promise of escape or resolve, in a harrowing narrative of decline. Marek's life is a protracted series of humiliations and beatings; he experiences forced and paid sexual encounters, drugs, AIDS anxiety, and abandonment. Marek is initially noticed by a predacious pimp as a possible trainee productive prostitute. From this early point in Grodecki's *Mandragora*, life declines for Marek, with two extended shot sequences realistically illustrating his painful existence: at the home/worksite of a porno film director, and later, in the public bathroom that his father enters, ironically, while searching for his son.

In a private home-worksite dwelling—a concealed site—a producer-director of hard-core male porno films introduces Marek to these violent industrial staples that create generous amounts of capital. To Marek, this sequence is a grotesque parody of the filmmaking process, and he recoils at its suggestive, sadistic enactments; in Grodecki's *Mandragora*, this director might be the most dangerous figure in the film, as he uses young men like disposable props. Later, as a nearly broken Marek enters a public bathroom infused with drugs and exhausted by life, his father unknowingly enters the same area, but the two are divided by a stall. Grodecki splits the fame—these are two separate, yet simultaneous spatial realities—and as Marek slowly collapses onto the floor, his father finishes urinating and exits from the shot, and likely, from Marek's life. The wall between them is never breached. Grodecki realistically and symbolically documents the troubled life of an abused, ruined runaway. Just as the botanical analysis of the mandrake, an attractive, poisonous plant that frequently induces sleep and acts as a painkiller, and is noted for its human-like appearance, Grodecki's *Mandragora* details the poisoned, plucked life of a striking young man, numb and lost, in a dark urban place.

In André Téchiné's *J'embrasse pas/I Don't Kiss* (1991), a handsome young country boy, Pierre (Manuel Blanc) leaves his home and travels to Paris in search of a new life, preferably as a stage performer. He initially gets a job as a dishwasher, recalling the pre-New York City employment of future male prostitute, the Texan Joe Buck (Jon Voight), in John Schlesinger's *Midnight Cowboy* (1969). Whereas Joe Buck planned to entertain women in his decidedly heterosexual career in the city, Pierre wants to be a discovered, successful actor there. Both Joe Buck and Pierre labor as prostitutes, initially engaged with women, but each eventually discovers that survival in the urban jungle means career compromise, since their sexual magnetism also attracts male clients.

Pierre labors as a "rent boy" who works in public spaces—pick-up places—such as remote areas in the city park at night. His one steadfast rule, as if to preserve a notion of heterosexual distancing, remains the "never kiss" policy with his male clients. Téchiné's study of a young man's failure to acclimate to city life and his overall struggle to survive includes a near-suicidal gesture on a highway overpass—not a river bank—when Pierre's despondence increases as reality intrudes upon his dreams. At one point, Pierre is raped violently by the pimp of a female friend, another prostitute, with whom he shares his unhappiness. The consistent, isolated space and time of the anonymous urban setting—Téchiné's dreary naturalist vision of Paris—creates a prostitute narrative for a city of broken dreams and lost people. In a later, questionable act, Pierre enlists in the army, which he conceives as an alleged refuge to halt his depressing decline. Shown standing alone on the beach, Pierre will soon follow orders not from directors or clients, but from authoritarian men in uniform.

Rosa von Praunheim's *Die Jungs vom Bahnhof Zoo/Rent Boys* (2011) is a documentary depicting the problematic labor and survival strategies of young male sex workers in Berlin. Von Praunheim's interviews and on-site location shots examine a series of horrific personal recollections—narratives of abuse—experienced by street hustlers plying their trade. In medium and close-up shots, recollections of painful moments recall experiences with HIV, diabetes, child abuse, and harrowing instances in the trade. Berlin is a pivotal presence throughout the production, as von Praunheim reveals the street, sounds, and overall sites of an exposed city. As in Paris, New York City and other urban venues, male hustling remains an underground activity ironically plied openly: attractive youth as a worthy purchase. Novelist and male hustler John Rechy discusses the sexual, marketable presumptive pose and relates how he "learned too that to hustle the streets you had to play it almost-illiterate."[30] In *Rent Boys*, these hustlers assume a contrived, engaging identity, appearing as a noticeable purchase, without revealing the non-essential qualities, including expressions of threatening intelligence.

The assorted hustlers in Von Praunheim's film present nearly identical personal narratives; those who were once young, promising, and striking are now reduced to medically and emotionally compromised figures, barely alive and in constant search of capital. These are disposable, atypical laborers; many of the hustlers are transvestites whose survival and experiences are even more precarious. Von Praunheim's sexual outlaws conjoin in a naturalist study, observations of peril and decline.

Henrique Goldman's *Princesa* (2004) examines the personal travails and labor of a young transgender sex worker in Milan. In *Princesa*, Brazilian hustler Fernando/Fernanda (Ingrid de Souza) is a troubled, pre-transitional person working the streets in search of lonely men's capital to arrange for a sex-change procedure. In Goldman's foreshadowing pre-credits shot sequence, composed of close-up and two shots, a child and her father sit inside a train car and either stare at or forcefully attempt to ignore Fernanda, who sits opposite them. As the authorities enter the area to inspect passports, Fernanda's passport documents her identity as Fernando, which prompts her immediate humiliating removal from the train. As the authorities and Fernanda travel across the platform, the father and daughter witness the event with the window separating them. In *Princesa*, this public humiliation is a recurring act of demeaning sexual categorization, which then leads to the questioning officer in charge forcing Fernanda to expose her breasts and demanding oral sex as her entry fee. The painful, brief shot sequence differs from Andy Warhol's avant-garde, single-shot close-up of enraptured facial expressions of a serviced man (DeVeren Bookwalter) in *Blowjob* (1964); in *Princesa*, the act of forced fellatio is an indicative sign of abusive power relations with a disempowered person, like a trapped prisoner and her jailer.

Fernanda soon meets Gianni, a married man full of unkept promises who drives a car in search of something else in life, which he discovers in Fernanda, until Gianni's wife becomes pregnant and Fernanda decides that the relationship is over. Things consistently go badly for Fernanda, as she and the other transgender workers are constantly harassed, while each labors on open, volatile streets. At one point, as a client explores Fernanda's body, he throws her out of the car once he discovers her male member, although she is nearly undressed and in a sequestered location. Fernanda is soon pimped out by an older, established woman running a private service, which she eventually leaves.

In Goldman's *Princesa*, Fernanda suffers from dangerous pick-up encounters and personal disappointment. In voice-over messages—mail sent back home to her mother that Fernanda signs as Fernando—she expresses hopeful optimism, although, after multiple setbacks, Fernanda contemplates suicide as she stands on the roof near the ledge of a building. She is persuaded down and returns to the streets to re-engage in familiar routines. Her life is a series of mediated highs and mostly lows. As Fernanda returns to her former pimp, stating: "I'm a good whore," the pimp admits her back into the fold but threatens to return her "to the jungle" should this reoccur, as the exploitive cycle continues.

Sean Baker's eccentric melodrama, a transgender Christmas film *Tangerine* (2015), examines the pre-holiday labor-related experiences of two sex workers on the streets of Los Angeles. Noted for its use of hand-held (Apple iPhone 5) camerawork, with a pervasive sense of location realism, as the film is shot on the streets of a city at night, *Tangerine* juxtaposes multiple personalities in crisis. There is the married immigrant cab-driver in love with one sex worker, her cheating pimp boyfriend, the dreams of a saloon singer looking for recognition, and the recurring physical dangers of the profession. Throughout Baker's film, the language and urban action are full of slang, abusive insults, and frequently comedic, including a sequence featuring a fellatio sequence in a busy car wash. In *Tangerine*, the donut shop, a business staple found in most cities, becomes a semi-stationery meeting and pick-up site where trade is established: a sugary, neon-illuminated public brothel. In *Tangerine*, setting and time—the city of Los Angeles, mostly at night—produce new sexual birth.

Brothels/Factories

In Jean-Louis Forain's painting, *Le Client or Maison Close* (1878), a fleshy assemblage of prostitutes poses like a hearty meal for likely consumption before a lumpish male. The viewer gazes upon what the man seemingly ignores; Forain's canvas is a carnal display of imaginative pleasure, not involving idealized beauty or love, but suggesting commerce and purchasing power. A confirmed naturalist trope involves the subaltern working world of the male-female prostitute in the brothel narrative. These narratives historicize setting to provide realistic readings of a subaltern culture; they are visually suggestive period pieces of proscribed carnality, set within credible parameters.

Vasilis Georgiadis' *Ta Kokkina Fanaria/Red Lanterns* (1962) examines the intersecting lives of female prostitutes—all Greek nationals with one Romanian immigrant—laboring in a bar-brothel serving Piraeus, a port city within the Greater Athens area, prior to the closure of brothels by the local government. The lives of several sex workers are highlighted in the historically infamous red-light district, like the Tenderloin district in both San Francisco and New York City, and in Storyville, New Orleans. *Red Lanterns* features a coterie of shiftless clientele, replete with blaring music and endless rounds of alcohol in a carnivalesque atmosphere, interacting in both serious and comedic sequences involving class, sex, and cash. Georgiadis' *Red Lanterns* is a film about a disappearing local industry, and several shots in Georgiadis' *Red Lanterns* recall Paul Cadmus' censored canvas *"The Fleet's In!"* (1934), which features semi-grotesque renderings of prewar sailors and a marine on leave openly socializing in Manhattan's Riverside Park area with likely prostitutes, as the women "have repeatedly been identified as prostitutes since 1934 by historians, critics, and the general public."[31] The sailors are apparently drunk and aggressively looking for fast company, while the marine solicits a cigarette from an encoded homosexual figure. The painting signals anticipatory pleasures of all sorts.

Georgiadis' *Red Lanterns* begins in an amusement park, a public site, with two lovers, Petros (Dimitris Papamichael) and Eleni (Jenny Karezi), enjoying frugal moments. Eleni, the alienated immigrant forced by circumstance into the profession, secretly works in the brothel as a means of desperate survival and is nicknamed "princess" by the other women as she is viewed as haughty and remote. While few of these women ignore the reality of the profession, their labor does not demean them. As the brothel is later forcibly closed, the furniture, the clients, and the sex workers find other venues and resources: the profession endures.

In *Red Lanterns*, Madam Pari's garish bar-brothel, unlike Clint Eastwood's version of the saloon-brothel in *Unforgiven* (1992) and the competing saloon-brothel establishments run by Cy Tolliver and Al Swearengen in David Milch's HBO Western series, *Deadwood* (2004–6), in *Red Lanterns*, the most tranquil site is the bedroom, in which personalities converge and cautiously reveal themselves. Other brothel sites in intermedial narratives profess a refined, relaxed atmosphere in contrast to raucous settings. One notable brothel site is set in the basement-cellar of a home, a surreptitious carnal "underworld."

Gaston Bachelard notes, "As for the cellar, we shall no doubt find uses for it. It will be rationalized and its conveniences enumerated. But it is first and foremost the dark entity of the house, the one that partakes of subterranean forces."[32] Playwright Sholom Ash's controversial melodrama, *Got Fun Nekome/God of Vengeance* (1907),[33] is set in the turn-of-the century Eastern European home of a religious family operating a brothel in the cellar. In naturalist cinema, the home, when reconfigured as a brothel, is a destabilized site in which secrets are exposed and sex is marketed. In Edward Dmytryk's *Walk on the Wild Side* (1962), the fashionable bordello-home, the ironically labeled "Doll's House," in which assorted Depression-era prostitutes labor, is well-ordered and well-kept by the intense Madame Jo (Barbara Stanwyck). Among the most interesting aspects of Dmytryk's naturalist narrative is the intimated relationship between Jo and the conflicted prostitute, Hallie (Capucine). Jo's obvious strong sexual desire for Hallie accesses for her a place of privilege, a relaxed work standard, and personal attention. Hallie, the artist-prostitute, would become the house special reserved for Jo, who continually desires, placates, but eventually loses Hallie to mindless violence. For several shot sequences, Hallie fitfully lounges in an attractive bedroom, physically eclipsing the lives and labor of the other sex workers. According to Dan Callahan, Jo is "unrequitedly in love with … prostitute Hallie … She's [Jo] a predatory hawk, a woman who swoops down on unhappy or destitute girls and installs them in her elegant New Orleans bordello."[34] Hallie, viewed by Jo like a rare jewel, is frequently shot by Dmytryk sequestered from others in the frame. Hallie remains depressed and exasperated by life, until an old lover arrives, but fails to rescue her. In *Walk on the Wild Side*, nobody is redeemed; there is always another bordello.

Louis Malle's *Pretty Baby* (1978) is the dramatic recreation of a period in the early twentieth century in which high-end brothels, frequently former mansions, were endemic to the sexual subculture of New Orleans in the Storyville section of the city. Malle's film suggestively mixes the factual with the fictional to produce a concocted soft-core fantasy as cultural history. The allegedly physically disabled E. J. Bellocq (Keith Carradine), the photographer of the sex workers, is prominently featured in the film; Carradine's Bellocq is a handsome, reserved figure committed to his craft, while he is eventually swayed by the alluring appeal of the "pretty baby," the wild child Violet (Brooke Shields), the twelve-year old daughter of a prostitute who labors in the bordello. Like Zola's nubile Nana, there is a nascent, sexual energy that makes Violet appealing and upon maturing, desired —literally, to be auctioned—as an object for male consumption.

According to historically based recreations of racial and class prerogative, Malle accurately portrays local Black and White cultures at the bordello; there are those white men and women with capital and means to attend parties and to participate in illicit activities and those individuals, mostly Black, who serve as support staff and musicians. One especially noteworthy figure is the "professor" (Antonio Fargas), the Black piano player working in the bordello who witnesses the demeaning auction of Violet's available-for-purchase virginity to the highest bidder. In this shot sequence, Violet is literally carried into the bordello's lush dining room while perched on a serving tray, a sumptuous offering of flesh to be devoured like a holiday meal. Malle's cut-away shot from the ongoing auction to the professor's face in medium close-up suggests that he recalls the language and dread associated with slave auctions. His facial expression is one of troubled historical consciousness, an awareness, as the older white men exercise their sense of entitlement. Violet is literally purchased for four hundred dollars, and after a few moments, a subsequent off-screen scream indicates her deflowered status as a sex worker.

In the bordello, Malle documents the women moments before and after their work upstairs, as they gossip, eat, and spend time busily with the daily chores of life, until Bellocq arrives and photographs them as subjects, rather than engaging them as objects. Bellocq is obsessive in the documentation of prostitutes in Arbus-like "look-back-at-you" poses, as if revealing the lives of working women in their natural habitat. According to Neil D. Isaacs, "Malle's Bellocq is transformed into a man of repressed sexuality but reasonable attractiveness, accepted by the women primarily because they enjoy his pictures and posing for them."[35] Violet impulsively attracts Bellocq's reticent desire, and he behaves like one of the older Nana's idiotic attendees; eventually, Bellocq and Violet illegally marry, as she is still underage.

Bellocq's photographs are now categorized as aesthetic, historical documents; his series of posing prostitutes, described by Susan Sontag as "inmates of a brothel,"[36] are the subject of an unresolved mystery, as the faces of several of the women are scratched out, leaving only the body and the imperfect face. Along with the results of this censorious gesture, the question as to why the posing image of the female nude, an artistic staple with a precedent history in photography and postcard culture, was not wholly destroyed remains unresolved. Zeese Papanikolas speculates:

> We do not know if [Bellocq] scratched out the heads of his subjects out of anger or cruelty or to protect the privacy of these women, who might have been his friends, and who might one day slip back across that tenuous line between the District and the respectable world of proper houses.[37]

Scratching out the sex worker's face is a cruel, metonymical instance of violence against women, which is graphically imposed on the face of the sex worker in Eastwood's *Unforgiven*, in which the prostitute, Delilah (Anna Thomson), while working in a brothel upstairs in the saloon callously controlled by her pimp, is attacked by an angered client with a knife and left horribly scarred. This violent act renders her sexually "useless," like damaged goods, a ruined presence fit for menial labor according to the terms of her cited contract.

A similar facial scarring incident occurs in Bertrand Bonello's turn-of-the-century Parisian erotic drama *L'Apollonide (Souvenirs de la maison close)/House of Tolerance* (2011). As one of the bordello's prostitutes, Madeleine (Alice Barnole) is obligingly tied up by a familiar client; he suddenly disfigures her face with a knife in a Gwynplaine-like series of cuts, leaving her impaired and shunned by the clientele or later used as a novelty, a sex-toy, with her veil removed to reveal the broken doll spectacle.

Some decades later, streetworkers and shots of bordello night life are the subject of Brassaï's photographic series, *Le Paris Secret des Années 30/The Secret Paris of the 30s* (1976), which features, as noted by Tomasz Ferenc, graphically revealing images of criminal and sex workers' culture:

> It is not just the silhouettes of Parisian prostitutes, standing in the archways and street corners; it is a bold reportage on the city's sex life. He [Brassaï] documented thriving jazz clubs, naked parties, portrayed semi-nude women waiting for their clients, visited by-the-hour hotels rented by lovers, immortalized ecstatic romps at Montparnasse, and opium dens.[38]

As noted by the investigative voice of Brassaï, violence was an occupational hazard for the sex worker: "Beneath their surface gaiety, these girls lived in perpetual anxiety . . . A prostitute's body has always fallen prey to stigmatization, but has also been constantly subjected to dangers such as disease and all forms of violence."[39] In *House of Tolerance*, Bonello documents the lives and misfortunes of working prostitutes in a turn-of-the-century historical setting, which includes referencing the Dreyfus affair and the hardcover publication of H. G. Wells' *The War of the Worlds* (1898). The recreation of this high-end brothel's furniture and formal clothing, set in a former mansion, initiates a sense of realistic escapism, enabling clients to lounge or to hide, even in masks.

In his discussion of Parisian bordellos, Brassaï notes, "The madam, also known as the landlady, the Lady Pimp, played the main role in the house's reputation, its orderly management."[40] Like the champagne freely consumed and opium smoked by workers and clientele, in *House of Tolerance* there are no limits to capital's purchasing prerogatives, including role playing and violence. The madam keeps the books and registers debt as the rise of the streetwalker and low rent brothels directly compete with her stylish establishment and her rising rent. The madam must consistently refresh her stock and conjure new delights for product differentiation and competition.

In Bonello's film, the prostitutes are not only attractive but intelligent and supportive of each other as they meet in the lounge and converse. In Brassaï's "House of Illusion" section, he describes the entrance rituals practiced in the bordello known as the "Suzy":

> At Suzy, a bell went off as the client opened the door, and he found himself in a kind of booth, as though he had gone to vote. The madam appeared with a wide, salacious grin. All the girls ... would form a tableau vivant: the shortest, sometimes kneeling, in front, the others, standing behind them. The visitor could thus make a considered choice among the bodies before him.[41]

In *House of Tolerance*, as a new client enters, Bonello shoots from the male's point of view as he walks through the bordello; the women line up for exposure in a tracking shot that looks like an assemblage of featured products in a department store. Brassaï observed "the most flourishing whorehouses in Paris were the ones known in slang as the 'slaughterhouses' ... Every movement there was calculated, measured, tailored, charged for, as in an assembly plant."[42]

In *House of Tolerance*, women are not disposable merchandise, but each one is susceptible to various acts of exploitation, deception, potential acts of violence, and work-related illness, especially venereal disease. During a requisite medical examination, which is impersonal and intrusive, Julie (Jasmine Trinca), one of the workers, is revealed to have syphilis. Bonello's shot sequence cuts from images of a pleasant young woman protesting this illness to her lying on a slab in the morgue, with disfiguring pock-marks that resemble documentary-like images of the deceased in Andres Serrano's *Morgue* series.[43]

In a notable deconstruction of the space and time in the bordello setting, Bonello frames a quadrant of intersecting images of painterly wholeness as a unified composite, in which each part of the frame comments on the other:

in the top left quadrant of the frame, three women slumber in one bed, as if reconceiving Courbet's site of the dormant desire of two nude women sleeping together in *Le Sommeil/Sleep* (1866); at the top right side of the frame, a woman actively reads to children; at the bottom left side of the frame, a woman stolidly cuts meat on a kitchen counter, and at the bottom right side of the frame, several brothel women sit together and play cards, while in the background of the shot, a painting of a reclining female nude hangs on the wall, as if commenting on the foreground's reality. As the shot progresses, Bonello reconstructs and links these four separate spaces across time: one of the women in bed descends into the shot of the woman cutting meat and one of the children leaves the reading and enters the frame of the card players, thus conjoining the images while remaining visually interdependent. Bonello then cuts to a medium shot—a triptych of three women—in simultaneous time in movement from left to right. One woman sits in a chair, smokes, and fixes her hair in the mirror, one woman pushes a curtain aside and sunlight flows in to illuminate her, and one woman stands alone with her opium pipe, walking out of the frame and into the shot of the women playing cards. Bonello's pyrotechnic stylization in *House of Tolerance* positions a painterly sensibility in the lives of the workers not working.

At the end of *House of Tolerance*, as the Parisian brothel's rent and its competition demands are overwhelming, the remaining women are literally sold away or simply leave to become common streetwalkers. In an act of cognitive "homage," Bonello's narrative departs from the original brothel setting and cuts across space and time to reveal contemporary Parisian streetwalkers working on the streets. One of the sex workers is identifiable as the "symbolic descendant" of the aging, opium-addicted Clotilde (Céline Sallette). The viewer considers this image as evidence of a generational recycling of the sex worker's decline narrative.

Lizzie Borden's *Working Girls* (1987) is set in attractive apartment house–bordello and focuses on the daily labors of three prostitutes, all of whom have lives outside their employment, working in a midtown bordello in New York City. As noted by Karen Jaehne, "The lack of marquee value in Lizzie Borden's *Working Girls*, with its ho-hum nudity, makes it breathtakingly naturalistic, photorealistic,"[44] which makes behavior in the brothel appear mundane while interesting. Russell Rouse's prostitute-brothel bio-pic, *A House is Not a Home* (1964), set mostly in apartment houses during the Depression era in New York City, features "old Hollywood" studio performers. Shelley Winters portrays the infamous Polly Adler, the one-time madam of a successful brothel. *A House is Not a Home* traces the unusual immigrant narrative of brothel madam Polly Adler's requisite "rise-and-fall" career, from her impoverished early life laboring in the factory sweatshop, vicious sexual assault, and consequential introduction to organized crime, featuring corrupt police and politicians and historical figures such as New York's well-known pimp-murderer, organized crime's Lucky Luciano (Cesar Romero). According to Campbell, *A House is Not a Home* exposes "the life of the notorious New York madam Polly Adler [and] focuses on her ties with a bootlegger attached to Lucky Luciano's gang."[45] In this era, when urban, gangster cultures thrived in New York City, the brothel was a reliable source of income and employment for young women, unlike inaccessible skilled factory labor.

Situated under the introductory flow of credits, a series of Bellocq-like photographic images of alluring female talent is presented as potential objects of cataloged consumption: a preview of fleshy merchandise. After this display of stock, *A House is Not a Home* cuts to the present setting; Polly Adler is entertaining at an elegant brothel party in an apartment during which faux "can-can" dancers flash their obscured genitalia region to entice and engage the clients. Adler's voice-over enables the drama to flash back to the extensive origin sequence that constitutes the bulk of the film narrative. Adler states, "I'm the madam of a brothel," to which she adds shortly, "The only unforgivable sin was to be poor." The narrative pursues this biographical trajectory as it mixes the historical events of the era, featuring Brooklyn and Manhattan corrupt "club" politicians, Prohibition, the speakeasy, and the Depression, intermingled with sexually charged escapades. Although pursued by a musician, Adler consistently rejects the "love-marriage" reformation formula, as she believes that she cannot be forgiven for pimping.

Adler states that her stable of prostitutes were "chosen for beauty, manners and taste." This high-end operation excludes streetwalkers in order to cautiously service the socially and politically well-connected array of males. The women are trained to act like models and pleasant party-girls, although they reveal their collective loneliness during the New Year festivities, and one develops a drug habit and overdoses. According to Adler, "no woman is born a whore," but many may die as one, emotionally or physically scarred and disposable. As in Bertrand Bonello's *House of Tolerance*, in between daily events and appointed assignations, for these women there is a permeating sense of the perpetual, feckless present, like an extended break from the assembly line. After a series of setbacks and changing times, Adler's brothel enterprise begins to fade along with the gangster era, and *A House is Not a Home* cuts back from the flashback to the present party, where Adler ignores a phone call from her suitor from the past. For Adler, there is only the present and capital.

In Tomu Uchida's *Yôtô monogatari: hana no Yoshiwara hyakunin-giri/Hero of the Red-Light District* (1960), in a series of events that seemingly parallel Oedipus' unsettling origin, a child born with a pronounced facial birthmark is abandoned by his parents and adopted by successful merchants, a childless couple. The child grows into a thriving textile businessman, Sano Jiro (Chiezo

Kataoka), a man whom even the courtesans disregard, until he meets and courts in the bordello the unpopular, attractive parvenu, Otsuru (Yoshie Mizutani), who uses him in a scheme to become a celebrated figure and to improve her overall social standing in Yoshiwara, the red-light district. Otsuru, a sexual commodity to be purchased but not trusted, and her duplicitous married pimps conspire against and continually fleece Sano Jiro for piles of money. For his money and for her entry into local society, Otsuru finds Sano Jiro tolerable.

In several shot sequences, Uchida's tripartite setting juxtaposes the home, the factory, and the red-light area to contrast Sano Jiro's pathetic decline into a foolish, desperate figure. Uchida features several shots of the courtesans as exposed merchandise, peering at customers from behind gates—a reversal of the gaze—appearing imprisoned by rituals while waiting for work. Uchida's bordello shots reveal women eating, conversing, combative, and entrapped.

After squandering money and ignoring the business advice of friends, fellow subcontractors, and merchants, Sano Jiro is a broken, cash-strapped figure; Otsuru disgraces him in public and eventually ignores him, unaware of Sano Jiro's impending revenge. As if to restore his honor, Sano Jiro returns to the bordello area during a festival and kills several participants, the two married pimps, and even Otsuru, although Sano Jiro remains a broken figure of his former self, a man "scorned."

Notes

1. Sears Roebuck and Company, *Consumers Guide, Catalogue #104* (Chicago, Illinois, 1897), n.p.
2. Anonymous, *A Gentleman's Companion* (New York: 1870), 17. See https://www.nytimes.com/interactive/projects/documents/a-vest-pocket-guide-to-brothels-in-19th-century-new-york-for-gentlemen-on-the-go. Accessed April 12, 2023.
3. Ibid, 19.
4. Ibid, 19.
5. Ibid, 30–1, 41–2.
6. Ibid, 47.
7. Ibid, 54–5. Note: "Safes" is a slang term for male condoms.
8. John H. Girdner, *Newyorkitis* (New York: Grafton Press, 1901), 77–8. Note: the Tenderloin district is now known as the Chelsea section of Manhattan, and the italics are mine.
9. William Thomas Stead, *Satan's Invisible World Displayed, or Despairing Democracy* (London: William Clowes, 1898), 81.
10. Judith R. Walkowitz, "The Politics of Prostitution and Sexual Labour," *History Workshop Journal*, Vol. 82, No. 1 (Autumn 2016), 195.
11. Russell Campbell, *Marked Women: Prostitutes and Prostitution in the Cinema* (Madison: University of Wisconsin Press, 2006), 21.
12. Ibid, 9.
13. Sherwood's *Waterloo Bridge* was produced in two film adaptations: *Waterloo Bridge* (dir. James Whale, Universal Pictures, 1931) and *Waterloo Bridge* (dir. Mervyn LeRoy, MGM, 1940).

14. Reverend C. Maurice Davies, *Orthodox London: Phases of Religious Life in the Church of England*, second edition (London: Tinsley Brothers, 1876), 196.
15. This study favors the interpretation that Maggie was a murder victim and not a suicide. Murder was a common fate for the frequently unidentified and abandoned women of the working urban class who were forced into prostitution at this time in "progressive" history.
16. Stephen Crane, *Maggie: A Girl of the Streets* (1893 edition), ed. Christopher Gair (Nottingham: Trent Editions, 2000), 60.
17. Campbell, *Marked*, 305.
18. Peter Mathews, "The Mandatory Proxy," *Biography*, Vol. 29, No. 1 (Winter 2006), 46.
19. Ibid, 47.
20. Campbell, *Marked*, 384.
21. Heidi Schlüpmann, "The Brothel as an Arcadian Space? *Diary of a Lost Girl* (1929)," in *The Films of G. W. Pabst: An Extraterritorial Cinema*, ed. Eric Rentschler (New Jersey: Rutgers University Press, 1990), 87.
22. Timothy J. Gilfoyle, "Prostitutes in History: From Parables of Pornography to Metaphors of Modernity," *American Historical* Society, Vol. 104, No. 1 (February, 1999), 129.
23. Miriam Hansen, "Fallen Women, Rising Stars, New Horizons: Shanghai Silent Film as Vernacular Modernism," *Film Quarterly*, Vol. 54, No. 1 (Autumn 2000), 16.
24. Henry Bacon, Kimmo Laine, and Jaakko Seppälä, "Tulio and the Traditions of Melodrama," in *ReFocus: The Films of Teuvo Tulio: An Excessive Outsider* (Edinburgh: Edinburgh University Press, 2020), 31–2.
25. Eric Schaefer, "Exploitation Films: Teaching *Sin in the Suburbs*," *Cinema Journal*, Vol. 47, No. 1 (Autumn 2007), 97.
26. Grant Tracey, "Crosscuts: Brief DVD Reviews," *North American Review*, Vol. 296, No. 3 (Summer 2011), 45.
27. Campbell, *Marked*, 124.
28. Ibid, 136–8.
29. A special note of gratitude to Robert Beavers for making a rare copy of *Flowers of Asphalt* available for viewing. Also, a special "thank you" to John Mhiripiri and Alex Westhelle at the *Anthology Film Archives* in NYC for the generous use of their space and time.
30. John Rechy, *City of Night* (New York: Grove Press, 1964), 32.
31. Anthony J. Morris, "Paul Cadmus and Carnival, 1934: Representing the Comic Grotesque," *American Art*, Vol. 26, No. 3 (Fall 2012), 93.
32. Gaston Bachelard, *The Poetics of Space*, trans. Marian Jolas (Boston: Beacon Press, 1994), 18.
33. Sholom Ash is cited as Sholem Asch in other publications, along with several spelling variations of his name. The version cited in this study is: Sholom Ash, *The God of Vengeance*, trans. Isaac Goldberg (Boston, MA: Stratford, 1918). Note: according to the YIVO Encyclopedia, the play was written in 1907: see https://yivoencyclopedia.org/article.aspx/asch_sholem.
34. Dan Callahan, *Barbara Stanwyck: The Miracle Woman* (Mississippi: University of Mississippi Press, 2011), 174–5.
35. Neil D. Isaacs, "Malle's Eye for Rose's "Storyville," *Literature/Film Quarterly*, Vol. 24, No. 2 (1996), 224.
36. Susan Sontag, "Introduction," in *Bellocq: Photographs from Storyville, The Red-Light District of New Orleans*, ed. John Szarkowski (New York: Random House, 1996), 8.

37. Zeese Papanikolas, *American Silence* (Lincoln, NE: University of Nebraska Press, 2007), 92–4.
38. Tomasz Ferenc, "Nudity, Sexuality, Photography: Visual Redefinition of the Body," *Qualitative Sociology Review*, Vol. 14, No. 2 (2018), 109.
39. Brassaï, *The Secret Paris of the 30's*, trans. Richard Miller (New York: Pantheon Books, 1976), 96, 109.
40. Ibid, 112–13.
41. Ibid, 118.
42. Ibid, 115.
43. The reader is directed to the website https://andresserrano.org/series/the-morgue. Accessed April 24, 2023.
44. Karen Jaehne, "Two or Three Things We Know about Her: Hooker," *Film Comment*, Vol. 23 (May–June 1987), 26.
45. Campbell, *Marked*, 218.

5. FLESHY IMAGERY

Sharp Blades

Departing from the *actualités* format and producing a single-set medium-shot film, Louis Lumière's comedically fantastic composition *Charcuterie mécanique/The Mechanical Butcher* (1896), a silent film about labor and the futuristic technology of porcine butchery, features an amusing vision of the (dis)assembly line and its manufactured product. *The Mechanical Butcher* is an imaginary, Georges Méliès-like machine, set outdoors. In under one minute across the frame, workers load a large pig into a box-like machine with a spinning wheel behind it providing a power source as steam flows from an exhaust pipe. A prominent advertisement on the machinery, stating "The Mechanical Pork Butcher in Marseille" establishes both a screen title and a geographical setting. To the right side of the frame, a man wearing butcher's clothing removes from the machine various cuts of processed pork, while workers collect and place each consumer good on a nearby table, and another worker attends to the machinery in the background of the frame. The film rolls out on a vaguely realistic image of assembled workers, machinery, and pork products.

As if rephrasing the comedic mechanized component in Lumière's film, Fatty Arbuckle's *The Butcher Boy* (1917) introduces the stoic-absurd presence of Buster Keaton to American cinema in a supportive performance to Fatty Arbuckle's role as a butcher. *The Butcher Boy* is a film divided into two complementary sections: the former section features frenzied recreations of semi-skilled labor, customer relations, and the lure of romance; the latter section features threatened love, cross-dressing, criminal machinations, and a traditional chase sequence. Erik Bullot remarks that in *The Butcher Boy*, "it should be noted that the shortcomings of the Keaton character [Luke] are also generated by the space around him; it is unexpected, absurd, unstable."[1] As in Lumière's *The Mechanical Butcher*, Arbuckle's *The Butcher Boy* features imaginary space and time functioning in a comedic capacity, essentially involving labor practices: a close-up shot of a dog running on a treadmill controlled by Luke energizes a grinding process, and Luke as a "do-it-all" clerk glides briskly across the store as he fulfills his responsibilities. Arbuckle skillfully prepares meat products in the backroom-freezer; these sequences furnish a series of sight gags to absurd proportions, including Fatty tossing a knife into the air to artfully slice meat and talking to the meat products as they hang on a hook. At one point, Fatty enters the meat locker and emerges with sausages. As the customer exits with the hanging meat exposed, Fatty begins slicing sections from them as they freely dangle. Meat is in the air.

However abbreviated and humorous Lumière's narrative, *The Mechanical Butcher* initiates in silent film a direct and ongoing relationship with workers (assembly-line labor, butchers), animals (two- and four-legged), and meat-as-marker, the raw, exposed product. The following year, filmed in Chicago's stockyards, James H. White's *Cattle Driven to Slaughter* documented the final pre-processing moments in the lives of a herd of cattle as they were driven into the slaughterhouse from their pen by workers prodding them along with long sticks. In the article, "Robots Carve a Butchery Role," nearly one hundred years later, the art of butchery and predictions about meat consumption are presented: the mechanized preparation and packaging of meat products will be controlled by robots—not by humans—and advanced technology will guide the process:

> The meat processing industry is one of the hardest to automate. Meat is soft, sticky, and pliable, which makes it difficult to handle mechanically. And the fact that no two pieces of meat are exactly the same has created technical problems which have so far baffled robot designers. But now Bristol University's advanced manufacturing and automation research centre is developing a mechanical butcher which will cut joints and remove bones with the same dexterity as a human.[2]

Meat, a signifying naturalist trope recurring across intermedial and interdisciplinary narrative forms, appears in multiple configurations and preparations, especially in international film narrative, ranging from the documentary, melodrama, horror, and comedy genres, set primarily in the abattoir-slaughterhouse, to the local butcher's shop with the skilled butcher, and finally, in the morgue. This chapter analyzes the aesthetic, signifying presence of meat-flesh, whether placed on a dinner plate, in human meat pies, or as pulverized dismemberments, and the abattoir, the site of exposed, bloody labor; these are critical naturalist tropes.

Porcine Desire

In the fifth season of André Antoine's Théâtre Libre, playwright Auguste Linert's *Conte de Noël/A Christmas Tale* (1890) was staged on Christmas Eve.[3] The drama was considered a grotesque and astonishing production featuring rape, infanticide, and a terrifying moment when predatory porcine consume a small corpse. In the words of an observant critic:

> *Le Conte de Noël* played at the Théâtre-Libre is a nasty tale, a crime of infanticide that takes place on Christmas night. Mr. Linert saw the staging effects to be drawn from the contrast that can exist between the birth of Christ and that of the child of Rosa, a servant to the Janid farmers. Here, songs, lights, Christmas trees in honor of the Child God; there, silence and darkness, cries of pain, curses for the illegitimate child.[4]

At a critical juncture of Antoine's staging, the child dies. An old woman exclaims, "'Hush! it's over: it was already cold. So I threw it at the pig.' And over there the bell rings midnight, and voices cry out: *Come, let us worship!*"[5] Although the event is not witnessed by the audience, the cruel and abrupt act of human disposal is disruptively juxtaposed with overheard local holiday rituals and ceremonies. Antoine presciently notes after the initial staging of Linert's drama that "In this time of prosecution and bans, I'm afraid the noise around his work will cause him some legal trouble."[6] Theatrical historian Mel Gordon cites how "the Theatre of the Grand Guignol was one of several offshoots from the Naturalist movement on the Parisian stage that began in the late 1880s," featuring an exceptional "sordid realism," and how "The Grand Guignol's most significant influence on world culture can be found in the popular subgenres of the Hollywood film."[7] The noise and action of the unnatural and cruel thrive in naturalist cinema. Among other terrifying porcine dining venues are Ridley Scott's *Hannibal* (2001), in which the infamous Dr. Lecter (Anthony Hopkins) traverses a farmyard unscathed while engorged, massive pigs dine on flesh, and the HBO series, *Deadwood* (2004–6), featuring a pigpen belonging to the Chinese immigrant-entrepreneur, Mr. Wu (Keone Young) that serves as a diner for pigs and a final resting place for his enemies.

In Ramon del Valle-Inclan's macabre naturalist *Divinas Palabras/Divine Words* (1919), an *esperpento* (grotesque) drama of poverty, greed, adultery, exploitation, debasement, and savagery in an imaginary modern, rural Spain, the violent behavior of a few individuals affects the weak, ignored, poor peasants. In one compelling sequence, an intellectually challenged, abused hydrocephalic dwarf performs for slight renumeration as a traveling comic public spectacle. One night, as he is left alone outdoors in a cart amid farm animals, he succumbs to the predatory appetites of carnivorous creatures, and his remains are discovered in the morning:

> Marcia del Reino: ". . . Oh God! They've eaten his face! The pigs have eaten his face! He's had it!"
> Serenin de Bretal: "What's the world coming to. I never thought I'd live to see the day when animals turned into savages and devoured Christian souls."[8]

In naturalist narrative, in literal and allegorical manifestations, meat is a primary trope indicating the end product of the grinding tradition. Meat is the metaphorical correlative of the human nub. Valle-Inclan presents this darkly grotesque act in a naturalist context; the consumption of body parts—human meat—is a synecdochical parody of unabated capitalism. This exploitative form of brutal capitalist standards and practices is represented in Upton Sinclair's narrative of labor and its discontents, *The Jungle* (1906), which links the labor-related despair and primitive living conditions of the exploited immigrant working class, as experienced daily at the slaughterhouse factory's assembly line: "With one member trimming beef in a cannery, and another working in a sausage factory, the family had a first-hand knowledge . . . they use everything of the pig except the squeal."[9] In Sinclair's novel, set in turn-of-the century urban America, the factory is a site where two-legged animals rip apart four-legged animals as a standard operating procedure on the assembly line, a still contemporary staple of production.

Mo Yan's naturalist novel, *POW* (2003), is an allegorical fantasy of contemporary Chinese society, its political-dietary frailties, its corporate and state corruption, the meat industry and the ironies of flesh consumption. Luo Xiaotong, a young male, a predatory meat-eating creature of limitless appetite, exclaims this cogent insight into human nature: "life without meat isn't worth clinging to,"[10] and later, he asserts: "the relationship of meat to humans is very complex, and there are only a few people on this earth who understands it as well as I do."[11] Where Luo lives in China, there is a Carnivore Festival and people live in Slaughterhouse Village, where they work mostly in the factory for the corporation. Artist Zeng Fanzhi's painting *Meat* (1992) depicts the working conditions of factories described by Yan, as two skeletal butchers pose amid bleeding, hanging carcasses of beef, some covered in white sheets, draping puddles of invasive bright red, suggesting bodies in a morgue. As Yan declares, butchering is a "bloody business,"[12] and traditional ideology surrenders to a more carnal, capitalist nature.

In the article, "Eating Meat: Evolution, Patterns, and Consequences," Vaclav Smil notes the irresistible biological impulse that draws the human beast to the consumption of other beasts: "Meat eating is a part of our evolutionary heritage. Carnivorousness continues to evoke strong emotions, being not only a universal symbol of affluence, well-being, satiety, and contentment but for a minority also an object of scorn and moralistic disapproval."[13] According to Smil, the consumption process is a matter of social as well as biological evolution: "During the last four decades of the twentieth century, global meat production increased more than threefold."[14] Yet there is notable irony to this statistical insight, as Xiaotong declares, "People eat the flesh of pigs, dogs, cows and sheep; fleas and bedbugs eat the flesh of humans. This is known as the subjugation of one species by another or, simply, tit for tat."[15] In the cyclic process of meat production and consumption, nothing wholly ends. Only the grinding process is maintained in naturalist film narratives.

Abattoir

In 1866, Thomas F. DeVoe's presentation *Abattoirs: A Paper Read Before the Polytechnic Branch of the American Institute, June 8, 1865* evaluated the future of the meat industry in the United States as a centralized business like the European models, and focused on New York City as a local industrial template:

> The subject before us does not recommend itself for elegance, but rather as a necessity. To many, no doubt, it presents repulsive features; features even revolting to some persons. Abattoir, a place for slaughtering animals ... and the site of the first public slaughter-house, or Abattoir, would now be on the east side of Pearl Street, between Wall and Pine Streets.[16]

The film narrative of the slaughterhouse has no demarcating walls or avenues; whether set in an urban factory, a butcher's shop, a boxing ring, on a remote island, or at any relevant site of preparation, naturalist film narrative provides a canvas to expose and to indicate acts of consumerism and consumption. The human body is a site spectacle ground down like prepared beef by catalytic affective, genetic, or socially determinist agencies. Whether placed on the dining table or left rotting for parasites, meat indicates consumption and consuming. The individual eats or is eaten, for meat is a pictorial signifier and "there is little that is neutral about meat."[17]

According to John D. Smith, as described in *The Butcher's Manual*, butchered meat is a most pliable substance: "You can use most any kind of meat for bologna,"[18] to which he adds for future industrial posterity, "you must cook the meat, so that it will not fall to pieces"[19] and also, "If you want to keep hams over summer, you must hang them in a dark airy room, so the flies cannot get to them, or you can put them in sacks."[20] Instead of pigs and cattle, what are the industrial and narrative implications of prepared human dismemberments? As if revisiting the Grand Guignol theatrical tradition of "suffering and effects,"[21] Tobe Hooper's *The Texas Chainsaw Massacre* (1974) is a narrative about dreadful dining and living leftovers involving the abattoir, the home, butchering, and butchers. These intersecting tropes inform Hooper's *sui generis* naturalist narrative. As the film begins with an authoritative male voice-over, in mock documentary style, *The Texas Chainsaw Massacre* presents its falsified historical recreation of murderous events as a kind of re-enactment of before and after grisly experiences of violent death.

The decaying body is a potent naturalist image in *The Texas Chainsaw Massacre* and in the series of photographs by Andres Serrano, *The Morgue* (1992–3).[22] Serrano's grotesque close-up images of the dead in posed repose, and photographer Joel-Peter Witken's transgressive studies of the fragmented body-as-art, are enticing images of unattractive remains. Although the tradition of photographing the dead dates to the nineteenth century—including postcards—most of these earliest photographs address mostly a documentary aesthetic, a record of the lost and retrieved past, rather than the carnivalesque aesthetic that also attracted Diane Arbus to photograph the world of social outcasts and the dead. In *The Texas Chainsaw Massacre*, multiple photographic shots depicting dead bodies and body parts, in morgue-like poses, establish an atmosphere of human decay and grave danger, leading to the doomed travel experiences of lost young adults driving on a desolate road, as Hooper's film shifts from discomforting stillness to an apprehensive present.

Hooper's engagingly dark and frequently humorous study—as the viewer observes a family of murderous butchers who now survive as supplanted cannibalistic ex-workers from a nearby Texas slaughterhouse—renders the youthful travelers intrusive fodder for the hungry: two-legged cattle to be processed in the home-abattoir. As the travelers pass by cattle on the road, they remain unaware that they themselves are future cattle for insane locals. According to Carter Soles, Hooper's film successfully sutures the audience to both the victims and victimizer's points of view technically, via camera placement and shot composition, and thematically, as hunters, and their prey are seen as imperiled, expendable families:

> Wes Craven's 1977 rural slasher [*The Hills Have Eyes*] equates homicidal violence and cannibalism with the American class struggle and urban fears of the countryside and its denizens . . . films like *Texas Chain Saw* go out of their way to depict their rural killers as fully (if insanely) human,

characters with families, economic backgrounds, and a real need—i.e. survival—to do what they're doing[23]

With a dead armadillo planted on the road, a brilliant full moon in view, flies caught in a web, meat hooks, stacks of feathers, skeletons, and the unseen presence of an odiferous, deserted slaughterhouse, the sensory signs of horror are fomenting as flesh is later cut, cured, and even barbequed. This family of cannibal-displaced workers illustrates Bruce Kawin's observation that "some humans not only perpetrate horrors, but are horrors themselves. They are not supernatural entities in human form or allied with the spirits as witches are, and they cannot transform themselves like a Dr. Jekyll."[24] As an intergeneric narrative, *The Texas Chain Saw Massacre* incorporates a documentary-like framing, familiar horror tropes, popular 1970s' "road film" narratives, and moreover, as noted by Jerry D. Metz, Hooper's film may be viewed in a suggestively political context, as a "dark Marxist fairy tale"[25] involving disposable labor and survival strategies.

In *The Texas Chain Saw Massacre*, the travelers pick up an odd-looking hitch-hiker behaving strangely on the road. Hitch-hikers have an established, sinister precedent as dangerous cargo in American cinema; Ida Lupino's ominous postwar noir naturalist study of a damaging, invasive germ placed on a specimen slide in the desert, *The Hitch-Hiker* (1953), features two middle-aged married men on a fishing expedition who foolishly pick up Emmet Myers (William Talman), a psychotic hitch-hiker and escaped convict, while driving on the open road. Myers nearly manages to kill them both. His sinister appearance, with a Poe-like evil eye, and his continuous mockery of his two potential victims prefigure the initially undetected yet monstrous hitch-hiker in Hooper's naturalist horror narrative. In Patty Jenkins' *Monster* (2003), the prostitute and murderer Aileen Wuornos (Charlize Theron) ensnares most of her prey—guilty older male pick-ups—by marketing a measure of her sexual lure while she is available on the open road.

In *The Texas Chain Saw Massacre*, after dropping off this crazed hitch-hiker and pausing for provisions, the travelers stop on the road and approach a deserted home. Each member of the traveling party, save one, is eventually slaughtered, and they appear like unknowing animals entering the pen with no exit. There is a reversal of sorts in the bear–frontiersman assault in Alejandro G. Iñárritu's *The Revenant* (2015) in which hunter-explorer Hugh Glass (Leonardo DiCaprio) is violently attacked and nearly killed—ripped apart—by a large bear. In these films, the unexpected bodily assault on victims in the woods presents an animalistic violation of the flesh in which people are viciously struck. The near total silence of the immediate environment in both films shatters the "nature-escapism" trope to release significant terrors involving the violated body by both non-human and human predators.

Leatherface (Gunnar Hansen), perhaps the most intriguing character in *The Texas Chain Saw Massacre*, is a unique naturalist vision of *La Bête humaine*. Leatherface's hulking presence, like a two-legged bear, remains a nightmarish vision of rampaging need. He cuts and rips meat-flesh; therefore, he is working at his craft, however insane and violent the motivation and moment. Hooper directs this character's behavior to be alternately menacing—he is a human monster—as well as oddly sympathetic, as Leatherface seems lost in the world that no longer needs him. According to Carter Soles, "The connection between the Leatherface family's former profession and its current cannibalism is made clear throughout *Texas Chain Saw*. All the film's murders relate in one way or another to meat slaughtering."[26] In Hooper's film, the abattoir has departed from the industrial stockyards and entered the living room and secret places inside the home in which dead people and relevant body parts, including butchered farm animals, hang for future preparation and consumption. As one female victim, Sally (Marilyn Burns), escapes from the macabre dinner party—in which she would be later served—she flees into the woods, with Leatherface in pursuit armed with his chain saw. However alone and injured, Leatherface survives, as noted by James Rose:

> The film's final image is one of the most powerful in the history of horror cinema. In the maddening spinning, Leatherface is injured but alive. His crazed dance is ambiguous in its purpose, for it is potentially as much a celebration of his freedom as it may be an intense expression of his frustration at Sally's escape ... He is indeed, the grisly work of art, the mad and the macabre, the nightmare and the tragedy.[27]

The climactic performance of Leatherface's "danse macabre" of death is a complex, eccentrically engaging "naturalist moment," in which form—Hooper's gyrating, motion-filled medium shot—and essence—the ecstatic release of Leatherface's psychotic energy—produce a unique image in naturalist cinema. Some years later, as Arthur Fleck/Joker prances down the "step stairs" in his destitute South Bronx neighborhood, fully dressed in a garish clown costume near the climax of *Joker*, he releases himself in a transformative series of visually sensational moments. For Leatherface, in this climactic instance of pursuit and exposure, the human beast, slaughterhouse, butcher-butchering, and meat itself merge as a unified trope in his berserk, frenzied motion.

In James H. White's *Sheep Run, Chicago Stockyards* (1897), in a medium set shot, dozens of sheep run between two gates into the foreground of the frame until off screen, presumably to a violent fate. Eighty years later, Charles Burnett's urban melodrama, *Killer of Sheep* (1977), observes the daily lives of an African-American working-class family, its tedious routines and external distractions, as a skilled laborer, Stan (Henry Sanders), struggles to cope with

BEYOND REALISM

Figure 5.1 Tobe Hooper's *Texas Chain Saw Massacre* (1974)

a job he dislikes and living conditions in a substandard environment in which race and class encase the individual. According to Sarah O'Brien, *Killer of Sheep* is a complex, structured narrative plausibly linked to naturalist cinema's tropes of skilled, yet alienated factory labor with racial and class-based depictions of daily life:

> Because it is more of an expression of a time and place than a carefully plotted story, *Killer of Sheep*'s narrative resists retelling. It is episodic and consists of three outwardly disparate strands: mostly interior scenes of Stan, his family, and his friends engaged in the mundane details of domestic life and the prosaic activities of the neighborhood; interior scenes of Stan working at the slaughterhouse; and exterior scenes of children, including Stan's son and daughter, playing in back alleys, train yards, and razed lots.[28]

Over a musical soundtrack of familiar blues and jazz standards, which dominates sound effects such as running machinery and animal shrieks, Burnett films several shot sequences of sheep in crisis, as they are penned, processed, and slaughtered on the disassembly line within sight of dangling meat hooks and machinery. In one sequence, as a judas goat stands before them, the sheep move as one shuffling mass toward the inevitable.

In 1881, M. Walravens expressed his belief concerning the nascent industrial enterprise of the urban slaughterhouse in Paris: "The creation of a vast common slaughterhouse was in the public interest."[29] Images of industrial

FLESHY IMAGERY

Figure 5.2 Charles Burnett's *Killer of Sheep* (1977)

enterprise—entrapment and processing—endemic to the industry recall assembly-line practices from Lumière's *The Mechanical Butcher* and multiple slaughterhouse films, such as Georges Franju's *Le sang des bêtes/Blood of the Beasts* (1948) with its contrasting shots of a beautiful city and the daily slaughtering of animals, and Frederick Wiseman's documentary *Meat* (1976), in which laborers and the labored upon are rendered in grimly realistic, routine portraiture. Franju's *Le sang des bêtes* is visually overwhelming in its deployment of Naturalism's mimetic veracity to reproduce images of the standardized cruelty related to meat processing:

> In quick succession, cattle are rounded up on the ranch, put on the auction block, trucked, vaccinated, disinfected, penned, fattened, weighed, penned, stunned, hoisted by the hooves, and slit at the throat. Poor husbandry practices are realistically portrayed in all livestock handling scenes. Then, in an extensive sequence of slaughter and processing, cattle are beheaded, and the heads are processed in close-up detail. Cattle are eviscerated, skinned, split, sawed into sections, cut into pieces, mechanically tenderized, ground into patties, wrapped, boxed, and shipped.[30]

Franju's experimental documentary may also be read in a historically symbolic context. Produced only a few years after World War Two, in Franju's film, the horrors committed inside the factory (the camp) remain largely unseen yet quietly accepted by the local population. In a touch of ironic avant-garde filmmaking, Franju's cut-away shots of life in a waking and busy city contrast with graphic shots of revealed stunning horror. A slaughtered horse and processed cattle visualize violence in a near-aesthetic capacity, with a city in lyric, atmospheric counterpoint.

Vaclav Smil notes that "Meatpacking remains the country's most dangerous occupation. Some modern slaughterhouses process as many as 400 cattle per hour and some workers make up to 10,000 repetitive knife cuts every day."[31] The slaughterhouse, where preparing meat is a business, is a frequently dangerous worksite. Frederick Wiseman's documentary *Meat* is an immersive study in the rituals of modern meat processing, without highlighting "conventional notions of tact, breaking through what would otherwise be ideological constraints of politeness [and] queasiness in the face of the grotesque or taboo."[32] In *Meat*, Wiseman utilizes live-recorded sound, from diesel trucks to wailing cattle and salesmen's conversations, in a bleak, visually textured black and white series of images displaying meat processing as a business secured by ritual industrial acts of slaughter. Dennis R. Henderson and Bobby D. Van Stavern note Wiseman's layered, near-clinical documentation of the procedural horrific in *Meat*:

> Wiseman lets the sounds do the talking, including the bawling of the cattle, the auctioneer's banter, salesmen making deals in their peculiar jargon, the mechanized sounds of a meat plant, and a fixation on the sounds of diesel truck engines. In a sense, it's the story of the assembly line in reverse, beginning with the completed product and ending with the parts.[33]

In *Meat*, both the animal and the workers' pens are controlled areas in which the slaughtered-herded confront the laboring-herded. Without a controlling, authoritative narrative voice, in *Meat*, the reality of the moment speaks for itself via modified forms of continuity editing with no discernable figures other than the interacting, numb, living, and soon-to-be slaughtered animals. In both Franju's experimental documentary and Wiseman's *cinéma vérité* documentary, dismemberment is bleakly yet qualitatively authenticated as standardized labor practice, from postwar France to the USA.

During a grotesque extended shot sequence in Rainer Werner Fassbinder's *In einem Jahr mit 13 Monden/In a Year with 13 Moons* (1978), the transsexual occasional prostitute Elvira/Erwin (Volker Spengler) takes a tour with a friend inside the slaughterhouse where s/he once worked. In this astonishing "touring" sequence, during the documentary-like slaughter and processing of cattle, a conversation continues as the two friends walk casually across the factory site while animal throats are slit and blood drips extensively over the floor. In medium framing, Fassbinder's tracking shots follow two people who are seemingly impervious to the deconstructing assembly line, which juxtaposes a striking, ironic perception of space and time. As workers rip and cut away at the once living, Elvira evaluates conflicting personal, somewhat absurd issues during the preparation of carcasses for future dinner tables. *In a Year with 13 Moons* features the slaughterhouse, the working butchers, and the production of meat for consumers, three interrelated naturalist tropes involving labor and consumption.

Parts of the Whole

As a unique portrayal of the late nineteenth-century working world, Tim Burton's *Sweeney Todd: The Demon Barber of Fleet Street* (2007), adapts from the penny dreadful serial *The String of Pearls* (1846–7), earlier film versions, and contemporary musical theater, an unreal dark and graphic setting, depicting a frightful London as an unrelieved vicious slaughterhouse during the historical era of Robert Louis Stevenson's Jekyll and Hyde narrative. Burton's pictorial representation of the dusky, murky city conjures the worst admonitions of William Blake's vision of the city-as-hell, full of smoke, shadows, and terror: an urban wound. Both the murderous barber, Sweeney Todd (Johnny Depp), a "proper artist with a knife," who cuts the throats of his victims, and the friendly baker, Mrs. Lovett (Helena Bonham Carter), who laments the loss of these "nice plump frames," as waste(d) products in the grave, reside in the "great black pit," an alienating, corrupt city.

As he is falsely accused by authorities and nearly destroyed, Sweeney loses his family to the villainous and corrupt judge who coveted his wife and child and now hates the world; the lonely Mrs. Lovett, nearly as sinister as Sweeney, figures out that the best way to dispose of all the bodies Sweeney creates is to prepare them as meat pies for consumers. This is cannibalism as a consumer delicacy, and Lovett's baked goods not only enlarge the market for her retail business, they become a trendy product. Jennifer L. Jenkins notes:

> Consumption defines the city in the Sweeney narrative, represented by a series of machines: the commodity-producing factories (Sondheim's stage play begins with the shriek of a factory whistle); the corpse-producing barber chair; and the meat grinder. All are machines of ingestion and degustation ... The creative team on Burton's *Sweeney Todd*, from Sondheim on down, all insisted that the film be a wholly new conceptualization of the material—not a filmed stage performance.[34]

In Walter West's *Sweeney Todd* (1928), a late silent-era British adaptation, the industrious Mrs. Lovett (Iris Darbyshire) playfully responds to a portly customer's inquiry concerning the special ingredients in her meals: "that's a trade secret." Burton's *Sweeney Todd* is also a reflection of urban working-class experience. In Jack London's *People of the Abyss* (1903), a blending of literary Naturalism and travel literature, London describes the local inhabitants and living conditions in London's East End only a few years after the historical period of *Sweeney Todd* and recounts daily life on these streets:

> [The] ghetto pours them forth, and the festering contents of slums, stews, and ghetto are undiminished ... They overrun the country like an army of ghouls ... As they drag their squat misshapen bodies along the highways and byways, they resemble some vile spawn from underground ... their rottenness is a slimy desecration of the sweetness and purity of nature.[35]

Jack London's highly subjective class-based observations, "I saw a nightmare, a fearful slime that quickened the pavement with life, a mess of unmentionable obscenity ... It was a menagerie of garmented bipeds that looked something like humans and more like beasts," are followed by this leveling remark: "to complete the picture, brass-buttoned keepers [police] kept order among them when they snarled too fiercely."[36] This is a naturalist landscape. London describes a vicious and predatory environment with suspect keepers on patrol.

As Burton's Sweeney laments in song how "the vermin of the world inhabit" the city, he vows to eradicate them, especially the corrupt judge, who, "with a gesture of his claw, removed a barber from his place." Although the potential for his butchery is almost limitless, Sweeney is not a serial killer in the traditional sense. He is crazed with retributive anger, occasionally spurred on by consuming alcohol, and survives initial detection by being the smarter beast. This postmodern naturalist musical production, a blending of guignol-horror, romance, and noir's visual atmospheric conventions, follows the gushing blood and dangerous machines. In one compelling shot, blood completely fills the frame, an overwhelming red release of human slaughter. Jenkins notes that "Grand Guignol's effects—though not its means—appear from the first frame,"[37] to which she adds: "combined with the chair gears, the oven, and the pathways of drainage for the blood, this abattoir sequence well illustrates the mechanisms of death and vengeance that the tale to come will engage."[38] Burton's *Sweeney Todd* is a study of violence perpetrated by men and women in which the destroyed body is prepared as a newly butchered product to consume: meat pies.

Herman Yau's *Bat sin fan dim: Yan yuk cha siu bau/The Eight Immortals Restaurant: The Untold Story* (1993), a Category III film based on the documented experiences of a serial-killer butcher, Wong Chi Hang (Anthony Wong), features the police investigative drama and droll moments of humor informing the comedic-horrific naturalist narrative of cannibalism, decapitations, multiple homicides, sexual assaults, and specially prepared barbequed pork buns. In *The Untold Story*, Wong Chi Hang's violence is a relentless, compelling spectacle; Wong Chi Hang is Naturalism's predatory beast-as-chef, armed with pans, ladles, and knives for all sorts of deranged culinary preparation.

The first murder in *The Untold Story* involves Wong Chi Hang's attempt to cheat his boss out of money, which leads to a violent and protracted assault that concludes with burning the victim to death. An idyllic scene shot on the beach where multiple sets of carefully sliced body parts have washed ashore indicates the presence of a stalking beast who has traveled to avoid detection. In *The Untold Story*, as the chief investigative officer and his colleagues assigned to the case scrutinize the butchered remains of what was formerly a human being, the shot cuts to Wong Chi Hang slaughtering and butchering a pig, literally ripping parts from the carcass. This visually arresting ironic juxtaposition indicates that he is like a "Sweeney Berserk."

Wong Chi Hang's murderous assaults and butchering are crimes of enraged passion and economic opportunity. The restaurant he literally steals alternates as a crime scene, an abattoir, and a morgue. Like London's overworked Sweeney, Macao's Wong Chi Hang must find a way to dispose of the bodies he creates, so he cuts them up and cooks them, thus creating a new delicacy in the form of "pork buns" that even the police enjoy when they investigate and later catch him.

The shots of Wong Chi Hang working the butcher's meat grinder, as he prepares the raw flesh of his victims for consumption, are among the most overwhelming and masterful indicators of the metaphorical and literal naturalist grinding trope, not without its own grim humor. The master butcher really is the master butcher. He cannot resist his limitless rage. The grinding process has reached a cinematic zenith of representation as naturalist spectacle: *La Bête humaine*.

To speak of Wong Chi Hang as a skilled yet alienated worker might appear facile, but he expresses frustration at his lack of economic and personal advancement. He cheats at cards and mahjong as a response to his own perceived helplessness. At work, he reduces what was human to its barest state and later, the unsalvageable remains of carcasses are disposed of in garbage bins. He urinates on his hands to remove the blood, an animal behavior that marks territory and control. In the restaurant, the human-as-bun is the most popular item on the menu and his business becomes increasingly productive and prosperous. As the police catch him, a series of close-up shots of people eating the buns in the restaurant while he is questioned are among the most horrific and humorous in the film. People consume people.

Haim Tabakman's *Einayim Pkuhot* [*Einayim Petukhoth*]/*Eyes Wide Open* (2009)[39] is set primarily in an ultra-orthodox neighborhood inside a kosher butcher's shop in Jerusalem. Aaron (Zohar Strauss), the butcher, is a married middle-aged man with several children working in his deceased father's shop in an isolated community in which Aaron's feelings of discontent remain repressed but contained by his dutiful labor preparing and selling cuts of meat for local consumption. The butcher shop, like Aaron's life, is visually ascetic and lacks inviting color and recalls the bleakish setting of the Italian immigrant's turn-of-the-century New York City business location in Wallace McCutcheon's seminal gangster narrative *The Black Hand* (1906), in which occasional banners and advertisements appear as historical markers. In *The Black Hand* and, according to Stefanie Knauss, *Eyes Wide Open*, "[the] symbolic relevance of setting"[40] reflects the outlier status of both groups: the skilled working-class Italian and Orthodox butchers labor in urban communities, which seek to "preserve [their] boundaries,"[41] secure and regulated within their own ethnic-social group, unless unforeseen disruption occurs. Exposing crimes—legal or sexual—is threatening beyond the enclosure of the community.

As Aaron develops a work and personal relationship with an outcast from this enclosed society, Ezri (Ran Kahlil Danker), an artistic younger Orthodox man, they become attracted to each other as they note each other's loneliness and engage in a strictly forbidden relationship, including ritual bathing, sharing work–living space, and making love in the butcher's shop. Ezri introduces color drawings into the setting and expansive feelings into the austerity of Aaron's life. Knauss notes, "[there is a] striking contrast between the sterility of the shop and the passion of the men, they have sex in the same walk-in refrigerator for the first time, their carnal desire being satisfied in close proximity to big lumps of meat."[42] The symbolic contrast is evident; the frozen defrosts under heat.

After their prohibited intimacy is exposed, Ezri is forced to leave and Aaron faces the ridicule and rejection of his community, including a punitive economic response. Despite this decline in his personal and economic stature, Aaron tells his rabbi, "I was dead. Now I'm alive." Aaron later returns to the place where he bathed, partially covered, with Ezri. Now fully nude, Aaron immerses himself in the water. As the shot closes, Aaron remains under the surface of the water: will he emerge "freer," or end his life as an ostracized male? In *Eyes Wide Open*, complicated questions involving religious and sexual identity support an open-ended closure, facilitated by Tabakman's direction. *Eyes Wide Open* is composed of visually compelling close-up two-shots, and "its montage [combining] the realism and calm fluidity of tracks or pans with sudden cuts that leaves gaps."⁴³ Tabakman's film is notable as a naturalist narrative, for "the film's careful documentation of the details of daily life and ritual in this particular community";⁴⁴ Aaron's personal sexual values and religious customs are subjected to profound symbolic and revelatory grinding.

Julia Ducournau's *Grave/Raw* (2016) is a unique entry into the cinema of disability—both biological and psychological—in its portrayal of Justine, the sensitive cannibal in a family of cannibals. This dark naturalist film begins with an arranged accident in which a severe automobile injury entraps a motorist who is left exposed to an attractive young woman's criminal cannibalizing acts of consuming brain matter, literally, licking his wounds and blood. This is a fresh kill, shot in daylight somewhere on the open forest's road, as the hunter ensnares its prey.

In *Raw*, Justine (Garance Marillier) is ironically studying to become a veterinarian at a medical school, a kind of specialized abattoir, known for its cruel hazing (*bizutage*) rituals and vivisection practices. At one point, she even inquires, "do monkeys have rights?". Along with the woods, the medical school campus, the labs, dorm rooms, and hallways, *Raw* reveals unnatural covert practices in these (now) extra-legal sites in which brutalities are exposed, as if Dr. Moreau's remote island and laboratory full of vivisected horrors were to relocate. In *Raw*, Martine Beugnet and Emmanuelle Delanoë-Brun note, "the students are not protected by, nor bound to, the laws of normal student life, but have to follow a new set of rules with their own, mysterious logic,"⁴⁵ which suggests a vital naturalist correlation to the cannibalism. Beugnet and Delanoë-Brun observe, "the final scene suggests there is a genetic cause to Justine and her sister's transformation, that it is the manifestation of a hereditary condition inherited from their mother."⁴⁶ Justine's older sister (Ella Rumpf) is already a student at the school and she initiates Justine into its academic and non-academic practices, along with inflaming personal, odd desires. Justine discovers she is copying both her mother and her sister's formerly repressed, semi-active behavior—a taste for flesh—which emerges along with Justine's desire for sexual expression, linking two bodily experiences. After an accident, Justine literally licks her sister's severed finger and eventually consumes it. Justine's older sister's secret life as an intellectual cannibal is exposed in the film after a series of criminal acts, one involving a gay Arab male student who is sacrificed to sexual and carnivorous appetites, for which Justine's sister is sent to an asylum. In Ducournau's naturalist, dark comedy-drama, a conflicted, patient father later reveals to a horrified Justine scars running across his covered body, which provided evidence of hidden snacks for his wife. Although this family attempts to live as strict vegetarians, their secret involves a tainted matrilineal heredity.

According to Gunnar Rehlin, Anders Thomas Jensen's black comedy, *De grønne slagtere/The Green Butchers* (2003), displays "strong echoes of

'Sweeney Todd' . . . [the] ending is both dramatically satisfying and as politically incorrect as the whole movie."[47] *The Green Butchers* is a film about survival of the most adaptable in a consumer-driven culture. Set in a suburban city in Denmark, two semi-intelligent butchers, Svend (Mads Mikkelsen) and Bjarne (Nikolaj Lie Kaas), search for a product, "something that people will love." The butchers need to raise capital in order to maintain their fledgling business, and at one critical moment, an undetected man falls into the freezer and dies. The meat freezer frequently conceals a shocking discovery in naturalist cinema as a recurring site marker: in Martin Scorsese's chronicle of postwar urban ethnic-gangster culture, *Goodfellas* (1990), a delivery truck's freezer contains a frozen mobster, who needs to be defrosted over time for his corpse to be properly identified. In *The Green Butchers*, this fatal accident releases the butchers' inner "beasts," rendering the meat locker as an extra-legal site to produce the most desirable product—ground-down human flesh—as new carrion, although fresh bait would be required to resupply this popular product. In *The Green Butchers*, Jensen's eccentric naturalist narrative, two butchers remain undetected and darkly, humorously contrive to survive.

In *Canto Twelve* of Whitman's "Song of Myself," he describes a joyful moment between poet and laborer: "The butcher-boy puts off his killing-clothes, or sharpens his knife at the stall in the market'/I loiter enjoying his repartee and his shuffle and break-down."[48] Whitman's idyllic moment of poetic experience links the observer with the observed, a contemplative object of image consumption, a historicized presence involving labor and meat. Likewise, the anonymous photograph entitled "Negro butcher, Hill District, Pittsburgh"(1926),[49] features the fading figure of an African-American butcher in standard industrial garb who remains alone in the doorway of a shop, peering away from the camera. The paved street in front of his shop is clean but bare. In the large store-front window to the left side of the butcher are several prepared "cuts"—sections of chicken and possibly pork and beef—meant to attract consumers. Dangling outside the doorway, to his immediate right side, are additional selections for sale. A sole ceiling lightbulb illuminates the interior of the shop. In this historical image, the butcher and his business are a solitary presence in the community, working at his daily labor in animal flesh and animal blood.

André Antoine produced Fernand Icres' guignol revenge drama, *Les Bouchers/The Butchers* (1888),[50] a violent work that features simmering sexual intrigue, expressive jealousy, and murder amid the meat carcasses literally placed on stage in this Théâtre Libre production. Antoine later commented about this historical, unorthodox production: "In my desire for a characteristic staging, I had hung, in *The Butchers*, real quarters of meat which caused a sensation."[51] According to Stuart Liebman, this was a significant act of theatrical enterprise: "From his [Antoine's] first productions he replaced painted scenery and accessories with three-dimensional props whenever possible. (... Antoine insisted on using a raw side of beef in the butcher shop set of his 1888 production of Icrès' *Les Bouchers*)."[52] Icres' stage setting, despite its goriness, retains its authenticity.

In Icres' horror-melodrama, Titou, a massively strong, mentally challenged and exceptionally unattractive worker, butchers meat carcasses in the shop of Brunis, who once seduced and then abandoned Titou's sister, and for whom Titou has labored for years, planning his revenge. The audience focus remains on the troubled figure of an intellectually compromised, aroused brute, armed with sharp cutlery; in one heightened, self-reflexive moment, Titou addresses the audience and reveals his deranged plans for revenge as he links the slaughter of an animal with the slaughter of a man: "Ah! When I hold a calf, its foot tied up on the counter/Arms naked, neck outstretched, lower back stiffened/ Before starting the attack, I think to myself: If it were him!"[53]

The revenge melodrama concludes with Titou killing Brunis, vividly rendered upon the butchered carcasses of cattle and men. (In)sanity is restored amid the remains. Gaspar Noé's *Seul contra tous/I Stand Alone* (1998) is a continuation of Noé's short film *Carne* (1991), which begins in an abattoir in which a horse is slaughtered. *Carne* might be read as an ur-Faustian hypotext, an experiment leading to the more thematically evolved narrative *I Stand Alone*, which documents the grim realities of a two-legged virus. Adrienne Angelo notes:

> *Seul contre tous* was constructed as a feature-length sequel to Noé's short film *Carne* (1991), a film which introduced us to the protagonist, a figure that can be read a sort of anti-Everyman in Noé's cinema ... the spectator is asked to identify with an individual who places himself outside and against social norms—a fugitive on the run, a misanthropic racist who bemoans the current state of society, a transgressive loner. Yet we remain trapped as it were within his twisted psyche—via his interior paranoid rants in voiceover.[54]

Noé's film is a narrative of broad naturalist design featuring vigorous variations on tropes involved with a released savage: *La Bête humaine*. *I Stand Alone* deregulates the familiar reception of space and time to solicit a writerly, reactive response. Like Icres' guignol revenge drama, *I Stand Alone* observes the careening struggle of a desperate man, Jean Chevalier/"Le boucher" (Philippe Nahon), who begins life in France as a sodomized orphan and grows as a powerful middle-aged, working-class, skilled but frequently unemployed butcher of horse meat. He is profoundly alienated, brutish, and subject to the numbing reality of a socially and economically limited life with his disturbed, attractive, mute, and intellectually handicapped daughter, who is dangerously nearing puberty. Chevalier is sent to jail for committing a mindlessly violent crime against an innocent man, after which Chevalier experiences life as a former inmate looking for his place in a city that has displaced him with new minorities.

I Stand Alone explores the nightmarish life of an enraged predator, a fascistic older male handling a meat hook. Jane Giles concludes:

> Charting, through its central character Jean Chevalier, the relentless downwards spiral of a man who has already lost everything, *Seul Contre Tous* asks us to consider which may be the greater humiliation for a former horse butcher: to work as a charcutier in a delicatessen where an acned junior tells him to smile to sell second-rate salami, or in the slaughterhouse of his former supplier, who sits tight beneath an equine pin-up.[55]

In a series of protracted interior monologues, Chevalier's voice-overs provide comments and context for Noé's stationary camera and use of medium, point-of-view, and close-up shots. *I Stand Alone* establishes an atmospheric, full palate of urban ugliness to match the butcher's interior state of being, and Noé's Brechtian distancing effects, composed of abrupt edits, eruptive sound effects, and title cards effectively formulate a coherently grotesque naturalist narrative. *I Stand Alone* is a study of isolated male anxiety in decline, exposed in frenzied, spiraling frames.

The Morgue

A critical source for the recurring tropes of both the morgue and meat can be found in Zola's naturalist novel *Thérèse Raquin* (1867), a study of predatory human-animals. Zola's novel, an early entry into the naturalist literary canon, examines the intersecting, mundane working-class lives and sexual dispositions of struggling humans—untethered creatures: a cat, a bull, and a mouse. Zola's presumptive clinical posture records their status via its prose style and posited objectivity. When Zola asserts that "I wrote every scene, even the most passionate ones, with the pure curiosity of a scientist,"[56] he compels his readers and his critics to experience "the study of temperament and of the profound modifications of an organism through the influence of environment and circumstances,"[57] representative of the modern and objective clinical methodology. In *Thérèse Raquin*, a horrific murder occurring in a boat on a lake with the three principles, husband Camille, wife Thérèse, and her lover Laurent, provides a setting for the observation of triangulated dread.

In Zola's *Thérèse Raquin*, just prior to Camille's contrived murder, the cuckolded husband struggles like a small, snarling trapped animal against the assault of the vicious predator Laurent, a larger animal, in the seemingly pastoral lake environment: "He [Camille] could not understand what was going on but was gripped by a vague sense of terror ... with the instinct of a struggling animal, he got up on his knees and gripped the side of the boat ... [Laurent] held him up like a child."[58] This signals the bite-mark sequence of events: "As he [Laurent] bent his head forward, leaving his neck uncovered, his victim, mad with fear and fury, twisted round, bared his teeth, and dug them into the neck ... his teeth took away a piece of flesh. He [Camille] fell into the water with a scream."[59] After Camille sinks and rises a few times in the river, inevitably drowning, Thérèse faints and Laurent forces the boat to capsize in order to fake the scene of an accident.

Both Camille and Laurent are models of the wounded naturalist male; the former a weak, doomed specimen, and the latter an overweight, unemployable, abusive drinker with a festering red sore on his neck. The bite on Laurent's neck appears like an animal's tearing away of fleshy meat and is a wound-marker indicating guilt and damage. Like a scarlet letter, Laurent's wound compels the reader to set the gaze on a vulnerable spot, a gap of lost meat. As Linda Nochlin asserts, "the human body is not just the object of desire, but the site of suffering, pain and death,"[60] and Laurent intensely suffers from this lesion. Camille's missing, decaying corpse—a former whole reduced to a nub—is eventually retrieved and, as it remains unidentified, lies on a slab in the morgue. Like the butcher's shop and its arranged display of various cuts of prepared products, the morgue is an essential naturalist site of exposure. Laurent later visits the Parisian morgue apprehensively to identify the remains.

In Gilles Deleuze's *Francis Bacon: The Logic of Sensation* (1981), Deleuze discusses Francis Bacon's grimly expressive portrait *Figure with Meat* (1954), in which a screaming man—a blurred foreground nightmare—sits between two hanging, grotesquely split raw beef carcasses to suggest a literal view of meat-as-signifier. Deleuze concludes:

> This objective zone of indiscernibility is the entire body, but the body insofar as it is flesh or meat ... Bacon does not say, 'Pity the beasts,' but rather that every man who suffers is a piece of meat. Meat is the common zone of man and the beast, their zone of indiscernibility; it is a 'fact,' a state where the painter identifies with the objects of his horror and his compassion. The painter is certainly a butcher.[61]

Meat, whether fresh, putrefying, or mutilated, signifies a prior whole, part of a deconstructed present. In *Thérèse Raquin*, Camille's recovered corpse is placed on a morgue slab to be identified as well as observed. For Laurent, the cadaver is a potent signifying spectacle, to be experienced as a retrieved dreadful memory. Like attending an opera, gazing at odd creatures in the zoo, or attending a museum exhibit, Zola's prosaic morgue setting relates the experience of a popular urban activity, a form of pre-cinematic entertainment for all classes of Parisian society. According to Vanessa R. Schwartz, gazing at rotting, semi-preserved human flesh—meat on a slab—was a fashionable social event:

> Crowds of as many as 40,000 a day gathered at the Paris Morgue to see dead bodies publicly displayed behind a large glass window in the salle d'exposition ... The new building's interior heightened the institution's theatrical quality. A green curtain hung at the window's sides and was used to close it off during a change of scene, when a body was either removed from or put on display ... Why did this show attract so many visitors? ... The vast majority of visitors probably did not go to the Morgue thinking that they actually might recognize a corpse. They went to look at real dead bodies under the pretense of acting out of civic duty. This was public voyeurism ... the Morgue satisfied and reinforced the desire to look that permeated much of Parisian culture in the late nineteenth century ... [it] stemmed from the public interest in "reality."[62]

The informed consumer scans the butcher's counter for the best cut of sirloin, the parasite enters the body for a gourmet feast, and for many people, the morgue was the public site to witness flesh on display, however rotting. According to Mark Seltzer, "the public fascination with torn and opened bodies and torn and opened persons, a collective gathering around shock, trauma, and the wound," indicates a near pathological fascination with the culture of victim and victimized, violence, and spectacle, as well as the public's "mass attraction to atrocity exhibitions" in contemporary society.[63] The public's fascination with visual morbidity is evident in multiple art forms.

Ruminating over the photographic aesthetic in relationship to violence and bodily decay, Roland Barthes concludes:

> In Photography, the presence of the thing (at a certain past moment) is never metaphoric; and in the case of animated beings, their life as well, except in the case of photographing corpses; and even so: if the photograph then becomes horrible, it is because it certifies, so to speak, that the corpse is alive, as a *corpse*: it is the living image of a dead thing.[64]

In July 1960, *Esquire* magazine published a series of photographs, six portraits of New Yorkers, entitled, "The Vertical Journey: Six Movements of a Moment within the Heart of a City," by Diane Arbus.[65] One photograph by Arbus shot in the morgue of New York City's Bellevue Hospital is a grainy composition of a body lying under very bright two lights with the feet of the corpse placed in the foreground of the shot and a toe-tag on the right foot's big toe. The body, covered by a shroud, remained unclaimed and unknown. According to Arbus biographer, Patricia Bosworth, Arbus found the morgue: "a place of dank tiles and refrigerated corpses. In the autopsy room, the air was heavy with the smell of decomposing flesh, of viscera open for examination . . . [and Arbus] began to collect information about death and dying."[66] As if to augment her appreciation of the deceased, Arbus examined police files containing information and anecdotes about the dead, "yellowing police records," containing observable details and objects from past lives, and most importantly, Bosworth notes that Arbus was beginning to "[define] her special interest in photography as a sort of contemporary anthropology,"[67] suggesting a relationship between Arbus' naturalist themes, her technological composition, and a revealing anthropological-historical context.

Formalist considerations of Marcel Carné's *Thérèse Raquin* (1953) clearly align the film to an atmospheric, black and white noir aesthetic. There is a Brassaï-like photographic quality of 1930s–1940s Paris to Carné's mise-en-scène, in which a preponderance of shots are composed in a medium and semi-wide frame depicting a working-class city. There is also an abundance of two shots in *Thérèse Raquin*, which fill the frame with a dynamic tension between lovers Laurent (Raf Vallone) and Thérèse (Simone Signoret). Carné's *Thérèse Raquin* emphasizes the dark within the dark, as many sequences are shadowy and low-lit, even when set during the daytime. These noirish images suggest a linkage between claustrophobic, stifling settings and the determinist sense of entrapment. The story of a failed marriage and murder is realistically composed in the opening shot sequences: in the bedroom, after Camille is put to his sick bed, Thérèse, apparently and frustratingly resolved to her abusive state of domestic entrapment, gazes out of the window, exposing to the audience her longing and anxiety. This gaze shot recalls the placement of the adulteress Vicki (Gloria Grahame) before a window in Fritz Lang's *Human Desire* (1954), an adaptation of Zola's *La Bête humaine* in which Vicki exposes her internalized longing and stress. For Vicki, murder is a viable option for her sexual and economic unhappiness.

In Carné's *Thérèse Raquin*, Thérèse is the nursemaid–sex worker for her husband, the mousy Camille. Although Thérèse works, in Carné's 1950s urban setting, the trope of the unhappy bourgeois wife was integral to the melodramatic presence in the narrative. Laurent, the foreign-born truck driver who befriends Camille and becomes Thérèse's lover, is portrayed as a sturdy member of the more physical working class. Handsome, strong, sexual, all the things Camille is not, Laurent is the antidote to Thérèse's frustrations and entrapment. Marcel Carné's *Thérèse Raquin* is a film about violent crime, illicit passion, and consequences in desperate spaces.

In Simon Langton's BBC production *Thérèse Raquin* (1980), the grimly realistic rendering of Camille's murder and later, the display of his rotting corpse in the morgue suggest a certifiable presence. Jean Mitry specifically noted:

Lifted from its context, *Thérèse Raquin* is no longer *Thérèse Raquin*, but simply the story of two lovers who get rid of an annoying husband and later feel remorse about it. This is a story which could happen anywhere, in any way, at any time—but we miss what Zola provides, we miss his people whose very existence is a function of the epoch and milieu in which they live and struggle.[68]

Mitry insightfully links *Raquin* narratives to a space and time in which naturalist conflict manifests. Camille's murder sequence in Langton's *Thérèse Raquin* is set on a placid lake full of atmospheric white clouds and greenery with a spacious, brightly lit feeling lessening the tension-filled moments prior to the murder. Langton's narrative recalls the Impressionist era's light-filled and airy afternoon seascape paintings by Georges Seurat in *La Seine a Courbevoie* (1885–6) and *La Seine at La Grande Jatte* (1888) as the film saturates the frame with descriptive, realist images. However, the lover's contrivances and the inevitable struggle for survival vitiate the colorful, peaceful setting. Thérèse (Kate Nelligan), like a trapped jungle cat, has nowhere to go in order to survive except to her stifling job and loveless marriage, a traditional cage. Laurent (Brian Cox), her lover, is a bull untethered by convention and unabated desire. Camille (Kenneth Cranham) is a victim in the making, a specimen to be consumed by dangerous organisms. Langton's painterly palate, composed of reflective sunlight and natural sounds produced by birds, carefree people, and rolling river water, dramatically shifts from the images of idyllic friends to one of a crime scene.

Prior to the murder, while on land, as Camille rests, Thérèse and Laurent seem to lie peacefully near her husband, but the efficacy of the moment and its illusions are nearly ruptured as Laurent, in a medium shot, rises and then towers over the smaller body of Camille. As Laurent raises his foot as if to stamp out the life of an annoying insect, he stops, realizing that it is not the place or the moment. Thérèse recoils from the sight of this near-homicide but does nothing to stop it; the river shortly beckons. The pastoral quality of the moment is further enhanced by other sets of boaters and picnickers casually appearing. As hunger leads the triangle to a restaurant, only to be delayed for approximately an hour before seating, Laurent suggests that time spent row boating would be pleasant, although Camille prefers a drink. It is Thérèse who decides to take the ride, again, aware of the potential for the murderous scenario, as Laurent indicates to her to follow his lead. The spider–fly stratagem ensues.

Langton depicts the violent rupture of the shoreline's normalcy shortly after the three characters get on the boat. Thérèse, ever silent in cat-like repose, positions herself on one side of the boat and masks her anticipatory anxiety by appearing distracted and looking elsewhere. Laurent, in the middle of the boat, rows away from the shore and from the sight of others. Laurent watches his passive prey, Camille, as he drifts off into sleep, sitting on the other side. Clouds gather overhead, the sky gets darker, and as tension mounts, Laurent stands and moves toward Camille and lifts him up, nearly overhead. Once Camille realizes this is not a moment of male bonding, he begins to struggle, like a terrified lab rat. Thérèse expresses yet controls her fear; she never tries to stop the assault. The two men struggle on the boat, as it is a one-sided conflict, Laurent lifts the smaller, weaker man, who impulsively bites Laurent on the neck, leaving a disfiguring wound. Like a fish unworthy of storing, Camille is tossed overboard, and Thérèse faints. Her gesture is neither a standardized theatrical pose nor a melodramatic flourish; Thérèse is overcome by the physical, emotional toll, a flourishing of anxiety.

Langton's medium shot of Camille slowly sinking and gasping in the water amid the reeds and drowning like a large trapped fish is horrific and pathetic. While the lovers, now murderers, remain in the boat, Laurent touches his fresh, bloody neck wound and sees that Thérèse has passed out as another boat approaches. In another example of his apish, brutish strength, Laurent swiftly lifts Thérèse and succeeds in capsizing the boat. After an unsuccessful attempt to retrieve Camille's body by the advancing party, the corpse is left in the river, only to later resurface as a tell-tale casualty in the morgue sequence. Other adaptations of Zola's novel revise the murder of the "Camille figure" according to narrative design; whether considered as an old man or depicted as his younger self, even if not later discovered in a morgue, the husband must be eliminated.

Contrived acts of violence leading to murder are a recurring, eruptive trope throughout naturalist film narrative. Multiple international adaptations of the popular roman noir, James M. Cain's crime novel *The Postman Always Rings Twice* (1936), itself a hypertextual renewal of Zola's *Thérèse Raquin* (1867), reconceive and ingeniously renew the plotted beating and drowning of Camille, Thérèse's weakling husband, the disposable figure in an asymmetrical sexual triangle. Select cinematic adaptations of Cain's novel, Luchino Visconti's *Ossessione/Obsession* (1943), Tay Garnett's *The Postman Always Rings Twice* (1946), Robert M. Young's *Caught* (1996), and György Fehér's *Szenvedély/Passion* (1998), renew and significantly revise both Zola's climactic boat struggle and Cain's roadside assault, while conceptualizing the spider–fly stratagem in which the deceived husband cannot escape the criminal machinations of the plotting, illicit lovers.

Visconti's *Ossesione/Obsession*, a neorealist production permeated with a sense of violent urges and fulfilled lust between adulterous lovers is a narrative of triangulated decline. Via the conventions of the melodrama, *Ossessione* is a case study of naturalist grinding theory, as its final image is a trapped, broken male, alone and bereft of purpose. In *Ossessione*, homeless derelict Gino

(Massimo Girotti) and unhappy worker-housewife Giovanna (Clara Calamai) find no relief except when surrendering to their passion; their adulterous affair leads to the murder of her unsympathetic, abusive husband, tavern owner Bragana (Juan de Landa), the isosceles side of the triangle. *Ossessione* presents sexual excess as a catalytic presence. No character in *Osessione* is innocent, but some are guiltier than others. According to Angelo Restivo, "Visconti's film is such a stumbling block to the writing of the history of neorealism that nobody seems to know quite what to do with it. [It is] marked by a fascination with melodrama."[69] Visconti's absorbing narrative negates melodramatic resolution and initiates darker naturalist preoccupations with desire and the déclassé.

In *Ossessione*, neorealist-formalist tropes of production, such as long shot sequences, location footage, non-professional actors, and intrinsic lighting, focalize Visconti's examination of ordinary working-class people made extraordinary by circumstances that they cannot completely understand, responding to complex stimuli that destroys them. When Bragana is violently murdered off the road, off screen, his death barely elicits sympathy. Bragana is the necessary fatality to facilitate the rise of future disaster; he is a catalytic presence producing multiple negative effects, for only by his death can the couple's destruction be realized. The murder of another disagreeable, aging husband is requisite in Tay Garnett's *The Postman Always Rings Twice* (1946), the adaptation conceived within the stylistic conventions of film noir, an industrial production mode associated with Naturalism's deterministic bent. James Naremore has noted that James Cain "specialized in Dostoyevskian narratives of criminal psychology, transposed into lower-class America and strongly influenced by the naturalism of Theodore Dreiser."[70] Whether depicting the experiences of a drifter, a dissolute worker, or a frustrated gas station attendant, in film noir, environmental and psychological catalysts are subsequently linked with violent consequences for members of the working class.

In Garnett's *The Postman Always Rings Twice*, Frank (John Garfield), the handsome drifter who arrives at an out-of-the-way gas station–restaurant, and Cora (Lana Turner), the unsatisfied housewife-worker married to Nick (Cecil Kellaway), an unsympathetic older man, discover that there is no escape from endemic class and gender proscriptions. Adulterous passion leads to Nick's murder. After a failed initial attempt, in another plan, the lovers get the husband drunk while driving along a dark and isolated road. As the car is shut down in a remote area to prevent overheating, Cora's drunk husband sings out into the canyons, but his echo soon outlives him. In a series of medium close-up shots, Frank picks up an empty bottle, clutches it firmly, and delivers the fatal blow as he strikes Nick, who is off screen, over the head. The camera cuts to Cora's reaction, an image and instance of apprehension mixed with release. Only Nick's echo remains.

In Courbet's allegorical series of self-referential paintings, *The Trout* (c. 1872), and *Three Trout from the Loue River* (1873), the artist depicts symbolic images of death, profiles of finality, as trout have lost their struggle for existence. On the former canvas, an entrapped trout lies lifeless; on the latter canvas, three fish, two hanging from hooks and one set upon the ground, suggest incipient decay and future consumption. Traditional interpretations of Courbet's series of these naturalist images, representing an interaction between nature and man, have metaphorical and politicized associations involving the artist's own post-Commune imprisonment in 1871. Courbet adds an indicative inscription in (blood) red, at the bottom of the first *Trout* painting, "In viculus faciebat"/"It was made in chains."

Young's *Caught* (1996) opens with a compelling series of images suggesting struggle and ensnarement, as an unsuspecting fish is fatally netted. This metonymic image of entrapment visualizes, as it foreshadows, the lives of three characters in Young's naturalist narrative of the working class. Set in the urban laboratory of 1990s gentrified Jersey City, in a fish store business, *Caught* expands the melodramatic parameters of the ill-fated romantic triangle as it renews the structural and thematic design of James Cain's appropriation of Zola's Naturalism.

In Young's *Caught*, Nick (Arie Verveen), an attractive and young homeless immigrant states in an introductory voice-over, "it's amazing how you get into things." Nick literally stumbles into the snare of two seductive modes involving semi-skilled labor and adultery; he becomes a willing worker and the eventual lover-victim of a troubled marriage in the home of Joe (Edward James Olmos) and Betty (Maria Conchita Alonso), the owners of the store. Young repeatedly focuses on shot sequences documenting the working class grinding away at unseen, unrewarded labor, sweeping the floors, cleaning and scaling fish, as workers daily hustle for survival. Like Zola's shopkeeper, Thérèse Raquin and Cain's waitress, Cora, Young's Betty, a lonely and sensual middle-aged woman, experiences repressive domesticity in the form of a stultifying marriage and her own ignored labor, as she sits in her fish-designed wallpapered apartment. Betty's marriage and life are both flat, but Nick, like Zola's energetically sexual Laurent and Cain's dynamic and available Frank, is a revitalizing distraction for Betty. The predictable affair between Nick and Betty leads to a sordid and violent outcome: Joe's death from a heart attack and Nick's death, as his throat is slit, like a gasping carp prepared for dinner, by Joe and Betty's troubled, abusive son. *Caught* is a post-noir, melodramatic, naturalist narrative of the ensnared working class.

Fehér's adaptation, *Szenvedély/Passion* (1998) presents a long car drive with the three, triangulated principles—the wife, the husband, and the man—claustrophobically traversing the countryside in an aging automobile on a lonely road. All three sit together without a single word expressed among them; there are only the natural sounds associated with car travel. Fehér's side-angle shot framing these three people inside the automobile shifts to extended points-of-view shots from the passenger seat and through the unclean windshield, since the road offers little attraction. Fehér's camera pans to the right to reveal both the metallic structure of the car and the left side of the old man's head, in shadowy near-silhouette portraiture. At one point, the other man-driver stops the sputtering car and lifts the hood to examine faltering machinery, and the older man gets out to help; while the old man inspects the equipment under the hood, he moves off screen. After a few seconds, the other man raises his arm to reveal the murder weapon, a tool, which he uses to strike three times and kill the older man. The man's violent striking action is shot through the windshield, a framing within the frame, and as the man closes the car's hood, it recalls the closing of a coffin.

In Langton's *Thérèse Raquin*, the Parisian morgue shot sequences, in which a mannered Laurent goes in search of his victim's body, effectively utilize muted, dark colors in a clinical display of the horrific as medical spectacle: a realistic exhibition of rotting corpses. The experience of viewing decomposing flesh, the sound of the running water over the bodies—an act to preserve further decay—has an eerie, unsettling resonance that links it with the crime scene. The morgue attendees witness this quasi-social activity in death's waiting room for various, frequently eccentric reasons. Vanessa Schwartz notes, "A large and socially diverse audience went to the morgue."[71] Some people attend the morgue's display of unclaimed corpses for curiosity's sake or voyeuristic pleasure, while Laurent goes to the morgue for evidentiary finality. Camille's disintegrating remains tell their own tale, as Langton's close-up shot of Camille's rotting head suggests a near grinning ironic awareness, as if the head knowingly mocks its guilty spectator.

Broken Up

Oliver Stone's *Trümmerfilme*, *World Trade Center* (2006) examines the political climate of post 9/11 cinema with images of broken bodies and fragmented flesh. In one extended shot sequence, after the historic collapse of the towers, two police officers (Nicolas Cage, Michael Peña) are trapped below the lobby in a crippling darkness, punctuated by bursts of light from explosive fires and bullets discharged from overheated ordnance. The building has become a consuming block of debris—a metaphorical mouth crunching people and objects—and in a series of compelling close-up and medium shots, the cropped heads, hands, and body parts of both officers recall Théodore Géricault's series of amputated limbs and lifeless torsos, as each shot reveals what is left of a broken, severed existence.

Much of *World Trade Center* is set inside the crumbling structure where bodies are fragmented; the coherence of the body politic as well as the literal bodies of workers becomes an observational focal point. The initial act of violation is followed by a re-conjoining of the workers' bodies—some are saved—as well as the body politic. *World Trade Center* is a wound narrative; Stone's film, a political-horror-melodramatic intergeneric blending, features broken bodies within its metaphorical morgue. Costa-Gravas' *Missing* (1982), another historically based political-horror film narrative, reveals the plight of Ed Horman (Jack Lemmon), a naïve middle-aged man who goes in search of his socially active, presumably murdered son, missing after the Chilean junta in the 1980s that eliminated progressive undesirables. The shot sequence in another *ad hoc* morgue, a former sports stadium, reveals a distraught father stepping over and around the bodies of hundreds of slaughtered people. These nameless, uncovered victims facilitate an encroaching mood of despair and resignation in this makeshift morgue.

Like the butchered and reassembled remains of the failed actress Elizabeth Short, discovered off the road in Brian De Palma's *The Black Dahlia* (2006), human remnants indicate some perverse realities. De Palma's film, a semi-fictional detective-romance-history narrative involving two policemen and one woman, establishes triangular sexual tension among principles, along with additional sexual liaisons and plot intrigues, as a fictional framing story explores the murder of Elizabeth Short (Mia Kirshner), the black dahlia, a woman vainly seeking employment in the postwar Hollywood film industry. Short's decline into soft-core pornography and very possibly prostitution informs her infamous murder. *The Black Dahlia* features mutilated bodies, with frequent visits to the morgue and to the bedroom, and significantly highlights visually based technology: photography, mugshots, and films, both commercial and pornographic. Photographs of the mutilated body of Elizabeth Short serve as historical markers as well as disturbing psychological catalysts for both detectives. Pornographic films, as well as screen tests, provide information about Short's decline from working-class woman, to alleged prostitute, to butchered victim, as she speaks into the camera documenting her enactment-confessional as a struggling actress and her sexual encounters. In the morgue-autopsy shot sequence, De Palma places the camera directly above Short's body on the dissecting table while the camera slowly moves downward, tightening the shot on her body which is surrounded by policemen, as the doctor in charge discusses the removal of her organs and the general pattern of her mutilation.

In Marc Schölermann's *Pathology* (2008), before the graphic appearance of the Hippocratic Oath enters the frame, an introductory sequence reveals a series of extreme close-up shots of a doctor's hands moving the lips of dead bodies inside a traditional morgue while humorously lip-synching a voice, per body. As one female corpse is made to simulate the sounds of a sexual climax, the reanimation of the dead is depicted as a comedic routine, a joke, in the performance space of the morgue. In *Pathology*, a crime-horror narrative, coercive images of naturalist decay and death inform the violated human bodies on display. The morgue is uniquely envisioned as an adult playground—a violent fun house—as the camera tracks back to reveal amused medical professionals. Flesh, whether fragmented, putrefying, or mutilated, expresses meaning.

According to Michael F. Miller, in Stan Brakhage's *The Act of Seeing with One's Own Eyes* (1971), for thirty-two minutes in Brakhage's silent film, "we observe an Allegheny County coroner hard at work as he measures, examines, slices, peels away flesh, discards viscera, and scoops out the brain matter of four different anonymous corpses."[72] Brakhage's experimental documentary was shot with several film stocks in the autopsy room. *The Act of Seeing with One's Own Eyes* reveals the graphic ongoing dissection of several bodies in close-up and medium shots and non-stationary camera movement; the audience views the remains of the anonymous human. Brakhage's point-of-view shots remain clinical while being artistically gory. As forensic specialists eviscerate the human body, the viewer experiences informative details being uncovered. According to Juan Carlos Kase, the classification of Brakhage's film as a documentary is aesthetically debatable:

> Produced on a personal and artistic precipice, this unprepared, unrehearsed film was, quite literally, an experiment . . . By choosing the most difficult, almost unbearable visual spectacle of the dead as his subject, he was interrogating the medium's capacity to register subjectivity and affect without the imposition of a guiding rhetorical directive.[73]

Kase later concludes that in *The Act of Seeing with One's Own Eyes*, "Brakhage produced a filmic experiment that provoked and transcribed extreme encounters of somatic tension and ontological crisis to reveal the fault lines between human bodies and the technologies that circumscribe them in art."[74] An alternative reading of Brakhage's film considers it an experimental narrative exposing the human, observed and experimented upon in compelling clinical moments of naturalist documentation. All that remains will be inventoried.

Notes

1. Erik Bullot, "Keaton and Snow," trans. Molly Stevens, *October*, Vol. 114 (Autumn 2005), 21.
2. Anonymous, "Robots Carve a Butchery Role," *The Engineer*, Vol. 273, No. 7066–7 (August 29, 1991), 38.
3. Samuel M. Waxman, *Antoine and the Théâtre Libre* (1926) (New York: Benjamin Blom, 1964), 81. Note: This would be Christmas Eve, 1890–1.

4. U. Saint-Vel, "*Conte de Noël*—Mystère moderne," *Revue D'Art Dramatique*: Tome XXI, No. 122, Janvier–Mars (Paris: 1891), 111.
5. Rodolphe Darzens, *Le Théatre Libre Illustre* (tome deuxième) (Paris: Libraire de la Société des gens de lettres, 1890), 95. Note: Italics are in the original.
6. André Antoine, *"Mes Souvenirs" sur le Théâtre-Libre* (Paris: Arthème Fayard, 1921), 211.
7. Mel Gordon, *The Grand Guignol: Theatre of Fear and Terror* (New York: Amok Press, 1988), 8–9, 41.
8. Ramon del Valle-Inclan, *Divinas Palabras*, in *Three Plays: Divine Words, Bohemian Lights, Silver Face*, trans. Maria M. Delgado (London: Methuen, 1997), 64–7.
9. Upton Sinclair, *The Jungle*, 1906: this excerpt is from chapter 14. See https://www.gutenberg.org/files/140/140-h/140-h.htm. Accessed May 12, 2023.
10. Mo Yan, *POW*, trans. Howard Goldblatt (New York: Seagull Books, 2012), 54. Note: Yan's novel was published earlier but made available in English in 2012.
11. Ibid, 146.
12. Ibid, 117.
13. Vaclav Smil, "Eating Meat: Evolution, Patterns, and Consequences," *Population and Development Review*, Vol. 28, No. 4 (December 2002), 599.
14. Ibid, 628.
15. Yan, *POW*, 49.
16. Thomas F. DeVoe, *Abattoirs: A Paper Read Before the Polytechnic Branch of the American Institute, June 8th 1865* (Albany: Van Benthuysen & Sons' Steam Printing House, 1866), 3, 7.
17. Smil, "Eating," 599.
18. John D. Smith, *The Butcher's Manual* (Kansas: Democrat Book Print, 1890), 7.
19. Ibid, 10.
20. Ibid, 19.
21. Bruce F. Kawin, *Horror and the Horror Film* (New York: Anthem Press, 2012), 65.
22. The reader may wish to peruse the following website: www.art-forum.org/z_Serrano/gallery.htm. Accessed March 12, 2023.
23. Carter Soles, "Sympathy for the Devil: The Cannibalistic Hillbilly in 1970s Rural Slasher Films," in *Ecocinema Theory and Practice: Theory and Practice*, ed. Stephen Rust, et al. (New York: Routledge, 2012), 234, 239.
24. Kawin, *Horror*, 152.
25. Jerry D. Metz, "Headcheese and a Side of Benjamin:" Aura and *The Texas Chain Saw Massacre* (1974)'s Working-Class Gaze," *Irish Journal of Gothic and Horror Studies*, Vol. 11 (June 30, 2012), 71.
26. Soles, "Sympathy," 242.
27. James Rose, *The Texas Chain Saw Massacre* (Great Britain: Auteur Publishing–Liverpool University Press, 2013), 86.
28. Sarah O'Brien, "Nous revenons à nos moutons: Regarding Animals in Charles Burnett's 'Killer of Sheep,'" *Cinema Journal*, Vol. 54, No. 3 (Spring 2015), 26.
29. M. Walravens, *Abattoir* (Bruxelles: n.p., 1881), 15. "La création d'un vaste abattoir commun était conforme a l'intérèt public."
30. Dennis R. Henderson and Bobby D. van Stavern, "*Meat* by Frederick Wiseman," *American Journal of Agricultural Economics*, Vol. 59, No. 3 (August 1977), 601.
31. Smil, "Eating," 628.
32. Bill Nichols, "Fred Wiseman's Documentaries: Theory and Structure," *Film Quarterly*, Vol. 31, No. 3 (Spring 1978), 16.
33. Henderson and Van Stavern, "Review: *Meat*," 601.

34. Jennifer L. Jenkins, "A Symphony of Horror, The Sublime Synesthesia of *Sweeney Todd*," in *The Philosophy of Tim Burton*, ed. Jennifer L. McMahon (Lexington: University Press of Kentucky, 2014), 173–4.
35. Jack London, *People of the Abyss* (New York: Grosset & Dunlap, 1907), 168.
36. Ibid, 284.
37. Jenkins, "Symphony," 179.
38. Ibid, 181.
39. The film was produced with both Hebrew titles.
40. Stefanie Knauss, "Exploring Orthodox Jewish Masculinities with *Eyes Wide Open*," *Journal of Religion and Film*, Vol. 17, No. 2 (October 1, 2013), 13.
41. Yael Friedman and Yohai Haka, "Jewish Revenge: Haredi Action in the Zionist Sphere," *Jewish Film & New Media*, Vol. 3, No. 1 (Spring 2015), 49.
42. Knauss, *Eyes*, 16.
43. Ibid, 13.
44. Ibid, 12.
45. Martine Beugnet and Emmanuelle Delanoë-Brun "Raw Becomings: Bodies, Discipline and Control in Julia Ducornau's *Grave*," *French Screen Studies*, Vol. 21, No. 3 (2021), 206.
46. Ibid, 209.
47. Gunnar Rehlin, "Film Review: *The Green Butchers*," *Variety* (December 15–21, 2003), 53–4.
48. This excerpted verse appears in Whitman's "Song of Myself," first edition (1855), as well as in the "death-bed" (1892) edition.
49. The photo appears in Scott Nearing's *Black America* (New York: Vanguard Press, 1929), 93. This file is from the New York Public Library: https://digitalcollections.nypl.org/items/510d47de-1a35-a3d9-e040-e00a18064a99. Accessed July 10, 2023.
50. Icres' work may be accessed at http://gallica.bnf.fr/ark:/12148/bpt6k625660. Accessed July 14, 2023.
51. André Antoine, *"Mes Souvenirs" sur la Théatre-Libre* (Paris: Arthème Fayard, 1921), 117–18. "Dans mon désir d'une mise en scène caractéristique, j'avais accroché, dans *les Bouchers*, de véritables quartiers de viande qui ont fait sensation."
52. Stuart Liebman, "André Antoine's Film Theory," *Framework: Journal of Cinema and Media*, No. 24 (Spring 1984), 35.
53. Icres, *Bouchers*, 24. A very special thank you to Marcelline Block for the translation from the French: "Ah! Quand je tiens un veau, pied lies sur la banque/Que je suis-la, bras nus, cou tendu, reins roidis/Avant de commencer l'attaque je me dis/Si c'était lui!"
54. Adrienne Angelo, "Contextualizing Transgression in French Cinema at the Dawn of the Twenty-first Century," *Irish Journal of French Studies*, Vol. 12 (2012), 170–1.
55. Jane Giles, "The White Horse, *Seul Contre Tous* and Notes on Meat as Metaphor," *Vertigo* Vol. 1, No. 9 (Summer 1999), 1.
56. Émile Zola, "Preface to the Second Edition (1868)," in *Thérèse Raquin*, trans. Robin Buss (London: Penguin Books, 2004), 6.
57. Ibid, 7.
58. Émile Zola, *Thérèse Raquin*, trans. Robin Buss (London: Penguin Books, 2004), 62–3.
59. Ibid, 63.
60. Linda Nochlin, *The Body in Pieces: The Fragment as a Metaphor of Modernity* (London: Thames & Hudson, 1995), 18.

61. Gilles Deleuze, *Francis Bacon: The Logic of Sensation*, trans. Daniel W. Smith (New York: Continuum, 2003), 22–4.
62. Vanessa R. Schwartz, "The Morgue and the Musée Grévin: Understanding the Public Taste for Reality in Fin-de-Siècle Paris," in *Spectacles of Realism: Body, Gender, Genre*, eds Margaret Cohen and Christopher Prendergast (Minneapolis: University of Minnesota Press, 1995), 268–93.
63. Mark Seltzer, "Wound Culture: Trauma in the Pathological Public Sphere," *October*, Vol. 80 (Spring 1997), 3.
64. Roland Barthes, *Camera Lucida*, trans. Richard Howard (New York: Hill & Wang, 1981), 78–9, original emphasis.
65. The reader may review some of this photographic series in *Diane Arbus: Magazine Work*, eds Doon Arbus and Marvin Israel (New York: Aperture Books, 1984), 11–13.
66. Patricia Bosworth, *Diane Arbus* (New York: Alfred A. Knopf, 1984), 173–4.
67. Ibid, 174.
68. Jean Mitry, "Remarks on the Problem of Cinematic Adaptation," *Bulletin of the Midwest Modern Language Association*, Vol. 4, No. 1 (Spring 1971), 5.
69. Angelo Restivo, *The Cinema of Economic Miracles* (Durham: Duke University Press, 2002), 24.
70. James Naremore, *More Than Night: Film Noir in Its Contexts* (Berkeley, University Press, 1998), 83.
71. Schwartz, "Morgue," 270.
72. Michael F. Miller, "Stan Brakhage's Autopsy: *The Act of Seeing with One's Own Eyes*," *Journal of Film and Video*, Vol. 70, No. 2 (Summer 2018), 52.
73. Juan Carlos Kase, "Encounters with the Real: Historicizing Stan Brakhage's The Act of Seeing with One's Own Eyes," *The Moving Image: Journal of the Association of Moving Image Archivists*, Vol. 12, No. 1 (Spring 2012), 6, 8.
74. Ibid, 13.

6. DARWINIAN DISCONNECTIONS

Growth Signs

According to Gaston Bachelard, "A house constitutes a body of images that give mankind proofs or illusions of stability. We are constantly reimagining its reality: to distinguish all these images would be to describe the soul of the house; it would mean developing a veritable psychology of the house."[1] The Lumière brothers' *Repas de bébé/A Baby's Meal* (1895), a seminal home movie/*actualité* set in a garden, suggests a painterly canvas of moving, interrelated moments of domesticity revealing the unedited footage of a family, not at work, but rather reveling in the everyday while anticipating a future: signs of happy heredity. Constant Girel's *actualité Repas en Famille/The Family Meal* (1897) is shot in Japan and features, in one medium set shot, three adults and two children all tastefully dressed, eating and drinking tea outdoors on a sunny afternoon in a peaceful setting. Bachelard shares his own pastorally inflected reflections about the garden and being outdoors:

> How many times, in my garden, I have experienced the disappointment of discovering a nest too late. Autumn was there, the leaves had already begun to fall and in the fork of two branches there was an abandoned nest. To think that they had all been there: the father bird, the mother bird and the nestlings. And I had not seen them![2]

In *A Baby's Meal*, for an attentive thirty-three seconds, Louis Lumière's fixed-camera medium shot reveals in the foreground of the frame his brother's "nested" family—father, baby, and mother—as they feed and entertain the baby, who interacts with both solicitous parents while leaves silently rustle in the background. Patricia Vigderman discusses the playful moments in *A Baby's Meal*:

> It's a comical and messy event: the spoonfuls that miss their mark, gustatory anxiety, parental distraction. Because the unblinking machine is running, the film continuous frame after frame catching every smile and gesture; and simultaneously time is running out . . . The frameless actuality of it leads to a little shock when we are left mid-meal as time hurries on, the film runs out. This bit of celluloid, this composition in front of that solid corner of the house, this slightly shaky medium shot of generational happiness, this brief sequence of feeding the future, is all that's left of that moment.[3]

Moving from the outside space of the two Lumière productions into the indoor setting of a contemporary family, naturalist painter Émile Friant's *Le repas frugal/The Frugal Meal* (1894) is a study of six members of a working-class family barely making interpersonal contact and about to consume an unappealing meal. Unlike *A Baby's Meal*, the Lumière brothers' *actualité*, in Friant's painting, there appear to be no pleasantries exchanged among family members; sitting to the left of the frame, the sole male's back is turned away from the viewer while the women and children sit to the right side of the table waiting for the plate to be placed on the table. The kitchen itself is unpretentiously adorned; Friant's color palate, especially his use of brown and red, make the room credibly realistic as it reveals decorative items but not wealth. According to Richard Thomson, "Friant . . . preferred to operate within the generous parameters of naturalism . . . [Friant was] an artist whose aesthetic was scrupulously observed naturalism."[4] Friant's canvas of a working-class family depicts the frugal, uncelebratory present.

In Rainer Werner Fassbinder's *In A Year with 13 Moons* (1978), he juxtaposes transexual Erwin/Elvira's (Volker Spengler) unconventional gendered alienation in an extended shot sequence that recalls the pastoral, home movie-like setting in the Lumière brothers' *A Baby's Meal*. As Erwin/Elvira is separated from their ex-wife and daughter—a conventional middle-class family—they all meet and sit together in a spacious garden setting where they might convene and dine al fresco. This inadvertently produces troubling, awkward flashes for Erwin/Elvira, as their return to a remote past life within the immediacy of the moment cannot genuinely occur. Milan Pribisic notes how in Fassbinder's *In A Year with 13 Moons*, "each scene is an episode in Elvira's cautionary tale in which she tries to connect her journeying self with an original self. It is a trip backward, a journey of reconstruction to her origin."[5] These moments in the garden reveal a discomforting clash between Elvira/Erwin's past and present life, in which the present exposes their past's loss. Although they gently tell the daughter to eat, as Lumière might request of his child, Erwin/Elvira eventually stands and then runs out of the frame, as if sensing the garden scenario is too late, an impossible reality now too distant to sustain in the present.

The Lumière brothers' *A Baby's Meal* is an *actualité* about the future. In *A Baby's Meal*, there is an indicative aleatory shot, a *Barthesian* punctum within the space of the frame that suggests a cinematic linkage, a *symbolic* suturing relationship with future film narrative. In one moment, there is a discernable shift of focus by the baby, making an errant gaze outside the frame, as the baby lifts her hand while holding a cookie.[6] To whom does the baby offer her cookie: the camera technician, unknown personnel, or is it a meaningless gesture? If, however, the Lumière brothers' production is read *figuratively* by the present audience as a link to the cinematic past, might the baby's outward gaze and gesture while holding the cookie in the *actualité* be construed as leading to the future? According to Patricia Vigderman, in the Lumière brothers' *A Baby's Meal*, "The moving frames carry us further and further away from their images."[7] Three stages of signifying realism demonstrably coexist in the space and time of *A Baby's Meal*. The gentle offering of the Lumière brothers' toddler-muse's gaze forward, breaking the illusionary boundaries of the frame from its initial sighting, invites a reading of past realities (1895), in the present ("now"), and the future ("later"). The "staring baby" moment suggestively traverses the frame.

In this section, as it involves the family, home, and applications of imaginative genetics, a theoretical reading of naturalist film narrative initially focuses on clinical, critical suppositions revealing ghosts from the past in the present and implied uncertainties in the future, as formerly encoded, now that exposed interactions of heredity—the space and time of the gene—are rendered. As subsequent naturalist films reveal, genetic material and heredity yield a field of narrative play. Babies grow up. The second focus of this section involves the home setting, which also includes the housing project and "hood"—all territorial sites of imagined interaction—as the dynamic locus of naturalist revelation of personal and social complications. The Lumière brothers' *A Baby's Meal* provides this writerly platform of narrative intertexts.

Gene Pool

In a letter addressed to his colleague, dated April 18, 1905, British scientist-researcher William Bateson discussed the need to formulate a new word, a term, in order to establish and sponsor a university professorship to examine a compelling new branch of science: "Heredity and Variation ... No single word in common use quite gives this meaning. Such a word is badly wanted, and if it were desirable to coin one, 'GENETICS' might do."[8] The letter soon refers to heredity and "cognate phenomena,"[9] an alluring phrase suggesting a range of perceptual applications for both the clinical and creative communities. "Genetics" has remained a central concept on multiple levels of academic and artistic discourse, in an *a priori*, mystique-like presence historically fixed to and associated with the mystery of heredity, a predetermined conceptual "fate" ripe for imaginative prognostication. In naturalist cinema, genetics—heredity's platform—signifies a presumptive, clinical, anti-supernatural, biologically "fated" form of affective presence to be factored with socio-economic agencies. Invisible DNA strands comingle with social agencies. What Zola might have imagined in his clinically predisposed novels of family and society now possesses a firmer entry point into clinical logos. The presence of the "scientific" layering of clinical discourse involving genetics in naturalist film narrative is an essential, extensive part of film history.

Edwin S. Porter's *The Whole Dam Family and the Dam Dog* (1905) has been categorized as an amusing trifle with an ironic surname, an appropriation from the contemporary vaudeville theater, without depth or distinction: "This film can hardly be said to contain a narrative as such."[10] This brief film opens with the screen title, "Do you know this family?" and then cuts to a series of close-up shots in patrilineal order of the entire middle-class Dam family, concluding with the Dam dog. These facial caricatures (playful mugshots), ranging from the near-grotesque to the playfully annoying, present the unromantic, subversive vision of the effects of heredity in this short humorously contrived naturalist film narrative, and may be considered a case study of disappointing genetics.

The Whole Dam Family and the Dam Dog depicts an unappealing family like a failed, awkward series of revelatory photographs in an album: the father rubs his nose and sneezes repeatedly as he stares into the camera; the mother never stops gabbing into the camera; the older daughter apparently is in love with herself; the older son arrogantly smokes in his ill-fitting clothing; one young daughter wears a stylish, inappropriate hat while the next daughter in line unappetizingly chews gum, and the male baby cries persistently, perhaps aware of his immediate environment. The whole Dam family looks at you looking at them, self-consciously aware but unconcerned. Porter's film is a comedic, visual declension of unsettling images of the modern middle class. The framing screen title has supplied the audience with a response to the question it initially posed: we very likely *do* know this family, even the Dam dog.

In two of Porter's more creative shot sequences following the crass family portraiture, a series of jumbled, shifting letters "unjumbles," and upon recomposing, spells the "whole Dam family." Charles Musser concludes this is a popular film technique of the early silent era:

> Among Porter's most successful cinematic innovations of this period were "jumble announcements," animated intertitles whose letters and shapes swirled around the black background, finally forming words and silhouettes ... These were used extensively in several comedies ... *The Whole Dam Family and the Dam Dog* ... adapted images from a postcard that was then enjoying wide circulation.[11]

Like a descriptive caption to the family portrait; this unstructured lettering also resembles—perhaps for future audiences—symbolic genetic coding, the hereditary strand-substance of DNA, which when energetically formulated creates a family line. Nearly fifty years prior to its clinical conception, this DNA-like animated lettering is as amusing as it is suggestive, and it is followed by the lengthy family dinner table sequence, in Porter's static medium shot, in which the Dam dog ruins the meal as it pulls the tablecloth out and away.

In John Frankenheimer's *The Island of Dr. Moreau* (1996), Kyle Cooper, creator of the film's title sequence, presents in approximately 160 seconds of shuffling, colorful graphics, *sans* identifiable scientist, a foundational process of clinical observation for the ensuing narrative. According to Jose Van Dijck, "The opening scene of the movie features a collage of cells, DNA helixes and enlarged microscopic pictures, symbolizing the control of humans over evolution through intervention at the molecular level."[12] Cooper's title sequence, a collage of intersecting visual signifiers, introduces Moreau's narrative of failed experimentation. The display of cast and credits shares the screen with rearranged DNA-like shifting letters/symbols—the patterns of life changing—and the focalizing, recurring image of an open, synecdochical eye, as if it were peering into a microscope, suggesting that someone is observing as well as being observed. The incessant motion of the title sequence then reformulates in a paratextual capacity visual markers from the Moreau narratives: the island, the sea, and unknown bestial life forms rising from experimentation of microscopic origin. In this title sequence, like an artist's layered canvas, Cooper's close-up and medium shots frame the elements of a botched experiment in the making while invoking for the audience a nascent sense of dread in Frankenheimer's adaptation of interspecies vivisection and genetic malformation in an extra-legal environment, surrounded by a spectacular ocean.

In *Cinema 1: The Movement-Image* (1983), Gilles Deleuze specifically refers to naturalist cinema and how narrative sequencing of time is "subordinate to naturalistic co-ordinates," in which time "unravels in derived milieux"; consequently, time "confers upon it [the originary world] the role of a destiny which cannot be expiated."[13] Whether in the jungle, prison, brothel, slaughterhouse, mining camp, or dining room, these familiar settings are foregrounded, recurring catalytic spaces: affective co-ordinates. Destiny and classic notions of fate are reconfigured as experimental sites of naturalist narrative discourse engaging foregrounded genetic activity in the visible field of heredity. In multiple international naturalist film narratives, these sites and settings function as agencies to facilitate the revelation—frequently, the exposure—of impulsive expressions, genetically based and inherited moments of deleterious human behavior, ranging across genre and movements, from the comedic to the bestial, in traditional and popular culture platforms. As noted by Dijck, "Genetic thinking has apparently dethroned social determinism as a dominant social force, and has percolated into all aspects of society and culture,"[14] for which he posits a direct relationship with narrative:

> The power of narrative is that it serves as a code of cognition without it being itself recognizable as an interpretive framework ... Every story on genetics ... displays essential ingredients of narrative ... the gene, finally, is most commonly explicated through models and metaphors ... popular representations of genetics are articulated through the *characters of geneticists*, the *plots of genetics*, and the *metaphors of genes*.[15]

In Tom Shadyac's *The Nutty Professor* (1996), the seriously obese Professor Klump (Eddie Murphy), an experimental geneticist, must cope with family stress, academic politics, renewed funding concerns, and an alluring female colleague. Murphy plays multiple roles, depicting one African-American family in the Rabelaisian-inflected dinner table sequence. Shadyac's fluid close-up and medium shots reveal the eccentricities and comically grotesque moments of a family dinner at home, complete with a series of gaseous exchanges and threats. David Kirby notes that Shadyac's *The Nutty Professor* raises complex issues associated with genetic technology, clinical cultures and religion:

> The genetic changes in *The Nutty Professor* (1996) straddle the line between treatment of a genetic disorder and genetic enhancement. In the film, the hyper-obese Klump alters his genome and in the process becomes the slender 'Buddy love.' In keeping with the anti-eugenic themes of past science fiction films, *The Nutty Professor* implies that any change to the human genome is an intrusion into God's realm. Rather than producing a better version of himself, Klump's genetic manipulation unleashes the testosterone-overloaded Buddy love, reminiscent of an earlier Mr. Hyde in his behavior.[16]

Alexandre Aja's study of violent, disposable humanity, *The Hills Have Eyes* (2006), a remake of Wes Craven's eponymous film (1977), is a satirical horror film that engages the American myth systems associated with the nuclear family. It is also a film narrative depicting defective genetics in the family of isolated desert mutants-as-monsters, and the effects of the American post-nuclear age—the recent past as experienced in the present—on an allegedly normal family. *The Hills Have Eyes* examines issues involving alienated, surplus workers, and particularly a guignolish mixture of horrific-playful acts of consumption, in which one family struggles to survive while lost and the other family struggles to survive being found, in an intergeneric narrative about the loss of civilization and identity, and reversion into primitivism and cannibalism, all enacted under a broiling sun in a perilous, forgotten Nevada landscape. In Aja's *The Hills Have Eyes*, James Rose concludes that violence is a compelling spectacle signifying both literal and symbolic acts:

> In both Craven's film and Alexandre Aja's remake ... repressed rage is poked, cajoled, and pushed until it is released through an act of stark and primitive violence ... As the violence escalates the bourgeois family reverts back to a primitive state and commits violent acts in retribution for the equally primitive and violent acts perpetrated against them. Throughout the narrative both groups are paralleled and then finally become interchangeable through their violence. Progress, technology and modern civility are suddenly undermined and then made redundant as they are perverted by primal response.[17]

Aja's film may be read in a hypertextual capacity as exhibiting the inherited information of Craven's formative film, yet Aja's film is not a duplicate of Craven's production. Aja's *The Hills Have Eyes* remake is a renewal of intertextually based source narratives, displaying an information load of familiar naturalist tropes, spectacle-driven plot points, and generic formulations. Aja's remake of the Craven original may be considered conceptually as an activated issue of a genetic line and a replenishment exhibiting and recalling familiar traits and related data, but unique as its own film narrative. In a protracted series of visual juxtapositions between two families competing against each other in order to survive, Aja presents abandoned desert mutants—surplus humanity—and the Carter family, full of children and presided over by a gun-toting patriarch, "Big Bob" (Ted Levine). The entrapped Carter family unknowingly serves a culinary purpose, as they are constantly watched by a family of unseen others: freakish leftovers, disposable workers from the 1950s era of atomic experimentation sites in the American southwest, who have succumbed to cannibalistic practices in order to survive. The abandoned town where the mutants live is a functioning abattoir, a significant naturalist trope, which exhibits fragments of the recent past—wrecked automobiles, abandoned homes, and other relics—that recall the bountiful postwar era but now decorate the fractured landscape with its angry, hungry surviving mutants.

In *The Hills Have Eyes*, the past will consume the present, barbeque style. In several horrific-humorous shot sequences, Aja reveals in medium and close-up how the malformed live as isolated cannibals. One of the mutants watches the television and sings along to the "Star Spangled Banner"; another mutant watches reruns of the popular American television series *Divorce Court*, while others go about working their daily chores, which includes transforming fresh bodies into mangled meals. One of the cannibalistic workers exclaims: "your people destroyed our homes ... We went into the mines ... You made us what we became." *The Hills Have Eyes* is a study of the walking wounded, discarded workers and their families. The tainted family line, with expressively cruel animalistic behavior, is a naturalist film narrative staple.

Imperfect Beings

In his analysis of the horror film, Bruce Kawin notes, "some realities are impossible to show completely or in their full, transcendent horror. There must be room for transcendent suggestion, for the shot whose implications go beyond what it can put on the screen."[18] Kawin concludes:

> The screen can be a window ... It is a look at the frightening, put in a frame ... Within the frame of fiction, the horror film's images and events touch on the genuine fear and revulsion that may be inspired by our imagination, by our apprehension, by the expectations we hold of the genre and its recurring visual and narrative traditions and by our knowledge of what can happen in reality.[19]

Director J. V. Durden's *Heredity and Man* (1937),[20] a short film narrated by evolutionary biologist-eugenicist Julian Huxley on behalf of the Eugenics Society, is an intergeneric political-horror blending presented as an educational documentary that outspreads its purportedly edifying scientific messaging involving the individual, family, medical, psychological, and related socio-historical consequences. The racial, class-based misapplication of scientific principles linked to genetics, heredity, and society is viewed through a clinically compromised, obfuscated perspective, communicated via encoded images.

Like Dr. Jekyll (Fredric March) addressing frame-filling rows of medical students from a high-angle lectern in Rouben Mamoulian's *Dr. Jekyll and Mr. Hyde* (1931), in *Heredity and Man*, Julian Huxley's patriarchal presence on screen and authoritative voice-over creates a controlling social Darwinist narrative, establishing a tone of falsely progressive discourse. Huxley exemplifies the "great man" at work as he discusses the conceptual and historical realities of eugenics. The informative tone of the entire documentary reeks of a racially based sense of privilege, a "them and us" style of establishing the factual. *Heredity and Man* conflates color-coded graphics, first-person testimony, incomprehensible charts, and most significantly, a display of visually charged contrasting social contradictions separating the healthy and the ill, the privileged, and the undesirable. *Heredity and Man* exploits the notions of natural selection, survival of the fittest, and purification of the species, and falsely illustrates Darwinian evolutionary theory and Mendelian genetic concepts. In "Darwinism and Social Darwinism," James Allen Rogers notes, "the central problem in the relation of Darwin to what was later called Social Darwinism lies in the highly metaphorical concepts in which Darwin expressed the theoretical aspects of natural selection."[21] Huxley's problematic film couches its misinterpretations of human "pedigree" and a class-based, pseudo-scientific application of eugenics as a measure of progress, confirming eugenicist Lothrop Stoddard's terrifying notion, "scientific realism is racial reality."[22]

The pro-eugenics melodrama-horror-documentary intergeneric blending of disturbing images and fascistic ideology, *The Black Stork* (1917), co-directed by Leopold and Theodore Wharton, retitled, slightly revised, and re-released as *Are You Fit to Marry?*,[23] is a polemic in support of eugenics that rivals Nazi imagery and racist film narratives. In the opening shot sequence of *Are You Fit to Marry?*, a family of obvious class privilege sits in front of a palatial home, invoking images of domestic bliss recalling Lumière's *Feeding the Baby*. Martin Pernick concludes:

> *The Black Stork*, like many early health-education movies, was a feature-length melodrama. And like most health films, it attempted not simply to educate the public about medical facts, but to persuade people to change their personal lives and behavior . . . [using] shock, fear, and revulsion as central persuasive techniques.[24]

The film, critiqued for its unpleasant subject matter and "aesthetic concerns,"[25] launches into a frame narrative, as an older man relates a tale of infamy to his naïve potential son-in-law about a doomed marriage and its consequences. As the topic of marriage is introduced in their conversation, a hesitant father takes Claude (Hamilton Revelle), his prospective son-in-law, to two sites: an animal breeding farm and a hospital-asylum. These are naturalist environments in which tropes associated with reproduction, slaughter, illness, and crime are set in impactful space and time as an observational process. At the breeding farm, in one superimposition image, the head of a bull is juxtaposed with the head of a virile man within the shot to concretely indicate healthy breeding.

Once the visit to the breeding farm is complete, the duo arrives at a hospital-asylum, where screen titles such as "mentally warped" and "tour of hell" create a clinical editorial presence to complement horrific images of human suffering. It is suggested that the parade of sick, physically deformed inmates, frequently shot in close-up, are undesirable social and economic drains on society since they survived beyond the initial discovery of their affliction; this is the eugenic message of the film, a message common to Nazi hygiene and race films. *Are You Fit to Marry?* exhibits direct, immediate parallels with several Nazi film productions, including Herbert Gerdes' *Erbkrank/Hereditary Disease* (1936) and *Alles Leben ist Kampf/All Life is Struggle* (1937). Martin Pernick considers that, "[These] films feature stark visual contrasts between loathsome, expensive defectives and poor but healthy working people."[26] The Nazi party produced film *Erbkrank* was especially loathsome in its manipulative, close-up depiction of the mentally and physically afflicted, creating for its audience a series of emotionally charged images noted for their vicious, antisemitic, racialized tropes of discord. According to Pernick, *Erbkrank* did "feature crude photography of repulsive-looking institutionalized handicapped and mentally ill patients. *Erbkrank*'s silent intertitles provide these cases with individual price tags for their annual care. The film sought to foster disgust, resentment, and hatred."[27] Another fascistic narrative, *Geisteskrank/Mentally Ill* (1939), produced at the start of the war, urged the "merciful" killing of the chronically afflicted, both mentally and physically, and arguably parallels the message of *Are You Fit to Marry?*.

In contrast to these fascistic narratives, *Feind im Blut/Enemy in the Blood* (1931),[28] Walter Ruttmann's experimental film about syphilis, is an intergeneric blend of horror, avant-gardism, and the documentary. The film begins with familiar naturalist imagery as children, flowers, and fruit seemingly dissolve and rot away in Courbet-like images of decay. Animals are later seen in cages awaiting sanctioned experimentation, foreshadowing similar images of helpless, entrapped animals in John Frankenheimer's *The Island of Dr. Moreau* (1996). In a medium shot, Ruttmann later cuts to several sick children in bed as seen through the prison-like bars behind their metal bedframe, as both animal and humans are clinically disposed subjects. In case studies of afflicted adults and children, Ruttmann reveals the plight of still living victims in chilling close-up shots, which reach an inevitable conclusion in a series of death masks. One narrative thread concerns the passing of syphilis from a factory worker, whose arm is clearly marked with signs indicating the disease, to his wife, whose disastrous pregnancy delivers an afflicted baby and ends with her suicide. Close-up and medium shots detailing both labor and laborers inside the factory are assembled as associative images, an abstract montage leading to the revelation exposing the "spotted arm" of the afflicted worker. As a doctor later blames "alcohol and prostitutes" for the presence of venereal disease in proper society, Ruttmann's shots of prostitutes standing on the sidewalk and bars full of lonely men serve as familiar urban markers and recall Ernst Kirchner's *Strasse, Berlin/Street, Berlin* (1913) and *Strasse mit rote Kokotte/ Street with Red Streetwalker* (1914), which depict the presence of sex workers seeking employment. Unlike William Dieterle's bio-pic, *Dr. Erlich's Magic Bullet* (1940), in which the "great man" labors to conduct research and make his eventual scientific discovery, Ruttmann's *Feind im Blut* avoids the mythic recycling of reassuring patriarchal imagery and instead engages the pervasive expressionistic stylization of fluid experimentalism.

In the United States, expressions of populist ideology complement the eugenic sentiments; eugenicist Edwin Conklin states that the social and legal implications for modern society are fatalistically evident:

> We may confidently expect that in a very short time the marriage of the feeble-minded, hopelessly insane or epileptic, the congenitally blind, deaf and dumb, and those suffering from many other inherited defects which unfit them for useful citizenship will be prohibited by law in all the States.[29]

Conklin, a Princeton University professor, concludes, "If only the very worst are eliminated in each generation, the standard of a race is merely maintained, but the more severe the elimination is the more does it become a directing factor in evolution."[30] *The Black Stork/Are You Fit to Marry?* is a class and racially based admonition, an anachronistic jeremiad to be retrospectively critiqued as a kind of politicized horror film narrative.

As a political-horror film with its monsters in medical garb, *The Black Stork/Are You Fit to Marry?* demonstrates how the naturalist film narrative generates a transgressive space and time to record and render an asymmetrical realism that begins in logical states, devolving into moments of ideologically based shudders. Non-supernatural horror reveals human cruelty, violence, vivisection, alcoholism, sexual assault, intolerance, child abuse, and experientially based forms of destabilized existence involving gender, class, and racial maltreatment in society. As noted by Steven Jay Schneider,

> For a genre so traditionally fantastic in its iconography, hyberbolic in its display of violence, and conventional in its plot structures and character types, the horror film may seem like a pretty poor place to search for 'realism,' however this term is defined.

He later concludes, "The notion of 'realism' is a useful and important one for horror film studies in ways that go well beyond a discussion of the biology and psychology of specific monsters."[31] Whether involving generic industrial models such as horror, bio-pics, and adaptation, the naturalist-experimental narrative observes the darker, ugly, and complicated aesthetic of the real/almost real.

The ill-fated marriage of perennially despondent Claude, potentially carrying the "blood taint of an indiscreet ancestor," interpreted by the audience as the effects of congenital syphilis, could infect his wife and parallels, as a foreshadowing narrative, the framing story of genetic malfunction. Claude is even seen with a copy of Henrik Ibsen's *Ghosts*, a naturalist marker. Pernick notes that "[*Ghosts*] Ibsen's stage drama, depicting a victim of congenital syphilis, had been introduced to movie audiences [George Nichol's adaptation] only a year earlier. The reference both establishes Claude as a man terrified of his diseased ancestry and lays claim to serious cultural value for the film itself.[32] In a dream flashback sequence, Claude envisions the historical source of his illness, a depraved ancestor, a lordly figure sexually assaulting a seductive maid. The messaging is evident, as class mixing breeds disease:

> The ghost is identified as Claude's grandfather. Allowing an ample thirty years per generation would make him a figure from 1856. Yet he appears in powdered wig and brocade greatcoat and conducts his seduction in a canopied four-poster, more a character from a Hogarth print of the 1750s than a man of the mid-nineteenth century ... They also draw on a newer association between colonial days and contaminated heredity established by the highly publicized colonial-era pedigrees of such families as the 'Jukes' and 'Kallikaks.'[33]

Are You Fit to Marry? features a complex variation on the disabled yet horrific human monster referred to in the film as "the defective" offspring. If Shakespeare's prematurely born King Richard the Third, "rudely stamp'd ... cheated of feature by dissembling nature, deformed unfinish'd ... so lamely and unfashionable that dogs bark at me," relocated to an early twentieth-century American upper-class family, his fate, like the defective's, would have been no less incredible and effectively vile as both are "determined to prove a villain" owing to frustration and blatant scorn. As if emerging from a Kallikak genetic chartography, the defective man (Henry Bergman), with crippled arm and pronounced hunchback, is a product of Claude and Ann's unsound marital coupling. The defective learns to hate after years of failing as a social outcast among the repulsed privileged. The defective is a botched, losing gamble. As he matures, the figure of a modern ostracized Quasimodo-like male, the nameless defective, experiences several humiliating experiences. He is ignored and embarrassed at a formal party that his mother designs, recalling the celebratory Walpurgisnacht sequence in István Szabó's *Mephisto* (1981), in which upper-class party goers mingle with uniformed party officials while political-medical undesirables magically disappear into death camps. The deformed male tries to enlist into the army only to be told that "Uncle Sam demands perfection," again being defined and denied by his disability while noting that others shun him as they gaze at this ambulatory, ghastly outcast.

Pernick cites relevant details about Bergman's performance in a naturalist context: "actor Henry Bergman as 'the defective' and 'the monster,' the outcast crippled, adult cast apart from class and culture since he is consequently not medically disposed of at birth,"[34] is in many regards the sole sympathetic performance in the film. Dr. Dickey, the "gallant" practitioner who concludes it is better to dispose of the sick child right after birth—"God does not want that child to live"—is ironically depicted as a progressive thinker amid elder male medical figures, the established clan. As the adult version of the sickly child, Henry Bergman's performance is a naturalist spectacle during a clinically obtuse, sterile narrative:

> Henry Bergman ... played Claude and Ann's adult son, depicted the 'defective' as a tragic, even noble figure. Laboriously and meticulously dressing his bent body for a formal party, or vainly struggling to mimic a poster of a football hero in action, even shyly flirting with a derelict woman on a park bench, Bergman made his character appealingly human despite the titles that consigned him to an 'abyss of abnormality' filled with 'criminal desires.'[35]

Like Lon Chaney's vilified and enraged Blizzard in Wallace Worsley's *The Penalty* (1920), the defective descends into a life of crime and concludes that his parents, and especially the learned men who saved him from merciful Dr. Dickey's plan for his demise, are to blame for his misfortune. He attacks them and is sent off to jail. Once freed on parole, living like Joe Brown in his narrative of syphilitic displacement, the defective meets a fellow abandoned character, a woman, and they proceed to breed generations of equally defective children: Kallikaks in the making.[36] The narrative then cuts back to the earlier Dr. Dickey sequence with the infant; the "defective's tale" was imagined and the child, at the mother's behest, is allowed to die, and is promptly taken into the curative hands of the superimposed image of an adoring Jesus. Eugenics works in heavenly ways. In a moment of additional narrative incredulity, *Are You Fit to Marry?* cuts back to the frame story of the father and prospective son-in-law, still intending to marry the potentially defective bride-to-be. It was a case of mistaken eugenic terror; the girl was adopted and not genetically impure or damaged. In these films, everybody, except the physically or mentally ill, was fit to marry. Other provocative films like *The Black Stork/Are You Fit to Marry?* are linked to problematic permutations of the conceivable biological malfunction.

Growing Up

According to Cesare Lombroso, "The born female criminal is, so to speak, doubly exceptional, as a woman and as a criminal. For criminals are an exception among civilized people, and women are an exception among criminals . . . the criminal woman is consequently a monster."[37] The majority of contemporary serial killer narratives, in both fiction and film, are dominated by the presence of the male subject. William March's unique contribution to Naturalism, *The Bad Seed* (1954), is a novel about Rhoda Penmark, a charming, pig-tailed child serial killer. March's novel has extensive roots in naturalist ideology, with familiar images of entrapment, much like a genetic code.[38] June Howard has commented on "[Naturalism's] scientific fascination with the gene, its obsession with the predator" and later concludes that "an appeal to domestic ideology is incorporated in a number of naturalistic novels . . . and as so often in naturalism, the ultimate terror is the loss of stable personal identity, the collapse of self into Other."[39] This informs the naturalist taxonomy of *The Bad Seed*, the violent, predatory child and the bourgeois family in crisis. Mervyn LeRoy's adaptation of the March novel *The Bad Seed* (1956), released the same year as Nicholas Ray's *Bigger Than Life*, is similarly a generic blending of naturalist horror and melodrama infused with the spectacle of explosive violence.

The Bad Seed establishes its naturalist intertextuality as it recalls the complex and scientifically plausible yet imaginary theories associated with genetics as well as addressing immediate social and historical living conditions of the 1950s in American suburbia. It details incredible ruptures in a middle-class American family. Pre-pubescent Rhoda (Patty McCormack) violently murders her way through suburbia, attacking those who interrupt or challenge her need for social approbation and desire for rewards in the form of medals, jewelry, and near-continuous recognition. She has inherited the lethal "bad seed" from her infamous serial-killer grandmother, yet Rhoda's family, except for her grandfather, remains unaware of her identity, as Rhoda's mother was adopted and the secret kept from her to protect her in the future.

LeRoy's adaptation "renders a complex reading of socio-biological interrelations, as it displays atavistic action set within the postwar American, suburban milieu."[40] As Rhoda is detected in her role-playing by other children, her family, and especially by Leroy (Henry Jones), the sleazy, cellar-dwelling handyman, while she lies and cheats her way to achieve approval and rewards, she contrives violent forms of revenge, like a trapped animal would spring forward at the right moment. Rhoda beats a little boy to death with her shoe and starts a fire that fatally burns Leroy. These are just two of her victims; nobody is safe.

In one shot sequence, as Rhoda's mother looks directly into her child's eyes to finally see the monster behind the mask, Rhoda playfully smiles and performs as "the good girl" as her mother gasps in recognition. In Mervyn LeRoy's *The Bad Seed*, the home is like a petting zoo in which one of the cuter animals goes berserk.

BEYOND REALISM

Figure 6.1 Mervyn LeRoy's *The Bad Seed* (1956)

Frequently, genetic activity is manifest in deleterious social settings in which the environment functions as a catalytic parameter. Basil Dearden's *The Violent Playground* (1958), filmed on location in Liverpool, realistically documents the space and time of local tenements and their discontents, as it contrasts the streets and working-class lives of the adults and next generation surviving in cemented areas. In *The Violent Playground*, the very young play on public sites, but their school becomes an occupied place of violent hostage taking as one teenager, Johnny (David MacCallum), tries to escape from the police after a botched arson and manslaughter incident while failing to ignite an explosive flame in an act of perceived revenge, a gesture of class-slighting. In an all too familiar, grimly real series of events, Johnny, armed with an automatic weapon, entraps and sequesters himself and a room full of anxious children while overwhelmed parents and the authorities wait for the children's rescue or release. After some troubling events, the crisis is resolved and Johnny is led away by the police in a van rather than in an ambulance.

Paul Elliott considers that, "films like ... *Violent Playground* ... present a plurality of causes that, commensurate with their position as social problem films, were designed to engender debate rather than offer explanations."[41] Johnny is neither an anti-hero nor significantly sympathetic; according to

Alan Burton and Tim O'Sullivan, "Johnny remains the troubling figure; apparently, the film seems to suggest, propelled by psychopathology, inured to the interventions of church or education."[42] A viable comparison with Johnny would be Vic Morrow's portrayal of the vicious, unredeemed teenage hoodlum, Artie West, in Richard Brook's *The Blackboard Jungle* (1955). Dearden's crime–juvenile delinquent narrative more accurately focuses on the victimized school children, as "the film's conclusion is as much concerned with Mary and Patrick (Johnny's siblings) as with Johnny himself."[43] *Violent Playground* is a more open-ended narrative suggesting progressive potentialities.

The visually claustrophobic urban housing project is also a business site, confining as a genetic code, and functions as the setting of Matty Rich's *Straight Out of Brooklyn* (1991). Rich's film reveals the site as one in which the struggle to survive depends on the cleverness of enterprising thieves to elude armed drug dealers: stronger viruses. Poverty, racism, alcoholism, as well as forms of institutionalized neglect collectively serve as catalysts that destroy an African-American family. The robbery of local drug dealers, an upsetting of the corrupted social order of the streets, is a futile gesture by one young man, Dennis Brown (Lawrence Gilliard, Jr.), to alleviate his family's poverty and the pervasive sense of entrapment in a small apartment. One especially effective opening shot sequence places the camera below the window of the apartment in which the screaming and fighting can be heard, leading the camera to tilt upwards, inside to the calamitous series of sequences. Ironically, while their new-found capital, stolen from dangerous local dealers, enables the trio of thieves to leave the area, they remain in the same projects as perpetual targets, since nobody calculated where to go for escape. An expansive variation of *Straight Out of Brooklyn* is evident in the five seasons and sixty episodes of HBO's *The Wire* (2002–8), set primarily in the racially segregated area of the drug-addled city of Baltimore. *The Wire* may be read as a case study of intersecting naturalist negative tropes involving disenfranchised youth, gun-related violence, political corruption, racial divisiveness, chronic unemployment, and especially, the business of illicit drugs.

Salvatore Stabile's *Gravesend* (1997) is set within a volatile Brooklyn neighborhood. Behaving like the young violent males in Edward Bond's drama, *Saved* (1965), in Stabile's *Gravesend*, the near-narcotic allure of handguns rather than cavemen-like rock hurling demonstrates considerable racial and gender rigidity and codes of violence endemic to the White, male working class, as engrained codes of behavior inform social and personal life:

> Disenfranchised white youth in search of an evening's thrill drive about aimlessly and waste time and their lives as a form of escapist fun. [Stabile's] film reveals how these young men are consumed by boredom, guns, and literally, by themselves. These are the sons and nephews of

the alienated, dancing boys of the previous generation's *Saturday Night Fever* (1977). These locals could go anywhere but have nowhere to go. They do not even know what they want, only that they want it. For them, all roads lead back to the white ghetto and its determinist rigidities.[44]

In Lee Daniels' *Precious* (2009), teenage mother Precious (Gabourey Sidibe) lives in the same city and era as Chantel Mitchell (Ariyan A. Johnson), an intelligent African-American high school student, who makes first-person contact with the audience throughout Leslie Harris' *Just Another Girl on the I.R.T.* (1993). Unlike Precious, in *Just Another Girl on the I.R.T.*, Chantel is egocentric and aggressive, and her dreams of a career and escape from life as a "project girl" are illusory, as she is unhappily pregnant. The birth of Chantel's child occurs in her boyfriend's apartment, without adult assistance or medicine. This harrowing sequence is composed of alternating wide shots of Chantel writhing on the bed, in agony from her unmedicated premature labor, and close-ups of her horrified boyfriend's face as she gives birth. She refuses to acknowledge or look at the child, aware that the life she had imagined for herself is over unless the problem disappears.

In John Edgar Wideman's "Newborn Thrown in Trash and Dies" (1992), a blistering short story based on a real incident of urban infanticide, the reader is informed from an infant's point of view, "My mother is nineteen years old. The trash chute down which I dropped is forty-five feet from the door of the apartment my mother was visiting ... 911 is the number to call if you find a baby in the trash."[45] Like the fictional *Precious* and *Just Another Girl on the I.R.T.*, Wideman's short story merits classification as naturalist horror narrative of violent abuse. Whereas Precious arranges for her child "Mongo" to spend time with her grandmother as well as at home in the darkly lit room, Chantel compels her boyfriend to take away and then abandon the child. He reluctantly obeys her. The shot cuts back to the opening sequence of a bag clearly containing the baby, disposed of in a garbage can. Although Chantel's abandonment of her child is resolved via reluctant reconciliation, Chantel's carefree life is now markedly different; she is just another girl riding the train. This is not the case with Precious as she later develops AIDS, a penultimate biological mishap. Julie Phillips notes that "Harris makes Chantel not maligned and sympathetic, but abrasive and ungrateful."[46] Chantel's pleasures, aside from the sexual, are overwhelmingly material in nature and invoke the escapist consumer culture of the media-saturated young urban female of the era: cars, clothes, jewelry, and parties.

The escape trope also features prominently at the conclusion of Spike Lee's *Clockers* (1995), as "Strike" (Mekhi Phifer), a sickly, young African-American male drug dealer ostensibly lost in a dangerous Brooklyn housing project, enters "middle management" but is eventually labeled as a "snitch," thus forcing him to flee from the only life he has known into the unknown boundaries of Manhattan and beyond:

> The symptomatic social order closing in on the individual in crisis has strong parallels with the politicized space of the hood in Spike Lee's *Clockers* ... in which Ronald, 'Strike,' narrowly escapes from the Gowanus Housing Projects with his life ... Lee's film suggests that the individual, however stymied and classified by race and class, has the ability to confront the politicized fate of life in the projects.[47]

As African Americans, Strike, Precious, and Chantel experience the limitations of a class and seemingly enclosed racial social circulus. Diana Guzman, the Hispanic high school student/boxer in Karyn Kusama's *Girlfight* (2000), lives in Brooklyn in another housing project. "Diana is a project girl ... her personal conflict [is set within] a class and gender bound social milieu that discredits the aggressive female."[48] Her fists and "street-smarts" provide her means to dream of escape; Diana (Michelle Rodriguez) "lives in the projects but thrives in the ring. Her rise as an amateur featherweight is convincing and not romanticized."[49] For Diana, as for Maggie (Hilary Swank), the over-thirty-year-old waitress-turned-boxer in Clint Eastwood's *Million Dollar Baby* (2005), the only way out of class and gender-based entrapment is to achieve the unlikely: she must box in the ring or go home. In Maggie's case, she would return not to the projects but to her working-class environment for a programmed, unhappy life. Both films paraphrase familiar Darwinian-naturalist precepts as each woman struggles to survive amid despair, in this case fueled by male expectations of normative female behavior.

Whereas Kusama's film ends well for her fighter—Diana wins a boxing title and may even achieve romantic love, thus confirming that not all naturalist narrative ends "badly" for its principal characters—Eastwood's film grinds down Maggie, a formerly successful boxer, to a disabled nub of her former self as she is cheated in the ring and horribly hurt by her adversary. Read as a naturalist narrative, *Million Dollar Baby* denotes the "plot of decline ... a powerful ordering force."[50] While in a physically degenerative state, Maggie is mercifully released from her suffering by her trainer/father figure (Clint Eastwood), as she chooses quality of life over its duration. With training and personal commitment, both Diana and Maggie learned how to transcend impediments by pummeling adversaries in the ring, yet with differing results.

Family Portraits

In Darwin's *The Origin of Species* (1859), he comments upon the binary nature of parasite–host relations and the perils involving both organisms' survival:

> The dependency of one organic being on another, as of a parasite on its prey, lies generally between beings remote in the scale of nature. This is often the case with those which may strictly be said to struggle with each other for existence, as in the case of locusts and grass-feeding quadrupeds. But the struggle almost invariably will be most severe between the individuals of the same species, for they frequent the same districts, require the same food, and are exposed to the same dangers.[51]

Naturalist film narrative is regularly a study of abnormal psychology set within the once-familiar structure of a home, suggesting a pathological human presence, and the generic blending includes familiar industrial forms such as melodrama, comedy, science fiction, and horror. The "haunting" is always human. In naturalist cinema, behavior is the product of activated impulses and inherited genetic, affective manifestations, localized with the environment and broader socio-historical milieu. In Paul de Kruif's *Microbe Hunters* (1926), he quotes the observation made by the scientist Dr. Gernez while peering into a microscope, expressed to Dr. Pasteur, while both were conducting laboratory research: "'It is solved,' he cried, 'the little globules are alive—they are *parasites!*—They are what make the worms sick!'"[52] Bong Joon-Ho's *Parasite* metaphorically deploys the critical gaze of the microscope in its observation of interacting, competing forms of life, from parasites to people. The South Korean film *Gisaengchung/Parasite* (2019) presents the rise-and-fall narrative of the Kim family, from slightly crooked fringe people—precariat labor—to nearly successful social poseurs, while juxtaposing the lives of two other families who temporarily coexist under the same roof in a parasitic state of relations: one conspicuously wealthy, and the other *lumpen*, poor working class.

In *Human, All Too Human* (1878), Friedrich Nietzsche's aphorism #356 describes the parasite as a person indicating "a complete lack of nobility of disposition when someone prefers to live in dependency, at the expense of others, merely so as not to have to work and usually with a secret animosity toward those he is dependent on."[53] Bong Joon-Ho's film is a study in class conflict and contrasting dependencies, "animosities," set in a house divided three ways. *Parasite* reveals triangulated parasitical relations in which the "host" is an unclarified, varying image of shifting power relations: everybody seems to exploit and is exploited. As the Park family, wealthy home owners who waste time and capital, are humorously deceived by the plotting Kim family, their beautiful home is the primary setting for a dynamic intersection among the caste-like divisions in a society which deems that one can smell class. In the case of the Kim clan, a working-class family of small-time crooks, as well as for the wealthy Park family, their respective genetic lines demonstrate a capacity for deception and cruel behavior. Whether deploying walkie-talkies, cell phones, computers, or surveillance technology, nobody sees anybody, especially the "ghost" in the basement. The Park's home setting is full of delusion and dependencies.

In *The Poetics of Space* (1957), Bachelard notes that the house is the site where personal experience bears expressions of subjective essence, becoming an intimate site of memory; in the case of *Parasite*, the memories are exposed as a series of concealments and duplicitous acts. *Parasite* features two contrasting sets of déclassé workers living in undesirable subterranean spaces. In a standard trope of the horror genre, the descent into the basement—a sequestered and subjectively pre-psychological, dark uninhabited setting—leads to consequences and a series of exposures, both humorous and horrific. Other films featuring foreboding yet darkly comedic basement settings and improbable "monsters" include a bewigged corpse, a failed comedian-kidnapper, a "gimp," and an inconceivable surgical re-assemblage: Alfred Hitchcock's *Psycho* (1960), Martin Scorsese's *The King of Comedy* (1982), Quentin Tarantino's *Pulp Fiction* (1994), and Tom Six's *The Human Centipede: First Sequence* (2009). These films share with Bong Joon-Ho's *Parasite* a revelatory emergence as the basement door opens and divulges its secrets. *Parasite* is thematically like the assemblage of inspired, scheming oddities in Woody Allen's *Small Time Crooks* (2000), in which conspirators and ex-cons, led by Ray Winkler (Woody Allen), build a tunnel from a restaurant's basement into the bank next door in order to rob it, but fail. In *Small Time Crooks*, the restaurant, transformed into a trendy cookie bakery popular with consumers in the 1990s, becomes a money-making franchise operation. Allen's film combines the heist narrative with a comedy of class-bound misfits whose work is crime. *Parasite* similarly casts divergent personalities as it blends familiar generic tropes. Allen's reading of the socially parasitical extends to the tasteful art dealer who leads Winkler's baker-wife away from the immediate social circle with the lure of class and experience, while cleverly using her for her new-found wealth, which is ironically stolen by crooked accountants who defraud them.

In *Small Time Crooks* and *Parasite*, exploitative practices are not reserved for any class or individual. *Parasite* advances the naturalist relationship between two film genres: comedy and horror. Bong Joon-Ho's allegorical reading of human disposability, parasitical relations, and alienated work is a narrative of socio-biological, interacting, frequently comedic malfunctions. Amy Taubin notes that *Parasite*

> seems to be a broad comedy in which the concept of the underclass is visualized as slapstick. That style will continue to the very end, but while gradually mixing with darker genre elements, and climaxing in a children's party that turns into a Grand Guignol massacre. This combination of comedy and horror is a genre film staple.[54]

Taubin's reference to the Guignol theatrical traditions of anti-supernaturalism and human grotesqueries is essential to *Parasite*, and links the film to the absurd presence of festering violence and undetermined identities, such as those in Harold Pinter's drama *The Birthday Party* (1957), which provides a contrasting claustrophobic setting for its wordplay of comedic deceptions, and a later celebration. A house is a requisite site, full of floors, rooms, and secrets, and those who live covertly below the surface assume a disguise, a latent presence, like genetic patterns slowly emerging in the body and evident in future generations.

Like the encroaching stink bugs that overrun the Kim's neighborhood, the Park home is invaded by various parasitic human agencies. However, the issue of host–parasite identification is complex and seemingly interchangeable; Taubin concludes, "who is the parasite depends on one's point of view."[55] Bong Joon-Ho's narrative deftly shifts this biological-metaphorical focus—the mutuality—among three competing families. Below-the-surface dwellings mask but also reveal presence; In *Parasite*, the former housekeeper's derelict husband, representing the poorest family, has been hiding for years from loan sharks while he lives in the wealthy Park family's former fall-out shelter, undetected in the sub-basement catacombs—a nearly interred Poe-like figure—like a brooding monster in the cellar. This squalid sub-existence is endemic to the criminal class across cultures. Describing the habitation of criminals in New York City tenements in 1908, Theodore A. Bingham links the observational with the biological in inflammatory terminology:

> The low-ceiled rooms of the squalid buildings in Doyers, Pell and Mott streets, and facing on the Bowery, many of them opening only into inside courts, are divided and subdivided into closetlike [sic] spaces that are rented for living and sleeping purposes, and in them are housed the very lees of humanity, black, yellow and white—Chinamen, honest and dishonest, but all the others—thieves, thugs and prostitutes, with their parasites.[56]

In *Parasite*, the housekeeper's husband is the traumatizing, violent, and alternatively comedic catalytic monster in the forgotten crypt. In Jack Arnold's science fiction narrative about molecular restructuring and the disappearing male body, *The Incredible Shrinking Man* (1957), the home, especially the basement, becomes the site of estrangement, decline, and unbecoming, a place where things are lost. As a result of a nuclear mishap, a middle-class shrinking man loses his job, wife, social identity, and fights or evades dangerous reminders of the natural world, a massive spider, floods, and obsessive hunger, as he vanishes from sight, a precocious essence in the basement, in contrast with the housekeeper's ghostly, pathetic husband. At some point, the basement exposes its secrets.

The former housekeeper, who lives above ground and maintains the diet and survival of her sequestered husband, is also the keeper of secrets involving the Park family and the house itself. In the climactic party sequence, her husband, the beast, escapes from his chthonic exile, and now finally visible, assaults several people, killing the Kims' cruel daughter only to be slain himself; ironically, one beast will replace another: Mr. Kim, now a wanted criminal, assumes the former monster's place and becomes the newly undetected basement dweller, as if replacing the original. The nineteenth-century physiognomist-moralist Max Nordau described the presence and nature of undesirable specimens like the housekeeper's husband in modern society as "another unhealthy variation from the normal human type—who can only live by the work of others, and who, to appease all their lusts, unscrupulously overpower every human being who crosses their path."[57] Nordau's condemnation of these social "parasites"[58] is both inflammatory and histrionic:

> Like bats in old towers, they are niched in the proud monument of civilization, which they have found ready-made, but they themselves can construct nothing more, nor prevent any deterioration. They live, like parasites, on labour which past generations have accumulated for them; and when the heritage is once consumed, they are condemned to die of hunger.[59]

The Kim family is depicted as a struggling, corrupt working-class family of misfits who adapt to the Park's near-limitless alcohol and class prerogative. Prior to advancement, subsisting like social parasites while living in an out-of-the-way neighborhood in the economic miracle of modern Seoul, the Kim family role-play but are regressive social outcasts; they exist but do not contribute, so they take, and then take more. The criminal-parvenu Kim family lives conditionally, alternating between the Park estate and their flooded, unattractively cramped apartment. Through a series of well-conceived lies, the Kim family role-play, performing as professionals in order to gain employment, and wriggling their way into the lives and the home of the Park family.

One essential aspect of the Kim family's working-class lives and identity involves their odor: the *hoi polloi* Kim family smell different than the more discerning Park family. Foul odors play a significant sensory role in *Parasite*: outside of the Kim family's apartment, the smell of multiplying stink bugs leads to spraying insecticide; the smell of urine sprayed freely by a local alcoholic outside the Kims' window is horrible, as is the smell of flooding sewer water; the smell of specially concocted delicacies compared with boxed preparations denotes class privilege; and the smell of laboring, sweaty people like

Mr. Kim denotes one's place. *Parasite* sharply delineates between those who work and those who smell people who work. When the youngest child in the Park family—himself an unleashed oddity—smells an unpleasant odor present among the disguised Kim family, exclaiming how "they smell the same," the exasperating messaging is clear: one cannot escape one's class. It is interesting to note that this same spoiled child dresses in a stereotypical "savage" native American costume at his party and consistently misbehaves.

Jonathan Reinarz has analyzed the politics of odor in world culture and indicates its lack of prominence in the ordering of the senses: "The sense of smell remains at the bottom of the sense hierarchy, where it has lingered for centuries,"[60] to which he adds, "Nearly every history of smell has demonstrated how scents have divided groups by erecting concrete boundaries ... [O]dor reputedly distinguished blacks from whites, men from women, and ... laborers from the leisured classes."[61] Like a recurring genetic defect, odoriferous scents reassert themselves as a class and cultural marker over space and time, with labor as a critical catalyst for its emergence and detection: "Like race and gender discrimination ... olfactory codes enforced class boundaries, often functioned subconsciously, and were quickly regarded as truisms, impervious to rational challenges."[62] *Parasite* observes these codes of signifying discourse; the sense of smell indicates sets of ideologically consequential assumptions: who detects whom denotes social identity.

Almost Human

"With the publication in 1859 of Darwin's *Origin of Species by Means of Natural Selection*, the theory of evolution became the most controversial topic of the age,"[63] and ironically remains so in many political and religious circles today. Darwin indicates that men lived in a struggle for survival against other animals, including men, via a process of natural selection. This was a revolutionary scientific and social posture, to be limitlessly referenced by naturalist literature, art, and later film. Furst and Skrine spare no accolade: "[i]n the development of [n]aturalism Darwin's theory is without doubt the most important single shaping factor."[64] Darwin's publication was soon followed by *The Descent of Man* (1871), which introduced the fundamental evolutionary notion "that man was closely related to apes ... [and was] profoundly shocking [to the] Victorians' [sense of] self-possession."[65] The very notion that the human being descended from lower forms of animal life and was not made in the image of a supreme being, a supernatural entity, removed celestial aspirations and fundamentally placed people and society in a non-idealized posture. Human behavior now had an evolutionary perspective, and this invoked fundamental concepts of determinism and genetics.

In *The Book of Imaginary Beings,* Borges references an intriguing comment: "Descartes tells us that monkeys could speak if they wished to, but they prefer to keep silent so they won't be made to work."[66] In David Lynch's black and white film, a seventeen-minute surreal foray into noir dialectics, *What Did Jack Do?* (2017), set in a small room in a train station, a detective (David Lynch) grills a capuchin monkey about a murder and thwarted love affair with an amorous chicken. As the intent detective contemplates the guilt of his seated suspect, the audience overhears Jack's declamation, in a moment of unguarded pique during his questioning: "who is going to believe an orangutang?" The mystery of simian intelligence and its capabilities becomes a dramatically absurd concept in Lynch's surreal narrative.

A century earlier, in Robert Louis Stevenson's anti-vivisection short story 'The Scientific Ape,' another simian plausibly answers Jack's rhetorically charged inquiry "Why are not apes progressive," as hominids engage in philosophical discourse and comment on anthropoid inhumanities.[67] Ralph Parfect notes the ironic tone of Stevenson's story about loquacious, querulous simians:

> 'The Scientific Ape' is one of the author's funniest stories ... although the use of anthropomorphized apes as characters seem to invoke Darwin, there is no implicit fear of man's devolution or degeneration ... Stevenson exposes the absurdity and hypocrisy of commonplace sayings by inverting their terms.[68]

Likewise, Lynch's film is an experimental hybrid, preposterous while eccentrically dramatic:

> The screenplay by Lynch is one that can either be nerve wracking, hilarious, or both simultaneously ... the dialogue is filled with animal and food related puns that are delivered with deadpan seriousness, creating a tension in the viewer that not only confuses them about the subject matter ... [and] the way in which they should be reacting.[69]

In effect, Lynch defamiliarizes the totality of the image; this is evidence of Lynch's technical mastery of the unfamiliar, the "dream logic" associated with a surreal anti-aesthetic, which leads to Jack, the guilty capuchin. Jack is under the scrutinizing eyes of the law, like Kafka's Josef K., and of the audience, like scientists observing negative catalysts interacting during an experiment.

Why a capuchin? Apes are stronger; orangutangs are reputedly smarter, but capuchins are notably "restless."[70] Recent clinical research notes, "capuchins [are] prone to the development of psychopathologies when kept in captivity":[71]

> Capuchin monkeys ... are receiving increased attention in primatological, psychological and anthropological literature due to their striking cognitive capacities such as: combinatorial tool use skills, cooperative and pro-social propensities in food sharing, triadic awareness with increased social learning in tolerant social organisation, and exhibition of behavioural traditions ... Furthermore, capuchins with different personalities vary in their boldness to novel stimuli, as measured by their willingness to voluntarily participate in cognitive experimental sessions.[72]

Perhaps most ludicrous and oddly compelling, as it suggests a link between Jack's bestial amorous desires and Lynch's atmospheric absurdities is the prattle-as-dialogue: Jack's interrogation. Jack's performance is obsessively engaging to witness, like a nervous figure about to burst. Ian Aitken has provided the critical linkage between Surrealism and, as suggested in Lynch's narrative of comical despair and desire, Naturalism's grinding propensity to render nerves exposed: "Surrealism's concern for the determining power of sexuality and the unconscious is, in many respects, comparable to the emphasis placed on the determining power of the subconscious genetic inheritance within naturalism."[73] Jack, like his human predecessors in literary and film culture, cannot escape the impulses of his physical as well as psychological being. Jack is a wild, occasionally nasty subject.

During the interrogation process, Jack, like the guilt-ridden Raskolnikov in Lev Kulidzhanov's *Prestuplenie i nakazanie/Crime and Punishment* (1970), unravels and reveals information; like recessive genes emerging in a tainted biological system, something becomes unbalanced. Saera Yoon and Robert O. Efird discuss multiple film adaptations of Dostoyevsky's novels and cite Kulidzhanov's *Crime and Punishment* as one of the few compelling, successful adaptations, referring to other adaptations as "dull mediocrities."[74] Kulidzhanov's film adaptation is a confessional narrative composed in medium and close-up shots, like Lynch's framing. There is suggestive intertextuality, both formal and thematic, between Kulidzhanov's guilt-ridden, deflated Raskolnikov (Georgiy Taratorkin) and Lynch's obsessive Jack, however incongruous the notion. Both figures unfold. In Kulidzhanov's *Crime and Punishment*, the film begins with long shots of a man running, as if being pursued by something dreadful, complemented by exaggerated sounds of footsteps, tolling bells, and running water, with an infrequent, atmospheric soundtrack. The audience intuits that this man, Raskolnikov, experiences a disquieting dream-time; freeze-frames confine his image, placing him in unnatural, haunted, Cesare-like poses, as if derived from Robert Weine's *Das Cabinet des Dr. Caligari/The Cabinet of Dr. Caligari* (1920).[75] Raskolnikov runs away from something, on streets, under arches, and finally across a bridge, as he dodges the pursuing police by jumping into the water below, in slow motion. The shot cuts to Raskolnikov as he awakens in his bed—like Kafka's Josef K. awakening from expressions of his inner estrangement—into a close-up shot of Raskolnikov gazing directly at the audience, a portrait of conflict coming to consciousness. Raskolnikov's face, like Jack's, is an affective study in anxieties to be revealed; this condition is a palpable pre-physical presence near guilt's metaphorical boiling point.

In *What Did Jack Do?*, Jack's facial expressions and nervous fidgeting, however endemic to the species, reveal similar states of perturbation. Whereas Lynch sets his narrative in a desolate train station, and Jack's crime of passion occurs off screen, Kulidzhanov's film engages a bleak city with saloons, prostitutes, and living conditions associated with urban poverty. These naturalist tropes create a visual context for Raskolnikov's on-screen violent double murder. As Lynch's interrogation sequence between Jack and the detective is an absurd study in power relations between two figures in a dream-like setting, composed in close-up and medium two-shots, Raskolnikov's final interrogation with the inspector is also visualized in a series of close-up and medium two-shots. Kulidzhanov's compositional framing encases the dynamics leading to an eventual confession as the tension associated with unmasking the beast inside Raskolnikov is presented as a game-like experience, an intellectual discussion, unlike Lynch's comical verbal inanities and impossible, playful meanings.

In *A Companion to Dada and Surrealism*, Jonathan P. Eburne's "Crime/Insurrection" cites a direct historical linkage between Naturalism and Surrealism, as he notes the surrealists' abiding interest in violence, crime, and popular cultures, especially fiction and cinema, as an expression of aesthetic experience:

> In the *Manifesto of Surrealism*, for instance, André Breton notably singled out a general ideological condition of 'absolute rationalism that is still in vogue,' epitomized by literary naturalism; such fiction 'allows us to consider only facts relating directly to our experience,' serially reproducing such experiences in turn. Yet it was the very hypostasis of this endless reproduction, in the guise of serial crime fiction, that offered a medium, in turn, for disrupting this ideological 'vogue.'[76]

Eburne later concludes, "Crime is not a static concept; nor, for that matter, is 'surrealism,' or its political or artistic practices."[77] Eburne's commentary confers upon Lynch's film the aura of the avant-garde in contemporary cinematic practice; *What Did Jack Do?* is an intellectually restless, eccentric, oddly erotic composite of dream-like imagery. In "Avant-Garde Art and the Problem of Theory," Nöel Carroll considers the avant-garde film as a "maieutic" work of art:

> It provokes the recognition of theoretical points by spectators by initially disorienting them through its elliptical and obscure structure. The avant-garde artwork is didactic, but it educates by inducing the participation of the spectator. The audience fills in the fragmented, often juxtapositional work by postulating a theoretical insight which not only makes sense of the work at hand, but which has implications for art or representation in general.[78]

For Carroll,

> Avant-garde artworks may refer or allude to theories, but this doesn't make them theoretical ... Avant-garde artists in creating their artifacts ... are not engaged in theoretical work. At best, they obliquely refer to such work. One might wish to say that in this they are intertextual.[79]

What Did Jack Do? "refers" to the rigorous tradition of Naturalism's grim dénouement as the entrapped figure of a capuchin in crisis, as he and the audience experience the surrealist illogic of the nearly real in cinematic space and time. According to Peter Bradshaw, "The closeups on Jack's face and head movements contrived by Lynch and cinematographer Scott Ressler give us a bizarrely convincing sense of someone defiant, yet haunted and evasive, and also pleadingly wide-eyed."[80] The emotive performance style and seeming self-awareness expressed on the capuchin's face, complemented by deepfake, imposed lips and a human (male) voice-over cohere as affect shots suggesting stress, fear, shame, and anger. These absurd images are off-putting yet oddly sympathetic, as they establish an atmospheric mood of guilt and entrapment, however irrational the premise, prompted by the detective's incessant grilling.

Is Jack guilty? In Robert Louis Stevenson's story, an ape asks a fellow ape: "Can apes descend to such barbarity?"[81] In *Planet of the Apes* (1968), Franklin J. Schaffner's cinematic view of a barbarous, dystopian future is augmented by tribalized, primitive humans comingling in a subservient capacity with fierce gorillas, sly orangutangs, and sympathetic chimpanzees, all of whom speak perfect English. In Schaffner's film, the suspension of disbelief is characteristic of the sustained credibility afforded by the audience to science fiction's allegorical narratives; in Lynch's film, those consistently unsettling medium two-shots and close-ups of Jack and the detective reshape the audience's perceptions: space and time seem something lifted from the unnerving landscape of a protracted dream.

The perturbed capuchin is weirdly a sympathetic figure, as Lynch's shot–reverse shots invoke the interrogation sequences of noir classics such as Jules Dassin's *The Naked City* (1948) and Alfred Hitchcock's *The Wrong Man* (1956), in which questions are posed systematically to alleged suspects. In a review of Lynch's film, Maciej Pradziad references "the true beauty of this fever dream," and cites "the interplay between gritty noir realism and off-the-wall Surrealism,"[82] as especially effective atmospheric contrivances. In Gary D. Rhodes' definitive history of the American horror film, he notes the ongoing presence of simian-related, silent film narratives:

> Monkeys, orangutans, and apes appeared onscreen repeatedly during the early cinema period ... more commonly, these moving pictures focused on humor ... some of these comedies cited Darwinian evolution by dressing monkeys and orangutans and placing them in situations akin to the daily lives of humans.[83]

Rhodes cites films produced as early as 1896, an era that initiates the rise of the avant-garde featuring Dada's non-sequiturs of prattle-based conversations and the ensuing surrealist dream imagery of the comically erotic in international culture. Kafka's clinically absurd short story "Ein Bericht für eine Akademie/Report for an Academy"(1917) utilizes a realistic tone and professional language as an ape relays his process of humanization to an audience. The ape amusingly confesses his delights involving his newly achieved progress and work ethic: "When I come home late at night, after banquets, from learned societies, from social get-togethers, I have a little semi-trained lady chimp waiting for me, and I let her show me a good time, ape-fashion."[84]

What Did Jack Do? is an avant-garde film narrative of intersecting aesthetics in which Naturalism and Surrealism convene on the *Lynchian* landscape. The audience observes Lynch's enigmatic, investigational narrative of pre-human anxieties in an unfamiliar dreamscape. As Borges concludes how a child might grasp potential imaginative encounters, the initial incomprehensibility of seeing strange animals in the zoo:

> He sees for the first time the bewildering ... spectacle, which might alarm or frighten him, he enjoys. He enjoys it so much that going to the zoo is one of the pleasures of childhood ... How can we explain this everyday and yet mysterious event?[85]

Apes, capuchins, humans, and their biological "derivations" share the imaginative space of expressive emotions in naturalist film narratives.

Early Sightings

In W. K. L. Dickson's history of emerging cinematic technology, he discusses his first-hand experience observing, photographing, and projecting images of specimens set on a watery microscope slide common in hitherto unseen nature landscapes, from bugs and beyond:

> The enlargement of animalcule in a drop of stagnant water proved a most exacting task, but ... we will suppose that the operator has at last been successful in imprisoning tricky water-goblins on the sensitive film ... A series of inch-large shapes then springs into view magnified stereoptically to nearly three feet each, gruesome beyond power of expression and exhibiting an indescribable celerity and rage. Monsters close upon each other in a blind and indiscriminate attack, limbs are dismembered, gory globules are tapped, whole batallions [sic.] disappear from view ... An unseen enemy is usually voted to be peculiarly undesirable, but who would close their eyes to the unimaginable horrors which micro-photography reveals in connection with the kinetoscope?[86]

Dickson's "unseen enemy" assumes multiple forms in modern visual culture. In the opening shot sequence of John S. Robertson's *Dr. Jekyll and Mr. Hyde* (1920), an early film adaptation of Robert Louis Stevenson's novella (1886), a scientist identified as Dr. Jekyll (John Barrymore), framed in a side-angle medium close-up, establishing for the audience a presence of the working, engaged researcher, sits in his laboratory and peers into a microscope onto a watery slide containing a colony of microbes. This is an experience of unmediated observed facts for both the doctor and the audience. In a close-up shot, from the doctor's point of view, the viewer sees this diffuse mass of life under the microscope, and then a medium reaction shot frames the amazed Dr. Jekyll responding to the scientific miracle he has just witnessed. Robertson's film adaptation is an example of naturalist cinema blending its source narrative with melodramatic staples involving threatened domesticity, identity, and unfettered sexuality, and the horror genre's animal-like, subhuman transformation into something predatory, introducing a unique intertextual presence into the Jekyll/Hyde narrative for future adaptations.[87]

As Robertson's film displays microbes, previously invisible clinical phenomena, in realistic stock footage, the shot creates a suggestive field of play in a naturalist context: the chemical-biological becomes an accepted aspect of the unknown. The audience sees Jekyll reacting to the microbes and the mystery these rudimentary forms of life imply to the critical mind at work, denoting scientific progress in action and the power of examination. Paul de Kruif notes, "The last ten years of the nineteenth century were as unfortunate for ticks, bugs, and gnats as they were glorious for the microbe hunters."[88] Robertson's initial shot sequences into the microscope may be configured as symbolic shot–reverse shots, mirror images of a sort, implying a process of linked portraiture: a before-and-after framing of life in stages of development.

DARWINIAN DISCONNECTIONS

Figure 6.2 John S. Robertson's *Dr. Jekyll and Mr. Hyde* (1920)

In this experimental-observational practice, who or what is watching whom, and which is the more profound, unfolding phenomenon—the microbes or the man?

Robertson's *Dr. Jekyll and Mr. Hyde* presents the life and death of one complex, albeit unbalanced man, as an observed experiment. The spectator is the interpreter of naturalist data: activities in the bar and the laboratory, and the narrative's allusions to predatory sexuality. The Jekyll/Hyde narrative, in any one of its abundant cinematic hypertexts, depicts and juxtaposes lower and higher forms of life struggling to survive, whether in the shape of quivering, silent microbes or in the violent, troglodytic figure of an almost-human being.

Robertson's *Dr. Jekyll and Mr. Hyde*, Rouben Mamoulian's *Dr. Jekyll and Mr. Hyde* (1931) and subsequent Jekyll/Hyde film narratives are examples of the natural world gone awry, failed experiments, a botched process and all that it potentially signifies. The naturalist film narrative frequently introduces substantially flawed human products. In Robertson's *Dr. Jekyll and Mr. Hyde*, seconds later, in the same laboratory, Dr. Lanyon, an authoritative figure of contrasting temperament, described in the intertitles as "conservative," appears disinterested, even hostile, to the amazing, unfolding world of unseen ancestral life forms. Lanyon sits behind Jekyll and is finally cajoled into looking into the microscope, only to feebly suggest afterwards that Jekyll is "tampering with the supernatural." Lanyon is incorrect; this is the natural world. The audience is not positioned to see these moments just as moral and artistic arbiters; the interpellated audience functions as corroborating clinicians in a preconstructed analytical positioning. In Robertson's adaptation, Lanyon serves as a counterpoint to Jekyll's progressive scientific model while female characters are abused stereotypes. Hyde's eruptive violence and menacing sexuality contrast with Jekyll's repressed romantic, heterosexual desires; the audience intuits that this is one man in conflict with both himself and his society—the rigors of morally proscriptive Victorian England—that he struggles against, and the pleasures of the deregulated night, with its bars and available sexual pleasures, to which Hyde succumbs.

Paul de Kruif states, whether referring to malaria, mitochondria, or microbes:

> Searchers, the best of them, still do no more than scratch the surface of the most amazing mysteries, all they can do (yet!) to find truth about microbes is to hunt, hunt endlessly ... There are no laws! an interpretive process is initiated,[89]

which instigates a model of clinical positioning and reception. In the laboratory, unknown mysteries of life are observable quantifications; in Robertson's film adaptation, the insidious Mr. Hyde, Jekyll's entrapped self, is a calculation of the living, grotesque unknown. Considering the Jekyll/Hyde trope of the binary, yet divided self—these two men *are* one man—the audience qualifies and accepts human variations, however perverse or eccentric.

For Stevenson, Mr. Hyde is a primary metaphor for repressed and dissolute passions, not without character, only possessing an unsettling, displeasing presence and form. He is an evolutionary and psychological throwback. Mr. Hyde is seen and experienced by others but hardly describable, an amoral abstraction of repulsive but human plausibility. If it is true that "monsters are meaning machines,"[90] Mr. Hyde is one monster that means a great deal, to both the filmmaker and the audience. Mr. Hyde is an image of contextual anxieties that are released, visible, and potentially real. Mr. Hyde, a deflated counter-symbol of selfhood, is the symbolic structure of the deconstructed self, a product of his transformation. In various film adaptations, Mr. Hyde has been depicted as a leering degenerate, a hydrocephalic, a violent Black male, a sexual predator, a drug addict, a nutty professor, a blood-lusting female serial killer, and more.[91] Mr. Hyde, the simian-like lesser male, replaces Dr. Jekyll to generate narratives incorporating significant issues of race, class, and gender in multiple film adaptations.

Rouben Mamoulian's *Dr. Jekyll and Mr. Hyde* reconstructs the idea of late nineteenth-century urban London, with its working-class neighborhoods and bars filled with brassy music and people, to suggest an overall seedy, foreboding environment: Hyde's world. Implied superstructural economic and historical considerations are located in the set design, including landscape and bodies. Class-based economic and historical models are visually juxtaposed by contrasting shots of high ceilings, fancy furniture, and stylish clothing, elaborate parties with classical music, and related images of wealth and privilege afforded to the upper class and all it can control: Jekyll's world. In Mamoulian's adaptation, Stevenson's Victorian historical milieu and all it connotes activates visual tropes of signifying discourse which register with the contemporary Depression-era audience. Mamoulian's *Dr. Jekyll and Mr. Hyde* features medium and wide shots recalling a painterly and photographic series of class-based images that mediate, for the engaged viewer, an imaginary reality.

Mamoulian's celebrated introductory first-person point-of-view shot sequences leading to the revelation of Dr. Jekyll's identity when reflected in a mirror, and the montage sequence contrasting Dr. Jekyll, two women, and images of sexual repression-expression, with Mr. Hyde's facial disfigurement and lusty grin, solicit a reading of the body politics of physiognomy, race, sexuality, and class privilege.

James Baldwin has suggested that: "the question of identity is a question involving the most profound panic."[92] Who or what is Mr. Hyde? In her essay on Mamoulian's film adaptation, Virginia Wright Wexman astutely comments on the politically and historically charged image of Mr. Hyde (Fredric March): "racial overtones are inescapable in Mamoulian's conception of Hyde as a primitive man ... the racial overtones inherent in the representation of Hyde are intimately associated with his physical repulsiveness."[93] This racially charged conception is made evident by theatrical makeup in the form of darker skin, thick lips, wiry hair, and a broad nose. The Depression-era audience was exposed to embedded racial imagery in film productions such as Merian C. Cooper and Ernest B. Schoedsack's *King Kong* (1933). In Mamoulian's centering Jekyll/Hyde film narrative, Mr. Hyde is an encoded representation of both Stevenson's and Zola's *La Bête humaine*, the conception of a menacing Darwinian evolutionary predecessor.

Charles Darwin wrote in *The Expression of the Emotions in Man and Animals* (1872), "our emotions are so closely connected with their expression that they hardly exist if the body remains passive."[94] In Mamoulian's adaptation, these transformation sequences, an active reversion from the human to a lesser animal state, facilitate the release and display of aggressive emotions. Darwin further suggests that the contemptuous glance and snarl, as displayed by Mr. Hyde in Mamoulian's film and in several adaptations, has its root in a more primitive form: "our semi-human progenitors uncovered their canine teeth when prepared for battle, as we still do when feeling ferocious."[95]

Mr. Hyde is horrific because his transformation and anti-social behavior invoke individual and collective anxieties; he is recognizable as the crack in the mirror that distorts but still reflects a de-centered image.

As a recurring Darwinian symbol, Mr. Hyde generates meaning as the product and central metaphor of the transformation, the naturalist *moment*, the site spectacle indicating a tragic, linked image of progress/failure. Philip Rosen indicates how the indexical sign, like the faltering Hyde, attests to the existence of something, suggesting an existential connection, a form of prior knowledge, between a specific referent and signifier"[96] activated by an intertextual process of inference and reading. This experience of knowledge is "based on a kind of history of the sign, for at least some of the referential presence occurred before the time of the reading."[97] Rosen suggests that "cultural configurations" are the agencies for diffusion of that prior knowledge for this indexical signification.[98] In whatever narrative form s/he appears, the naturalist individual, whether a prostitute, worker, criminal, or clever monster, initiates a process of signification. While "absorbing" its immediate literary and cinematic predecessors in an intertextual capacity, Mamoulian's *Dr. Jekyll and Mr. Hyde* is a naturalist film. In reality, the Jekyll/Hyde transformation trope from civilized man to uncivilized lesser man, and the ensuing personal and social manifestations of chaos recreated in multiple naturalist film narratives, are products of scientific research and development, which repeatedly lead to the precipitous, atavistic decline of the individual.

Raj Tilak's Jekyll and Hyde adaptation, *Chehre Pe Chehra/Face to Face* (1980), may be read as a palimpsestic tracing of Mamoulian's naturalist narrative. *Face to Face* recalls familiar plot contrivances, including a respectable scientist, laboratories, repeated displays of class and social-gender prerogative, and the decline of an inquisitive professional betrayed by chemicals, which are revised along Bollywood industrial standards.[99] The Jekyll/Hyde character Dr. Wilson/Blackstone (Sanjeev Kumar) in Tilak's film is neither parody nor facile; the initial transformation features a montage sequence of swirling, slightly out-of-focus images superimposed over close-up shots of standardized characters that recalls Mamoulian's flow of thematically interrelated attractive or displeasing personalities. Two distinctive women—one from the upper class and the other a member of the "disposable" lower class—cohere in a binary oppositional strategy to engage and lure Dr. Wilson's decline into Blackstone. Tilak's narrative rarely disengages from Mamoulian's sequencing; Wilson/Blackstone becomes even more inappropriate and facially disfigured as he devolves over time and expressions of desire. One especially inventive shot sequence occurs after the transformational swirling stops, as Wilson peers into the mirror and sees his new self, exposed, with extended sharp fingernails. He eventually breaks into laughter and grins. *Face to Face* is an intercultural realization of a concept critical to film Naturalism as it references Darwinian thematics: the submerged-released beast, *La Bête humaine*, especially as a failed experiment in progressive humanity.

In Jekyll and Hyde cinematic hypertexts highlighting unreal special effects, one thematic imperative educes that Jekyll and Hyde is nearly one man, not two men. In Ken Russell's *Altered States* (1980), drugs and sensory deprivation facilitate the transformation sequence of another Jekyll-like scientist (William Hurt). In Russell's film, a compellingly violent and atavistic form of human being, stripped of centuries of social progress and physical formation, has been released in an experiment; primitive, encoded expressions of race memory in a physical, deaccelerated nub of his former self are the product. In Louis Leterrier's *The Incredible Hulk* (2008), a brutish, enraged, and nearly invulnerable figure, resembling a muscular green man on a spiraling steroid regimen, performs impossible leaps through the air, lands, and destroys advancing military units and biotechnical weaponry of which he once was a creation. This hypertextual renewal of the Jekyll/Hyde narrative is a popular-culture study of the human beast, a projection of male power fantasies as futuristic weaponry, which portrays the Hulk comic character as a product of dangerous industrial and government-sponsored military research.

As a victim of a failed experiment—literally, an accident—the nuclear physicist researcher Dr. Banner (Edward Norton), the pre-Hulk, becomes the overpowering monster. Banner's transformation into the Hulk releases uncontrollable anger and anxiety. *The Incredible Hulk* is conceived as a special-effects driven narrative, essentially renewing the Jekyll and Hyde transformation trope, and as a study in psychological duality associated with male identity issues. The emotional struggles of Dr. Banner, the human side of the Hulk, as well as his betrayal by the military, for whom he labored, serve as plot points to facilitate the emerging beast. Leterrier's Hulk is a reading of the destabilized human, transforming unpredictably into a fierce thing that is perceptibly human, an intertextual appropriation of themes and tropes from the "cinemas" of Stevenson's *Jekyll and Hyde*. In *The Incredible Hulk*, which focuses on a failed experiment, exposed rage, and career alienation, the naturalist narrative is mediated within a super-hero, science fiction, even melodramatic generic blending.

Like Louis Leterrier's thematic appropriation, Serge Bozon revitalized the familiar Jekyll/Hyde theme in the adaptation *Madame Hyde* (2017), which introduces a feminist slant to the narrative, especially involving the transformation trope.[100] *Madame Hyde* features an unromantic view of working women and their daily discontent. Having labored for years at Arthur Rimbaud High School as a distraught, disliked, and generally ignored teacher in contemporary France, Mrs. Géquil (Isabelle Huppert) struggles to cope with an unremarkable life and career while mocked by her native and immigrant students during her science classes. Several classroom sequences realistically invoke and ironically contrast with the unrivaled adulation afforded the lecturing, authoritative male Dr. Jekyll from his high-angle podium in Mamoulian's *Dr. Jekyll and Mr. Hyde*. Bozon's *Madame Hyde* exposes troubling experiences associated with teaching, especially as it depicts unacknowledged labor and a near relentless, gendered alienation.

Mrs. Géquil undergoes a radical, unnatural, and transformative change that deleteriously affects her life and the lives of her students. As Mrs. Géquil is accidentally electrified by one of the classroom science projects in her inaccessible laboratory, this transforms her into the glowing red and powerfully menacing Madame Hyde.[101] Although these two women are uniquely different in personality and performance, Mrs. Géquil and Madame Hyde are one woman.

One significant shot sequence focuses on Mrs. Géquil's physics experiment with electricity, a symbol of intense energy. The project involves the theoretical analysis of a Faraday Cage, an object—like a large box or cage—that blocks the flow of electromagnetic fields inside the cage, making it a kind of hollow conductor, which suggests a comparison with the imminent transformation infusing the unhappy Mrs. Géquil with furious power. As she transforms into a released presence, she frees herself from her own cage. She becomes charged and newly visible. As Madame Hyde emerges, she threatens her neighborhood, kills a violent local thug and two dogs, and ignores her husband. She states, prior to an eventual arrest, "every object seeks balance," which she has discovered because of her unbalanced experience. Consistent with the Jekyll/Hyde narratives, progress is frequently rendered potentially transgressive. She is also a failed experiment.

Notes

1. Gaston Bachelard, *The Poetics of Space*, trans. Marian Jolas (Boston: Beacon Press, 1994), 17.
2. Bachelard, *Poetics*, 94.
3. Patricia Vigderman "The Two-part History of a Time-based Art," *Southwest Review*, Vol. 90, No. 3 (2005), 344.
4. Richard Thomson, "Regionalism versus Nationalism in French Visual Culture, 1889–1900: The Cases of Nancy and Toulouse," *Studies in the History of Art*, Vol. 68 (2005), 218, 220.
5. Milan Pribisic "Carousel: Erwin, Elvira, Armin, Fassbinder, and All the Others' Auto/Biographies," *Biography*, Vol. 29, No. 1 (Winter 2006), 77.
6. This "incident" occurs (approximately) 23 seconds into the film.
7. Vigderman, "Two-Part History," 343.
8. A copy of this pivotal historical document, and the direct quote, may be accessed at https://dnalc.cshl.edu/view/16195-Gallery-5-William-Bateson-Letter-page-1.html. Accessed July 12, 2023. Note: GENETICS appears in caps in the original letter. This is further discussed in Siddhartha Mukherjee's *The Gene: An Intimate History* (New York: Scribner Publishers, 2016), 62.

9. This phrase and additional information may be located at https://dnalc.cshl.edu/view/16196-Gallery-5-William-Bateson-Letter-page-2.html. Accessed July 12, 2023.
10. Kristin Thompson, "Narration Early in the Transition to Classical Filmmaking: Three Vitagraph Shorts," *Film History*, Vol. 9, No. 4 (1997), 413.
11. Charles Musser, *The Emergence of Cinema: The American Screen to 1907* (Vol. I), (Berkeley, University of California Press, 1990), 393.
12. Jose van Dijck, *Imagenation: Popular Images of Genetics* (New York: New York University Press, 1998), 1.
13. Gilles Deleuze, *Cinema 1—The Movement-Image*, trans. Hugh Tomlinson and Barbara Habberjam (Minneapolis: University of Minnesota Press, 1986), 127.
14. Van Dijck, *Imagenation*, 5.
15. Ibid, 15, 17, original emphasis.
16. David A. Kirby, "The Devil in Our DNA: A Brief History of Eugenics in Science Fiction Films," *Literature and Medicine*, Vol. 26, No. 1 (Spring 2007), 103.
17. James Rose, "Review: *The Hills Have Eyes*," *Offscreen*, Vol. 10, Issue 10 (October 2006), n.p.: see https://offscreen.com/view/violence_undoes_man. Accessed May 20, 2023.
18. Bruce F. Kawin, *Horror and the Horror Film* (New York: Anthem Press, 2012), 206.
19. Kawin, *Horror*, 207–8.
20. This film may be viewed at https://digirepo.nlm.nih.gov/ext/hmdvid/hmdvid-101514101/hmdvid-101514101.mp4. Accessed June 17, 2023.
21. James Allen Rogers, "Darwinism and Social Darwinism," *Journal of the History of Ideas*, Vol. 33, No. 2 (April–June, 1972), 268.
22. Lothrop Stoddard, "The New Realism of Science," *Racial Realities in Europe* (New York: Charles Scribner's Sons, 1924), 237.
23. *Are You Fit to Marry?* is the film primarily discussed in this section.
24. Martin S. Pernick, *The Black Stork: Eugenics and the Death of "Defective Babies" in American Medicine and Motion Pictures Since 1915* (New York: Oxford University Press, 1999), 120. Note: Access to *Are You Fit To Marry* was graciously provided by the John E. Allen Archive.
25. Ibid, 121–2.
26. Ibid, 165–6.
27. Ibid, 164.
28. *Feind im Blut/Enemy in the Blood* (Praesens-Film, 1931) is difficult to locate but does exist in DVD format.
29. Edwin Grant Conklin, *Heredity and Environment in the Development of Men* (Princeton: Princeton University Press, 1917), 303.
30. Ibid, 297.
31. Steven Jay Schneider, "Introduction, PT. I: Dimensions of the Real," *Post Script*, Vol. 21, Issue 3 (Summer 2002), 3, 4.
32. Pernick, *Black*, 147.
33. Ibid, 147–8.
34. Ibid, 150.
35. Ibid, 145.
36. Henry Herbert Goddard's *Feeble-Mindedness: Its Causes and Consequences* (1912) (London, Forgotten Books, 2012) is recommended.
37. Cesare Lombroso, *The Female Offender* (New York: D. Appleton, 1897), 151–2.
38. See Robert Singer's "'Error Bred in the Bone': *The Bad Seed*," *Horror Studies*, Vol. 6, No. 2 (2015).

39. June Howard, "Preface and Casting Out the Outcast: Naturalism and the Brute," in *Documents of American Realism and Naturalism*, ed. Donald Pizer (Carbondale: University Press, 1998), 394–5.
40. Singer, "'Error Bred," 178.
41. Paul Elliott, *Studying the British Crime Film* (Liverpool: Auteur Publishing, 2014), 141.
42. Alan Burton and Tim O'Sullivan, *Cinema of Basil Dearden and Michael Relph* (Edinburgh: Edinburgh University Press, 2009), 223.
43. Elliott, *Studying*, 146.
44. Robert Singer, "What Grows in the Hood: Projects, People and the Contemporary Brooklyn Film," *The Brooklyn Film: Essay in the History of Filmmaking*, eds John Manbeck and Robert Singer (Jefferson, NC: McFarland, 2003), 52.
45. This story may be located at http://serichardson.com/Readings/Wideman.pdf. Accessed August 29, 2023.
46. Julie Phillips, "Growing Up Black and Female: Leslie Harris's *Just Another Girl on the IRT*," *Cinéaste*, Vol. 19, No. 4 (1992), 86.
47. Singer, "What Grows," 66.
48. Ibid, 67.
49. Ibid, 68.
50. Howard, "Preface," 401.
51. Charles Darwin, "Chapter 3: Struggle for Existence," in *On the Origin of Species* (First Edition) (London: John Murray, Albemarle Street, 1859), www.gutenberg.org/files/1228/1228-h/1228-h.htm#link2H_4_0005. Accessed August 31, 2023.
52. Paul de Kruif, *Microbe Hunters* (New York: Harcourt Brace Jovanovich, 1954), 47.
53. Friedrich Nietzsche, "Man in Society," *Human, All Too Human*, trans. R. J. Hollingdale (Cambridge: Cambridge University Press, 1996), 143.
54. Amy Taubin, "A House Divided," *Film Comment*, Vol. 55, No. 5 (September–October, 2019), n.p.
55. Ibid, 30.
56. Theodore A. Bingham, "Foreign Criminals in New York," *North American Review*, Vol. 188, No. 634 (September 1908), 391.
57. Max Nordau, *Degeneration* (New York: D. Appleton, 1895), 155.
58. Ibid, 155.
59. Ibid, 540.
60. Jonathan Reinarz, *Past Scents: Historical Perspectives on Smell* (Illinois: University of Illinois Press, 2014), 5.
61. Ibid, 174.
62. Ibid, 145.
63. Lillian R. Furst and Peter N. Skrine, *Naturalism: The Critical Idiom* (London: Methuen, 1971), 15.
64. Ibid, 16.
65. Ibid, 15.
66. Jose Luis Borges with Margarita Guerrero, *The Book of Imaginary Beings*, trans. Norman Thomas di Giovanni (New York: E. P. Dutton, 1978), 126.
67. Ralph Parfect, "Robert Louis Stevenson's 'The Clock Maker' and 'The Scientific Ape': Two Unpublished Stories," *English Literature in Transition, 1880–1920*, Vol. 48 No. 4 (2005), 401. According to Parfect, "The Scientific Ape" has not been conclusively dated but is likely to have been written in the mid-1880s.
68. Parfect, *Stevenson*, 393, 394.

69. Maciej Pradziad, "Film Review: What Did Jack Do? A Surreal Noir," *Trinity Tripod* (February 21, 2020), n.p. See https://tripod.domains.trincoll.edu/arts/what-did-jack-do-film-review-a-surreal-noir/. Accessed August 30, 2023.
70. Renata G. Ferreira et al., "Coping Strategies in Captive Capuchin Monkeys," *Applied Animal Behaviour Science*, Vol. 176 (2016), 124.
71. Ibid, 121.
72. Ibid, 121.
73. Ian Aitken, "Distraction and Redemption: Kracauer, Surrealism and Phenomenology," *Screen*, Vol. 39, Issue 2 (Summer 1998), 139.
74. Saera Yoon; and Robert O. Efird, "Final Words, Final Shots: Kurosawa, Bortko and the Conclusion of Dostoevsky's Idiot." *CLCWeb: Comparative Literature and Culture*, Vol. 21, No. 4 (2019), n.p. See https://doi.org/10.7771/1481-4374.3204. Accessed February 12, 2023.
75. The reference to Weine's *Das Cabinet des Dr. Caligari* (1920) is a notable intertextual link to expressionist cinema. A presence of Expressionism's unsettling, nervousness is evident in Lynch's narrative.
76. Jonathan P. Eburne, "Crime/Insurrection," in *A Companion to Dada and Surrealism*, ed. David Hopkins (John Wiley & Sons, Incorporated, 2016), 259.
77. Ibid, 267.
78. Nöel Carroll, "Avant-Garde Art and the Problem of Theory," *Journal of Aesthetic Education*, Vol. 29, No. 3 (Autumn 1995), 7.
79. Ibid, 11.
80. Peter Bradshaw, "Review: *What Did Jack Do?* David Lynch's surprise Netflix short is pure, surreal style," *The Guardian* (January 20, 2020). See https://www.theguardian.com/film/2020/jan/20/what-did-jack-do-review-david-lynch-netflix-short-film. Accessed April 12, 2023.
81. Parfect, *Stevenson*, 403.
82. Pradziad, "What Did Jack Do?"
83. Gary D. Rhodes, *The Birth of the American Horror Film* (Edinburgh; Edinburgh University Press, 2018), 239.
84. Franz Kafka, "*Ein Bericht für eine Akademie/A Report to an Academy* (1917)," trans. Michael Hofmann. Located at https://artviewer.org/wp-content/uploads/2019/05/A-Report-to-an-Academy_Franz-Kafka_EN.pdf. Accessed March 12, 2023.
85. Borges, "Imaginary," 15.
86. W. K. L. Dickson and Antonia Dickson, *History of the Kinetograph, Kinetoscope and the Kineto-Phonograph* (1895) (New York: Museum of Modern Art, 2001), 41–3.
87. The Jekyll–Hyde film narratives frequently incorporate material from the multiple stage adaptations of Stevenson's source novella in their inclusion of the "threatened female" trope, along with religious tonalities.
88. Paul de Kruif, *Microbe Hunters* (New York: Harcourt Brace Jovanovich Publishers, 1954), 135.
89. Ibid, 145.
90. Judith Halberstam, "Parasites and Perverts: An Introduction to Gothic Monstrosity," in *Skin Shows: Gothic Horror and the Technology of Monsters* (NC: Duke University Press, 1995), 21.
91. Some other significant Jekyll and Hyde adaptations include: *Dr. Jekyll and Sister Hyde* (1972, Dir. R. W. Baker), *Dr. Black and Mr. Hyde* (1976, Dir. W. Crain), and *Edge of Sanity* (1989, Dir. G. Kikoïne).
92. James Baldwin, *The Devil Finds Work* (New York: Dial Press, 1976), 77.

93. Virginia Wright Wexman, "Horrors of the Body: Hollywood's Discourse on Beauty and Rouben Mamoulian's *Dr. Jekyll and Mr. Hyde*," in *Dr. Jekyll and Mr. Hyde after One Hundred Years*, eds William Veeder and Gordon Hirsch (Chicago, University of Chicago Press, 1988), 288–9.
94. Charles Darwin, *The Expression of the Emotions in Man and Animals* (New York: Philosophical Library, 1955), 237.
95. Ibid, 251–2.
96. Philip Rosen, "History of Image, Image of History: Subject and Ontology in Bazin," in *Rites of Realism: Essays on Corporeal Cinema*, ed. Ivone Margulies (Durham: Duke University Press, 2003), 48.
97. Ibid, 50.
98. Ibid, 50.
99. This author does not speak or understand written Hindi. As the film was reviewed, the visual qualities of Tilak's work made it possible to "read" the film as a silent Jekyll/Hyde narrative (although the sound was always on). *Face to Face* is available on *Youtube* at https://www.youtube.com/watch?v=hMa1KKerpqU. Accessed April 14, 2023.
100. There have been many other feminist reworkings of the Jekyll/Hyde theme.
101. Bozon's adaptation recalls a segment from the second series run of Rod Serling's original *The Twilight Zone*. The broadcast on November 8, 1985, entitled "Teacher's Aide," is co-directed by Robert Downey, Sr. and Bill Norton. The segment features an abused high school teacher transformed by a demonic presence—an intimidating gargoyle on the school building's ledge—into a vengeful, raging instructor who nearly kills one of her students.

7. MOREAU NARRATIVES

Beastly Derivations

In *Murder, Inc., and the Moral Life: Gangsters and Gangbusters in LaGuardia's New York* (2016), historian Robert Weldon Whalen's account of urban criminals and underworld syndicates focuses on a particularly violent gang and gang member:

> Murder, Inc., refers to a gang of hoodlums, led by Abe Reles, that flourished in Brooklyn's Brownsville neighborhood from 1931 until 1940. Reles and his gang, there were maybe twenty or so full-time members of the gang, engaged in a whole range of criminal activities, including murder. No one knows how many people the gang killed; the best guess would be several hundred.[1]

The most infamous assassin for hire in this organization was their leader, the apish, sadistic Abe Reles, well known to the public as a dangerous figure. Reles was feared for his pathological disposition, physical strength, and predatory outbursts against any perceived enemy. As noted by Edmund Elmaleh, "Abe Reles was a living, breathing nightmare ... a 'gorilla-like figure' ... he was capable of unimaginable brutality."[2] After years of murder and racketeering, upon his inevitable capture for several criminal activities, Reles was scheduled to testify in court as a government witness against leaders of the still unknown underworld to lessen his own sentencing. In a series of extensive interview-confessions, Reles provided assistant district attorney and prosecutor Burton Turkus with multitudes of damning information. Right after these revelations, while still under police protection, Reles died while trying to "escape" from a hotel window by climbing out on a bedsheet. This act of underworld retribution, defenestration from a window, has never been solved.

The confessions and testimony of Abe Reles was a legendary betrayal of the criminal code of misconduct and was vividly recreated in Burt Balaban and Stuart Rosenberg's gangster narrative, *Murder, Inc.* (1960). Prior to the window shot sequence in the hotel, Abe Reles (Peter Falk) sits in a prison cell, temporarily calm and pondering an improbable deal with the authorities, which he discovers will not happen as he imagined. Like Jake LaMotta (Robert De Niro) awkwardly contemplating his life in Martin Scorsese's *Raging Bull* (1980) and "Charles Bronson" (Tom Hardy) ironically singing lyrics from the popular song "please, release me," in Nicolas Winding Refn's *Bronson* (2008), Reles will soon yield to splenetic outbursts, suggesting his realization of entrapment, with little chance of resolution, priming the release of the inner fulminating beast.

In *The Expression of the Emotions in Man and Animals* (1872), Darwin discusses the simian species in general and notes parallel notions of self-expression: "Many display their anger by suddenly advancing, making abrupt starts, at the same time opening the mouth and pursing up the lips, so as to conceal the teeth, while the eyes are daringly fixed on the enemy, as if in savage defiance."[3] After mock-heroic outbursts and his violent assault on a more cooperative witness, Reles decides to talk to the authorities. As he is led into the cramped office space where he will give testimony in hopeful exchange for a lighter sentence, in a medium shot, Reles sits opposite Turkus at his desk as the stenographer copies Reles' every word and a policeman stands apart, but fully engaged. At one point, Reles states, "I've got plenty to say to you," and when asked about what, Reles calmly notes, "murder." A series of shot–reverse shots reveal a cooler, momentarily interesting violent man discussing horrible anecdotes in graphic detail. The focus is primarily on Reles' face and reaction shots across the room; in a voice-over, Turkus states, "he sang a full-length opera," as Reles betrays every known criminal associate over a period of six days without stopping, filling twenty-five notebooks. The most striking aspect of the shot sequence is Reles' placid recollection of relentless, conspiratorial violence performed like a thoughtful memory about incidents at work and other workers.

Murder, Inc. presents the image of a vicious, simian-like gangster version of *La Bête humaine* that predates Barbet Schroeder's documentary *Koko, le gorille qui parle/Koko: A Talking Gorilla* (1978), featuring Koko, the gorilla who mastered and communicated to humans in sign language. In both films, linked representations of simian strains are evidence of naturalist propensities involving behavior and consequential sociability, or its notable lack. Ironically, Koko is more sympathetic—perhaps more identifiably human—than Abe Reles, the murderer. There is an additional presence, an experimental life form, a recurring trope evident in multiple naturalist films: *the Moreau narrative*.

Dark Hearts

In 1896, H. G. Wells published *The Island of Dr. Moreau*. As author Peter Straus ponders in his introduction to this scientific novel of naturalist design, "what kind of book is it?"[4] Satisfactorily labeled neither as a travel and shipwreck narrative like Shakespeare's *Tempest* and the adventurous fantasy of Robert Louis Stevenson's *Treasure Island* (1883), nor as an examination of violence and colonial exploitation like Joseph Conrad's *Heart of Darkness* (1899), Wells' *The Island of Dr. Moreau* may be viewed by the contemporary reader as an intricate work of fiction that reproduces elements of the aforementioned narrative schema, but now, more specifically, as a seminal indexical referent of the naturalist paradigm. *The Island of Dr. Moreau* is read in an intertextual, theoretical capacity as an experimental novel, one that sustains and advances Zola's naturalist discursivity into the speculative range of the political-horror narrative. *The Island of Dr. Moreau* may be viewed as a popularized reading of Darwinian science and theories involving eugenics, evolution, and extreme survivalist strategies, a study of "bad" experimental science involving the spectacle of the isolated human, imperfect bodies, and the beast, and as an ideologically suggestive exploration of power relations involving vivisection, master/slave relations, atavism, labor, language, extra-legal sites, and especially as a literary text that solicits multiple film adaptations.

The Island of Dr. Moreau refutes sustaining illusions of civilization as the narrative voice acts like a witness to past crimes, revealing specific horrors to an incredulous listener. In *The Island of Dr. Moreau*, the island's bestiary, a disposable worker-slave population, foreshadows realities of subsequent historical depravity, from the extra-legal scientific laboratory to the dehumanized extermination site as the novel reveals the primitive behavioral, animal ancestry presence in the civilized. *The Island of Dr. Moreau* and its hypertexts examine the *presence of absence*, in the form of moral, social, or legal authority, as suggestively fascistic power systems, affected by a human being and some things *like* a human, which emerge and deflate. These isolation narratives are studies in violent, failed experiments that produce despair. The naturalist milieu of the jungle-island, its physical setting and respective historical period, induces expressions of dread in the observer who steadily evolves into an interpellated witness to the events. The Moreau narratives, regardless of immediate generic classification, suggest a naturalist reading, especially when linked to modernism's discredited pseudo-sciences, enacted ideologies of class exploitation, and consequential acts of brutality. These narratives skewer notions of progress via emplotted acts of social engineering; the sequestered naturalist environment makes humans into monsters and, inversely, the monsters more human.

In a demonstrable capacity, Moreau's island is a formative concentration camp, as Wells' narrative suggests how the needless cruelty of experimental, animal vivisection leads to more grotesque, historically unregulated realities when applied to the human subject. The comparison between the concentration camp and the jungle setting is neither cursory nor inconceivable, for Moreau's island and the concentration camp are both extra-legal, radically dystopian sites:

> The camp as a space of exception is a paradox. The camp is a piece of land which is placed outside the normal juridical order, but it is not simply an external space ... The camp is ... the structure in which the state of exception—on whose possible decision sovereign power is founded—is realized normally ... [e]very question concerning the legality or illegality of what happened there simply makes no sense.[5]

Wells' *The Island of Dr. Moreau* is structured in the form of a published memoir, a retrieved modern captivity narrative, although the tale is "without confirmation."[6] For a framing, distancing device, the narrative begins with the nephew of a shipwreck survivor publishing the story of his uncle, Prendick, an exhausted, withdrawn Marlow-like figure.[7] Wells' novel also suggests a parallel with Stephen Crane's short story "The Open Boat" (1897), as both narratives cast presumptively civilized men against nature in a struggle for survival, adrift and threatened, nearly lost to the sea. In *The Island of Dr. Moreau*, the reader discovers that Prendick, as if modeled on the student career of Darwin, has a university background in biological science and that he had an interest in "natural history."[8] Prendick recounts his survivor's tale to Montgomery, his rescuer and Moreau's co-conspirator aboard a ship heading toward Moreau's island with its cargo of various wild animals. The reader discovers that Prendick had nearly participated in the act of cannibalism while adrift with others of whom he alone survived, but Prendick did not degenerate into savagery, just a lingering case of numbing incredulity.

Wells' *The Island of Dr. Moreau* stresses operative, interpretive notions of Darwinian science and theories involving evolution and survivalist strategies, as a study of depraved experimental science, specifically applied vivisection and eugenics linking the spectacle of the human, the body, and the beast. Wells' *The Island of Dr. Moreau* is an ideologically suggestive exploration of shifting master and slave power relations. The Moreau narrative and its hypertexts, set in the remote island and jungle of the reader's imagination, are studies in isolation and the corrosive social conditions that lead toward the emergence of the immediate naturalist crisis. These are isolation narratives in which the central figures are absented from allegedly progressive, modern civilization, so a functional, often grotesque parody of a social order is established in its stead to extend naturalist themes into horrific and politically perverse narratives.

Like Kafka's visitor to the nominally progressive islet located *In the Penal Colony* (1919), who attempts to flee but hardly escapes, or to the spectator of the concentration-labor camp sites evident in twentieth-century history, the sense of an absence generates a reflexive, annexing, and destabilizing susceptibility. In *Heart of Darkness* (1899), as Conrad's Marlowe sits on a boat in the river pondering the horrors he has witnessed in the Belgian Congo, a product of the civilizing qualities of European industrialists and royalty, and in William Golding's *Lord of the Flies* (1954), as little schoolboys revert to tribalism and violent sacrificial rites, the observer notes the presence of rapacious two-legged animals roaming in the menacing naturalist jungle; often, the beasts wear uniforms and work in laboratories or for corporations. Prendick has ingested his experiences; he may have escaped from Moreau's nightmarish colony, yet he remains consumed by recollections of time past and restrictive space. The Moreau film narrative and its multiple hypertexts are naturalist studies in the struggle, isolation, and decline of the human or near-human.

Lost Cities

In an interview published in *Film Comment*, James Gray notes his muse-like source informing *The Lost City of Z* (2016), a film set in the remote region of the ominous, exotic Brazilian jungle. Gray states, "we looked at a lot of paintings. We looked at Henri Rousseau and Claude Lorrain. For the jungle, Rousseau was our guy—the jungle as a dream."[9] In the interview, Gray's comments are accompanied by reproductions of paintings, particularly Rousseau's *Jungle with Setting Sun* (1910), a naïve, *imagined* jungle landscape, which suggests that amid the forestry are severe, threatening hazards—a tiger—awaiting the unexpected. In a series of paintings by Henri Rousseau, *The Hungry Lion Throws Itself Upon the Antelope* (1905), *Fight Between a Tiger and a Buffalo* (1908), *The Equatorial Jungle* (1909), and *Horse Attacked by a Jaguar* (1910), the artist creates a series of jungle landscapes that depict the perilous nature of struggle and survival in the jungle of the imagination. Animals attack other animals in violent encounters, suggesting that the verdant landscape contains creatures that wait patiently and then act to entrap and destroy prey. However disquieting, these are natural events, in direct relationship with environmental order; in naturalist film narrative, there is the unnatural world of a troubling, problematic near-human reality. In *Cinema 2—The Time-Image* (1985), Gilles Deleuze concludes:

> We see that the cinema of reality sometimes claimed objectively to show us real settings, situations and characters, and sometimes claimed subjectively to show the ways of seeing of these characters themselves, the way in which they themselves saw their situation, their setting, their problems.[10]

The Deleuzian "cinema of reality" is an edifying aesthetic principle as it addresses naturalist film narrative. In the Moreau narrative, the physical space of an island and its traditionally unregulated jungle environment and occupants are not reductively rendered as the verdant, romanticized site of wild animals and dense forestation as travel brochures and romance novels might indicate. Remote island sites are frequently depicted as inaccessible and foreboding, and despite the presence of teeming life and movement, reveal themselves bereft of order and enforced, stabilizing social systems. The jungle setting is a primary naturalist site engaging the spectacle of human despair and decline. Either presented as an exotic wilderness on a secluded Pacific Ocean island, or on the overpopulated, menacing island of Manhattan, the jungle as a conceptual naturalist setting contains complex, representative life forms subverting the notion of modernist progress and projecting another, darker side to cinematic reality. Whether fictionalized or in real life, this anticipatory anxiety has its roots in lucid images of Darwinian natural selection, moments in the struggle for survival and a creative reconfiguring of the evolutionary process as it reveals its biological misfires. The monsters are not always monstrous, but they are isolated.

Erle C. Kenton's *The Island of Lost Souls* (1932) was a controversial film. According to Stephen Prince, *The Island of Lost Souls* was banned in at least eleven countries due to its violent subject matter and potential blasphemies.[11] The source of this blasphemy involves Dr. Moreau's irreligious, imperious rhetoric, criminal activities, freakish images of laboring, suffering near-humans, and the pre-code inclusion of the seductive Lota, the panther-woman. David Kirby notes particularly how disturbing the beast people were to the Depression-era audience:

> The Beast People are indeed horrific reminders of humanity's tainted animal origins. Their ability to walk on two legs, their human clothing, and their rudimentary speech are human-like, but their hairy features, fangs, and pointy ears betray their animal origins. The makeup was so horrific, in fact, that it, along with the vivisection and bestiality themes, contributed to the film being banned in Britain and parts of the United States.[12]

The Island of Lost Souls begins with the ghostly, fog-laden atmospherics of a mysterious large ship framed in an opening shot that cuts to a wide shot of a man, foreground in the frame and to its left, sighting a smaller boat.[13] He yells out that there is a "derelict afloat with a man on board," thus initiating the rescue narrative. After the initial shipwreck rescue, on board the SS *Covena*, Parker (Richard Arlen)—Wells' Prendick—sees animals in cages as well as animals–near-humans at work. The most violent of the animals is the abusive, alcoholic captain of the ship, who is hauling cargo to Moreau's island. After the captain strikes one of the workers for a minor incident, Parker runs over to him and discovers in a close-up shot the worker's now visible non-human, hairy ear. Once the worker is resuscitated, he compulsively and violently attacks the captain in a manner that recalls repressed atavistic tendencies, its animal ancestry.

After the cargo and Parker are dispatched from the ship, various shots of Dr. Moreau (Charles Laughton) managing the ship and the crew at work, suggest an encoded racialist patriarchal symbol in which White authority figures, rather than darker colored laborers, control events. The autocratic Moreau, a vengeful, fascistic godfather, frequently behaves like a mad Prospero, cursing and controlling his compromised Calibans with a whip instead of magic. Moreau's whip, a weapon associated with slavery, signifies his power over his dual bestiaries: the private collection of jungle animals and the created social order of experimental animals on the island. In one symbolic shot, Kenton cuts to the beast people working in the background of the frame, as they stand upon a wheel and turn it with their legs, with the image completed by bars across the frame in the foreground, thus suggesting imprisonment and punitive labor. Manet's naturalist seascape painting *Toilers of the Sea* (1873) dispassionately documents working men on a boat, identifiable as laborers who work to survive, but they are men. Kenton's evocative close-up and medium shots feature pitiable laboring creatures, members of a herd-like mob.

One of the remarkable achievements of *The Island of Lost Souls* is the that beasts are often more human than the original humans. The beast people evoke audience sympathy far more than their creator, who at one critical point asks an astonished Parker: "Do you know what it means to feel like God?" In a series of powerful shot sequences inside the house of pain, where bodies are disassembled and reassembled, Parker witnesses the standardized applied torture as he exclaims, "they're vivisecting a human being," almost correctly identifying the unfortunate victim. As Moreau and Montgomery hover over the afflicted animal's strapped down body, the lighting appropriates an expressionist design, suggesting an alignment of the internal state of anxiety with the external experience of the horrific and repulsive.[14] The two-shot of these culpable scientists cutting up a living thing without the benefit of anesthesia comments directly upon the lawless nature of the encampment and the power of the whip, despite the mindless recitation of the rules of law by the victims of these flawed experiments in evolution.

BEYOND REALISM

Figure 7.1 Erle C. Kenton's *The Island of Lost Souls* (1932)

Kenton's adaptation recalls historical and ideological preoccupations with fundamental survival, menial labor, power relations, and race in several significant films from the Depression-era 1930s: Tod Browning's *Freaks* (1932), with its portrayal of isolated others, laboring wound-spectacles; Merian C. Cooper and Ernest B. Schoedsack's *King Kong* (1933), with its exploitative characters, stereotypical representation of Africans, and movement from foreboding Kong island to an equally foreboding Manhattan island; and Irving Pichel and Ernest B. Schoedsack's *The Most Dangerous Game* (1932), with its shipwreck, predatory sharks, and humans, the enforced struggle for survival on a remote island, and the abusive, deranged Count Zaroff.

The Most Dangerous Game is a naturalist film that features a cultured, brain-damaged recluse in a tuxedo living in imperial-style isolation with an assortment of servants on a remote island in which he may hunt the most challenging of all prey: men. Count Zaroff (Leslie Banks), whose name and behavior signals a decadent, old-world European class and manner, and the rugged, attractive American, Bob (Joel McCrea), are both skilled hunters presented as inverse reflections. The Count's scarred, skull injury—a marker-explanation for his eccentric violence—was the product of a failed hunt: "a cape buffalo gave me this head wound." The Count's trophy room, like a Nazi museum for extinct races or a butcher's shop, features the heads and body parts of hunted animals.[15] At one point, Zaroff reveals the competition: "here on my island, I hunt the most dangerous game," and to guarantee obedience, he displays a torture device with prominently sharp needles, which recalls the commandant's device for labeling prisoners in Kafka's *In The Penal Colony*. As the Count enthusiastically states, "kill, then love. When you have known that, you have known ecstasy," he invokes the predatory, atavistic sexual inclinations of Zola's Jacques Lantier in *La Bête humaine*. In *The Island of Lost Souls*, love—in the form of an anticipatory reproductive act—signifies Parker's living value and the subject of Moreau's game.

In *The Island of Lost Souls*, Lota (Kathleen Burke), a wholly invented character for Kenton's adaptation, is manipulated by Moreau to seduce Parker in order to produce a more genetically sound experimental offspring. Lota, an alluring, child-like character, resembles other female attractions introduced in theatrical and film adaptations of Stevenson's Jekyll and Hyde hypertexts and suggests a thematic shift from dramatic, horrific narratives to the romantic and melodramatic, which engages a broader audience. In subsequent Moreau variations, Lota, as the sexualized, post-animal, nearly human character, is an image of engaging, sympathetic decline, an evocative figure introduced into the naturalist bestiary. As the cat-as-woman, Lota functions not only as a sexual marker but concurrently as naturalist derangement. She is the nearly successful experiment to come out of Moreau's laboratory, and he misleadingly states to Parker that she is "pure Polynesian . . . the only woman on the island," but this is just another racialized lie. Like Prospero's daughter, Miranda, who marvels at the sight of a man—Montgomery functions more like a co-creator, a demigod on the island—Lota experiences an instinctive sexual awakening when she discovers Parker. Moreau believes he can control this breeding experiment, but he cannot, as her emotional impulses refute his authority. She unexpectedly helps Parker and others to escape.

Lota, a dark, sensual creature, functions as a naturalist derangement that destabilizes the fascistic experiment as she joins with Parker against the will of her creator-tormentor, and tries to help him escape. Lota serves as purposeful oppositional strategy in the narrative for the well-dressed, blonde fiancée left behind by Parker, who also assists in his escape as she goes out in search of her lost man to reclaim him for civilization. Both women, absent from the source novel, make sacrifices for Parker, and all flee from Moreau and his bestiary. Like the exotic and disturbing Irena (Simone Simon) in Jacques Tourneur's *Cat People* (1942) and Irena (Nastassia Kinski) in its remake, Paul Schrader's *Cat People* (1982), there is danger in unfettered sexual longing. Moreau wants Parker to arouse within Lota a desire to breed, thus enabling Moreau's experiment to succeed in ways he had not originally anticipated.

He could theoretically create legions of working, self-generating slaves. This measure of success, the breeding plan, would justify for Moreau in his mind his viciousness and illicit experimentation. While the animals in the zoo respond negatively to Irena's presence in both *Cat People* narratives, and the beast people lecherously gaze upon Lota, Parker remains attracted but hesitant, slightly aloof.

In *The Island of Lost Souls*, the startling, repetitious images of the beast people, a vivisected collection of flawed near-humanity, created because of uncontrolled scientific experimentation on an extra-legal site, constitute a constant thematic trope indicating atavistic regression in all Wells' Moreau adaptations. The bestial images of suffering humanity have roots in Lombrosian presentations of Darwinian natural selection—the failed struggle for survival—and a creative maladjustment of the evolutionary process. In Kenton's adaptation, Dr. Moreau is a prototypical fascist with the power to discipline, an unrivaled autocratic presence, like a camp commandant surveying inmates.

While a typical jungle may be dangerous for the uninitiated, Moreau's jungle is especially hazardous. The beast people turn against their creator in a form of mad, worker revolt, mocking the rules of the imposed fascistic social order, and bring Moreau to the house of pain to die as violently as he has lived, recalling the commandant of Kafka's penal colony turning the machine against himself as the narrator flees. Lota, the nearly-human, sacrifices herself to save the man she thinks she loves. As Moreau is vivisected by the vivisected, the perverse products of his experiments in anthropological biology burn alongside him; "law no more." The real jungle will annex this transgressive site, and all that remains will be ruins and oddly shaped skeletal formations.

Don Taylor's adaptation *The Island of Dr. Moreau* (1977), set near the beginning of the twentieth century, dispenses with both the framing story and the rescue sequence and establishes in an aerial, wide-medium shot that zooms out to a long shot, a small adrift craft illuminated by encroaching moonlight. The ship becomes a distant speck, a strand of life lost on the sea. With the arrival of daylight, the shot cuts to a series of medium to close-up shots of three exhausted men on board. When two men discover that the third man is dead, they toss the carcass overboard. The shot sequence reverts to more drifting-on-sea shots, in a series of medium and close-ups, until the next cut establishes the sighting of land from the point of view of an engineer, Andrew Braddock (Michael York). This opening series of shots suggests the crisis of dislocated sensibility and survival instinct, when one must locate a safe landing. As in the case of Robert Zemeckis' *Cast Away* (2000), the island offers imaginable succor; the sea is a baking death.

Before long, Braddock realizes he is not in paradise. He has found his way to Dr. Moreau's island, another transgressive site operating outside of the law it actively proclaims. Moreau's island is one huge experimental laboratory in which progress is measured by pain, as he seeks to jump-start the nascent science of genetic engineering by controlling the evolutionary process of life formation on a cellular level. Moreau (Burt Lancaster) introduces a serum into living organisms in order to add a new set of genetic instructions, abetted by surgical procedures conducted in the house of pain, in order to erase natural instincts that modify the body and produce humans. Moreau seeks to "reach for the control of heredity," yet he creates a multitude of malformed bodies. Other malformed bodies appear in Teruo Ishii's eccentric, surreal renewal of Moreau thematic motifs via the Poe mystery-revenge narrative in *Kyôfu kikei ningen: Edogawa Rampo zenshû/Horrors of Malformed Men* (1969), which features an opening shot sequence of a wandering male on a beach shoreline, an array of topless near-grotesque bodies of wild women, and other unfathomable figures on a violent extra-legal site with a controlling male figure. As Braddock concludes of these misshapen near-individuals, "they're human enough to pity," and like Ishii's bizarre concoctions rampant in his remote setting, all are perversely alive in Moreau's extended bestiary.

In Taylor's adaptation, Moreau shares similarities with a uniformed descendant, the Nazi Dr. Mengele, since both accept inflicting inhuman levels of pain and their own sadistic impulsiveness to a dreadful end for perverse research. The seductive female presence on the island, Maria (Barbara Carrera), a former child prostitute saved by Moreau before her natural beauty would make that implausible, has been recast in this Moreau hypertext as a recovered victim rather than an experimental product. Not long afterwards, Moreau taunts an imprisoned Braddock as he becomes a subject for the reverse scientific procedure—man into animal—exclaiming with gleefully raised expectations, "you've lost control. You are an animal." Braddock, now a violent, hairy, barely competent speaker is rescued by the woman whose sympathy he invokes. Ironically, Moreau does succeed to some degree in this reversal of evolution, and he was not a total failure when the original, animal-into-man experiments were conducted. Taylor's Moreau was close to achieving his hideous goals.

John Frankenheimer's controversial adaptation of the Moreau narrative *The Island of Dr. Moreau* (1996), set somewhere in the Java Sea, begins with a narrator's voice relating the tale as a past series of events, thus co-opting the framing device from Wells. The narrator informs the audience that "our plane crashed" and establishes the crisis of survival as a wide aerial shot frames the speck in the center of the frame, his ship. As the voice-over delineates the details of this struggle, relating that "on the sixth or seventh day" things became insufferable, the shot cuts to two of the three men on board fighting, with the narrator eventually participating in the struggle. The two combatants, now bleeding, fall overboard, becoming shark bait. The sharks always win. A series of medium and close-up shots then establish the narrator's exhaustion and dehydration, nearly leading to his death, as a shot of a blazing sun recalls the desert heat that bakes McTeague in *Greed*, slowly roasting the human, until in a daze, his head rises to gaze upon his rescuer in the form of a modern pirate ship. Is he saved? Edward Douglas (David Thewlis), the narrator and survivor, will inevitably land on Moreau's island.

As Douglas slowly recuperates with the assistance of Moreau's colleague, Montgomery (Val Kilmer), who ironically informs Douglas that he is "more like a vet" than a practicing doctor, Montgomery snaps the neck of a rabbit as he is calmly stroking it to the revulsion of Douglas, who slowly intuits that he is not on an island paradise. Montgomery acts like one of the regressive, violent boys in William Golding's *Lord of the Flies* (1954) and as Douglas enters Moreau's compound, like Kafka's unnamed traveler who arrives on the island to witness legal proceedings in the penal colony, Douglas will become more exposed to and aware of the standardized cruelty and encroaching insanity of the immediate environment and its despotic, all-powerful regime. As Moreau (Marlon Brando) enters the compound on a "burnished throne," in kabuki-makeup style, like a vision of a recalled Colonel Kurtz from performances past, Moreau's papal white imagery broadly caricatures his role as the atypical father. His eventual death at the hands/paws of his betrayed children, upon whom he levels recurring jolts of electrifying pain to control their obedience, is both horrific and justified. As Moreau is literally consumed by rebellious experimental offspring, he lives on as a digested source of meat protein.

Frankenheimer's postmodern adaptation is a reconceptualization of the Moreau narrative along several critical lines: as a self-conscious, parodic revision of its narrative antecedents, as a study of worker/slave, island/prison, and class privilege/anarchistic rebellion, and as a blending of the comedy, horror, and political film genre. Susan McHugh concludes:

> Thus updating as well as situating Moreau in the late twentieth century with this latest incarnation, the film narrative's environment shifts from a vivisectionist nightmare involving painful cross-species grafting to a eugenic transgenic experiment involving primarily subcutaneous interventions: manipulations of protein strands to design creatures, followed by injections of endorphins and hormones to prevent their regression as well as the implantation of electrodes to stabilize the social interactions of these new forms.[16]

Moreau's scientifically created extended family of near-humans dine with him in a sequence recalling the wedding celebration in Erich von Stroheim's *Greed* (1924) and in Tod Browning's *Freaks* (1932); the dining table and its occupants are strangely human, but not quite wholly civilized, although Moreau's guests do not consume meat.

One of Moreau's more successful children, introduced in Frankenheimer's adaptation as a sympathetic, yet regressing cat-woman is Aissa (Fairuza Balk), a sensual, dancing inhabitant of the island, theoretically to be bred with Douglas. In Kenton and Frankenheimer's adaptations, the female specimen is depicted not so much as a romantic resource but more as a critical segment in Moreau's plans. To sustain her desirability and remain as a potential mate, Aissa needs more experimental drugs, as some recessive animal touches slowly but visibly emerge. Like humans, these creatures consume varieties of drugs to control mood and to regulate survival. Aissa will be destroyed by other less successful experimental inhabitants of the island, as will Montgomery, but a few do survive. As Susan McHugh notes,

> As befits this scion of Faust, the premise in the 1996 film remains the same, namely that the doctor's immediate success entails his ultimate failure. However, this time the creatures live collectively beyond the experimental context, suggesting that the doctor's eugenics and not necessarily the creatures' transgenic status provide the basis of failure.[17]

While Douglas ambles about the compound, he enters the "house of pain"—the surgical platform where Moreau and Montgomery perform unnatural, torturous acts upon their subjects in the name of progressive medical, scientific research. In the Moreau cinematic hypertexts, the house of pain is depicted as the extra-legal site within the extra-legal site, a space for illusory redemptive measures, literally, physical torture within a penal colony, like undisclosed activities in covert military encampments. Both literature and history demonstrate how uncontrolled extra-judicial procedures subvert their assumed qualifying intentions in the guise of security and reformation. Scott McClintock presents a direct relationship between Kafka's monstrous inscriptive device in the colony and Moreau's torturous surgical procedures in relationship to clandestine historical events:

> The Harrow in Kafka's tale . . . has an archaic quality about it that makes it all the more suitable as an emblem for what is most contemporary about Kafka's story, with its prison island setting geographically and chronologically outside of modern penal practice and jurisprudence . . . Prison islands, of course, are always at the limits of national boundaries. They inhabit the space between juridical and extra-juridical bounds.[18]

Prisons in cities, prisons on islands, racialized ghettos, brothels: any space located in narrative time situated apart from or against judicial observation exists potentially as a naturalist observational site—a slide under the microscope—at its perceived moral-legal limit, one whose success is facilitated by unchecked power relations and isolation. *The Senate Intelligence Committee Report on*

Torture (2014), a congressional investigation publication documenting extra-legal practices conducted as covert national security measures taken against perceived terrorists/"monsters," reported that outlawed waterboarding was conducted in foreign countries in order to avoid legal restraints by government agency professionals: training for waterboarding was frequently carried out by medical staff. One such site, "Detention Site Cobalt," was sequestered in a foreign country to avoid extenuating legal circumstances.[19] Another less remote island site, located in Brooklyn's Coney Island neighborhood, grimly reanimates a narrative of power and pain contrasting with Frankenheimer's Moreau adaptation. In a parodic, gruesome exhibit in 2008, *Waterboarding Thrill Ride*, artist Steve Powers solicited his audience to gaze behind the glass opening placed on a store-front at the mock set-up of an imagined, yet factually sound sequence of events in which an animatron performs a waterboarding session upon a hooded, chained prisoner/animatron.

According to Sara Brady, "Water participates in a spectacle of pain: in between an active body and an incapacitated body, water performs."[20] Brady astutely links the observer of these proceedings with the simulated experiment in covert torture: "As installed, the *Waterboarding Thrill Ride* isn't about a simulation of waterboarding. It's about the spectator becoming a participant. As she rises to peer through the prison bars, she must decide: put in a dollar or not?"[21] The focalizing gaze of the viewer and his/her reaction to its recreation of the horrific realpolitik act informs the experiment as much as the process it depicts, as if stepping inside the house of pain during a procedure.

Frankenheimer's *The Island of Dr. Moreau* is an intergeneric naturalist narrative, a study in unchecked madness, isolation, and decline; perhaps its most disturbing quality is its suggestively plausible relationship to theoretical genetics, experimental methodologies, DNA/RNA research advances, and clinically created "breeding" technologies. As Frankenheimer's film concludes, a montage of newsreel inserts reveals a cataloging of violent images and bestial behavior—all human—suggesting to the observer that Moreau's island exists across the globe (even Coney Island). The Moreau narrative subverts the evolutionary process in the form of a demented series of experiments; this is not nature, but rather the product of flawed human nature creating imperfect forms of life, not born, violent criminals, but experimentally concocted, pathetic readings of life. The creatures habituating Moreau's island are fearful creations resembling their creators. As another dangerous creature, Abe Reles, stalked the streets of New York City, Moreau's jungle might be demonstrably constructed in steel and concrete. And then there are the Moreau hypertexts, naturalist studies in experimental "morbid anthropology,"[22] in which the jungle-island setting and its extra-legal propensities render numerous variations on themes of survival, brutality, and what it means to be (almost) human.

Isolationism

"Could the relative dearth of Darwin cartoons have been a manifestation of the eclipse of Darwinism?"[23] In Otto Messmer's animated cartoon, *Felix Doubles for Darwin* (1924), images associated with Darwinian theory and its ideological implications are masked as subtexts in the form of men, monkeys, technology, and a signifying magical cat. In Messmer's cartoon, one simultaneously registers both amusement at playfully surreal images and an annexing sense of perplexing racialized messaging involving evolution and the simian presence. As Constance Clark queries: "Why, when there were so many evolution cartoons in the 1920s, were so few of them Darwin cartoons? Darwin's photograph appeared regularly."[24] Animated films like *Felix Doubles for Darwin* exemplify a loosely structured, popularized Darwinism in which fundamental conceptual precepts associated with his theories were already registered in critical and popular discourse systems, like Freudian theories evident in the 1940s cinema involving the Oedipal complex and proscriptive sexualities, as an interpretive presence in the historical cultural logos. Patricia Vettel Tom suggests: "the Felix the Cat films have a place within the framework of aesthetic modernism, and as cultural artifacts, they were eagerly consumed by a public that left little empirical evidence as to the desires Felix seemed to satisfy."[25] Aside from the successful marketing strategy of animation's entertainment value, these cartoons suggestively address an unspoken desire that involves how the audience perceives a comedic, playful distancing from serious issues involving race and identity.

Felix Doubles for Darwin exhibits particularly discomforting naturalist images and issues via the comedic. Upon what Darwinian premise and its misapplication is the *Felix Doubles for Darwin* cartoon predicated? The response involves evolutionary theories, survival strategies, and historicized anxieties; the infamous *Scopes Trial* was only months away from the cartoon's release date.

In *Felix Doubles for Darwin*, an emaciated Felix desirous of sustenance is nearly consumed by a predatory fish who teases Felix into the water. After escaping, Felix meets a hurdy-gurdy performer with a monkey. The man gives Felix a newspaper in which he reads an advertisement: "Evolution Society offers a large reward for proof that man comes from monkey." This advertisement, which appears as a graphically realistic intertitle, leads to Felix's impossible journey inside the trans-Atlantic cable across to South Africa. Felix arrives in Cape Town, which then leads to perilous encounters with several jungle animals and a sign reading "Ape Town."

In "Ape Town," an area segregated from Cape Town, Felix sees monkeys joyfully dancing in a Charleston contest. Felix walks toward a large tree, the "Family Tree," where he sees more monkeys living on branches, some lounging, others cleaning clothes and caring for baby monkeys. As the camera tilts upwards, this dark assemblage appears like residents living on different floors in a boarding house. After calling one large monkey down from the tree, Felix shows him caricature-like images of White men in the newspaper, one a rotund "modern statesman" and then two encoded "modern cake-eaters,"[26] which makes the monkey laugh. As Felix then suggests an evolutionary linkage between species ("are these your relatives?") the monkey is visibly perturbed and calls out to other monkeys, "ye gods fellers . . . he says we're related to these," and they all angrily chase Felix, like a reverse lynch mob, back through the cable to civilization. Upon his return, Felix sees the hurdy-gurdy man, who asks: "well—do we come after monkeys?" Felix hastily and ironically replies, "the monkeys come after us," and as angry monkeys chase them, the cartoon iris closes.

Six years later, Felix made his return to the cartoonish jungle of the imagination. Otto Messmer's *Jungle Bungles* (1928) features Felix the Cat as an adventurous cameraman filming on location in the African jungle, where he encounters and disturbs several wild animals and a gathering of ludicrous-appearing cannibalistic Africans, who chase him away in an *illusionary* depth-of-field medium shot recalling the same blocking of the enraged monkeys in *Felix Doubles for Darwin*. Felix outsmarts the famished horde by magically exhibiting close-up screen images of rampaging animals coming into the Africans' space, forcing them to retreat in the other direction.

Felix Doubles for Darwin and *Jungle Bungles* are multi-layered narratives, cartoons categorized as animated, industrial productions from the silent film era by a celebrated studio featuring a well-known character, but both are controversial narratives containing naturalist precepts drawn from a racialized alteration of Darwinian concepts, involving issues associated with evolution, simian ancestry, race, even the struggle for survival. This was not an uncommon misrepresentation of Darwin's conclusions according to David Livingstone Smith and Ioana Panaitiu:

> The representation of racial minorities as apes has been a persistent dehumanizing trope . . . The notion that black people were akin to apes suffused the writings of the intelligentsia as much as it permeated popular culture. During the early twentieth century, scientists made confident pronouncements about the atavistic character of Africans, and racist cartoons routinely represented African Americans—including prominent athletes and entertainers—in simian form.[27]

In *Jungle Bungles*, one discovers that the filmmaking camera is the source of negative magic that transforms landscape and inhabitants—images of the real world, however much a cartoon—into a survival narrative.[28] William Golding's graphic study of survival, mob psychology, and the spectacle of atavistic reversion, *Lord of the Flies* (1954), in which schoolboys revert to tribalism and violent sacrificial rites after surviving a plane crash, links degenerating human behavior to extreme isolation suggesting a hypertextual linkage with *The Island of Dr. Moreau*. According to Richard Costa, "*Lord of the Flies*, like *The Island of Dr. Moreau*, traces the defects of society back to the defects of human nature."[29] These defects, whether located in an aging, perverse scientist, hybrid animal-human creatures, or violent school boys, reveal naturalist tropes including a hazardous jungle setting on a remote island. Both novels are survival narratives of lethal consequences, studies in naturalism's paradigmatic grinding tradition, the wearing away of humanity from the human, until a beast is revealed. Costa states, "both authors develop, in the mythopoeic way that is their trademark, the idea that man is a savage, not intrinsically different from the Paleolithic brute,"[30] as respective studies in atavistic human reversion. The difference between them is that Wells reveals what is beastly in man in the figure of a deranged scientist and the failed vivisectionist products of extra-legal experimentalism, while Golding uses the human-as-larvae, in an isolated, unregulated environment to rediscover the repressed core of the beastly. Both novels assault modern socio-biological imperatives, belief systems associated with civilization, human identity, and progress in case studies of naturalist isolation and decline.

In Hector Babenco's *Pixote: A Lei do Mais Fraco/Pixote* (1981), Pixote (Fernando Ramos da Silva), an abandoned pre-teenage boy, commits murder and robbery and deals drugs in the streets and alleys of Sao Paulo, living a feral existence in his struggle to survive as an unwanted human in an urban jungle. Babenco's grimly naturalist study is a fall-to-greater-fall narrative in which rampant violence is a way of life, and Pixote learns how to subsist despite crooked police and dangerous friends. After he commits homicide and robbery, there is really no place or solace left without significant danger, and in *Pixote*, this painful existence involves other lost juveniles. Babenco's shot sequence, set in the state-sanctioned juvenile facility in which a young boy is raped while other boys in the room sleep or feign sleeping, remains brutally horrific in observation and detail. Irving Epstein notes:

> [I]n *Pixote* the lives of street children are presented in ways that reflect the horror and violence of Latin American authoritarianism ... For director Babenco, street life simply becomes an extension of the brutality of the state, as symbolized by the youth's treatment in the reform school and in the adult prison. There are absolutely no redeeming characteristics to these state institutions, and, in fact, all pretense with regard to their legitimacy of purpose or function is lacking from the very start ... in *Pixote*, it is the brutality of the state that is later reproduced on the street.[31]

Pixote encounters predatory streets in an ongoing series of dangerous incidents. Similarly, David Baguley describes the pivotal incident in Golding's *Lord of the Flies* as "the ritual hunt by the boys on the desert island," which at first aims at the capture and slaughter of a sow, but later at another little boy as a preferred sacrificial offering. According to Baguley, "The scene represents the final release of the demonic capacities in man, which human moral systems only superficially constrain."[32] Like the primal situations experienced by frightened, violent youths in Babenco's *Pixote*, fear of isolation, fear of hunger, and fear of each other facilitate a restoration of primal, destructive tribalism. In *Lord of the Flies*, Jack, the most dangerous of the stranded youngsters, confronts the more intelligent Piggy and Ralph's socializing schema, exclaiming, "'Bollocks to the rules. We're strong—we hunt! If there's a beast, we'll hunt it down! We'll close in and beat and beat and beat—!'"[33] This leads to the death of Simon.

When American filmmaker and photographer Gordon Parks visited the Brazilian favela in 1961 with the assignment to visually document daily life and the struggles of the inhabitants of the economically isolated site, he observed: "the noon sun baked the mud-rot of the wet mountainside. Garbage and human excrement clogged the open sewers snaking down the slopes"; Parks later compares sites of poverty in America and abroad, "none of them had prepared me for this one in the favela."[34] Describing his departure from the favela, Parks notes, "[it] was no place for strangers after sundown. Desperate criminals hid out there. To hunt them out, the police came in packs, but only in daylight."[35] Fernando Meirelles' *Cidade de Deus/The City of God* (2002), set in an extremely violent extra-legal site, the favela slum district in Brazil's Rio de Janeiro, presents the indigenous, furious and exploited poor and focuses on lost tribalistic children in the *Lord of the Flies* drug culture narrative. Through his examination of the city's recent past, Meirelles' *The City of God* begins with an allegorical sequence of events: a chicken escapes from imminent slaughter and is cornered between corrupt police searching for local gangsters and those armed hoodlums in pursuit of an escaped meal. Blood, warfare, and consequential acts of butchery frame the observed activities of the daily life of drug dealers, murderers, and the occasional innocent in a place where few wholly emerge. In one early shot sequence, after robbing a local motel-brothel, the young criminals hide in the nearby jungle, a reversion to primitive origins.

One gangster, an especially dangerous drug dealer and murderer, Li'l Zé (Leandro Firmino), provides the counter-narrative for Buscapé, "Rocket" (Alexandre Rodrigues), the young photographer from the favela who documents crime scenes in the daily life he witnesses in Weegee-like photographs, initially as an amateur, but later as a working professional for the newspaper. As Rocket peers through the lens, the audience perceives expressions of human distress. Rocket's escape narrative, via labor, from the criminal activities of the favela contrasts with Li'l Zé's rise-and-fall narrative, as he kills his way to the top of the gangster culture. In a clinical context, the critical focus on a dangerous germ, Li'l Zé, who spreads across the controlled concrete spaces of the favela, indicates the remote island tribalism and Jack's primitive power design in Brooks' *Lord of the Flies*. In the favela, there is no adult supervision, since the local police are as dangerous as the criminals, who frequently labor in assembly-like production workplaces producing cocaine as the drug-of-choice.

In *The City of God*, age and gender figure in one's place and status; male teenagers effectively run most of the daily criminal activities. The ever visible "runts" are those children too young to work for gangsters such as Li'l Zé, except in minor, supportive roles, but they are the most threatening, nascent germs in the immediate environment: destabilizing potential derangements. The gang of deceptively uncontrollable runts are the faces behind an emerging, rudderless future in Li'l Zé's present criminal empire. As the runts repeatedly watch or even commit violent acts, they learn and adjust to the drug-saturated situation in the favela while plotting how to survive against both friends and enemies: kill.

Neither rival gangsters in the favela nor the police successfully eliminate Li'l Zé. A concluding shot sequence of Li'l Zé's final moments features his capture and release from the trunk of a police car after a gang war kills dozens in the streets. The corrupt police anticipate a windfall of profit for the arranged "escape," but as he is weakened and unarmed, Li'l Zé is repeatedly shot, mostly off camera, by a gang of runts he formerly used for minor activities. He is literally executed, as he lies on the ground, by the next generation of murderers and drug dealers he infected, thus begins the future in the present, as the runts walk off into the favela in armed triumph, neither rescued nor redeemed in the concrete jungle.

Peter Brook's *Lord of the Flies* (1963), a black and white low-budget film adaptation of Golding's novel, utilized non-professional actors on an island setting to portray the stranded, privileged school boys, and may be viewed as a (post)neorealist narrative aligned with a clinically naturalist structure in a horrific experimental context. Brook's use of long shots and natural low-key lighting contributes significantly to the sense of near-microscopic observation, as if witnessing the decline of a colony of self-devouring specimens. Jackson Burgess refers to the "pell-mell pace of the film," which is "horrendously exciting"[36] in a dreadful manner. Brook insightfully juxtaposes the lush island setting with the nascent emergence of the boy's appalling, nearly playful acts of violence in a communal desire for leadership and survival. If Ralph (James Aubrey), an older boy representing structure and order for the group, must cope with Jack (Tom Chapin), whose strength and instincts lead to a less advanced, more violent, and primitive survival strategy do clash, it is inevitable that one side should emerge victorious. Other boys, such as the intelligent

"Piggy" (Hugh Edwards), brutally murdered by the mob, sensitive Simon (Tom Gaman), and bullying Roger (Roger Elwin), align themselves according to disposition and survival-efficiency.

In Brook's film, the ritual slaughter of Simon is a frenzied, terrifying extended sequence. After Simon encounters the decaying head of a stuck pig, full of buzzing flies, Brook's shot and reverse extreme close-up shots between the boy and the gazing remains suggest who is watching whom. Soon, Simon discovers the body of a lost parachutist from the same flight, solving another mystery and providing knowledge to disseminate to the bifurcated groups. As the evening and the storm begin to settle in on island and sea shore, Jack's aggressive hunters steal, somewhat playfully, the burning logs from his perceived rival tribe—the non-hunters—to provide the necessary fire for cooking meat. These hunters, with sharp spears and painted faces functioning as signifying, identifying tribal markers, suggest a lapse into a more primitive, clannish gathering. As the meat-eating, increasingly violent boys begin to feast and utter nonsensical phrases and sounds, the other group approaches and is allowed to join after gaining permission from the leader. These two sides represent the attempt to imitate organizational strategies. According to Geertz, "Savages build models of reality . . . by ordering perceived particulars into immediately intelligible wholes . . . these become structural models representing the underlying order of reality as it were analogically."[37] On both sides, these boys adapt to their survival crises in an imitative fashion, one group seeking structured order and individual discipline, the other responding with the immediate, instinctive, primal action of the strongest. Brook never resorts to artificial sentimentalities; instead, the film narrative's brisk pacing and neorealistic dark-to-darker setting lead to credible, inevitable human horror as the sides clash.

The boys sing, dance around aimlessly, bang on objects and scream aloud as the night removes lingering daylight; only the campfire and moonlight are left to illuminate the immediate environment. As the storm continues to rage and the sea surges, Brook alternates between medium and close-up shots to suggest the rapid motion of a released chaos. As the boys chant gibberish and animal noises, some scream, "kill the beast," Simon returns from his fruitful excursion, crawling through the dense brush, only to be seen, attacked, and slaughtered like a trapped animal by stampeding boys, now a crazed hunting party in feverish, atavistic assault. This extended, revelatory shot sequence concludes with the image of a dead body just off shore, as Simon listlessly floats partially submerged.

Brook's adaptation of *Lord of the Flies* reveals, in its use of a realistic, natural setting and lighting, non-professional actors, and an overall documentary approach to Golding's horrific narrative of decline, how naturalist film advocates a "way of seeing" in an experimental context, what potentially remains of the human. For these boys, extreme physical separation from a regulatory social setting facilitates the removal of proscriptive norms. Geertz concludes,

> Savage ... modes of thought are primary in human mentality. They are what we all have in common. The civilized ... thought patterns of modern science and scholarship are specialized productions of our own society. They are secondary, derived ... artificial.[38]

Aside from modes of thought, hunger reduces the human, and survival emerges as the unifying principle. On the microscopic slide, one virus will consume the weaker other.

Beyond Moreau

How may a horror film transcend its generic parameters? Erle C. Kenton's *The Island of Lost Souls* (1932) adaptation of Wells' novel depicts botched experimental life forms, near-humans, and as the revised title suggests, the posturing of progressive humanity that is untraceable in this study of fascistic power, the subjugated grotesque, literally, Darwinian incongruities. *The Island of Lost Souls*, set in a nebulous time period somewhere in the sea of the mislaid, is a landmark narrative in naturalist cinema as it popularizes complex Darwinian precepts via the generic specifics of the horror film. The Lombrosian imagery of the misshapen beast people—a vivisected, experimental humanity—and the horrors of unabated, politicized science is an informing presence in *The Island of Lost Souls*, released at the height of the Depression in the United States. The beast people suggestively invoke images from newspapers and newsreels of legions of the unemployed and unemployable, the sickly and socio-economically imperfect masses, male and female precariat labor, struggling to survive, but still alive. Whether framed in close-up or medium shots in *The Island of Lost Souls*, brutish images of sauntering, stooped misery remind the audience of what they are not: the others in their midst who do exist. This functional gaze, set upon a vision of oddly realistic horror, what the audience is not, creates a deflective gap between the observer and the observed, a common distancing process that initiates narrative and historicized perspective, a situational response. Kenton's adaptation of Wells' novel reveals multiple intertextual parallels.

Politicized, plausibly Lombrosian images of the downtrodden and socially, racially undesirable, documented others from the Depression era, were produced, very likely by studio executives at the powerful MGM studio. In *California Election News* for the "Inquiring Cameraman," the staged newsreel inferentially warned the audience against voting for the author of *The Jungle*, socialist Upton Sinclair, for governor of California in 1934. Sinclair plausibly lost the election when close-up and medium shots of the poor advocating their support for him flashed on the theater's screen.[39] These visibly disturbing class and racially suggestive signs initiate a distancing reaction. Years later, documentarian Frederick Wiseman's *cinéma vérité* study of social betrayal and isolation *Titicut Follies* (1967), a controversial narrative about disabled human beings, mentally handicapped men who are warehoused as inmates in a hospital for the criminally insane, was so disturbing as to be banned from release for decades on ostensibly legal grounds. As a study in sequestered humanity, *Titicut Follies* remains a troubling documentary to witness; however historical the images, the abnormal suffering and dehumanizing living conditions of inmates are detailed in relentless, clinically objective framing. Are they not men?

Imprisonments

Humans are not bugs, but may be bug-like. In Aristotle's *History of Animals*, he notes: "The most laborious of all insects, if compared with the rest, are the tribes of ants . . . and their other congeners."[40] Aristotle states that a literal and symbolic relationship involving labor and temperament extends beyond other cited species such as "hornets and wasps,"[41] into the domain of mammals, specifically, the human animal, in which an observable capacity toward violence links the aforementioned species known for aggressive behavior. According to the *Smithsonian Magazine*:

> modern societies resemble those of certain ants much more than our nearest relatives, the chimpanzee and bonobo. No chimp has to create highways, traffic rules, and infrastructure; participate in assembly lines and complex teamwork; or allocate a labor force for effective division of labor . . . When considering the often-striking similarities between humans and social insects, one fascinating parallel is the existence of warfare in both.[42]

Naturalist film repeatedly engages the trope of the human-as-animal, a violent, predatory juxtaposition, and specifically extends the metaphorical range into the insect world, even to the smallest specimens engaged in survival strategies. Byron Haskin's remote plantation melodrama, *The Naked Jungle* (1954), set in a South American jungle environment in which armies of ants labor, attacking and destroying whatever edible is found in their path, may feature prominent actors such as Charlton Heston and Eleanor Parker, but the focus is arguably on the eruptive appearance of hordes of little monsters: the ants. Like an advancing army, the dreaded ants—the "marabunta"—act as one primitive mind obeying instinctual drives, but are eventually extinguished by a single plotting man. An anthill is a place in nature where ants live and frequently die, a place to labor and to defend.

Along with references to attractive peacocks and trench rats, in *Paths of Glory* (1957), Stanley Kubrick's study of class, mendacity, and martial conflict, ironic expressions of human misery and cruelty are set during a needless, ill-fated military campaign in World War One. *Paths of Glory* chronicles the lives of three sacrificed soldiers who fail to advance upon the "anthill," a geographic land mass located between warring armies. These three men devolve from serving soldiers to sacrificial offerings to assuage a disappointed military hierarchy and stimulate media coverage; what is the life of a few two-legged bugs? In novelist Roy Rigby's *The Hill*, set during World War Two, a neglected naturalist study of military justice, illogical codes of conduct, racism, imprisonment, and general states of moral decay in North Africa, men who were once soldiers are now prisoners of the army each once served for various reasons. The prison is run more like a vicious penal colony in which the men are treated like trained fleas as they are forced, in assembly-line fashion, to build and then hurriedly, repeatedly to climb on and over a steep hill under a blazing sun as a form of punishment; according to the jailers, "[it was] a splendid hill, specially constructed for defaulters and the awkward squad."[43] The construction of the hill is described as a meaningless, overwhelming activity designed to control and to humiliate the imprisoned:

> All day long trucks roared into the prison grounds and deposited sand, and slowly the hill began to take shape. The prisoners, bare to the waist and sweating in the intense heart, shoveled away in silent fury. More prisoners carrying heavy rocks staggered onto the hill, dropped the rocks, ran down the hill and collected more rocks and returned and dumped them on the hill; the prisoners with shovels buried the rocks in sand, and so the hill grew.[44]

Prisoners are viewed by the authorities as a problematic infestation. Another prisoner, the former officer Joe Roberts, resists the indoctrination and inhumanity of his jailers: "Roberts wearily clawed his way to the top of the hill, heaved himself upright and walked on, then his legs suddenly gave away and his mouth was full of sand again."[45] In *The Hill*, the prisoners labor like dispirited, entrapped insects.

Sidney Lumet's adaptation of Rigby's novel, *The Hill* (1965), examines the demoralization and consequential violence of those judged guilty. In Lumet's *The Hill*, soldiers mindlessly drill, march, line up, and obey orders about work in a military prison in which the commanding officers are cruelly sober by day and pathetically drunk at night. Near endless shots of physical activity establish a sense of both visual and social order, like a backdrop of obedience training for animals or trained fleas in a circus performance. The brutality is a platformed response, not even a corrective, but rather, a surveillance system set under a sweltering sun. In effect, the imprisoned men function like mindless ants entering and leaving the hill of their own making. Roberts (Sean Connery) serves as a dramatic focus in the adaptation as a soldier who obeys a moral code rather than absurd orders whenever possible; Roberts is the non-conforming ant. Another prisoner, Jacko King (Ossie Davis), is a Black man in an identifiably White man's army that abuses him. He is subjected to humiliating, virulent racist treatment and language, In one shot sequence, after Jacko receives one insult too many, he rips off his clothing and confronts the authorities in their office in a manner that unsettles them while he remains casually lounging, smoking, but nearly nude, as they gasp in reaction. Although treated like a dehumanized spectacle—he is derisively referred to as a "monkey"—Jacko humorously subverts the relentless insistence of his otherness among others, with dignity and self-assurance.

In *The Hill*, Sergeant Wilson (Harry Andrews), a pivotal symbol of prison authority, concludes that he must break Roberts to assert authority and force him to obey the law of the hill and behave like a complacent ant, which does not occur, leading to an unforeseen, riotous and violent ending for Roberts and his cellmates as they extract revenge on one especially brutal jailer: "Lumet distorts the planes of Andrews' face at the end of the film and establishes a visual correlative for the soldier's disintegrating sense of power, as what he imagines as a rationally imposed order crumbles into savagery and madness."[46] In Lumet's naturalist narrative about military prison life, brutality, alcohol abuse, and racism, only some ants survive. The anthill remains.

Anton Chekhov's *The Island; A Journey to Sakhalin* (1893) describes the daily routine and life of the prisoners he personally witnessed at this infamous pre-revolutionary penal colony, and makes the following observations about the relationship between convict life, labor, and the idea of the punitive gesture: "Digging out stumps in the forest, building houses, draining swamps, fishing, mowing, loading, and unloading cargo on ships are all types of convict labor which have necessarily merged with the life of the colony."[47] Chekhov's description of laborious corrective and time-consuming routines are significantly displayed in both Kenton's *The Island of Lost Souls* and Mervyn LeRoy's synchronous film release, *I Am a Fugitive from a Chain Gang* (1932), which presents convicts, not as monsters, but as brutalized, isolated creatures, barely surviving in a state-sanctioned, albeit extra-legal site. The socially progressive *I Am a Fugitive from a Chain Gang*, an intergeneric blending of the bio-pic, historical, fictional, and especially, popular prison/criminal film narrative of the respective production era, is a case study in sanctioned cruelty and nub theory.[48] LeRoy's decline narrative examines the life of engineer James Allen. The socially superfluous James Allen (Paul Muni) is introduced as a returning veteran seeking employment. As Allen is represented to the Depression-era audience, his struggle to survive embodies one failure among millions in a collapsed world economy. Allen returns from the war to face the tedium of a numbing factory job incommensurate with the life-changing experiences of global conflict; after a series of failed efforts to re-establish himself, Allen travels aimlessly around the country. His postwar male anxiety renders him restless and vulnerable as a psychologically displaced worker.

I Am a Fugitive from a Chain Gang is a naturalist film narrative about the decline and dehumanization of an individual, alienated labor, and extra-legal sites. The trope of the conflicted worker is a serial presence throughout LeRoy's film: first, the dislocating effects of war itself, the identification of Allen's anxiety in his reluctant return to familiar prewar employment in the factory, and especially, as Allen experiences the disciplinary chain gang and his failed attempts at escape/reform. Like the humiliating, grinding experiences director Gerhard Lamprecht's ex-convict Robert Kraemer suffers in *Die Verrufenen/The Slums of Berlin* (1925) as he fruitlessly searches for redemptive employment, Allen's decline in social and economic standing is marked by his unkempt appearance, his identifiably lower-class-criminal company, and even where he sleeps. Near the bottom of the status-barrel, in a familiar Depression-era flop house, Allen foolishly accepts an offer of a handout dinner, but his companion robs the restaurant at gunpoint. Although depicted as innocent in the film, Allen becomes the property of the state and is sent to serve in the forced labor of the chain gang. Like a galley slave in a Roman epic film, Allen toils in this agrarian-based nightmarish narrative of modern slave labor. Work is portrayed as interminable and punitive, and Allen's survival depends on his skill breaking rocks and clearing roads, laboring like a mule that pulls a wagon and carries loads. For both animals, survival was dependent on acclimation, not reform, but Allen is capable of unharnessing his yoke, and he does escape from the chain gang, although temporarily. While Allen's social status is temporarily restored as he successfully labors in Chicago, Carl Sandburg's celebrated "City of the Big Shoulders,"[49] he remains a fugitive.

In Käthe Kollowitz's drypoint line etching, *The Ploughmen*, sheet 1, "Peasants War" (1907), she depicts, moving from right to left, two men toiling like anonymous harnessed mules, bent over and likely exhausted, pushing the plow forward in the foreground of the frame.[50] The relationship between laboring animals, especially mules, and incarcerated individuals is a recurring naturalist trope in cinema. In *I Am a Fugitive from a Chain Gang*, LeRoy's shot of the harnessed, laboring mule juxtaposed with images of the chained prisoners is a compelling indexical sign of naturalist imagery: men as animals. There are metaphorical implications to this trope. In Clint Eastwood's *The Mule* (2018), an older, alienated man with limited economic resources becomes a drug cartel's "mule"—a transport animal—and he toils like a subjugated figure, driving across long roads delivering illegal products while encountering treacherous people in order to raise capital for his family. Earl (Clint Eastwood) is an absent father and husband and portrayed as selfishly unsympathetic. He belatedly realizes his own failures. Earl's decline into contemporary drug culture and his eventual capture by the authorities lead him to prison. In concluding shot sequences, Earl is viewed cultivating flowers in the garden. Eastwood's haggard face and stooping frame are signs of vestigial presence; like an old, nameless mule, he is put out to pasture, no longer viable in the technical world. In these naturalist films, for four-legged and two-legged animals, survival is dependent on acclimation, not reform. In *I Am a Fugitive from a Chain Gang*, Allen surreptitiously unharnesses his yoke and escapes from the chain gang, however temporarily, like a runaway animal.

It is noteworthy that in *I Am a Fugitive from a Chain Gang*, after Allen first escapes from the chain gang, traditional male prerogatives are re-established by a dynamic that energizes the progress machine; Allen is an intelligent, middle-class male ascending the heterosexual "success" ladder. After Allen escapes from the chain gang for the first time, he finds some traditional prerogatives re-established by the social dynamic that energizes the progress-myth machine, as Allen is an educated man and, as depicted in a series of time-clock markers noting his working the way up the labor-ladder, resourceful and industrious: the encoded Depression-era promise of restored normalcy. Guy Debord concludes, "myth is the unitary construction of the thought which guarantees the entire cosmic order surrounding the order which this society has in fact already realized within its frontiers."[51] Familiar myths associated with capitalism, individuality, progress, and especially social justice are refuted, restored and subject to observational scrutiny in *I Am a Fugitive from a Chain Gang* as a human being is hunted like an animal.

In 1861, Courbet's *Le Cerf forcé/Stag at Bay*[52] foregrounds against an ominously dark canvas a stag pausing at a water source in the forest, feasibly seeking respite from advancing, menacing sources such as hunters and packs of dogs.[53] The animal appears not to be at peace, as its head arches upwards as if responding to distant sounds, perhaps thunder or voices, barking, or gunshots in the distance. Courbet's *Stag at Bay* is an arresting image, a disturbing moment observed in the natural world of the stag's presumptive awareness before some encroaching danger. In his analysis of Courbet's extensive series of hunting paintings, Shao-Chien Tseng notes that "Courbet concentrated on two aspects of the hunt—the capture and suffering of the quarry and the hunter's peaceful and reflective moment afterward,"[54] to which he adds, "Courbet's paintings engage with the notion of hunting as a native heritage and masculine sport."[55] Perhaps the hunting party—death—will soon arrive.

Dimitri Kirsanoff's *Death of a Stag/La Mort du Cerf* (1951)[56] is an avant-garde film produced in France that appears like a Courbet painting metamorphosized as it depicts the sport of death. The sense of menace the animal intuits in Courbet's painting is visibly present in Kirsanoff's film as a flow of ironically juxtaposed close-up and medium shots of the uniformed, privileged few joyously hunting, with traditional horn playing and bland commentary functioning in the background. The celebratory moments afforded to the hunters—eating, gossiping, and preparing for the kill as they gallop off after the dogs trained to detect and to destroy animal life—are set against the natural environment of the woods, water, sky, and the terrorized creature in flight, a stag. As *Death of a Stag* begins by establishing shots of the forest, which lead to fading tapestry illustrations of hunting scenarios, recollections of a stagnant old world order are rendered in the here-and-now of the narrative. The film depicts an anachronistic sporting activity as a stylized, clinical study of violent rituals.[57] Like Courbet's hunting paintings, in which "a dialectic of life and death runs through the uncanny process Courbet employed to picture animals in hunting scenes and game pieces,"[58] Kirsanoff's *Death of a Stag* documents the relationship between pleasure, social exchange, and indifference to slaughter. The stag is finally trapped, shot, dragged by a chain, and skinned, and the raw flesh of its carcass is left for the dogs to consume eagerly. Soon, refreshments are served. The stag, a frightened, exhausted beast, never had an opportunity to flee from its circumscribed space; Kirsanoff's pack of humans is as merciless as clichéd nature. The death of Kirsanoff's stag has disturbing artistic and historical parallels in another postwar, suggestively experimental naturalist film narrative.

Naturalist film adaptation narratives do not depend on the habitual fidelity-to-source dialectic or even its wholesale creative revision as an evaluative measure of aesthetic-historical cinematic merit. More specifically, Albert Band's *Face of Fire* (1959) is a transnational production of Stephen Crane's novella, "The Monster" (1898). Crane's narrative chronicles the disgraceful decline and ostracism of Henry, a Black man in a small American town whose face is disfigured by fire as a result of saving a White child. Eventually, the intimidated townspeople turn against the sight of Henry's monstrous visage, the result of his heroic act, and he lives a diminished, sequestered life. Band's film adaptation alters Crane's examination of the community and its values by eliminating the racial element. Henry, now renamed as Monk, becomes a White man wearing a mask after the scarring incident to cover his grisly appearance, thus lessening Crane's significant, immediate social messaging. Yet Band's adaptation simultaneously introduces issues associated with disability studies and censorship. Both Crane's fiction and Band's adaptation are credible, distinctive naturalist narratives.

Despite its mixed critical reception, Pierre Chenal's *Sangre Negra/Native Son* (1951), however low the budget or imperfect in stylistic composition, may be read in an alternative context without focusing primarily on the eponymous source novel by Richard Wright. Page Laws contemplates, "Perhaps *Native Son* has proven so hard to adapt successfully because ... it is essentially unadaptable."[59] In retrospect, Chenal's film interpretation of Wright's novel may be viewed in a more experimental, cinematic context, as a coherent fictional document about perverse race and class relations and historicized agit-prop, much like Eisenstein's overt social messaging produced during the post-revolutionary era. In its repressive urban, neorealistic setting, Chenal's *Native Son* is a clinical study in the volatile decline of a racially constructed man rendered as unharnessed human beast.

A framing voice-over informs the audience that Bigger lives in a place, "a prison without bars," identified as Chicago. According to Ellen Scott, "*Native Son*'s violence displays the morbid fascination and unsentimental detachment that critics developing the concept of noir admired."[60] Although *Native Son* is primarily produced in Argentina, the noir setting is the Chicago of the imagination, evident in contemporaneous productions such as John Aueur's *City That Never Sleeps* (1953) and Henry Hathaway's noirish *Call Northside 777* (1948).

In *Native Son*, Bigger (Richard Wright) is introduced as a Black man without employment or measurable capital living with his family in a run-down tenement. In one unsettling shot sequence, while the family is cramped together in their rented home, Bigger chases down and kills a large rat running across the floor. There is no escape for the detested creature, a metaphorical, naturalist allusion; this hunting sequence is chillingly recreated as, after his crime of murder is publicized, the police and informers search for the fleeing Bigger across entangling locations in which he too struggles to survive. As he scurries through buildings and alleys, and climbs to a rooftop and water tower with "William's Funeral Garden" neon signage illuminating the sky, Bigger pauses in an overwhelming moment of anxiety as he hears horns, gunfire, and voices; he is a man at bay sensing impending doom.

In LeRoy's *I Am a Fugitive from a Chain Gang*, James Allen barely survives in the imagined setting of the cinematic "South," while chained to other convicts; in Chenal's *Native Son*, Bigger's chains, invisible markers of his race and class, also endure despite the efforts of sympathetic figures. Bigger is hired as a uniformed chauffeur—a marker of labor and status—to escort a young White woman as she indulges class-entitled fantasies, mostly after hours, and this inevitably leads to multiple deaths and damnation. It is important to note that Bigger accidentally suffocates the drunk, exhausted White woman, Mary Dalton (Jean Wallace), not out of a sense of sexual arousal or its frustration, but rather from the fear of detection and likely accusation of rape once her blind mother enters the bedroom and "senses" his presence. Bigger is not Zola's Jacques Lantier, whose compulsion to kill, once aroused is of a dim, ancestral origin; Bigger unwittingly kills because of uncontrollable, terrifying panic, and later, he kills his girlfriend because of his fear of betrayal. Bigger is not biologically predisposed to murder, but he is arguably conditioned via the eternal machinations of a relentlessly bigoted social milieu. Bigger and Jacques are different specimens.

Perhaps the most shocking shot sequence in *Native Son*, edited from the film prior to its commercial release, involves an act other than noir's familiar criminal intrigues or violence. In cinematographer William Heise's *The Kiss* (1896), in a medium close-up shot, after some conversation, an older couple, a White man and woman, kiss. Two years later, in William Selig's *Something Good—Negro Kiss*, in a sustained medium shot, a Black couple repeatedly kiss and enjoy each other's company. The racial, heterosexual divide between films is maintained. Over fifty years later, in Chenal's *Native Son*, the norm is emotively shattered; a censored shot of a passionate kiss between Bigger and the inebriated, reclining Mary occurs seconds before her mother enters the room to witness—although she is blind—the social taboo nearly without parallel, not to be depicted in mainstream cinema until the relaxation of the Hollywood Code in the 1960s. According to Thy Phu:

> Bigger's desire finds its most explicit expression in Wright's film in a kiss with Mary—a kiss that would nonetheless have been just as shocking and explicit as the novel's representation of black male sexuality. This kiss, however, did not make the cut, and though a still photo hints at what the final form might have been, the film itself had to settle for the image of Bigger supporting a drunken Mary to hint at this forbidden physical intimacy.[61]

This image of forbidden exchange resonates in several capacities as a sexual as well as political act; "the [edited] kiss between Mary and Bigger, was, for the film at least, tantamount to the kiss of death."[62] Bigger is a failed human experiment in the culture of alterity; he is the "other" unredeemed, aware of his impending fate like a foregone conclusion. In grim naturalist tradition, Bigger lands in the prison from which there is no escape, save his scheduled death, like a tracked, executed stag.

Bigger's execution is the end-product of a racially proscriptive society and his own unrestrained fury. Bigger is not innocent, but his violent behavior is partially a by-product of absorbed public toxins that reflect decades of inherited biases; in this sense, Bigger is a compromised part of a dreadful whole, a to-be-discarded, near-invisible man. Along with an excess of racial epithets, intoxicants, cool music, a televised boxing match, and the dynamic contrast between ghetto life and the life of the privileged many, *Native Son* is a unique, unsettling recovered film narrative, a film about the hunt:

> The film is visually dark but the stylized, high-contrast noir cinematography is missing. In its place is a blunt, frank darkness. Minimal editing and many medium-long shots leave spectators' vision remarkably undirected. Nor do we have a sense, as we do in many noir films, of the fecundity of urban space ... It gives spectators a radical approach to Black-white relations and Black subjectivity in an era characterized by conservative approaches to—and imaginings of—integration.[63]

Pierre Chenal's *Crime et châtiment/Crime and Punishment* (1935), an adaptation of Dostoyevsky's novel, released the same year as director Josef von Sternberg's *Crime and Punishment*, features an unusual expressionistic black and white set design with shadows, staircases, windows, and frames with stylized angles and geometrics, like Hitchcock's prison cell sequence in *The Wrong Man* (1957) featuring Manny's collapse. As Bigger's depressingly empty prison cell and unattractive urban environment reflect his social status, Chenal's Raskolnikov is also entrapped by poverty and his own consuming class resentment. He kills two women with an ax to steal a small sum of money. Engels notes:

> There is, therefore, no cause for surprise if the workers, treated as brutes, actually become such; or if they maintain their consciousness of manhood only by cherishing the most glowing hatred, the most unbroken inward rebellion against the bourgeoisie in power.[64]

After Raskolnikov confesses his guilt to the authorities, Chenal's synecdochic image of prisoners' shackled feet marching off and across the frame, like yoked animals, serves as a naturalist image.

In *I Am a Fugitive from a Chain Gang*, shots of the abusive treatment of both Black and White convicts—mostly disenfranchised laborers—toiling at road construction and forms of menial activity suggest labor's function as punitive corrective, an ironic redemptive exploitation of entrapped human beasts. A recurring linkage of shots between harnessed toiling animals and incarcerated humans occurs in *I Am a Fugitive from a Chain Gang*; in one shot sequence, as convicts prepare for the early morning ride to the next work location, the blank stare in close-up of chained workers is dryly juxtaposed with images of yoked mules. Most passively chained workers seethe silently, but obediently; Allen remains perceptibly incredulous while resistant to brutalizing expressions of power and control. Engels observes that

> they are men so long as they burn with wrath against the reigning class. They become brutes the moment they bend in patience under the yoke, and merely strive to make life endurable while abandoning the effort to break the yoke.[65]

Allen's refusal to accept his imposed fate, like Prendick's rejection of Moreau's insane social order on his isolated island, leads to Allen's eventual escape, his return to the chain gang. Like the semi-fictional film adaptation of convict Henri Charrière's multiple escape efforts from Devil's Island in the 1930s in Franklin J. Schaffner's *Papillon* (1973), the desperate individual, despite brutalizing conditions and enforced isolation, struggles, and continues attempting his escape. In René Cardona's *La Isla de los hombres solos/The Island of Lonely Men* (1974), the isolation and brutality endemic to the Moreau narrative blends with the prison genre film. Cardona's stylized, reality-based Moreau narrative invokes LeRoy's *I Am a Fugitive from a Chain Gang*, Schaffner's *Papillion*, and other Devil's Island narratives, with the added presence of Kafka's compulsively deranged commandant from *In the Penal Colony* as a sadistic figurehead. *The Island of Lonely Men*, with its mutilations, rape, murders, and systemic violence is a horrific political critique of the excesses and perversion of justice, as men dream of escape and make the effort. In *The Island of Lonely Men*, the worst criminals wear uniforms in support of a flawed system.

At the conclusion of *I Am a Fugitive from a Chain Gang*, the audience discovers that the state prison system—the bureaucratic part representing the ideological whole—hoodwinks Allen, who voluntarily returns to prison only to be betrayed. Allen must escape once again and learn to live like a thief; therefore, Allen is made into a criminal, identifying the narrative as a polemical tract, a call for social and penal reform. While standing alone in the dark space of a city street in medium shot, as the iris slowly shuts down to an encompassing black, Allen states to his former girlfriend that, "I steal," in his conclusive, transformative declaration. Allen is a naturalist nub, a product of the grinding process in a controlling, impersonal society.

Notes

1. Robert Weldon Whalen, *Murder, Inc., and the Moral Life: Gangsters and Gangbusters in La Guardia's New York* (New York: Fordham University Press, 2016), 1.
2. Edmund Elmaleh, *The Canary Sang but Couldn't Fly* (New York: Union Square Press, 2009), 3–4.
3. Charles Darwin, *The Expression of Emotion in Man and Animals* (New York: D. Appleton, 1897), 136. See http://darwin-online.org.uk/converted/pdf/1897_Expression_F1152.pdf. Accessed June 19, 2023.
4. H. G. Wells, *The Island of Dr. Moreau* (New York: Modern Library, 1996), ix.
5. Giorgio Agamben, "The Camp as *Nomos* of the Modern," in *Violence, Identity, and Self-Determination*, eds Hent De Vries and Samuel Weber (Stanford: Stanford University Press, 1997), 109–10. Note: Italics appear in the original.
6. Wells, *Moreau*, 4.
7. Comparisons to Conrad's *Heart of Darkness* (1899) are evident: an unreliable narrator relates the primary information, a remote, exotic jungle setting, racial exploitation, extreme violence, and questions of moral insanity.
8. Wells, *Moreau*, 11.

9. James Gray, "Inspired: Tropical Malady," *Film Comment* (November-December, 2016), 6.
10. Gilles Deleuze, *Cinema 2—The Time-Image*, trans. Hugh Tomlinson and Robert Galeta (Minneapolis: University of Minnesota Press, 1989), 149.
11. Stephen Prince, *Classical Film Violence* (New Jersey: Rutgers University Press, 2003), 67.
12. David A. Kirby, "The Devil in Our DNA: A Brief History of Eugenics in Science Fiction Films," *Literature and Medicine*, Vol. 26, No. 1 (Spring 2007), 89.
13. The cinematography is by the Karl Struss, the expressionist *extraordinaire*.
14. There is another effective expressionist shot (one of many in this film), with shadows looming larger in the background of the shot as the lovers flee from the encampment, that recalls cinematographer Karl Struss' shot composition in his other adaptation from 1932, Mamoulian's *Dr. Jekyll and Mr. Hyde*, in which Hyde's shadow, as if alive, expands across a building's wall as he flees from the authorities.
15. See Bernard Weinraub's "Trove of Judaica Preserved by Nazis to Tour U.S.," *New York Times*, September 20, 1983, Section A, p. 18.
16. Susan McHugh, "The Call of the Other 0.1%: Genetic Aesthetics and the New Moreaus," *AI & Society*, Vol. 20 (2006), 74–5.
17. Ibid, 77.
18. Scott McClintock, "*The Penal Colony*: Inscription of the Subject in Literature and Law, and Detainees as Legal Non-Persons at Camp X-Ray," *Comparative Literature Studies*, Vol. 41, No. 1 (2004), 157–8.
19. *The Senate Intelligence Committee Report on Torture* (Brooklyn: Melville House, 2014), 54, 58.
20. Sara Brady, "'It Don't Gitmo Better': Scenes from the Coney Island *Waterboarding Thrill Ride*," *TDR*, Vol. 53, No. 2 (Summer 2009), 142–3.
21. Ibid, 144.
22. Eugene S. Talbot, *Degeneracy: Its Causes, Signs, and Results* (1898), (NY: Garland Publishing, 1984), 13.
23. Constance Areson Clark, "'You Are Here': Missing Links, Chains of Being, and the Language of Cartoons," *Isis*, Vol. 100, No. 3 (September 2009), 586.
24. Ibid, 586.
25. Patricia Vettel Tom, "Felix the Cat as Modern Trickster," *American Art*, Vol. 10, No. 1 (Spring 1996), 65.
26. The "Free Dictionary" defines the (anachronistic) *cake eater* as "a winsome, effeminate young man, apt to socialize." See https://idioms.thefreedictionary.com/cake-eaters. Accessed June 15, 2023.
27. David Livingstone Smith and Ioana Panaitiu, "Aping the Human Essence: Simianization as Dehumanization," in *Simianization: Apes, Gender, Class, and Race*, eds Wulf D. Hund, Charles W. Mills, and Silvia Sebastiani (Zurich: Lit Verlag GmbH, 2015), 77–8.
28. I am grateful for Gary Rhodes for informing me of this complementary Felix the Cat cartoon.
29. Richard Hauer Costa, *H. G. Wells* (Boston, MA: Twayne Publishers, 1985), 17.
30. Ibid, 18.
31. Irving Epstein, "Street Children in Film," *Curriculum Inquiry*, Vol. 29, No. 3 (Autumn 1999), 380–1.
32. David Baguley, "The Function of Zola's Souvarine," *Modern Language Review*, Vol. 66, No. 4 (October 1971), 794.
33. This quote, located on page 130 in *Lord of the Flies*, may be accessed at https://d2ct263enury6r.cloudfront.net/X2bpH13Xnjn4ZJspWQzb5LMu7BGp5CUGaPGFQqVXvLT2M1AW.pdf. Accessed June 16, 2023.

34. Gordon Parks, *Voices in the Mirror: An Autobiography* (New York: Doubleday, 1990), 180–1.
35. Ibid, 183.
36. Jackson Burgess, "Review: *Lord of the Flies*," *Film Quarterly*, Vol. 17, No. 2 (Winter 1963–4), 32.
37. Clifford Geertz, *The Interpretation of Cultures* (New York: Basic Books, 1973), 352.
38. Ibid, 357.
39. This remarkable staged newsreel may be viewed at https://www.youtube.com/watch?v=TkIq9eIIAq4. Accessed June 12, 2023.
40. Aristotle, *History of Animals*, trans. Richard Cresswell (London: George Bell & Sons, 1883), 258.
41. Ibid, 258.
42. Mark W. Moffett, "When It Comes to Waging War, Ants and Humans Have a Lot in Common," *Undark Magazine* (May 14, 2019). See https://www.smithsonianmag.com/science-nature/when-it-comes-waging-war-ants-humans-have-lot-common-180972169/. Accessed June 11, 2023.
43. Roy Rigby, *The Hill* (New York: Dell Publishing, 1965), 9.
44. Ibid, 6.
45. Ibid, 59.
46. Frank R. Cunningham, *Sidney Lumet: Film and Literary Vision* (Lexington: University Press of Kentucky, 2001), 201.
47. Anton Chekov, *The Island: A Journey to Sakhalin*, trans. Luba and Michael Terpak (New York: Washington Square Press, 1967), 40.
48. Robert Burns, *I Am a Fugitive from the Georgia Chain Gang!*, reprinted 1931 (Georgia: Beehive Press, 1994). Note: "Georgia" was eliminated from the film title.
49. The Sandburg poem may be located at https://www.poetryfoundation.org/poetrymagazine/poems/12840/chicago. Accessed June 11, 2023.
50. See https://www.kollwitz.de/en/sheet-1-ploughmen. Accessed August 30, 2023.
51. Guy Debord, "127," in *Society of the Spectacle*, trans. Ken Knabb (Canada: Bureau of Public Secrets, 2014), 69.
52. Courbet's painting is also known as: *Le Cerf à l'eau, chasse à courre*.
53. According to the Musées de Marseille website, the painting may also be read as an allegorical representation of Courbet's career and his critical reception. See https://musees.marseille.fr/le-cerf-leau-dit-le-cerf-force. Accessed August 30, 2023.
54. Shao-Chien Tseng, "Contested Terrain: Gustave Courbet's Hunting Scenes," *Art Bulletin*, Vol. 90, No. 2 (June 2008), 220.
55. Ibid, 219.
56. The film is also known as *Une Chasse à Courre*.
57. The Hunting Act of 2004 banned the hunting of wild mammals in the UK. Fox hunting and the hunting of other mammals are only partially banned in France, where hunting is still considered a sport.
58. Shao-Chien, "Contested," 220.
59. Page Laws, "Not Everybody's Protest Film, Either: 'Native Son' Among Controversial Film Adaptations," *Black Scholar*, Vol. 39, No. 1/2 (Spring–Summer 2009), 28.
60. Ellen Scott, "Blacker than Noir: The Making and Unmaking of Richard Wright's 'Ugly' *Native Son* (1951)," *Adaptation*, Vol. 6, No. 1 (October 2012), 97.
61. Thy Phu, "Bigger at the Movies: Sangre Negra and the Cinematic Projection of *Native Son*," *Black Camera*, Vol. 2, No. 1 (Winter 2010), 43. Note: A still image of the censored frame is on page 44 of Phu's article.

62. Ibid, 45.
63. Scott, "Blacker than Noir," 93–4.
64. Frederick Engels, *The Condition of the Working-Class in England* (1892), (London: Panther Books, 1974), 144.
65. Ibid, 144–5.

8. NATURALIST COMEDY

Painfully Funny

Demanding physical activities, such as removing bricks and breaking down walls, have humorous potential when set in motion. The Lumière brothers produced the experimental *Démolition d'un mur/Demolition of a Wall* (1896), a brief film that depicts labor and unidentified workers in a two-fold generic format, ranging from credible images of routine work to the inventively *Dadaesque* comedic. Naturalist cinema's link with this seminal avant-garde movement, and other ensuing historical avant-garde film movements and styles, including Expressionism (and noir), Surrealism, and a postmodern palimpsestic aesthetic, demonstrate how Naturalism is absorbed as a presence within interrelated experimental and industrial models. In *Demolition of a Wall*, the viewer perceives in a fixed medium shot routines associated with traditional work that are, illogically, technologically inverted into a series of atypical impossibilities, but the viewer accepts these images as narrative data, linking Naturalism's labor narrative with the comedic. In the Lumière brothers' *Demolition of a Wall*, contrary to narrative expectations, the natural flow of images is reversed and the wall improbably returns.

Along with the contemporaneous and celebrated efforts of Méliès' playfully humorous productions, *Demolition of a Wall* depicts labor in a comedic narrative. As laborers demolish a wall, at midpoint the film is reversed to playfully initiate a Dada-like nonsensical performance, an alteration of logical space and chronological time; this technologically created visual absurdity links Naturalism's narrative of people-at-work with the comedic. According to Todd McGowan,

> The film depicts a group of workers knocking down a wall following the orders of Auguste Lumière in the film, but then after 45 seconds, the forward chronology of the film ends, giving way to a reverse chronology of the event . . . But *Démolition d'un mur* shows the capacity for atemporality existing in the most basic structure of cinematic temporality—the actuality.[1]

As a formative example of the cinema of attractions, *Demolition of a Wall* bifurcates narrative parameters, temporally, spatially, and thematically, along documented routines of realistic physical labor to the unrealistic playful. Among Naturalism's most significant contribution to international cinematic cultures is its presence in the film comedy genre, particularly films by Charlie Chaplin and Jerry Lewis. The persistent realities of the modern world of work, images associated with the impersonal factory, human-as-machine labor, are mischievously subverted within the naturalist film's imaginary landscape.

In Lumière's *Demolition of a Wall*, an *actualité* that operates as an avant-garde narrative, Deleuze's "small form" actions and characters create a sense of the familiar, the real, while depicting a labor-related situation; the short film then humorously disrupts the audience's perceptions. Work can be seriously comical. According to Jakob Ladegaard, "Comedy is a contested genre that seems particularly resistant to theoretical conceptualisation."[2] However, as Tristan Tzara notes in the *Dada Manifesto* (1918), "Logic imprisoned by the senses is an organic disease";[3] *Demolition of a Wall* contests the logic and rituals of physical labor as it destabilizes visual expectations of a rational process. Demanding physical activities involving semi-skilled labor, such as breaking down or building up walls, even gathering bricks, display sobering or humorous potentialities in film narrative.

Charlie's Labors

According to Jennifer Wild, "Beginning in 1920, the ubiquitous mobility of Chaplin's star is demonstrated in a host of works and texts that corroborate the Dada ethos and attitude, and that mimic the circulation flow of Chaplin's image and films to artists spread across Europe."[4] In 1922, director-actor Charles Chaplin released *Pay Day*, his last "two-reeler" film production. Like the Lumière brothers' *Demolition of a Wall*, Chaplin's comedy is fundamentally divided into two parts. *Pay Day* depicts experiences in the working day of a laborer at a building site, and then his evening spent drinking. According to William Solomon,

> The first half of the film focuses on the antics of the Chaplin character at the building construction site where he is employed, while the second concerns the character's struggles to make his way home to his wife after a night of heavy drinking with friends at the 'Bachelor's Club.'[5]

Chaplin designates himself as the "laborer," a semi-skilled employee in the film. The film is a "day in the life" narrative focusing on the routines of the laboring male.

Pay Day is a comedy that incorporates familiar naturalist tropes: images of physical labor, a working-class home environment, and the saloon's deleterious effects of alcohol on "drinking men." Chaplin utilizes a consequential special effect, which renews the Lumière brothers' comedic bifurcation of construction site reality. *Pay Day* reverses footage of tossed bricks to Chaplin/the laborer standing on a platform above the street, rendering his labor illogical in ballet-like motion. The unfeasible is visualized; Chaplin performs, in a machine-like series of motions, catching bricks tossed upwards at him by two men. At one point, he is not even facing them. Like the Lumière brothers' Dada-inflected wall suddenly rising and recreating itself, in *Pay Day*, the playfully impossible is comedically rendered via the motion of a machine-like laborer who later drinks too much alcohol. Michael North assesses Chaplin's *Pay Day*:

> [It is an] infantile comedy. Pervaded as it is by the machine, reality simply ceases to be unitary and consistent, and if there is bewilderment in the arbitrariness of it there is also a certain measure of freedom. Chaplin is Benjamin's symbol of popular enjoyment of this condition, an enjoyment of deflation and disorientation that dada had tried to bring about with much more limited success.[6]

If it is true that, "In Russia he [Chaplin] was the darling of the futurists; in Germany he was a model for the Dadaists."[7] Germane naturalist tropes—rote, physical labor, saloon-life, and trouble in the working-class home—frame the comically revealing narrative in *Pay Day* as a positioning of the realistic against the ridiculous.

Naturalist comedy is an essential presence in international cinema. Throughout modern and contemporary art, there is frequent linkage established between depictions of labor and narratives of naturalist discontent, as the world defines gradations of success and failure by capital, class, and corresponding conflict. Naturalist comedy posits a thriving space for these depictions as it is associated with malfunctioning labor and personal complications rendered in states of class and social (im)mobility. The naturalist comedy launches a platform for varieties of labor-related or personal experiences that do not necessarily end "badly" for individuals, as impossible, embarrassing situations may lead to conditional physical resolve and emotional states of (self) recognition. The individual or group's efforts are observed and exposed either working or not working, and stages of awkward or humiliating moments may be humorous while rarely being fatal.

In *The Poetics*, Aristotle refers to the genre of comedy as exhibiting "an imitation of men worse than the average; worse, however, not as regards any and every sort of fault, but only as regards one kind, the ridiculous, which is a species of the ugly. The ridiculous may be defined as a mistake or deformity not productive of pain or harm to others."[8] In Zola's *L'Assommoir* (1877), Gervaise is a case study in the naturalist declension of a family's matriarch; the marginally handicapped Gervaise lives the spiraling life of a laundress–mother–alcoholic–prostitute. Despite the deleterious conditions framing her personal narrative, there are two exceptional sequences of comedic value involving her wedding party and later, her unwelcome husband's drunken accident in the bedroom that are linked to public and private moments of class-related embarrassment and bodily malfunctions.

As an entertainment contrivance for the sake of her guests, Gervaise's wedding party journeys through the Louvre in a post-ceremonial event. While gazing at paintings and sculpture, the gathering experiences a variety of reactions to unfamiliar images of a traditionally inaccessible space and contemplative time rarely afforded to the working class. Robert Lethbridge notes that "critical reflection on the [Louvre] scene has seldom been extended beyond the further evidence that it provides of the impossibility of escaping the environmental fatalities to which Zola's working-class characters succumb."[9] To the observer of those observing, "Centuries of art passed before their dazed ignorance ... And the wedding party ... clattered their heels on the noisy floors, like the trampling of a herd running amock [sic] in the bare and solemn grandeur of the galleries."[10] The visit to the Louvre fails to leave a trace of heightened aesthetic perception or overall appreciation of their cultural environment.

After a series of cataclysmic personal events later ruins Gervaise and Coupeau's marriage and lead to his alcoholism and her economic peril and prostitution, Zola describes a broadly humorous, gross encounter between Gervaise and her returning drunk husband, lying in deep sleep in their bed:

> Gervaise ... realized she was walking in something wet. When she managed to light a candle a pretty sight met their eyes. Coupeau had thrown up in the lot: it was all over the room, the bed was coated with it and so was the carpet, and even the chest was splashed.[11]

Whether grossly scatological, displaying some corrupted bodily function, or rendered as class-related critique in a satirical vein, comedic naturalist film narrative functions as signifying spectacles ranging from the amusingly absurd to the Rabelaisian grotesque. In René Clément's *Gervaise* (1956), Zola's comedic passages are succinctly visualized in humorous shot sequences.

During a rainstorm, in Clément's Seurat-like images of people in motion, Gervaise's wedding party leaves for the Louvre for an afternoon's entertainment. With its masterpiece collection on full view, the wide open spaces of the museum are juxtaposed with medium shots of the shepherded-like movement of the arriving party guests, who wear wet clothes and muddy shoes. These visitors comically react to minor details rather than responding critically to the collection. Off-color comments highlight the child-like, amused reactions of the startled guests. The party is a directionless mass. Clément's shot sequence at the Louvre is composed of eleven different camera set-ups and features a variety of medium-wide shots, pans, and side-angle framing of those observing.

In a series of medium shots composed in swiftly edited panning motion and dolly movement, Clément incorporates Zola's infamous vomiting sequence as a horrific experience not witnessed but revealed afterwards, as if an absent animal's odiferous presence was detected inside an enclosed space. As Gervaise (Maria Schell) and her former lover Lantier open the door to her bedroom, a displeasing smell advances upon them as they look and see her husband, asleep and lying in a vomit-stained bed. Coupeau is literally corpse-like in drunken immobility and cannot be moved in order to remove the sheets. The shot sequence is coarsely comical. In naturalist comedies, personal weakness, ignorance, and hapless situations are means to expose society, and laughter is not always the actualized response.

Celebrating Idiots

In his discussion of Aristotelean comedy, Malcolm Heath notes, "For Aristotle, comedy is by definition a representation of morally inferior people . . . and if one is to represent morally inferior people, one must (logically) represent them doing and saying morally inferior things."[12]

While reveling in chaotic, ill-fated comedic exploits in their perennial search for employment and service, few performers may claim to represent unexceptional individuals and the consequences of class intermingling as well as the "Three Stooges" in their extensive series of Columbia Pictures short films. In Del Lord's *Hoi Polloi* (1935), at an upper-class social gathering, two professors discuss issues and make wagers about the impact of biological versus environmental factors on character formation. *Hoi Polloi* satirizes the issue of genetic determinism as it broadly parodies class divisiveness. *Hoi Polloi* is set mostly during a banquet in a lush, privileged home, and contrasts with the daily experiences of the Depression-era audience while functioning as the observational site of the pseudo-scientific experiment: residence as laboratory. The subjects of the experiment are the precariat laborer Stooges, initially working as garbage collectors. They accidentally dump a massive load of empty metal cans from a truck onto a car and are subsequently caught, and solicited to participate in the experiment as observable specimens. Since they fear imminent unemployment, the Stooges agree; for these unskilled laborers, this suggests capital and lunch. The Stooges will be instructed in etiquette, literacy, and refined dancing to impress their superiors. According to Don Morlan, in many of the Stooges' films produced at Columbia Pictures, social interaction fomenting parodic class contrast was a common thematic design:

> The Three Stooges were natural and obvious candidates for taking on the values of high society and the aristocracy in the Depression era. Most of the roles they portrayed were somewhere below the common denominator in American society. They were unemployed or in jail or total bumblers in any job they might temporarily hold ... Conflict between the upper and lower strata of society was the theme in a total of 34 of the 190 Stooges' Columbia shorts from 1934 to 1958.[13]

As the Stooges mimic the behavior of the privileged, even copying their language—"how is the countess?"—the banquet becomes a site of farcical destruction, abetted by sound effects including slaps, bangs, and screams indicating a humorous dimension to screen violence. The carnivalesque sequences include flying bugs buzzing down the dress of a woman who proceeds to dance madly, and, as instructed, the Stooges following her riotous prancing about until all jump from a window into a pond below. Although the Stooges are a trio of performing, clownish, even flirtatious figures unlikely to succeed at anything, their films reveal subtle ideological messaging concerning social prerogatives and carnivalesque culture. According to Geoff King, "one of the key aspects of carnivalesque humour for Bakhtin is the representation of the human body as a source of the grotesque."[14] In particular, Curly's rotund, seemingly impervious body, emitting improbable sounds and sustaining repeated, bruising physical acts is a focalizing site of exaggerated pain and punishment. Curly is a living cartoon. In *Hoi Polloi*, Lord's medium shot focuses on a prop gag involving a couch spring accidentally connected to Curly's posterior, which, as a very large woman he is dancing with knocks him to the floor, effectively bounces him up. This gag, a reversal of chronological film footage, recalls Lumière's *Demolition of a Wall* and its reversal of the wall falling and rising. The professors' experiment and the social event are ruined, but as the Stooges exit, the attendees begin to act like the déclassé subjects of the failed experiment; the Stooges' limited grasp of social reality ironically initiates a reversal of experimental expectations.

In Preston Black's *Ants in the Pantry* (1936), the frazzled owner of a pest control business demands that the Stooges, his workers, engage new clients or be fired. Although directionless, the Stooges arrive at an upper-class home full of partygoers and peer through a window to behold the upper class. The Stooges instigate their plan to attract business and capital; mice, ants, cats, and assorted bugs are surreptitiously released across the mansion, creating chaotically comedic effects abetted by sound and sight gags. There are cats hidden inside a piano, disrupting a performance; a mouse is placed inside a woman's shoe, and moths eat away at an expensive dress. In *Ants in the Pantry*, the spectacle of ants crawling across a fancy baked cake recalls Luis Buñuel's Surrealism in *Un Chien Andalou* (1929) as ants crawl on a man's hand; both film images are bizarrely amusing while marginally disturbing.

As the party goes off on a fox hunt, the Stooges subvert this callous expression of class privilege. In shot sequences anticipating the slaughter of a stag in Dimitri Kirsanoff's avant-garde *La Mort du Cerf /Death of a Stag* (1951), Preston Black has Curly blow his nose, which exaggeratedly sounds like a horn's call to the hunt. As a skunk substitutes for the trapped fox, a horse literally faints, and all related sporting and social activities lapse into playful chaos. The Stooges' films satirize Depression-era class stratification and prerogative as each film subverts normative behaviors involving labor and the displaced social other; the Stooges' films reveal how the unexceptional individual comically exposes the supposedly exceptional.

In a film about skilled labor and male anxiety, Ben Stiller's stalking narrative *The Cable Guy* (1996) examines the paradoxical invisibility of a psychologically damaged worker, the "cable guy," Chip Douglas (Jim Carrey), an emotionally desperate and manipulative figure. Alan Hájek notes how in contemporary society people respond to the near arrival of this prized technician: "The Cable Guy is coming. You have to be home in order for him to install your new cable service, but to your chagrin he cannot tell you exactly when he will come."[15] In Stiller's film, Chip installs, legally and illegally, relevant media technology, but few recognize his face or bother to learn his name until Chip's inner rage and alienation reveal themselves in the midst of providing access to consumers. Chip's baffling personality, abetted by a slight speech defect, is a generated response fashioned by childhood neglect and the absorption of countless meaningless images recalled from previous television broadcasts, which are invoked to imbue identity gaps as he struggles to survive in a society that utilizes his skill set but avoids the awkward man. He is a purposeful function, casually employed in a controlled space and time, but not noticed as a person. Stiller's *The Cable Guy* is a darkly humorous naturalist narrative, a critique of a media-saturated society in which Chip's emotional and psychological deprivation—however bizarrely it may be enacted in public—is measured against the false sincerity and privilege of those he serves. Chip is a released, clever pathogen.

As noted by Christopher Beach, Stiller's film

> [is] one of the most provocative comedies of the 1990s ... the film displays a mastery not only of the American comic tradition but also of various other film and television genres, any of which are fair game for its brilliant postmodern pastiche.[16]

Beach concludes that Carrey's performance as Chip should be "read in terms of Bakhtinian carnivalesque."[17] For example, during the farcical karaoke performance by the cable guy in his apartment, he sings and grinds to a ridiculous rendition of the Jefferson Airplane's "Somebody to Love," while Steven (Matthew Broderick), his friend-victim, saunters into another room with an attractive guest, a prostitute brought to the event for Steven's unknowing pleasure. After a few moments, the door bursts open, and while guests and the cable guy enter, he takes a picture of the illicit interlude. At breakfast the next morning, as the cable guy and Steven sit opposite each other in a two-shot at the table, the attractive guest is revealed to be a prostitute to a distraught Steven, who does not recall the photograph documenting an injurious moment. In this shot sequence, Carrey's complex performance is entertaining while disturbing as he exhibits aspects of a predatory, pathetic, and comical personality. James Parker notes Carrey's ability to make the audience feel relatively unnerved:

> His [Carrey's] great scenes, his great fits and flare-ups, come jumping out of his often half-baked movies like spikes on a lie detector or surges on a Ouija board. Chip Douglas, the stalker/parasite/no-man of *The Cable Guy*, is constructed entirely out of such peaks: between the freak-out karaoke version of Jefferson Airplane's 'Somebody to Love' and [later at] the armored showdown at Medieval Times, he barely exists.[18]

But the cable guy does exist as a grasping menace in Stiller's darkly comedic narrative of a disturbed worker. In a later series of calculated mishaps, Steven winds up in jail. In the prison-visiting sequence, the cable guy poses as a lawyer calling on Steven. Stiller's shot–reverse shots and two-shots are set mostly in tense close-up. A feigned homoerotic bond, signaled by the exposure of the cable guy's nipple pressed upon the reinforced glass wall separating them, produces an even more frightened Steven and references Alan Parker's *Midnight Express* (1978) with its sadistic, prison-house sexual encounters. The sequence is simultaneously terrifying, as Steven gazes upon his damaged adversary on the other side of the glass, and comedic, and illustrates the reduction of Steven's life into an incoherent mass. Steven is a nub of his former self. In *The Cable Guy*, the humiliating, grinding process of the privileged individual is initiated by a skilled worker already ground down in a lonely world.

In Woody Allen's comedic study of second-rate performers in the entertainment industry, *Broadway Danny Rose* (1984), talent agent Danny Rose (Woody Allen) is portrayed as a mild failure who continues his losing streak of working while cultivating the strained talent of a frequently drunk and foolish entertainer, Lou Canova (Nick Apollo Forte). *Broadway Danny Rose* largely functions in confined space and time, full of unlikely talent who are more embarrassing than entertaining. Peter J. Bailey notes:

> *Broadway Danny Rose* is as well-made a film as Allen has produced, in addition to being an object lesson in Allen's conception of the conditions necessary to the creation of artistic closure in film narrative ... Far from achieving anything approaching perfect art, the performances of a number of Danny's clients—his blind xylophonist, one-legged tap dancer and one-armed juggler—must be judged primarily on the basis of their success in overcoming the disability to which their acts unerringly draw attention.[19]

Allen establishes in a framing opening sequence, in medium and close-up shots and voice-overs, a series of recalled memories presented over lunch by a gathering of gossipy comedians in a New York City delicatessen, who comically extol the exploits of the helpless yet sympathetic Danny. The comedians reference Danny's bygone notions of loyalty and responsibility that fail to register for him any sign of economic or industrial progress. Danny is continually betrayed by second-rate talent in the sordid milieu of booking agencies and public venues by the same talents he gently nurtures. Danny is a functioning nub.

As Danny markets less desirable talent to the wary consuming public, he remains unaware that his clients are sadly pathetic spectacles, yet he delivers the talent while maintaining careers surviving on the industry's fringe. The opening shot sequence in the delicatessen, performed by real comedians, lends an aura of authenticity to the film and prompts the rise/fall narrative for both Canova, who is destined to perform erratically and wind up second-billed in second-rate hotels and touring on cruise ships, and Danny, who links himself to Canova's unpromising career. Ironically, once Canova begins to gets some bookings, Danny will be dropped as his manager at the behest of Canova's déclassé girlfriend, a sexualized, ethnic stereotype endemic to the gendered tropes of New Jersey gangster culture to be reconceived in the HBO series *The Sopranos*.

At Danny's Thanksgiving party he invites an eccentric gathering of clients to feast on frozen turkey dinners and reaffirms his belief in a future in which his and their success is getting closer. According to Brian Henderson, this shot sequence in *Broadway Danny Rose* "is photographed in harsh, Arbus-like black-and-white ... the Allen character has joined the freaks. When Danny makes Thanksgiving dinner for his grotesque-seeming clients, their grotesqueness and his disappears."[20] Those performers marginalized by society and their profession have a moment of solidarity on the outskirts of recognition. Peter Bailey inquires, "What makes Danny Rose a loser?"[21] Losers have a place in naturalist cinema. *Broadway Danny Rose* is an observable study of gentle, incongruous fringe people as slightly visible performance spectacles.

In another study of assorted others in the entertainment business, Tim Burton's *Ed Wood* (1994), the comedic, subversive, and parodic bio-pic of a singularly devoted filmmaker also features a revelatory celebration at a party of entertainment and industrial oddities, in which Ed (Johnny Depp) performs a fan dance in drag to the delight of observers, except his girlfriend. Both Danny Rose and Ed Wood are driven to achieve a measure of success for themselves as well as for other others, despite little industrial recognition and questionable talent pool. Burton's film never condescends while representing skilled labor and its industrial ambiguities. *Ed Wood* observes, in both comedic and dramatic sequences, the naturalist conditions of survival in the culture of creative disappointment. Wood and his performers strive, however embarrassing or foolish in appearance, and do make a film. According to Colin Odell and Michelle LeBlanc,

> *Ed Wood* takes the biopic formula and subverts it by concentrating on someone who was spectacularly unsuccessful. It is so easy to see how this material could have become a sneering mocking comedy, laughing at someone else's ineptitude, but fortunately it doesn't.[22]

Ed Wood probes the parodic element in naturalist cinema as it documents the fictionalized presence of fringe talent in the late era of studio production in Hollywood; Ed Wood is an oddly sympathetic, foolish figure and, like Danny Rose and Chip Douglas, these flawed men labor in an embarrassing realistic social milieu, in which failure remains a perceived option.

Bell Ringing

Expressionist artist Chaim Soutine's portrait of consumptive umbrage, *Bellboy* (1925), reveals a young man staring directly from the frame, beyond the presumptive routines and responsibilities associated with his mundane and usually thankless labor. The bellboy poses hands akimbo, his deflated physique covered by a baggy uniform suggesting temporary respite from uncelebrated semi-skilled labor. According to Tim Catkins, the bellboy is a familiar sight:

"the bellhop's short, cylindrical cap is what instantly identifies his lowly occupation in the hotel."[23] A bellboy remains a boy, regardless of age; his uniform defines his workplace status. Soutine's bellboy's outward gaze and comportment plausibly infer an internalized sense of discernable resentment, a self-awareness of status emanating as defensive contempt, a response to identity defined by incessant, ignored labor. As it concerns the bellboy's functional presence in the economic system, Robert Klara concludes, "Bellboys lift the luggage, fetch the messages, deliver the flowers. Whatever thankless, menial thing needs doing, they stand at the ready."[24] Bellboys serve to live, laboring without name or viable presence.

Naturalist comedy involves the near invisibility of the working subject, an unnoticed body in motion in situations involving labor. Roscoe Arbuckle's *The Bell Boy* (1918) introduces the figure of the necessary yet peripatetic, powerless, and mostly gendered figure of the bellboy at work, serving something or someone. In Arbuckle's silent, slapstick film, both Fatty Arbuckle and Buster Keaton labor as nameless bell boys at ritualistic responsibilities while serving the guests in a hotel. In one sight-gag sequence, Keaton polishes the glass in a phone booth although there is no glass present; it is not only the absence of the glass that is humorous but also, the effort of Buster's intense, robotic labor that is effectively absurd. According to Sarah Jane Bailes, the gag in cinema is an effective method to register altered perceptions of the real with its audience:

> The gag is widely recognized as the moment in which all that is seemingly coherent and correct about a given world begins to go horribly and irreparably wrong. But by analyzing the gag as a strategic technique, the disruption it generates suggests alternative ways of thinking through the unlikely coupling of continuity and uncertainty.[25]

Deleuze concludes how action image, particularly the silent era "small form" film, transforms the narrative as a flow of successive character-driven images that shape and initiate perception to create and affect assumptions. In naturalist cinema, the gag destabilizes the space and time of the real as it comedically comments on significant labor and class-related issues. According to Bailes:

> It is important to identify, therefore, the modernist qualities of fragmentation and discontinuity that gag insists upon in relation to a history that posits narrative continuity as the dominant organizing principle of film. Formally, the gag contests dominant ideology through its chaotic structure (which foregrounds formlessness), its independence from narrative, and especially through its capacity to revolt.[26]

The Bell Boy exposes routine labor practices associated with daily responsibilities at the hotel such as cleaning the floors, helping guests check into the hotel, and especially, operating the (dis)functional elevator, as child-like and (Dada) playfully escapist. In Arbuckle's medium close-up shot, as a woman somehow lands and hangs on top of a mounted elk's head, it repeatedly winks at the sight of her shapely, dangling foot; in another sequence, while working as a barber, Arbuckle shaves the facial hair of an eccentric client, and the head undergoes a series of successive comedic transformations into known historical figures. This sequence invokes the comical imagery of Georges Méliès' *Un homme de têtes/The Four Troublesome Heads* (1898) and *L'Homme à la tête de Caoutchouc /The Man With The India-Rubber Head* (1901), as the head–face is dislocated and rendered playfully ridiculous. In *The Bell Boy*, spectacle and narrative cohere under the labor platform in a state of suspended realism as the audience experiences the effects of these gags. Bailes notes:

> Buster Keaton, the iconic vaudeville and silent-movie actor and one of slapstick's most intriguing performers, was an expert interrogator of the mechanics of the gag, attracted by the limitless potential its excess offered him as a performer. Towards the end of his life, Keaton was claimed as an actor as much by the avant-garde and the surrealist movement as by the populist mainstream (cinematic) tradition he thrived in.[27]

Both Keaton and Arbuckle labor in a real world of impossibilities. Arbuckle includes a requisite chase sequence, romantic developments, and a robbery in which all conflict is resolved. In a layering of familiar action, one late sequence involves the free-throwing of stolen cash that resembles the pie throwing associated with comedic cinema. In a film composed primarily in medium shots displaying relentless movement in recognizable yet defamiliarized space and time, Arbuckle examines labor practices and the comedically mundane.

The Bellboy (1960) is a comedic naturalist study of alienating labor—Dada-in-motion—and the silence of a mutable, *socially* disabled working-class body. Director Jerry Lewis portrays Stanley, the bellboy, lifting, running, and negotiating reality as he is surrounded by voices and sounds, while remaining silent and barely visible. *The Bellboy* is considered by some as formless and embarrassing commercial cinema, with a series of interconnected routines leading from one sight-gag after another to propel Lewis' plotless narrative, without a sole reference to the naturalist context of this comedy. Geoff King concludes, "Narrative tends to be a minor component in the [film] . . . *The Bellboy* (1960), a solo Lewis feature, is an extreme example, making a gag out of its own status as little more than a pure sequence of gags."[28] An alternative reading of *The Bellboy* proposes greater narrative depth as a comedic survey of eruptive class disconnection and low-wage labor practices, as a nonsensical reaction to menial labor and a critique of the dull and dishonest affairs of the middle class, escaping from their lives from the bedroom to the swimming pool.

In his laboring efforts to please people, Stanley literally disrupts and destabilizes the landscape, the spatial-temporal continuum. Objects such as phones, cameras, chairs, even Stanley (when actor Lewis, playing Stanley, performs the meta-role of the real Jerry Lewis), become something "other," transcending the restraints of the real. Familiar events and objects actively refute perceptions of normalcy. In his analysis of Stanley's childish defacing of the still-unsettled clay bust of a woman in *The Bellboy*, Steven Shaviro notes, "It provides a carnivalesque release from the usual standards of responsibility, emphasizes grotesque inversions of hierarchical power relations and directly assaults the icons of social respectability."[29] However grotesquely misshapen, the revised bust is arguably more interesting than when it was a commissioned work of art. Stanley consistently yet inadvertently renders the serious as randomly ridiculous, the tone of *The Bellboy*.

Deleuze observes, "The cinema does not just present images, it surrounds them with a world."[30] This Florida hotel is a fantastic, glitzy, crass space in the world, in which the circus-staple "clown car" pulls up in front of the resort and releases a mob of personnel associated with the celebrated figure of Jerry Lewis, who emerges as the last body from the car. Chris Fujiwara notes, "In discarding the surface logic of narrative and verisimilitude, Lewis' cinema foregrounds its own structural logic. The viewer of a Lewis film follows the unfolding and application of the rules . . . that are independent of the demands of narrative."[31] Naturalist themes and tropes associated with invisible work and alienated labor are vitiated by Lewis' Dada-like playfulness. Stanley suggests a more considered reading than Deleuze's characterization of him as a "born loser . . . [in] a new age of electronics";[32] Stanley is a laboring product, a mobile machine in a comically defamiliarized environment. Geoff King notes that "In terms suggested by the social anthropologist Claude Lévi-Strauss (1968), popular cultural products can provide an imaginary way of dealing with real issues, often by the imaginary reconciliation of real and/or intractable oppositions faced by a particular culture or society."[33] Stanley deals with his assignments, however humorously unsuccessful, with disempowered acceptance and effort. Although he may not succeed, Stanley is not a loser. *The Bellboy* is a subversively comedic film about employment as experienced by interchangeable, unrecognized working individuals who respond to bells, finger snaps, and shouts, situated in an environment of superficial class, clients, and encroaching technologies: a world of imposed invisibility. These anonymous assembly-line workers perform real labor in an unreal environment.

Stanley exists in an imaginary environment situated in the real world of low-wage labor. *The Bellboy* comically depicts a life of unglamorized labor and the fantasies it generates as a form of escapism. Two-shot sequences focusing on Stanley's daily work routines and his reaction to these experiences suggest his nascent awareness as a malfunctioning apparatus as revealed in his reactive facial expression. Stanley's body is an awkwardness apparatus that portrays an expressive child-like sensory overwhelming of his social and sexual identity.

Once Stanley mistakenly enters a room, he stares directly into the camera as he encounters several scantily dressed women. He then clownishly covers the camera lens to signal his embarrassment, a voyeuristic discomfort at seeing nothing immoral except to a juvenile mind. As noted by Steven Shaviro,

> the effects of embarrassment and humiliation are central to Lewis's work ... [w]ithin the narrative situations of Lewis's films, embarrassment and abjection are the direct consequences of subordination: of being assigned a low position in the social hierarchy and being compelled to take orders.[34]

In contrast to Keaton's toiling bellboy, Lewis externalizes unsettling, embarrassing labor-related moments in a series of overreactive, comedic facial expressions.

One celebrated shot sequence involves Stanley setting up several dozen chairs in a large auditorium. Stanley's demanding and extended manual labor, performed in the real world of space and time, is comically defamiliarized. As Stanley enters this huge empty space, in a cut-away shot, other

Figure 8.1 Jerry Lewis' *The Bellboy* (1960)

bellboys comment on the difficulty that Stanley, the subject of derision, will experience in what would normally take hours to complete. Moments later, in Ionesco-like fashion, these bellboys enter the room to see folding chairs fill the entire frame of the medium-wide shot, all in effortless neat rows. Fujiwara notes:

> One of the most revolutionary aspects of *The Bellboy* is its reintroduction of the fantastic within a representational context defined (within and outside the film, by its genre) as naturalistic... in which the naturalistic—indeed, documentary-like—surface of the film is suddenly disturbed... *The Bellboy*, too, is a film of extreme depth of field. In a wide-angle shot of the empty ballroom that he must fill with chairs, Stanley enters from behind the camera and walks all the way to the back of the room, becoming tiny.[35]

Stanley, a consistently mute bellboy, is depicted as a technologically challenged male performing menial acts of labor. In intertextual citation with Arbuckle's silent film, Lewis' *The Bellboy* is an experimental quasi-silent film full of loud noises, music, and the voices of people other than Stanley. Fujiwara succinctly notes this unique, compositional absence:

> To counter this authoritarianism of language, Lewis uses languagelessness and other kinds of antilanguage. In *The Bellboy*, Stanley is silent 'because no one ever asked' him to talk. (Compensating for his character's silence, the entirety of Lewis's film is an extremely sophisticated utterance by its author; in Lewis's directorial debut, filmmaking becomes both a substitute for and the privileged metaphor for speech.)[36]

As the setting for this final sequence involves the discussion of a potential strike, Stanley's public verbal reaffirmation of social and psychological identity—his brief speech at the end of the film—fulfills *The Bellboy* as it enlarges Stanley's presence and simultaneously links him with the socially invisible labor he and others perform. As Stanley sits placidly among other bellboys who have expressed discontent with working conditions, the boss enters and ironically blames mute Stanley. After being queried about his lack of spoken interaction, Stanley finally comments, "certainly, I can talk, I suspect I can talk as well as any other man... no one ever asked me." With his voice heard, Stanley completes the stage to visibility as man and worker. *The Bellboy* is a naturalist comedy. Work is a struggle to survive, but it is also frequently comedic, even absurd, in a naturalist context.

NOTES

1. Todd McGowan, "Atemporality amid Lumière Temporality," *Empedocles: European Journal for the Philosophy of Communication*, Vol. 5, Nos 1 & 2 (2015), 62.
2. Jakob Ladegaard, "Laughing Matters: Four Marxist Takes on Film Comedy," in *Marx at the Movies: Revisiting History, Theory and Practice*, eds Ewa Mazierska and Lars Kristensen (New York: Palgrave Macmillan, 2014), 119.
3. Tristan Tzara, "Dada Manifesto, 1918," trans. Robert Motherwell: www.matesonart.com/tristan-tzara-dada-manifesto.aspx. Accessed June 1, 2023.
4. Jennifer Wild, "The Automatic Chance of the Modern Tramp: Chaplin and the Parisian Avant-Garde," *Early Popular Visual Culture*, Vol. 8, No. 3 (August 2010), 274.
5. William Solomon, "Second Technologies: American Modernism and Silent Screen Comedy Author(s)," *Interdisciplinary Literary Studies*, Vol. 6, No. 2 (Spring 2005), 81.
6. Michael North, *Reading 1922: A Return to the Scene of the Modern* (New York: Oxford University Press, 1999), 170.
7. Ibid, 163.
8. Aristotle, "Poetics," *The Complete Works of Aristotle: Volume Two*, ed. Jonathan Barnes (Princeton: Princeton University Press, 1984), p. 2319. See https://homepages.hass.rpi.edu/ruiz/AdvancedIntegratedArts/ReadingsAIA/Aristotle%20Poetics.pdf. Accessed June 14, 2023.
9. Robert Lethbridge, "A Visit to the Louvre: 'L'Assommoir' Revisited," *Modern Language Review*, Vol. 87, No. 1 (January 1992), 41.
10. Émile Zola, *L'Assommoir*, trans. Leonard Tancock (London: Penguin Books, 1970), 90.
11. Ibid, 266–8.
12. Malcolm Heath, "Aristotelian Comedy," *Classical Quarterly*, Vol. 39, No. 2 (1989), 2–3.
13. Don Morlan, "A Pie in the Face: The Three Stooges' Antiaristocracy Theme in Depression-Era American Film," in *Stoogeology*, eds Peter Seely and Gail W. Pieper (Jefferson, N.C.: McFarland, 2007), 124.
14. Geoff King, *Film Comedy* (London: Wallflower Press, 2002), 65.
15. Alan Hájek, "The Cable Guy Paradox," *Analysis*, Vol. 65, No. 2 (April 2005), 112.
16. Christopher Beach, *Class, Language, and American Film Comedy* (New York: Cambridge University Press, 2002), 205.
17. Ibid, 208.
18. James Parker, "The Existential Clown: Why Jim Carrey Makes Us Uncomfortable," *The Atlantic* (December 2008), 46.
19. Peter J. Bailey, "Woody's Mild Jewish Rose: *Broadway Danny Rose*," in *The Reluctant Film Art of Woody Allen* (Kentucky: University Press of Kentucky, 2010), 101–2.
20. Brian Henderson, "*Broadway Danny Rose*, by Woody Allen," *Film Quarterly*, Vol. 39, No. 3 (Spring 1986), 48.
21. Bailey, "Woody's Mild Jewish," 108.
22. Colin Odell and Michelle LeBlanc, "Angora, Bela, Cinema: The ABC Of *Ed Wood*," *The Pocket Essential: Tim Burton* (UK: Harpenden, Pocket Essentials, 2001), 57.
23. Tim Catkins, "The bellboy is really an iconic character because everybody is familiar with him. Advertisers have picked up on that." *Adweek*, Vol. 54, No. 11 (March 18, 2013), 65.

24. Robert Klara, "Here, boy! For at least a century, the humble bellhop has stood for temperance, obedience and service. Now, if he could only find his pants." *Adweek*, Vol. 54, No. 11 (March 18, 2013), 64.
25. Sarah Jane Bailes, *Performance Theatre and the Poetics of Failure* (London: Taylor & Francis Group, 2011), 39.
26. Ibid, 44.
27. Ibid, 41.
28. King, *Comedy*, 38.
29. Steven Shaviro, *Cinematic Body* (Minneapolis: University of Minnesota Press, 1989), 108–9.
30. Gilles Deleuze, *Cinema 2: The Time Image*, trans. Hugh Tomlinson and Robert Galeta (Minneapolis: University of Minnesota Press, 1989), 68.
31. Chris Fujiwara, *Jerry Lewis* (Chicago: University of Illinois Press, 2009), 16.
32. Deleuze, *Cinema 2*, 65.
33. King, *Comedy*, 55.
34. Shaviro, *Cinematic*, 108.
35. Fujiwara, *Jerry*, 48, 90.
36. Ibid, 62–3.

9. A JOKER'S WORLD

Unreal City

In Todd Phillips' *Joker* (2019), Arthur Fleck/"Joker" is a concealed creature, a broken, dejected man passing as an oddly sympathetic, violent clown, the result of past brutal interpersonal experiences. He is a real man but with a complex clinical lineage, as he transitions from Arthur, the unexceptional individual, into Joker, *La Bête humaine*, a disturbed, rampaging specimen of the human. *Joker* documents the stylized evolution of festering human duality in a specific socio-historical milieu, in this case, the New York City of the 1980s. The following case study introduces a suffering, surplus, drugged, lonely, and enraged man who emerges, in nefarious strokes of near-mythical violence, as a contrived naturalist specimen, a masked product. As Baudelaire observes "as for the grotesque figures which antiquity has bequeathed us—the masks—I believe that these things are full of deep seriousness."[1] *Joker* is a naturalist film narrative possessing a "deep seriousness" that needs to be unmasked.

Clown Time

In the 1876 November issue of *Scientific American*, an anonymous author provides illustrative insights into the imaginative possibilities of artistic composition available to the consuming public in the pre-cinematic device, the magic lantern, and how to best utilize its mechanical, fantastic potential to attract an audience: "[t]he best outlines are funny men and women, animals, birds, and grotesque figures, sheets of characters, clowns, harlequins."[2] Even before the celebrated era of the cinema of attractions emerged in the late nineteenth century, clowns, depicted as either humorous, delightful, or seemingly horrific images, were projected on walls, canvases, and later on screens.

The clown is a layered persona. According to Benjamin Radford, "The clown is a curious character partly because he or she combines the superficially contradictory human feelings of horror and humor."[3] The ghastlier image of the clown spectacle may be viewed as an exaggerated, grotesque spectacle, a distorted specimen of the human. The clown is a performer whether on or off stage, and there is someone, something, behind the mask, makeup, and flamboyant, exaggerated clothing. The clown's mask and clothing frequently render the formerly recognizable as something altered, ominous, and animated, all essential elements of the grotesque, which amuses as it unsettles the audience. Wolfgang Kayser characterizes the presence of the grotesque spectacle in Western culture as a sign, a signifying emanation of the familiar, processed into an image of-from the estranged world, in which the life we perceive is more fearful than death.[4] As this concerns the clown, no matter how painted, distorted, or humorous, the clown obscures both face and body, the clown–person is one, but layered. The shifting externals, the affectations of clothing and makeup are transitory; the individual is the presence, the essence behind the mask.

The signifying trope of the sad and violent clown is evident in Victor Sjöström's *He Who Gets Slapped* (1924), which features Lon Chaney's "He," a successful circus clown whose performance is predicated on repetitive public facial slaps. Frederick White's analysis of Leonid Andreyev's eponymous drama (1915) resonates with *Joker*'s characterization:

> In Andreyev's play and other works, a performance is employed to hide the main character's true emotions and psychological state. Even as he suffers on the inside, he plays the part of a clown and entertains the audience, demonstrating that people prefer the appearance of normalcy to the truth.[5]

The clown performs while remaining a troubled person below the makeup and mask. In Sjöström's film, Chaney's debilitated He is portrayed as a research scientist whose career was destroyed by a dual act of betrayal: a false, wealthy patron and his adulterous wife conspire against him. His makeup—a cosmetically applied mask—disguises his violent humiliation narrative of loss and decline. The mask, the makeup, the clown garb, sustain the unrevealed.

The signifying trope of the complicated clown in select film narrative expresses personal humiliation, rage, and decline. In Phillips' *Joker*, the emaciated figure of Arthur Fleck (Joaquin Phoenix), a repressed, disillusioned, urban working-class male is a naturalist specimen, a failed, breathing artifact surviving in the disintegrating imaginary socio-historical milieu of Gotham City: a reconceptualization of New York City in the early 1980s. Like Martin Scorsese's eruptive vision of an isolated, intense working-class man, Travis Bickle (Robert De Niro) in *Taxi Driver* (1976), and several other films ostensibly set in "Scorsese's New York City," Phillips' *Joker* is a film set in the same corrosive era, a space and time of urban decay.[6] An earlier Scorsese film, *Mean Streets* (1973) features "Johnny Boy" (Robert De Niro), a near-psychotic, explosive small-time hustler in 1970s New York City, who lives on other people's money and must then dodge their bullets since he never pays them back. Like Fleck/Joker, thin but powerful Johnny "unmasks" and reveals his loathing of others in a seedy bar-room sequence in which he pulls an unloaded gun on a loan shark. Johnny eventually reveals that beneath his clowning, childishly annoying behavior is a dangerous hoodlum. *Joker* will reveal that Fleck is weak while fierce, withdrawn while determined, a wounded, emaciated figure of an unimportant man, suffering from significant disability syndromes.

Weighty Issues

In a presentation delivered in 1873 by Dr. William Gull, who is credited with coining the medical term "anorexic," he states: "The want of appetite is, I believe, due to a morbid mental state ... I prefer ... the more general term 'nervosa,' since the disease occurs in males as well as females, and is probably rather central than peripheral."[7] While the anorexic subject has injudiciously been conceived as female, it is hardly scientific reality. If the symptom is removed from an historically gendered overview, the description is equally applicable to men. Contemporary clinician Chengyuan Zhang notes:

> Ever since the clinical term was first coined by Sir William Gull in 1873, anorexia nervosa has been bound to an inherently female nosology ... Yet, while still dominant in the years before and after the First World War, this orientation would be challenged from two different quarters: new psychiatric approaches, partly stemming from interest in war-related conditions, notably shell-shock, and in the socio-genic role of the family, [which] began to explore 'male anorexia.'[8]

In the cinema and visual culture of the twentieth and twenty-first centuries, the image of the anorexic or excessively thin male like Arthur Fleck, an incongruous counterpoint to the hypersexualized steroid-enhanced popular image of "real" manhood, appears to be a mistake, an unusual disability to consequently ignore, ridicule, or represent as physically infirm. The Swiss Expressionist artist

Hermann Scherer's *Self-Portrait* (1924–6) is an oil-on-canvas study whose subjective strokes reveal a haggard, morose subject. The surrounding nature-based landscape, rendered in blue, green, yellow, and red, exposes its subject as a sunken man, peering elsewhere, away from immediate forms. In both *Joker* and Brad Anderson's *The Machinist* (2004), the viewer is directed toward the figures of emaciated, socially disabled males surviving in a symbolic, dark, deregulated dreamscape.

Enraged, plotting, and pencil-thin: this is Arthur Fleck/Joker in Phillips' *Joker*. *The Machinist* presents the sleepless, morbid, and self-starving Trevor Reznik, a psychologically reduced and physically disabled nub of a man. However oddly sympathetic each character may be, Joker/Arthur Fleck and Trevor Reznik (Christian Bale) are screen images of the physically and psychologically disabled male: anorexics without the medical diagnostic labeling. Unlike the portrayal of the politically motivated male in Steve McQueen's *Hunger* (2008), the afflicted males in Jonathan Demme's *Philadelphia* (1993) and Jean-Marc Vallée's *Dallas Buyers Club* (2013), both films about AIDS and the failing body, the frail-appearing Arthur Fleck and Trevor Reznik are not evidently linked to sociopolitical causes. Fleck and Reznik are emaciated males responding to different conditions. In naturalist cinema, being emaciated is a genderless trope.

In the essay "The Philosophy of Toys," Baudelaire relates a spectacle of perverse delight as children from contrasting social classes gaze upon a rat trapped in a cage. Baudelaire describes the struggling creature as an amusement, "a living toy."[9] In Todd Haynes' low-budget, experimental "horror biopic,"[10] *Superstar: The Karen Carpenter Story* (1987), Barbie dolls, historical footage, and engaging music recreate a stylized documentary-like grinding narrative of anorexic decline. In Haynes' film, Carpenter is an entrapped, emaciated creature, with doll-like qualities, living in pain. Haynes' avant-garde bio-pic features hand-held photography, multiple point-of-view tracking shots, and dolls in conversation. Karen's dialogue includes, "I know I'm sick," and "have you ever heard of the word, anorexia?" as if to explain the mystery of the events. *Superstar* features naturalist cinematic tropes associated with illness, entrapment, and anxiety in a gendered, albeit fantastical series of deflating images of the human. In *Joker*, the mirror reflects and reveals its damaged living subject, rendering in close-up shots an image of contemplation, a defamiliarized, reduced presence amid glaring sounds and lights. As Fleck's internalized past involving abuse and neglect is externalized in the present as violent ruptures of his damaged self, his gaze focalizes a tortuous experience in a scraggly face and bony body. In *The Machinist*, the emaciated male body is also a laboring spectacle of decline.

Anderson's narrative exemplifies Naturalism's grinding tradition as it depicts and revitalizes the complex pathology of enacted guilt within a neo-expressionist setting. In *The Machinist*, Anderson's factory machinist Trevor

Reznik, a man like Kafka's macerated hunger artist hovering on the brink of his own extinction, states to his prostitute-neighbor: "I haven't slept in a year." Unlike the gaunt Cesare (Conrad Veidt), the prowling somnambulist in Wiene's *The Cabinet of Dr. Caligari* who sleeps until summoned, Trevor, like Arthur Fleck, remains dimly, constantly awake until drifting off into reimagined, self-made nightmares. In *The Machinist*, multiple mirror shots function as entry points into the imprecise space and time of a man on the edge of exposure in an increasingly unfamiliar world. Trevor and Fleck live in a world of isolated uneasiness. *The Machinist* is the protracted confession of a biological impossibility made visibly credible, as Trevor, an anorexic male, working in a machine factory among other laborers who do not like him, weaves in and out of multiple sets of frantic realties. Arthur Fleck is a failed clown, comedian, and street-sign hustler; the factory life and life beyond the factory gates do not accommodate either man.

In *The Disabled Body in Contemporary Art*, Ann Millett-Gallant refers to Diane Arbus' photographic images and concludes that "everyday and extraordinary people make spectacular spectacles of themselves in these images, enacting everyday life as theatrical, bizarre, and carnivalesque."[11] The eccentric, misplaced, unattractive individual—Arbus' frequent subject matter—merits a place in the naturalist film narrative schema that documents factually unidealized points of disorder. Clint Eastwood's *Richard Jewell* (2019) is a bio-pic focusing on the spectacle of a semi-skilled, uniformed figure. Unlike the emaciated Arthur Fleck, Jewell (Paul Walter Hauser) is a very overweight and overwrought man. Jewell labors as a low-wage security guard at the 1996 Olympics in Atlanta and is unjustly accused of a heinous crime. He is slowly and fatally ground into a public nub, humiliated on television and across the media. Eastwood frequently frames Jewell in close-up and medium shots to reveal and accent his girth. Jewell wears ill-fitting security guard clothing and does not register with the public in a sympathetic manner, which makes him a glaring specimen for relentless mockery by the media's late-night television hosts. This spectacle of humiliation resembles Arthur Fleck's taped nightclub performance on the Murray Franklin broadcast, which amused the audience as an exposed failure. Whether the scrawny Fleck, Reznik, or the obese Jewell, each suffers.

In contrast with films depicting the skinny-anorexic male is Mark Phinney's study of caloric self-abuse and loneliness in *Fat* (2013), a naturalist narrative of unregulated, self-destructive behavior. In *Joker* and *The Machinist*, the audience witnesses slow acts of social and physical starvation leading to obsessive decline; in *Fat*, the audience witnesses compulsive acts of addiction, including multiple face-stuffing sequences and alcohol consumption. *Fat* opens with the shot sequence introducing Ken (Mel Rodriguez), a very obese working-class suburban male. Ken is frequently depicted in close-up shots situated inside of his car, alone and overeating junk food, as other cars and people, like life, pass him by.

Perhaps ironically named after Ken, the Barbie doll's perfect male companion, Phinney's Ken is shot in claustrophobic close-up, a form of metonymical framing. Ken is morbidly obese, the obverse image compared to Joker and Reznik's emaciated portraiture, yet all are damaged males. Like Joker, Ken frequently peers into the mirror to receive a self-loathing reflection, and like Reznik, Ken cannot sleep peacefully, unless aided by a medical apparatus or pills. Ken is a gloomy spectacle in peril, without the promise of future resolution to his problems. He becomes ill with blood pressure complications, but he continues to eat, drink alcohol, take pills, and sit as a solitary figure in his car, a deflated naturalist male. In *Fat*, and the aforementioned "skinny" male films, there is no rescue or happy ending—no magic pill—for specimens in decline.

The jailed figure of disgraced, bloated ex-boxer Jake LaMotta (Robert De Niro) in Scorsese's bio-pic *Raging Bull* (1980), banging his fists in ape-like, irrational fury against the wall while ranting about his present state of public failure, recalls the final fleeting images of an enraged, pathetic Yank pummeling ghosts on the city streets in search of living targets in Eugene O'Neill's expressionist-naturalist drama *The Hairy Ape* (1922), only to wind up crushed by a gorilla in the zoo, who he refers to as his "brother." Yank, a hard-working coal stoker on a ship, wavers between comically ignorant and infuriatingly insightful, as, dying in a cage with fellow simians, he becomes aware of his outlier status; LaMotta, the big beast of the cage-like boxing ring, is doleful yet consistently unsympathetic, as Robert Kolker notes:

> In jail, the great fat man is alone and in the dark . . . [he is] a violent, emotionally fragmented figure, unable to make a mark on the world, with no one left to abuse, ultimately only able to take out his blind frustration on himself. A nobody whose only available target is his own body.[12]

As LaMotta performs later at a sleazy nightclub, in an act resembling Fleck's failed humorless live performances, he is most alone, having lost all except his delusional gaze into the mirror as he rehearses for a career as humiliation spectacle. Darren Aronofsky's *The Whale* (2022), set in a rural section of Idaho, begins with an absent image of online English instructor Charlie's voice emanating from the blacked-out, center-square frame of a live lesson. Charlie (Brendan Fraser) prefers not to be seen but would be heard. Charlie's obesity, which literally fills the frame in several shots, has left him increasingly disabled. Like Ben Sanderson's alcoholic descent into a pathetic death in *Leaving Las Vegas* (1996), in *The Whale*, Charlie, an intelligent, sensitive man overcome by depression and loneliness, is aware that his spiraling blood pressure and heart congestion constitute a veritable death sentence, but he consumes food without regard and basically sits. *The Whale* is a naturalist narrative of protracted, self-conscious suicide.

In *The Poetics of Space*, Gaston Bachelard notes that one essential feature of the home is to provide a site of emotional, psychological intimacies and succor: "For our house is our corner of the world. As has often been said, it is our first universe, a real cosmos in every sense of the word. If we look at it intimately, the humblest dwelling has beauty."[13] Bachelard later addresses the manner in which home life is significantly more memorable than the external social life of the individual: "Memories of the outside world will never have the same tonality as those of home and, by recalling these memories, we add to our store of dreams."[14] When viewed from the perspective of Bachelard's assessments, Lee Daniel's *Precious* (2009),[15] an intergeneric blending of horror, fantasy, melodrama, and potent strokes of negative, spiraling realism, details the nightmarish life of African-American teenager Claireece "Precious" Jones (Gabourey Sidibe), who lives in Harlem, New York City, in 1987. Charlene Regester notes that Daniel's complex film adaptation focuses on the sociohistorical experience of that era:

> Though *Precious* is not a horror film, it borrows from the horror genre and succeeds as horror because of the film's sociopolitical commentary that scares audiences. What makes *Precious* scary is that it directs our attention to issues such as bourgeois normality, obesity, monstrous mothers, welfare mothers, incest, socioeconomic disparity.[16]

Precious is extremely overweight, failing in traditional school, a rape victim who is pregnant with her second child (her first child, "Mongo," is mentally challenged), contracts AIDS, and is notably the target of relentless abuse from her violent, stalking mother. The predatory or ineffectual parent of any gender—living derangements—in naturalist film narrative is a core precept that incorporates relevant class, race, and gender-based configurations across genre and movements. The parent's deleterious actions frequently involve abusive, even deadly behavior emanating from some alcohol- or drug-related consideration or a more primitive, violent source, in a broken/breaking family setting. Precious works at surviving.

Mary (Mo'Nique), Precious' mother, is a foul-mouthed, extremely angry and aggressive chain-smoking, obese, and unemployed woman who resents her daughter, always mocks and torments her, and does nothing to help the family to advance or improve their lives. Mary calls Precious "a fat bitch," and threatens repeatedly "to kill her." When Precious is raped as a child by her drunken father, Mary does nothing except to blame Precious for the family being abandoned by the father, and screams at her, "you done took my man." Mary even tells Precious that "she should have aborted her," leaving Precious to withdraw to untenable fantasies in order to survive relentless hostility in a hostile home and neighborhood.

Precious thrives upon escapist fantasy as a survival mechanism. According to Mia Mask, "Like most teenagers, Precious is an unfiltered repository of media images. She is full of the cultural contradictions of mainstream American society regarding race, gender, sexuality, and class hierarchies. These contradictions manifest in her thoughts, daydreams, and private fantasies."[17] Mask considers *Precious* in an "Italian neo-realist"[18] framework. In *Precious*, the presence of the neorealist aesthetic complements the prevailing psychological fantasy-escape trope that signals observed, recurring expressions of gender, class, and racial discontent in an inhospitable environment at home, at school, and on the streets.

In scant peaceful moments, Precious exists outside of space and time; Precious resists. As Susan Sontag notes, "Nobody ever discovered ugliness through photographs."[19] In her photograph album, Precious repels the relentless grinding process of the world outside to escape into her recent, perhaps illusory past; while Precious peers into and internally relates to the story of these images, in voice-over, select photographs literally respond to her. These photographs are momentary safety zones. As Precious investigates objects such as the mirror, the paintings, and the photographs, and reacts to each experience imaginatively, she confirms that she is not just another anonymous, sad girl on the subway; nobody discovered ugliness through cinema.

In *Precious*, young men wasting time and generally starting trouble on the street stalk and menace Precious despite her constant objection and pregnancy. These are predatory, seemingly lost youth prowling the streets, endemic byproducts of urban cultures. In Edward Bond's naturalist drama of class-based barbarity and urban alienation, *Saved* (1965), a baby left in a carriage in a park is menaced and eventually murdered—lapidated—by a group of bestial local youth who know the baby and its mother. As the moronic hunters in the park gaze upon their prey in the baby carriage, one excitedly states to his friend, "Yer don't get a chance like this every day," as the stone is hurled.[20] In his introduction to his drama *Saved*, Edward Bond comments on the potentially primal origin of this released rage: "the murder of the baby shows the ... atavistic fury fully unleashed."[21] These aimless young men, who experience overwhelming boredom and lack of purpose, appear to imitate the behavior of pack animals cornering a victim; according to Bond, it is a rigid class stratification and sense of personal entrapment that afflicts these men: "They hate their situation rather than hate themselves."[22] *Precious* is a naturalist film; she lives on mean streets.

Glenn Ger's *Disfigured* (2008) is a study in contrasting female body types in urban culture: one obese woman and one anorexic woman portray common eating disorders. Ger's experientially based examination of unattractive realities reveals how both extreme physical realities of the female body live with pain and disappointment, from the bedroom to the workplace. Ger's close-up shots of obese heterosexual lovers in bed is neither pornographic nor comedic. *Disfigured* presents critical issues associated with the female body as experimental-surgical site, involving draconian diets and questionable procedures to reduce mass while featuring a supportive network of similarly challenged individuals as a survival strategy to cope with social ostracism. These are women who could access primary medical assistance and afford treatment for their perceived illness, a class and frequently racially based privilege, to secure their place at work and at home. These moments in the lives of the observed, afflicted individual, like Arthur Fleck, suggest the body as a site of deleterious consumption/ non-consumption, a consistent naturalist cinematic trope.

CRIMINALOIDS

Arthur Fleck/Joker lives in the imaginary, disturbingly near-real world of early 1980s New York City, in which he experiences the pervasive effects of abusive neglect and a fractured sense of self, complemented by frequent encounters with individual and mob violence: a New York of virulent, struggling specimens. Both *Joker* and several Scorsese films about a semi-imagined violent New York City depict the historicized mise-en-scène of near-hallucinatory moments in the lives of failed, yet oddly sympathetic men in possession of lethal weaponry. Kolker considers this a credible, historical image of the city:

> The mise-en-scène of *Mean Streets* [1973] . . . represents more than New York, a place of tough people, crowded streets, fights, and whores. They represent . . . a New York-ness, a shared image and collective signifier of New York that has little to do with the city itself, but rather expresses what everyone, including many who live there, have decided what New York should look like . . . Their [the violent] language is rooted in New York working-class usage, profoundly obscene and charged with movement . . . Scorsese's contemporary 'street' films are fashioned by a tension between two opposing cinematic conventions, the documentary and the fictional.[23]

Directors Scorsese and Phillips were not alone in depicting a dangerous urban landscape and violent portraiture of this era; Michael Winner's *Death Wish* (1974) is a narrative in which one man fights, with increasingly violent measures, against the war-zone atmosphere in a New York City full of murderers and criminals. This imagined threatening culture of New York City generated the publication of the anonymously written Council for Public Safety's infamous pamphlet, *Welcome To Fear City* (1975).[24] Referring to itself as a "Survival Guide," *Welcome To Fear City* was a widely distributed pamphlet bearing the death-like image of a smirking, hooded skeleton's head on its cover. This was

Fleck's imaginatively recreated space and time. In *Joker*, Phillips rarely utilizes light as an engaging resource; the predominant color pallet in his film is largely one of dark tones of brown, gray, and green, with some eruptive neon momentarily producing a jarring, glare-filled reaction. It is an atmospheric, uncolorful setting, replete with the worn colors of a decaying city and people. Within this conceptual era, the transformation of lonely Arthur Fleck into the vicious mob leader Joker is a reactive result, a product of discernable, calamitous causalities. Like an unfolding environmental-biological process, Fleck becomes Joker.

Like Arthur Fleck, Precious lives in a poor urban neighborhood during the 1980s; both have abusive mothers and live in cramped apartments, while each father is missing or predatory. Arthur and Precious suffer from repeated acts of violence and complicated medical issues, and both are repeatedly mocked or humiliated. While Precious fails as a student at her first school, Arthur fails at work. Both Arthur and Precious secretly remove case files—profiles and histories of catastrophic abuse—to learn more about themselves and fill in information gaps. The rail-thin Arthur and obese Precious are profoundly lonely people, constantly weaving between states of reality and escaping into a fantasy world of images as viewed in insipid television productions or emanating from the reflective gaze of a mirror.

For both Arthur and Precious, the mirror functions as an existential passageway that reveals the observed crisis of identity that each experiences but reacts to differently. Precious sees herself in the mirror, in a shot–reverse reflection shot, as a pretty White girl. Below the surface of her personal agony involving rape, incest, and public humiliation, Precious' imagined White face is a racialized marker to momentarily address her discontent. Precious does not want to be unattractive, obese, pregnant, and maltreated, so she selects her dynamic racial opposite as a case study in reflective irony.

Fleck keeps a notebook, a reflective mirror, in which he records and reads humorless anecdotes, aphorisms, jokes, and mysterious, disconnected observations about his life in an unreal, predatory urban environment, in which he is both prey and aggressor. In *Cinema 1: The Movement-Image*, Gilles Deleuze delineates the phenomena of a speculative, originary world in direct relationship to Naturalism:

> An originary world is not an any-space-whatever . . . [it] is recognizable by its formless character. It is a pure background . . . here the characters are like animals: the fashionable gentleman a bird of prey, the lover a goat, the poor man a hyena.[25]

In *Joker*, the city engages such naturalist potentialities. Deleuze suggests a visceral dynamic linkage between an applied socio-historical time and place—an era's marked specificities—and an exploratory presence. Deleuze later comments about the inhabitants of this abstract setting and makes a direct relationship to naturalist precepts:

> These are human animals ... The originary world is therefore both radical beginning and absolute end; and finally it links the one to the other ... It is thus the world of a very special kind of violence ... This is naturalism. It is not opposed to realism, but on the contrary accentuates its features in an idiosyncratic surrealism. Naturalism in literature is essentially Zola; he had the idea of making real milieu run in parallel with originary worlds. In each of his books, he describes a precise milieu, but he also *exhausts* it, and restores it to the originary world; it is from this higher source that the force of realist description derives. The real, actual milieu is the medium of a world which is defined by a radical beginning ... The originary world only exists and operates in the depths of real milieu, and is only valid through its imminence in this milieu, whose violence and cruelty it reveals.[26]

Like the sexually predatory and frequently violent setting in the almost-New York City of Stanley Kubrick's *Eyes Wide Shut* (1999), a film about class and gender masks/unmasking, this is Arthur Fleck's cruel world: where he lives, works, and discovers himself, the clownish-murderous Joker, a product and projection of Deleuzian originary culture:

> Even though it is localized, the originary world is still the overflowing location where the whole film happens, that is, the world at the basis of the social milieu which are so powerfully described ... the world does not exist independently of the determinate milieu, but conversely make them exist with characteristics and features which come from ... a still more terrible depth.[27]

The city of Gotham remains under the microscopic purview of the audience; Fleck/Joker is a fluid specimen viewed as he evolves like a microbe objectively scanned under the critical lens. Fleck, whether failing at work, relationships, or on the performance stage, is a clinical case study, an entry into a diagnostic notebook; he is a medicated and broken exaggeration of illegible male consciousness, a lonely, repressed, unskilled, pummeled man who fails to negotiate his survival in a hostile environment, and later, wears a clown's mask and makeup to indicate his otherness and signify/reveal his inner, brutish rage.

Fleck wears the distorted signifying mask–makeup of excessive guignolish horror set loose upon the space and time of his immediate environment. In her article on the Grand Guignol theatrical tradition, Tania Jurković concludes that "the moral man becomes a human animal in the finest naturalistic tradition,"[28] which suggests an overview charting Fleck's materialization as Joker; however, it is not just a matter of "who is Fleck/Joker?" The question is: "What is Fleck/Joker?" Todd Phillips' Fleck/Joker, who, like Dr. Jekyll/ Mr. Hyde, his naturalist predecessor, suggests the abnormal psychology and devolution of one man occupying the same space as two men, is a *man*, not an animation or the sub/posthuman creature. Phillips' Fleck/Joker differs from the comic book *Batman* DC series as well as his portrayal in prior superhero films and television programs.

Disorders

Joker was released in a year when multiple disability film narratives examined the suffering individual and how society views the afflicted; illness yields generic variations. Fleck likely suffers from trauma associated with the disease pseudobulbar affect (PBA); he cannot wholly control his body in public, and this leads to embarrassing outbursts of uncontrollable crying or laughter. As a result of these perceived ongoing humiliation spectacles, he can only secure menial, low-wage labor, where he remains less visible behind signs and masks. However, to Joker, these public afflictions are visible identity markers: simultaneously mocking and defiant. This medical condition is one of the affective agencies leading to Fleck's social ostracism but also to Joker's public approbation. Director/actor Edward Norton's film *Motherless Brooklyn* (2019) featured a distressed male in another period piece set in an imaginary noirish New York City who suffered from a socially alienating disease, Tourette's Syndrome, and *Five Feet Apart* (2019), Justin Baldoni's popular melodrama, features teenagers thwarted by the limitations imposed by cystic fibrosis.

Like Sjöström's humiliated "He," Fleck/Joker reveals both physical and psychological wounds. As generative causalities, wounds are revealed under deleterious or violent circumstances afflicting the character under the microscope. This is the case in Wallace Worsley's gangster film *The Penalty* (1920), an adaptation of Gouverneur Morris' eponymous novel (1913), in which Blizzard (Lon Chaney), the wounded sociopathic male, expresses his sadistic pathology as a product of the needless amputation of his legs when he was a child. This unfortunate event leads to personal and socially engulfing ostracism. While many wounds are purely of biological origin, Blizzard and Joker are created sickly detritus.

In *Joker*, Arthur Fleck is a reduced, frequently humiliated man, whereas Joker responds in a ferocious manner to perceived threats and initiates acts of violence. In Ilya Naishuller's action film *Nobody* (2021), "Hutch" (Bob Odenkirk) plays a lackluster middle-aged man who labors in a small factory, which he desires to purchase. Hutch's mask of middle-class propriety in suburbia is breached by a series of criminal acts threatening him and his family, resulting in incredible acts of formerly controlled male rage to be released, especially during the bus ride shot sequence when he nearly kills several thugs harassing people. *Nobody* displays naturalist themes and familiar tropes as Hutch responds to his work, family, and personal conflicts. While Naishuller's film later shifts in narrative tone and concludes as a male fantasy of super-heroic acts of revenge, *Nobody* explores secrets of the home, family, and contemporary worker.

David Cronenberg's *A History of Violence* (2005), an intergeneric blending of melodrama and gangster tropes, reveals how the Stall family, a threatened, "tainted" line, confronts past criminal indiscretions while indicating how these acts inform present and future crises. Tom Stall (Viggo Mortensen), the hard-working father of a small family, owns and operates a diner in a remote Indiana town. He will soon encounter two killers in need of cash in a late-night robbery, which, as an invasive presence, exposes the past life behind Tom's mask of middle-class domesticity. Tom Stall is a cached, dangerous virus. As the killers enter the diner, sit down, and demand service, the revelation begins. Cronenberg masterfully arranges the furious shot sequence of the diner robbery in a series of eruptive close-ups, medium shots, and rapidly edited perspectives. Like Arthur Fleck on the subway and Hutch on the bus, Tom's other side resurfaces in an encounter with violent, aggressive men, revealing who was behind the mask of assumed propriety.

Henry Slesar's short story "The Jam" (1958) features two men in a car eternally stuck in traffic inside a tunnel; hell is ironic immobility for these men who do not realize that they are dead. As one of the men pathetically asks the policeman for information about exiting from the tunnel, the officer responds that they will be entrapped, "Forever, of course. Eternity. Where the hell do you think you are?"[29] For Sartre, hell is other people; for many, hell is oncoming headlights and exhaust pipes. Joel Schumacher's naturalist narrative of decline, *Falling Down* (1993), begins with the extreme close-up shot of intense discomfort expressed on the face of a man stuck in traffic on a hot day. In *Falling Down*, the opening montage of chaotic sounds, including insects buzzing, faltering air conditioner knocks and irrationally honking horns, and a series of close-up and medium claustrophobic shots of entrapped people with contorted faces engulf "D-Fens," the nickname of the unemployed, perturbed figure, Bill Foster (Michael Douglas), the man falling. Like the non-functioning air conditioner, an overheated D-Fens literally grinds down to a nub of his former self as he abandons the immobile car in a futile attempt to return home, a place he no longer belongs. He has nowhere to go but attempts to restore his displaced life in a hostile, alien city.

According to Mark Seltzer, "The assumption that the cause of compulsive violence resides ultimately in childhood trauma has become canonical, in criminological and popular accounts."[30] Like Blizzard, another compelling example of severe biological-genetic trauma in childhood leading to pathological violence, criminal activity, and extreme alienation in cinema is found in Walter Hill's naturalist study of crime and disfigurement, *Johnny Handsome* (1989).

In the opening shot sequence of *Johnny Handsome*, as nameless figures walk through hazy, noirish urban streets, a figure emerges slowly from the crowd: the deformed criminal, Johnny Handsome (Mickey Rourke). *Johnny Handsome* presents a vision of the city of pre-Hurricane Katrina New Orleans that is rarely viewed by Mardi Gras tourists; this unromantic view of urban life parallels Phillips' recreation of 1980s' New York City in *Joker*, prior to the appearance of sparkly tourist centers and designer donut shops. *Johnny Handsome* blends several commercial film genres: the horror film, for Johnny's face is freakishly misshapen, and the gangster film, as extremely violent criminal acts occur within a post-Cocteau Disney "beauty and the (altered) beast" near-romance film. *Johnny Handsome* depicts a struggle for survival in the jungle of the city by a profoundly alienated man. As a study of the walking wounded, Johnny is capable only of severely slurred speech that alienates or amuses people, and he barely survives as a product of severe abnormalities, facilitated by his mother's drug addiction. He was reared in jail cells and survived by petty acts of street crime. Johnny's damaged genetic childhood and stunted maturation determine his social otherness in a lonely city where he cannot find legitimate work; he is an aimless nocturnal creature. Thomas Schatz has noted that "the gangster's milieu is the modern city, generally seen at night."[31] The local urban environment, full of bars, drugs, and more criminals, coupled with the problems associated with Johnny's chronic unemployment, although he later secures a position in a factory, creates an atmospheric mood of entrapment.

With its urban netherworld of dangerous outcasts, *Johnny Handsome* suggests a compelling relationship with *Joker*. In the shot sequence following his recuperation from a final plastic surgery operation, Johnny's public transformation from anti-social monster to man occurs in the presence of doctors, nurses, and the audience. After his surgical mask is removed and he sees his new face, Johnny fixes an unmovable gaze into the mirror, like Joker in his solitude, and Johnny states, "I still feel like I'm wearing a mask." Which face, what man, is the real Johnny?

The facial close-up as agency signifying space and time in flux is also characteristic of Scorsese's study of American gangster culture, *The Irishman* (2019), in which principal performers Robert De Niro, Joe Pesci, and Al Pacino are transformed, malleable male configurations via the technical, digital redesigning of industrial deepfake. An image, in this case, a younger version of the face and select body parts of an actor, generally replaces the older version of the same face/actor. Deepfake enables a form of synthetic masking in which

Scorsese augments flashback and flashforward motion, literally manipulating the facial and bodily features, the human geometry of the principal actors, to denote changes in historical setting.

In the opening sequence of *The Irishman*, Scorsese's point-of-view tracking shot slowly enters a nursing facility in the film's present to lead to the aged figure of an assassin, Frank Sheeran (Robert De Niro), as the camera focuses on the face that launched a thousand bullets. The voice-over segues into a flashback shot sequence and a more youthful version of the same man. According to Carolyn Giardina, Scorsese's technical manipulation of the face, hands, and body shapes, the aging/de-aging process, reveal versions of one's former self:

> septuagenarian screen legends Robert De Niro and Al Pacino will perform together as younger men in Martin Scorsese's gangster epic *The Irishman*. As visual effects technologies advance, filmmakers are rethinking the potential of digital humans, particularly as a tool for de-aging actors.[32]

Whether technically rendered or thematically recovered, one face leads to other faces, but it is the same face. Whether the face in close-up of a gangster, clown, or scientist, this special effect renders the biological—an unfixing of genetic inheritance—as a field of play, indicating a transitional presence of shifting selves.

In *Johnny Handsome*, Hill's narrative of decline leaves little space for unreal resolution; like Fleck/Joker, Johnny is not two men but one man with two selves. Following Johnny's placement from jail to a working-class job, an experimental, new life will take form. Hill's film posits oppositional sets of behavioral standards: deformed, criminal Johnny and handsome, working Johnny, as they coexist in one body. Yet Johnny lapses back into his former violent and damaged self.

Like Johnny, Fleck/Joker is also a psychologically and physically tormented man, a near-monstrous, oddly sympathetic criminal, a uniquely withdrawn figure. Fleck suggests a composite of distressful psychological factors emanating from deleterious genetic, physiological origins. Disastrous revelations involving Arthur's unknown identity are contained in a folder in a hospital for the indigent, buried along with other stories of surplus people. Ironically, when the truth about Arthur Fleck is secured by his theft of this folder, it enables him to release his inner Joker, a grotesquery with a painted, laughing face masking intensive pain, emanating from multiple levels of successive abuse and multiple prescribed medications. As Fleck concludes, "I used to think that my life was a tragedy, but now I realize, it's a fucking comedy." It is comedy, *sans* humor.

As Baudelaire notes about the complex emotions facilitating laughter, "Laughter is only an expression, a symptom, a diagnostic . . . laughter is the expression of a double, or contradictory feeling; and that is the reason why a convulsion occurs," and this suggestively refers to individuals, such as Joker, as "Fabulous creations, Beings whose authority and *raison d'être* cannot be drawn from the code of common sense ... The grotesque is a creation ... There is but one criterion of the grotesque, and that is laughter—immediate laughter."[33] Joker meets Baudelaire's criteria; Joker's laughter is not about humor; rather, it is painful and indicative, a formative indexical sign, eerily self-reflective. As Joker laughs, he acts.

According to the Swiss philosopher Max Picard, "A human face is so full of time that it seems all time must be in that one face."[34] In Victor Hugo's historical novel of carnivals, passion, and deformity, *L'Homme qui rit/The Man Who Laughs* (1869), Gwynplaine, a created monster, experiences a crippling life of social ostracism because of a sadistic facial mutilation when he was a child. Like Fleck/Joker, Hugo conceives of Gwynplaine as a complex, sympathetic figure:

> His disfigurement reached even his senses; and, while his conscience was indignant, his face gave it the lie, and jested. Then all was over. He was the laughing man, the caryatid of the weeping world. He was an agony petrified in hilarity, carrying the weight of a universe of calamity, and walled up for ever with the gaiety, the ridicule, and the amusement of others. All that was in him of generosity, of enthusiasm, of eloquence, of heart, of soul, of fury, of anger, of love, of inexpressible grief, ended in—a burst of laughter![35]

Joker's presence is an eruptive, malignant product of Fleck's prior abuse and disillusionment; the more Fleck discovers himself in Phillips' narrative sequencing, the more Fleck's distorted face reveals his bizarre self-awareness.

When Arthur Fleck is first on screen, he is a foolish-looking figure—a sad clown—hawking goods on a dirty street, surrounded by indifferent passers-by, who cannot bear to notice him. These grimy, menacing streets, a vision of a pre-gentrified, near-mythical 42nd Street area of porno shops, stores full of cheap merchandise, and theaters in the New York City of the 1970s–1980s, are Fleck's performance site, his initial stage. Fleck holds an advertising sign, yet appears like a foolish figure in this squalid setting, and he is soon pummeled by a roving band of thugs who steal his sign, leaving him beaten and prostrate in an alley. Fleck, the failed clown, is a contemporary variation of Lon Chaney's "He," the face that gets slapped professionally.

Eventually, when Fleck returns to his workplace office in the 42nd Street area, a colleague, whom he later murders, gives him a loaded gun to protect himself from the "fucking savages" and "animals"; the illegal acquisition of a firearm facilitates the fall of Fleck and the rise of Joker: Fleck, formerly a sensitive Pierrot, becomes Joker, a furious clown with a pistol in an ugly city. As revealed in Joseph Cates' *Who Killed Teddy Bear?* (1965), New York City's Times Square is a crowded site of tense seclusion for the socially marginalized in which "lonely men in shirtsleeves" traverse the midtown area's pornography palaces and seedy businesses. According to John Rechy:

> Times Square, New York, is an electric island floating on a larger island of lonesome parks and lonesome apartment houses and knife pointed buildings stretching up ... Times Square is the magnet for all the lonesome exiles jammed into this city ... the world pours into Times Square.[36]

In the 1970s and early 1980s, Fleck's employment site was this infamous, run-down area in Manhattan still known for its massage parlors and porno theaters; whether Phillips' location shots are set during Fleck's worktime hours or Joker's evening frolics, the immediate urban surroundings are grim and generally uninviting. The three-season broadcast HBO drama series, *The Deuce* (2017–2019),[37] is set largely in the historical space and time of *Joker*. *The Deuce* successfully linked criminal activities with the rise of the pornographic film industry and its exploited women and low-wage workers.

In Fleck's first significant act of violence, he shoots three well-dressed, abusive men riding in the same subway car who mocked him after humiliating a woman. These men assaulted Fleck because of his uncontrollable laughter and twitching, signs of his medical condition and social otherness. Disability exposes him. The gun supplied by the lying and abusive Randall serves as destabilizing weaponry, initiating the release of Arthur's inner self, Joker. This shot sequence recalls the historical incident in 1984 involving New York City's subway vigilante, the unimpressive Bernhard Goetz, who shot several alleged thugs who menaced him in this racialized skirmish. After Fleck is later fired from his job as a clown, in a significant act of compulsive frustration leading to symbolic resolution, he knocks the time clock from its place on the wall of his workplace; Joker will live in a different space and time from others.

In Fleck's subway incident, after the men remove his wig and mask, an emasculating, symbolic undressing, Joker, the violent and armed figure emerges. In a series of medium and close-up shots, defamiliarized space and time render a series of frenzied impressions, and after fleeing the site, alone in a bathroom and standing in front of a mirror, Fleck sees himself, like slowly emerging genetic encoding becoming visibly present. Phillips' stylized, neo-expressionist lighting, camera positioning, unappealing set design and muted colors recall a nightmarish venue, like a fleeing Cesare in Robert Wiene's *The Cabinet of Dr. Caligari* (1920) traveling across an imagined neo-gothic landscape that reflects his inner being. Fleck runs toward this bathroom and later emerges as Joker to damage an unreal world. Multiple mirror-reflection shot sequences in

Joker are critically revelatory; these shots indicate not just an image, but more significantly, the mirror is a space framing shifting identity formations leading to the emergence, the presence of Joker, the performance artist. In naturalist film narrative, the mirror is a transformative site, a visual trope suggesting the "before–after" of identity formations. In Scorsese's *Taxi Driver*, an armed and dangerous Travis Bickle peers into the mirror as he reviews dark, perplexing thoughts and practices drawing his weapons, all leading to violent episodes.

Despite several failed therapy sessions and ineffectual medication, Fleck cannot cope with the immediate, demanding world and is overcome by failure and rejection. Fleck is a troubled, repressed man, like Travis Bickle, but in a more complex way than even Fleck understands. His adoptive mother—the real abusive criminal in *Joker*—lives with him in a worn-out section of New York City, one that invites recycled populations of ethnically, socially disenfranchised people. Fleck's symbolic fathers, the Thomas Wayne of his imagination, as well as the untrustworthy television host Murray Franklin, both fail to understand that Arthur/Joker is a product of a brutal, deceptive society in which these men thrive, which spouts platitudes substituting for sincerity and wisdom. Both men, like the city at large, remain indifferent to their abandoned, troubled son.

Joker's climactic, deadly appearance on the Murray Franklin television show, a subject of Fleck's great delusions, recalls the protracted fantasies in related naturalist films: Martin Scorsese' tedious comic, Rupert Pupkin in *The King of Comedy* (1982), in which the inane Pupkin, via his criminal activity, makes an appearance on a Franklin-like talk show, and Darren Aronofsky's drugged and lonely Sara Goldfarb in *Requiem for a Dream* (2000), whose pill-induced fantasies lead her to believe that she is on a television game show only to produce humiliating hallucinations, resulting ultimately in her hospitalization. The staircase and steps near Fleck's apartment, where he dances like a medicated Fred Astaire epigone, serve as a passageway in which Fleck/Joker escapes from realities. Joker, the assassin, emerges on this site while engaged in a macabre dance of celebratory death, and his face seemingly externalizes his internal delusion: According to Picard, "The cinema-face is ghostly without reason ... like a true face, it seems to have ... presence."[38] Phillips frames several shots in extreme close-up to effect the presence of one man's layered suffering.

In Raoul Walsh's *White Heat* (1949), psychopath/gangster Cody Jarret (James Cagney) reveals in a startling close-up lap dissolve shot that his face, the visage of a murderer, *literally* merges with the face of his equally dangerous mother, conspiring in another location. Walsh's composite shot traverses space and time to suggest biological determinism and a linked, psychological predisposition, an expression of genetic relations, which in 1940s film culture would be intriguing for an audience discovering Freudian interrelations.

BEYOND REALISM

This abstract binary-composite image of the son–mother criminal is visualized as one face. Walsh's superimposition shot encapsulates the notion of the naturalist moment in which form (a transitional edit) and content (indexical sign of genetic flux and physiognomy) merge as singular, aesthetic perception. This fused shot, an image of dynamic angst, exemplifies naturalist film.

Performing Artist

Joker may be read as a hypertextual, grotesque construct evolving from Zola's determinist prose and Courbet's canvas:

> A new convention, like that of naturalism, for example, will become established because there are changes in the structure of feeling which demand expression, and which the most creative artists will eventually realize in their work. But by many these changes will be resisted, and bitterly attacked, in the name of accepted standards.[39]

In naturalist studies, and particularly naturalist cinema, nineteenth-century French realist-naturalist artist Gustave Courbet establishes a prominence

Figure 9.1 Raoul Walsh's *White Heat* (1949)

rivaled only by Zola. When viewed retrospectively as a progenitor of the naturalist aesthetic, Courbet is the artist of the landscape, both environmental and human; his is an indicative canvas. Naturalist art, especially Courbet's signifying canvas, literally or figuratively extends the realist frame of reference into the urban or rural working class as it depicts the life and experiences of the near-modern male and female worker, often in crisis, as well as the uninviting, unattractive socially problematic image. Peter Brook notes, in Courbet's art, "there is no transformation of an ugly reality in the process of its representation, no rhetoric of sentimentality to redeem it, no promise of transfiguration."[40]

Daniel Sipe references Courbet's connotations in his paintings and discusses Courbet-the-painter's "performance" as artist–laborer as an affective presence in his artwork.[41] Sipe specifically refers to Courbet's *Le Désespéré/The Desperate Man* (c. 1843),[42] and notes, "the depiction of mental illness had become an important part of the emerging Realist canon . . . Courbet's images represent a significant variation on the theme, for in them it is the artist himself who is a madman."[43] This also describes Joker, the mad artist. Sipe questions the traditionally asserted Romantic image of the "hypersensitive visionary"[44] in Courbet's self-portrait, and focuses on the analysis of "its aggressive proximity to the viewer as it is to the close observation it affords of the moment of personal crisis and despair that accompanies the artist's 'emergence.'"[45] According to Sipe, the space between the observed and observer is negligible: the "focal point of social interaction" has been redefined, and Sipe insightfully concludes that "to close this distance, even symbolically, is to posit the importance of art as focal point of social interaction."[46] Sipe concludes, "For the artist and his portrait appear to be trapped in a cycle of reflections and gazes to which we are only curious interlopers, surreptitiously occupying the creative space in front of the canvas,"[47] from which the viewer witnesses the spectacle, inviting reaction.

Courbet's self-portrait, a revealing, performative canvas of internalized anxieties, complements Joker's conflicted existence. In *Joker*, there is a close-up shot set in front of a bathroom mirror that recalls Courbet's celebrated self-portrait of discord and disquiet. *Joker*, a case study of a wounded, flawed character-as-product, enraged by social and material displacement, emanates mania and anxiety. In the case of *Joker*, the viewer "sees" but is uncertain what is seen, for the face is denormalized. The audience symbolically functions like a mirror into which Courbet and Joker settle an unsettling gaze. Both figures are male, human, and present but inconclusively understood—what do we see when we see?

In this reflective moment in Courbet's *The Desperate Man*, Courbet the worker enacts Courbet the artist, as Courbet the overwrought madman who exchanges gaze for gaze—a process of self-conscious performing-seeing.

Deleuze suggests a Bergsonian philosophical context for this "dual reflective" experience of the mirror image as coalescence:

> There is a formation of an image with two sides, actual *and* virtual. It is as if an image in a mirror, a photo or a postcard came to life, assumed independence and passed into the actual, even if this meant that the actual image returned into the mirror and resumed its place in the postcard or photo, following a double movement of liberation and capture . . .
>
> The indiscernibility of the real and the imaginary, or of the present and the past, of the actual and the virtual, is definitely not produced in the head or the mind, it is the objective characteristic of certain existing images which are by nature double.[48]

The perception of Courbet's anxious male and Joker's delusional art—is this personality or performance—suggests a shift in Realism's perspectivism. The naturalist image as self-portrait, a moment of representational madness, solicits sets of meaning; this image moves beyond the certifiable parameters of Realism's verisimilitude into an unclarified interpretive set of plausible responses. Courbet and Arthur, conflicted artist–performers, and Joker share in their abandonment of social propriety and enunciate their respective inner struggles in an exterior, presumptive pose. Unfamiliar but human eccentricities and outcasts locate space and time in naturalist film narrative.

In *Joker* and Tod Browning's *Freaks* (1932), the human spectacle is a performing chronic mishap. In *Freaks*, the sideshow and its players focalize the embarrassed gaze of the audience. Browning's film should be read as an experimental text, in particular, one that examines the world of work—the circus sideshow—as an unappealing naturalist site. In the written prologue to Browning's *Freaks*, the peritextual reference concludes, "never again will such a story be filmed, as modern science . . . is rapidly eliminating such blunders of nature from the world." Browning's *Freaks*, a study of bodily and social otherness in the lives of sideshow circus performers—ostracized genetic accidents—and like *Joker*, poses the question of who are the genuine grotesqueries in the narrative. In *Freaks*, the social and moral code of honor by which the unwanted and physically challenged live renders them sympathetic, perhaps more human, than the occupants of the intimidating world they perform for as amusing distractions. According to Roland Barthes, "What characterizes the so-called advanced societies is that they today consume images and no longer, like those of the past, beliefs."[49] Browning's freaks are images of "not me" to the audience. The freaks struggle to survive economically as manipulated attractions, laboring spectacles of misery in psychologically and sexually demeaning roles. As Deleuze succinctly notes, *Freaks* is a complex, socially reflective narrative:

> The monsters in *Freaks* are monsters only because they have been forced to move into their explicit role ... What we see in Browning is not a reflection on the theatre or the circus, as we will see in others, but a double face of the actor, that only the cinema could capture by instituting its own circuit.[50]

Joker is a performance artist, typical of the edgy late 1970s–early 1980s New York City and international art scene. Like artist-performers Andy Kaufman, Rudolf Schwarzkogler, Chris Burden, Tehching Hsieh, and Marina Abramovic, Courbet and Joker share the abandonment of social propriety, appearances of psychological normalcy, to enunciate their respective inner struggles in exteriorized, presumptive poses. Fleck's initial on-screen appearance as a colorful "walking billboard" and Joker's broadcast assassination of Franklin and later riotous presence in the 42nd Street and Times Square area suggest the constructivist color montage "notice me" art of Barbara Kruger and Jenny Holzer's aphorisms–reworked jokes, strikingly posted on theater marquees. According to Annie Ring Patterson, the densely visited New York City midtown area was an especially desired site for presenting art-as-spectacle.[51] During this era, clowns, carnival acts and freaks perform in displaced, offsetting space and time. Artist-filmmaker Bruce Nauman's overwhelming, multi-screen spectacle, *Clown Torture* (1987),[52] particularly features the repetitive images of an unstable clown in problematically alluring stages of buffoonery: "Bruce Nauman ... made a series of video and installation pieces in which a clown appears, foremost among them his 1987 installation Clown Torture ... Each screen and wall projection shows footage of a clown engaged in some absurd activity."[53] When Nauman's film is viewed in an intertextual capacity with Phillips' *Joker*, each work reveals the clown-artist in various phases of unsettling postmodern performance. Nauman's confrontational loop sequences are bizarre, alienating, and in effect torturous for both clown and spectator; Joker's festering aggression, like Phillips' performing artist, is controversial and disturbing.

In *Joker*, Arthur Fleck is a freak alone, never quite safe, even in his own conflicted mind. In one compelling moment, after Joker commits a brutal murder in his apartment, Joker spares the life of Gary, the little person and fellow-clown. In what might be considered an act of recognition and solidarity, Joker kisses Gary on the forehead. In contrast to this act of freak-camaraderie, the able-bodied Murray Franklin is not spared a violent death after Joker's truncated performance and feckless conversation once he is invited to sit on the couch with Franklin in what Joker intuited would be a protracted series of humiliating remarks aimed at him. As Joker ignores the pre-set conditions of power relations between host-guest, he controls his narrative.

After the Franklin assassination is broadcast on television, Phillips situates one of Joker's greatest performances, his temporary escape from a police car after a massive pile-up of crashed automobiles in the Times Square area. With his two fingers, Joker paints a grotesque, blood-stained smile on his face, signaling the emergence of the artist to the masses cheering him as they witness the rise from the near-fall. Unlike the feigned smile on brutalized Lucy's face to mask her anxiety and suffering in Griffith's naturalist study of child abuse and male rage in *Broken Blossoms* (1919), Joker's bloody visage is a mark of release. He invites applause and recognition.

A legitimate problem is that Fleck is never funny; his art is too personal and convoluted for the public, and he fails to perform successfully even when appearing on a less demanding local stage. Fleck fails at these performances because his audience, the mob, is not yet created, but Joker is in peak performance as he finally appears on television, to murder and to create for the small screen in a staggering live performance, thus ensuring a mob frenzy of activated popular reception. Like the pre-Joker Fleck, the aging song-and-dance man Archie Rice, playwright John Osborne's dishonest, anachronistic music hall performer in Tony Richardson's *The Entertainer* (1960) is also a study in decline in both career and social relations. Rice possesses a measure of self-awareness of his own diminished stature as he plays in third-rate venues: "we're dead beat and down and outs. We're drunks, maniacs, we're crazy, we're bonkers, the whole flaming bunch of us . . . We're a nuisance."[54] Both Archie and Fleck are ignored or rejected by the more officious elements in society. As Fleck specifically requests that he be called "Joker" before his broadcast introduction, he achieves the recognition Archie could only imagine, especially from the mob outside.

Some compelling shot sequences in *Joker* involve the crowd's evolution into a mob, an unidentifiable mass of enraged anonymous citizenry acting as one intense body and voice. In *Joker*, legions of rapt individuals find succor in self-reflective symbols of urban rage, an image Joker provides. Gustave Le Bon's *The Crowd* (1895) provides historical perspective into the nature of the de-individualized mass; "The crowd demands a god before everything else."[55] In *Joker*, multiple representation of enraged individuals begin as an assemblage, a crowd that develops along purposeful lines, in which a shift in tone and objectives occur. According to Le Bon, "When studying the imagination of crowds we saw that it is particularly open to the impressions produced by images . . . . All words and all formulas do not possess the power of evoking images."[56] Joker, a calamitous and unsettling image, produces impulsive, bestial behavior in the disaffected mass of people—a clown revolt.

In his comprehensive study *Faces of Degeneration* (1989), Daniel Pick refers to Le Bon and cites a critical passage that explicates this collapse of the social order: "the crowd was atavistic in behavior—a throwback to the evolutionary past of the individuals who composed it. The leader was usually a degenerate."[57] Joker, in his increasingly corrupt persona, fuels the animalistic release. As Joker enters a subway car packed with masked subway riders clad in semi and full "Joker" masks and regalia, he escapes from two policemen. There are more masked Joker-anarchists in riotous frenzy, attending a clown-rally later at City Hall. These crowds engulf the streets in hallucinatory images of an uncontrolled city-on-fire, suggesting a loss of individuality and acceptance of exposed rage, a class revolt of the superfluous. This is Joker's victory, and as Le Bon notes, "The unreal has almost as much influence on them as the real,"[58] in the recreated imaginary milieu of late 1970s–1980s' New York City. *Joker* is a clinically viable observed study of a troubled man in progressive decline adrift in an ugly society who increasingly reacts violently to his perceived dehumanization. In *Joker*, Phillips' conception of the Fleck/Joker character, his tortured humanity, ranks among the unique contributions to contemporary naturalist cinema.

Coda

From images of anonymous nineteenth-century women handwashing clothes by the river to stylized shots of a twenty-first-century costumed, violent man searching for himself in slums and subways, international naturalist cinema produces sites of imagined biological and social collaboration involving race, class, and gender. In naturalist cinema, whether the film narrative is set inside a bloody abattoir, foreboding basement, dim coal mine, oppressive chain gang or on an unkept urban street, familiar settings are foregrounded, recurring catalytic spaces: affective co-ordinates. The naturalist film is a "writerly" platform, demonstrably invoking intertextual sources, including artistic forms and interdisciplinary movements such as Surrealism and Expressionism, realist painting, grotesque photography, modern philosophy, and biological-evolutionary science. The viewer engages familiar tropes, such as *La Bête humaine*, alcohol, and conceptualized genetics (heredity's platform). In naturalist cinema, impalpable DNA strands comingle with social agencies and are reconfigured as sites of visual discourse. Naturalist cinema's experimental positioning is evident in cartoons, documentaries, fiction and non-fiction films—all industrial praxes—in both international and national markets and histories as observed phenomena.

In conclusion, Claude Bernard's *An Introduction to the Study of Experimental Medicine* (1865) asserts that "the experimental method is nothing but reasoning by whose help we methodically submit our ideas to experience—the experience of facts."[59] In order to establish a procedural norm, Bernard poses a process of clinical observation:

> Experiment is what teaches about facts [and comes] by sequence of reasoning . . . two things must therefore be considered in the experimental

method: (1) the art of getting accurate facts by means of rigorous investigation; (2) the art of working them up by means of experimental reasoning, so as to deduce knowledge of the law of phenomena.[60]

Phenomena is the critical term: "Observation is investigation of a natural phenomenon, and experiment is investigation of a phenomenon altered by the investigator."[61] The international naturalist film narrative extends the observational process into the world and experience of the exhausted, disturbed, defective, and jocose: the phenomena of the living.

Notes

1. Charles Baudelaire, *The Mirror of Art*, trans. Jonathan Mayne (Garden City, New York: Doubleday-Anchor Book, 1956), 141.
2. Anonymous, "To Draw and Paint Magic Lantern Slides Source," *Scientific American*, Vol. 35, No. 21 (November 18, 1876), 330.
3. Benjamin Radford, *Bad Clown* (Albuquerque, NM: University of New Mexico Press, 2016), 26.
4. Wolfgang Kayser, *The Grotesque in Art and Literature*, trans. Ulrich Weisstein (New York: Columbia University Press), 1981.
5. Frederick H. White, "A Slap in the Face of American Taste: Transporting *He Who Gets Slapped* to American Audiences," in *Border Crossing: Russian Literature into Film*. eds Alexander Burry and Frederick H. White (Edinburgh: Edinburgh University Press, 2016), 143.
6. Some excellent titles that review New York City's historical and cultural realities in the 1970s include: Allen Tannenbaum's *New York City in the 70s* (New York: Abrams Press, 2011); Edward Grazda's *Mean Streets: NYC 1970–1985* (New York: Powerhouse Books, 2017); Hillary Miller's *Drop Dead: Performance in Crisis: 1970s New York* (Illinois: Northwestern University Press, 2016).
7. William Withey Gull, "Anorexia nervosa, Apepsia Hysterica, Anorexia Hysterica," (October 24, 1873), reprinted in *Obesity Research*, Vol. 5 No. 5 (Sept. 1997), 500–1.
8. Chengyuan Zhang, "What Can We Learn from the History of Male Anorexia Nervosa?," *Zhang Journal of Eating Disorders* (2014) Vol. 2, Issue 138, 1.
9. Charles Baudelaire, "The Philosophy of Toys," (1853). *Essays on Dolls*, trans. and ed. Paul Keegan (Syrens–Penguin Publishing: London: 1995), 19.
10. Rob White, *Todd Haynes* (Chicago: University of Chicago Press, 2013), 13.
11. Ann Millett-Gallant, *The Disabled Body in Contemporary Art* (New York: Palgrave Macmillan, 2010), 113.
12. Robert Kolker, *A Cinema of Loneliness* (New York: Oxford Press, 2000), 215.
13. Gaston Bachelard, *The Poetics of Space*, trans. Maria Jolas (Boston: Beacon Press, 1994), 4.
14. Ibid, 6.
15. The film is also known as: *Precious: Based on the Novel by Sapphire*.
16. Charlene Regester, "Monstrous Mother, Incestuous Father, and Terrorized Teen: Reading *Precious* as a Horror Film," *Journal of Film and Television*, Vol. 67, No. 1 (Spring 2015), 44.
17. Mia Mask, "The Precarious Politics of *Precious*: A Close Reading of a Cinematic Text," *Black Camera*, Vol. 4, No. 1 (Winter 2012), 97.

18. Ibid, 106–7.
19. Susan Sontag, *On Photography* (New York: Farrar, Straus and Giroux, 1978), 85.
20. Edward Bond, *Saved* (New York: Hill & Wang, 1966), 55.
21. Ibid, 6.
22. Susana Nicolás, "'The Trigger of Truth is in Your Hands': Conversations with Edward Bond," *Contemporary Theatre Review*, Vol. 26, No. 2 (2016), 261.
23. Kolker, *Cinema*, 180–1.
24. Council for Public Safety, *Welcome to Fear City* (New York: 1975), n.p.
25. Gilles Deleuze, *Cinema 1: The Movement-Image*, trans. Hugh Tomlinson and Barbara Habberjam (Minnesota: University of Minnesota Press, 1986), 123.
26. Ibid, 124–5.
27. Ibid, 125–6.
28. Tanja Jurković, "Blood, Monstrosity and Violent Imagery: Grand-Guignol, the French Theatre of Horror as a Form of Violent Entertainment," *Coded Realities*, No. 1 (2013), 6.
29. Henry Slesar's short story may be located at: http://unfamiliartext.weebly.com/the-jam.html. Accessed June 14, 2023.
30. Mark Seltzer, "Wound Culture: Trauma in the Pathological Public Sphere," *October*, Vol. 80 (Spring 1997), 7.
31. Thomas Schatz. *Hollywood Genres: Formulas, Filmmaking, and the Studio System* (New York: Random House, 1981), 83.
32. Giardina, Carolyn, "The Dawn of the De-Aged Actor: 'It was time to try a digital human,' says Ang Lee of the steep challenge of creating a young Will Smith as Gemini Man and Scorsese's Irishman push new boundaries of VFX, budgets and, say some, ethics," *Hollywood Reporter*, Vol. 425, No. 33 (October 9, 2019), 54.
33. Baudelaire, *Mirror*, 142–4.
34. Max Picard, *The Face*, trans. Guy Endore (New York: Farrar & Rinehart, 1930), 137.
35. Victor Hugo, *L'Homme qui rit/The Man Who Laughs* (1869). See https://freeclassicebooks.com/Victor%20Hugo/The%20Man%20Who%20Laughs.pdf. Accessed June 12, 2023.
36. John Rechy, *City of Night* (New York: Grove Press, 1964), 21, 30.
37. The HBO-sponsored website is located at https://www.hbo.com/the-deuce. Accessed June 12, 2023.
38. Picard, *Face*, 129.
39. Raymond Williams and Michael Orrom, *Preface to Film* (London: Film Drama Limited, 1954), 23.
40. Peter Brooks, *Realist Vision* (New Haven: Yale University Press, 2005), 76.
41. Daniel Sipe, *Text, Image, and the Problem with Perfection in Nineteenth-Century France* (New York City: Routledge, 2016), 146–7.
42. This self-portrait is dated by art historians at 1843–4.
43. Sipe, *Text*, 146.
44. Ibid, 146.
45. Ibid, 146.
46. Ibid, 146.
47. Ibid, 146.
48. Gilles Delueze, *Cinema 2: The Time-Image* trans. Hugh Tomlinson and Robert Galeta (Minneapolis: University of Minnesota Press, 1989), 68–9.
49. Roland Barthes, *Camera Lucida*, trans. Richard Howard (New York: Hill & Wang, 1981), 118–19.
50. Deleuze, *Cinema 2*, 8, 72.

51. Alice Ring Peterson, "Jenny Holzer and Barbara Kruger at Times Square," in *The Urban Lifeworld: Formation, Perception, Representation*, eds Peter Madsen and Richard Plunz (New York: Routledge, 2001), 369–70.
52. An abbreviated version of Nauman's film may be viewed at https://vimeo.com/20303026. Accessed May 30, 2023.
53. Maxim Leonid Weintraub, "Clowning Around at the Limits of Representation: On Fools, Fetishes and Bruce Nauman's *Clown Torture*," in *Clowns, Fools, and Picaros: Popular Forms in Theater, Fiction, and Film*, ed. David Robb (New York: Rodopi Publishing), 2007, 71.
54. John Osborne, *The Entertainer* (New York: Penguin Books, 1983), 54.
55. Gustave Le Bon, *The Crowd* (1895), trans. uncredited (New York: Viking Press, 1966), 66.
56. Ibid, 102–3.
57. Daniel Pick, *Faces of Degeneration* (New York: Cambridge University Press, 1993), 91.
58. Le Bon, *Crowd*, 69.
59. Claude Bernard, *An Introduction to the Study of Experimental Medicine*, trans. Henry Copley Greene (New York: Dover Publications, 1957), 2.
60. Ibid, 11–12.
61. Ibid, 15.

INDEX

Abadie, Alfred C., 48
Abattoirs (1865), 110
Abel, Richard, 62
Acres, Birt, 15
Act of Seeing with One's Own Eyes, The (1971), 134
Aileen: Life and Death of a Serial Killer (2003), 73
Aileen Wuornos: The Selling of a Serial Killer (1992), 73
Aitken, Ian, 7, 54, 162
Aja, Alexandre, 143–4
Aldrich, Robert, 26
Allen, Woody, 92, 157, 219
Alles Leben ist Kampf /All Life is Struggle (1937), 147
Altered States (1980), 171
Althusser, Louis, 7
Anderson, Brad, 25, 231
Anderson, Paul Thomas, 63
Andreyev, Leonid, 229
Ang babaeng humayo/Woman Who Left, The (2016), 75
Angelo, Adrienne, 123
Animal Locomotion: An Electro-Photographic Investigation of Consecutive Phases of Animal Movements, 1872–1885 (1887), 35
Antoine, André, 2, 4, 5, 6, 34, 108, 122–3
Ants in the Pantry (1936), 217
Anzalone, John, 40
Arbuckle, Roscoe "Fatty", 106, 107, 221–2, 225
Arbus, Diane, 98, 111, 126–7, 220, 232
Aristotle, 61, 198, 214, 215
Arnold, Jack, 158
Aronofsky, Darren, 30, 32, 89, 233, 245
Arthur, T. S., 24
Ash, Sholom, 97, 104
Ashby, Hal, 65
Au Pays Noir/Tragedy in a Coal Mine (1905), 62–3, 64, 66
Aueur, John, 204
Avant-Garde Film, The (1978), 9
Avariès, Les/Damaged, The (1901), 36
Ayouch, Nabil, 83

Babenco, Hector, 27, 193, 194
Bachelard, Gaston, 97, 138, 157, 234

Bad Seed, The (1954), 154
Bad Seed, The (1956), 151–2
Bahrani, Ramin, 49, 50, 71
Baignade en mer/Swimming in the Sea (1895), 15
Bailes, Sarah Jane, 221, 222
Bailey, Peter J., 219, 220
Baker, Sean, 74, 95, 96
Bakhtin, Mikhail, 216, 218
Balaban, Burt, 178
Baldoni, Justin, 239
Baldwin, James, 169
Band, Albert, 203
Barry (2018–2023), 7
Barthes, Roland, 19, 126, 140, 248
Bat sin fan dim: Yan yuk cha siu bau/ Eight Immortals Restaurant, The: The Untold Story (1993), 118–19
Bateson, William, 140
Baudelaire, Charles, 228, 231, 242, 243
Baxter, John, 53
Beach, Christopher, 218
Bell Boy, The (1918), 220–1, 225
Bellboy (1925), 220
Bellboy, The (1960), 222–5
Bellocq, E. J., 98, 99, 102
Bellows, George, 15
Bergson, Henri, 248
Bernard, Claude, 251
Bête humaine, La (1890), 20, 28, 32, 113, 119, 123, 127, 169, 171, 178, 185, 228, 251
Bête humaine, La (1938), 20–4
Bigger Than Life (1956), 30, 151
Bingham, Theodore A., 158
Birthday Party, The (1957), 158
Black Dahlia, The (2006), 133
Black Hand, The (1906), 120
Black, Preston, 217
Black Stork, The (1917), 146, 148, 150
Blackboard Jungle, The (1955), 153
Blanchisseuse, La/Laundress, The (1863), 67
Blowjob (1964), 95
Bogle, Donald, 24
Böhme, Margarete, 85
Bolivia (2001), 60

Bond, Edward, 153, 235
Bonello, Bertrand, 99, 100, 101, 102
Borden, Lizzie, 101
Borges, Jose Luis, 1, 2, 161, 165
Borom Sarret/Wagoner, The (1963), 18, 50, 51
Bosworth, Patricia, 127
Bouchers, Les/Butchers, The (1888), 122–3
Bousquet, Stephen C., 39
Bozon, Serge, 171, 172, 176
Bradshaw, Peter, 164
Brady, Sara, 190
Brakhage, Stan, 134
Brassaï, 99, 100, 127
Breton, André, 63
Brieux, Eugène, 36, 37
Broadway Danny Rose (1984), 219–20
Broken Blossoms (1919), 28–9, 86, 250
Brook, Peter, 195, 196
Brooks, Richard, 153
Broomfield, Nick, 73
Brown, Clarence, 49
Brown, Joe, 35–6
Browning, Tod, 184, 188, 248
Bullot, Erik, 107
Buñuel, Luis, 13, 217
Burgess, Jackson, 195
Burkhardt, Rudy, 15
Burnett, Charles, 113, 114, 115
Burton, Alan, 153
Burton, Tim, 117, 118, 220
Busnach, William, 68
Byron, Lord, 91

Cabinet des Dr. Caligari, Das/The Cabinet of Dr. Caligari (1920), 162, 175, 232, 244
Cable Guy, The (1996), 217–18, 219
Cadmus, Paul, 96
Caetano, Adrián, 60
Cain, James M., 129, 130, 131
Call Northside 777 (1948), 204
Callahan, Dan, 97
Calnek, Roy, 24
Campbell, Russell, 81, 83

Cantet, Laurent, 31, 32
Capone (2020), 39
Capone, Al, 39
Cardona, René, 207
Carne (1991), 123
Carné, Marcel, 127
Carroll, Nöel, 163, 164
Cates, Joseph, 244
Catkins, Tim, 220
Cast Away (2000), 186
Castillo, Debra A., 66
Cat People (1942), 185, 186
Cat People (1982), 185, 186
Cattle Driven to Slaughter (1897), 107
Caught (1996), 131
Cerf forcé, Le/Stag at Bay (1861), 202
Chapin, Tom, 195
Chaplin, Charlie, 6, 53–4, 212, 213
Charcuterie mécanique/Mechanical Butcher, The (1896), 44, 106
Chase, David, 6
Chekhov, Anton, 200
Cheever, John, 16
Chehre Pe Chehra/Face to Face (1980), 170
Chenal, Pierre, 203, 204, 205, 206
Chien Andalou, Un (1929), 217
Chukwu, Chinonye, 71
Ciénaga, La/Swamp, The (2001), 17
Cinema 1: The Movement-Image (1983), 142, 237
Cinema 2: The Time-Image (1985), 181
City That Never Sleeps (1953), 204
Ciudad, La/The City (1998), 18, 57, 58
Cidade de Deus/City of God (2002), 194
Clark, Constance, 191
Clemency (2019), 71, 72
Clément, René, 215
Client or Maison Close, Le (1878), 96
Clockers (1995), 154–5
Clown Torture (1987), 249
Cocteau, Jean, 241
Companion to Dada and Surrealism, A (2016), 163
Conklin, Edwin, 148
Conrad, Joseph, 179, 181, 207

Conte de Noël/Christmas Tale, A (1890), 108
Cooper, Kyle, 142
Cooper, Merian C., 169, 184
Costa, Richard, 193
Costa-Gavras, 133
Courbet, Gustave, 4, 6, 8, 9, 15, 101, 131, 147, 202, 203, 209, 246, 247, 248, 249
Cowie, Elizabeth, 47
Cowie, Jefferson, 58
Crane, Stephen, 82, 83, 84, 88, 92, 93, 180, 203
Craven, Wes, 111, 112, 143, 144
Crime and Punishment (1935), 206
Crime et Châtiment/Crime and Punishment (1956), 83, 206
Cronenberg, David, 240
Crowd, The (1895), 250
Cry Macho (2021), 11
Cunningham, Frank R., 56

Dada Manifesto (1918), 212
Dahlberg, Andrea, 51
Dallas Buyers Club (2013), 231
Damaged Lives (1933), 37
Daniel, Lee, 234
Daniels, Jennie Irene, 17
Danks, Adrian, 30
Dardenne, Jean-Pierre, 59, 70, 71
Dardenne, Luc, 59, 70, 71
Darwin, Charles, 4, 8, 14, 16, 17, 19, 20, 21, 145, 146, 155, 160, 161, 165, 169, 171, 178, 179, 180, 182, 186, 191, 192, 197
Dassin, Jules, 164
Daumier, Honoré, 67
Davidson, Kief, 65
Davies, Reverend C. Maurice, 82
Dearden, Basil, 152, 153
Degas, Edgar, 58
De Palma, Brian, 133
De Sica, Vittorio, 11, 18
Deadwood (2004–2006), 7, 97, 108
Death Wish (1974), 236
Delanoë-Brun, Emmanuelle, 121
Deleuze, Gilles, 20, 33, 68, 74, 125, 142,

181, 182, 212, 221, 223, 237, 238, 248
Demme, Jonathan, 231
Démolition d'un mur/Demolition of a Wall (1896), 44, 211–12, 216
Dérobade, La/Memoirs of a French Whore (1979), 84
Descent of Man, The (1871), 160
Désespéré, Le/Desperate Man, The (c. 1843), 247
Deuce, The (2017–2019), 244
Devil's Miner, The (2005), 65
DeVoe, Thomas F., 110
Dhobi Ghat/Mumbai Diaries (2010), 52
Diaz, Lav, 75
Dickson, W. K. L., 165, 166
Dieterle, William, 147
Dijck, Jose van, 142, 143
Diligence dans la neige, La (1860), 6
Disabled Body in Contemporary Art, The (2010), 232
Disfigured (2008), 235
Divinas Palabras (1919), 108–9
Dmytryk, Edward, 97
Dr. Ehrlich's Magic Bullet (1940), 147
Dr. Jekyll and Mr. Hyde (1920), 36, 166
Dr. Jekyll and Mr. Hyde (1931), 145, 167, 169, 170, 172
Dreiser, Theodore, 130
Drunkard's Reformation, A (1909), 28
Ducournau, Julia, 121
Durden, J. V., 145
Dutt, Guru, 25, 26, 27

Eastwood, Clint, 11, 97, 99, 155, 201, 202, 232
Eburne, Jonathan P., 163
Ed Wood (1994), 220
Edison Manufacturing Company, 48
Einayim Pkuhot/Eyes Wide Open (2009), 120
Eisenstein, Sergei, 13, 59, 64, 204
Elliott, Paul, 152
Elmaleh, Edmund, 177
En el hoyo/In the Pit (2005), 59
Engels, Friedrich, 27, 49, 54, 62, 206
Enter the Void (2009), 13

Entertainer, The (1960), 250
Entre les murs/Between the Walls (2008), 31
Equatorial Jungle, The (1909), 181
Erbkrank/Hereditary Disease (1936), 147
Esslin, Martin, 52
"Etching-Leaf 4-March of *The Weavers*" (1897), 52–3
Expression of the Emotions in Man and Animals, The (1872), 169, 178
Eyes Wide Shut (1999), 238

Face of Fire (1959), 203
Faces of Degeneration (1989), 250
Fading Gigolo (2014), 92
Falling Down (1993), 240
Falzon, Christopher, 54
Fanzhi, Zeng, 109
Farocki, Harun, 45, 46
Fassbinder, Rainer Werner, 27, 28, 29, 116–17, 139
Fat (2013), 232
Fehér, György, 129, 131, 132
Feind im Blut/Enemy in the Blood (1931), 147, 148
Felix the Cat Doubles for Darwin (1924), 191–2
Fellini, Federico, 58
Ferenc, Tomasz, 99
Fifteen Years of a Drunkard's Life (1828), 23
Fifth Avenue, New York (1897), 79
Fight Between a Tiger and a Buffalo (1908), 181
Figgis, Mike, 25
Figure with Meat (1954), 125
Five Feet Apart (2019), 239
Flaubert, Gustave, 68
"The Fleet's In" (1934), 96
Flitterman-Lewis, Sandy, 28
Florida Project, The (2017), 74
Flowers of Asphalt (1894), 92
Flowers of Asphalt (1951), 93
Fofana, Amadou T., 50, 51
Forbidden Desire (1937), 37
Forty-two Kids (1907), 15

Found Drowned (c. 1848–1850), 82
Four Workers (1940), 58–9
Fournier, Alfred, 36, 38
Francis Bacon: The Logic of Sensation (1981), 125
Frankenheimer, John, 142, 147, 187, 188, 189, 190
Franju, Georges, 115, 116
Freaks (1932), 184, 188, 248, 249
Freud, Sigmund, 29, 191, 245
Friant, Émile, 139
Frost, Robert, 63
Fujiwara, Chris, 223, 225
Fuller, Samuel, 89, 90, 91

Garnett, Tay, 129, 130
Gastineau, Octave, 68
Gauthier, E. Paul, 21
Geertz, Clifford, 4, 196, 197
Geisteskrank/Mentally Ill (1939), 147
Gengangere/Ghosts (1881), 33–4
Gentleman's Companion, A (1870), 79
Georgiadis, Vasilis, 96
Gerdes, Herbert, 147
Géricault, Théodore, 132
Germinal (1885), 61, 62
Gerould, Daniel, 33
Gervaise (1956), 215
Ger, Glenn, 235
Ghosts (1915), 34, 38
Giardina, Carolyn, 242
Gibier de potence/Gigilo (1951), 91
Giles, Jane, 124
Gilfoyle, Timothy J., 86
Girard, René, 60
Girlfight (2000), 155
Girdner, John, 80
Girel, Constant, 138
Gisaengchung/Parasite (2019), 156
Gleaners, The (1857), 75
Goetz, Bernhard, 244
Gold Rush, The (1925), 6
Golding, William, 181, 188, 192, 193, 194, 195, 196
Goldman, Henrique, 94
Goodfellas (1990), 122
Goodwin, James, 35

Goose Woman, The (1925), 49
Gordon, Mel, 108
Got Fun Nekome/God of Vengeance (1907), 97
Grand Guignol, 108, 111, 118, 157, 238
Grave/Raw (2016), 121
Gravesend (1997), 153
Gray, James, 181
Greed (1924), 66, 188
Greenburg, Harvey Roy, 73
Greenwood, Walter, 53
Griffith, D. W., 28, 29, 86, 250
Grodecki, Wiktor, 93
grønne slagtere, De/Green Butchers, The (2003), 121–2
Gulf Stream (1899), 16
Gull, William, 230

Hairy Ape, The (1922), 233
Hallam, Julia, 8
Händler der vier Jahreszeiten/Merchant of Four Seasons, The (1972), 27–8
Hannibal (2001), 108
Hansen, Miriam, 86
Hapke, Laura, 57, 58
Harlan County, USA (1976), 60, 64
Harris, Leslie, 154
Has, Wojciech J., 25
Haskin, Byron, 198
Hathaway, Henry, 204
Hauptmann, Gerhart, 52
Hauser, Arnold, 8, 9
He Who Gets Slapped (1915), 229
He Who Gets Slapped (1924), 85, 229, 243
Heart of Darkness (1899), 179, 181, 207
Heath, Malcolm, 215
Heise, William, 205
Heller, Franziska, 15, 16
Henderson, Brian, 220
Henderson, Dennis R., 116
Heredity and Man (1937), 145–6
Herk, Aritha van, 67
Hill, The (1965, novel), 199
Hill, The (1965, film), 199
Hill, Walter, 241
Hills Have Eyes, The (1977), 111, 143

Hills Have Eyes, The (2006), 143, 144, 145
History of Animals, The (c. 350 BCE), 61, 198
History of Violence, A (2005), 240
Hitch-Hiker, The (1953), 112
Hitchcock, Alfred, 77, 164, 206
Hitchcock, Peter, 63
Hoi Polloi (1935), 215, 216
Holmes, Amanda, 60
Holzer, Jenny, 249
Home Box Office (HBO), 6, 7, 97, 108, 153, 219, 244
Homer, Winslow, 16, 40
homme de têtes, Un/Four Troublesome Heads, The (1898), 222
Honeymoon Killers, The (1970), 73
Hooker, Joseph Dalton, 14
Hooper, Tobe, 111, 112, 113, 114
Horse Attacked by a Jaguar (1910), 181
House Is Not a Home, A (1964), 101
Howard, June, 151
Human, All Too Human (1878), 156
Human Centipede, The: First Sequence (2009), 157
Human Desire (1954), 127
Hunger (2008), 231
Hugo, Victor, 243
Hungry Lion Throws Itself Upon the Antelope, The (1905), 181
Hunter, Colin, 16
Hurdes, Las/Land Without Bread (1933), 13
Huxley, Julian, 145, 148

I Am a Fugitive from a Chain Gang (1932), 200–2, 204, 206, 207
I Want to Live! (1958), 72
Ibsen, Henrik, 33, 34, 36, 37, 149
Icres, Fernand, 122, 123
In einem Jahr mit 13 Monden/In a Year with 13 Moons (1978), 116–17
In the Penal Colony (1919), 181
Iñárritu, Alejandro G., 112
Incredible Hulk, The (2008), 171
Incredible Shrinking Man, The (1957), 158

Introduction to the Study of Experimental Medicine, An (1865), 251
Irishman, The (2019), 241–2
Ironweed (1987), 27
Ishii, Teruo, 187
Isla de los hombres solos, La/Island of Lonely Men, The (1974), 207
Island, The: A Journey to Sakhalin (1893), 200
Island of Dr. Moreau, The (1896), 179
Island of Dr. Moreau, The (1977), 186
Island of Dr. Moreau, The (1996), 142, 147, 187, 188, 190
Island of Lost Souls (1932), 182–6, 197, 200
Isaacs, Neil D., 98

Jacobs, Lea, 66
Jaehne, Karen, 101
"The Jam" (1958), 240
J'embrasse pas/I Don't Kiss (1991), 93–4
Jenkins, Jennifer L., 117, 118
Jenkins, Patty, 70, 72, 73, 74, 112
Jensen, Anders Thomas, 121, 122
Jerrold, Douglas, 23
Jewell, Richard, 232
Joker (2019), 1, 3, 113, 228–51
Joon-Ho, Bong, 156, 157, 158
Jungle, The (1906), 109
Jungle Bungles (1928), 192
Jungle with Setting Sun (1910), 181
Jungs vom Bahnhof Zoo, Die/Rent Boys (2011), 94
Jurković, Tania, 238
Just Another Girl on the I.R.T. (1993), 154
Justice, Christopher, 37

Kabir, Nasreen Munni, 26
Kaes, Anton, 14
Kafka, Franz, 161, 163, 165, 181, 185, 186, 188, 189, 207, 232
Kammerspieltheater, 34
Kase, Juan Carlos, 134
Kastle, Leonard, 73
Kawin, Bruce, 112, 145

Kayser, Wolfgang, 229
Kazan, Elia, 31
Keaton, Buster, 106, 107, 221, 222, 224
Kenton, Erle C., 182, 183, 184, 185, 186, 189, 197, 200
Killer of Sheep (1977), 113, 114, 115
King, Geoff, 216, 222, 223
King of Comedy, The (1982), 157, 245
King Kong (1933), 169, 184
Kirby, David, 143, 182
Kirchner, Ernst, 147
Kirsanoff, Dimitri, 202, 203, 217
Kiss, The (1896), 205
Klara, Robert, 221
Knauss, Stefanie, 120
Koehler, Robert, 52
Kokkina Fanaria, Ta/Red Lanterns (1962), 96
Koko, le gorille qui parle/Koko, A Talking Gorilla (1978), 178
Kolker, Robert, 233, 236
Kollowitz, Käthe, 52, 201
Koppel, Barbara, 60
Kroik, Polina, 50
Kruger, Barbara, 249
Kruif, Paul de, 156, 166, 168
Kryczka, Piotr, 25
Kubrick, Stanley, 64, 65, 199, 238
Kuhn, Thomas S., 3
Kulidzhanov, Lev, 162, 163
Kurosawa, Akira, 37, 38, 39
Kusama, Karyn, 155
Kyôfu kikei ningen: Edogawa Rampo zenshû/Horrors of Malformed Men (1969), 187

L'Absinthe (1875–1876), 72
Ladegaard, Jakob, 212
Ladkani, Richard, 65
Ladri di biciclette/Bicycle Thief, The (1948), 18
LaMotta, Jake, 30, 32, 178, 233
Lampin, Georges, 83
Lamprecht, Gerhard, 201
Lang, Fritz, 85, 127
Lang, Robert, 28
Langton, Simon, 127, 128, 129, 132

L'Apollonide/House of Tolerance (2011), 99
L'Assommoir (1877), 68, 214
L'Assommoir: Drame en cinq actes et neuf tableaux (1881), 68
Last Detail, The (1974), 65
Lathe, Carla, 34
Laveuses sur la rivière/Washerwomen on the River (1897), 18, 44, 52, 67
Leaving Las Vegas (1996), 25, 233
LeBlanc, Michelle, 220
Lee, Spike, 154, 155
Lellis, George, 28
LeRoy, Mervyn, 151, 152, 200, 201, 204, 207
Leterrier, Louis, 171
Lethbridge, Robert, 214
Lévi-Strauss, Claude, 223
Levine, Caroline, 53
Lewis, Jerry, 212, 222, 223, 224, 225
L'Homme à la tête de Caoutchouc/Man with the India-Rubber Head, The (1901), 222
L'Homme qui rit/Man Who Laughs, The (1869), 243
Li, Yang, 64
Liebman, Stuart, 122
Linert, Auguste, 108
"Locomotor Ataxia Joe: A Human Document Founded on Facts" (1911), 35
Loden, Barbara, 68, 69, 70
Lombroso, Cesare, 23, 150, 186, 197
London, Jack, 118
Lord, Del, 215
Lord of the Flies (1954), 181, 188, 193, 194
Lord of the Flies (1963), 195
Lorrain, Claude, 181
Lost City of Z, The (2016), 181
Lost Weekend, The (1945), 26
Love on the Dole (1941), 53
Luc-Godard, Jean, 83, 84
Luca, Tiago de, 75
Lukács, György, 54, 55
Luks, George, 48
Lumet, Sidney, 56, 199, 200

Lumière Brothers, 3, 11, 15, 16, 17, 43, 44, 45, 46, 47, 48, 52, 56, 67, 70, 75, 106, 107, 115, 138, 139, 140, 146, 211, 212, 213, 216
Lupino, Ida, 112
Lynch, David, 161, 162, 163, 164, 165, 175

Machinist, The (2004), 231–2
Madame Bovary (1856), 68
Madame Hyde (2017), 171–2
Maggie: A Girl of the Streets (1893), 82–3, 84, 88, 104
Major Realist Film Theorists, The (2016), 7
Malle, Louis, 97, 98
Mamma Roma (1962), 89, 90, 91
Mamoulian, Rouben, 145, 167, 168, 169, 170, 172, 176, 208
Man Push Cart (2005), 49, 50
Manet, Édouard, 183
Mang jing/Blind Shaft (2003), 64
Manual de zoología fantástica/Book of Imaginary Beings, The (1957), 1
March, William, 151
Markopoulos, Gregory, 93
Marshment, Margaret, 8
Martel, Lucretia, 17
Marx, Karl, 4, 8, 40, 54, 58, 112
Mask, Mia, 235
Mathews, Peter, 84
Mayer, Hervé, 10
McCann, Bryan, 74
McCutcheon, Wallace, 120
McGowan, Todd, 15, 212
McHugh, Susan, 188, 189
McClintock, Scott, 189
McQueen, Steve, 231
Mean Streets (1973), 230, 236
Meat (1976), 115
Meat (1992), 109
Meirelles, Fernando, 194
Méliès, Georges, 44, 106, 211, 222
Mendel, Gregor, 146
Mephisto (1981), 149
Messenger, Carrie, 26
Messmer, Otto, 191, 192

Méténier, Oscar, 33
Metz, Jerry D., 112
Microbe Hunters (1926), 156
Midnight Cowboy (1969), 93
Midnight Express (1978), 218
Milch, David, 97
Miller, Arthur, 56
Miller, Michael F., 134
Millet, Jean-François, 8, 75
Millet-Gallant, Ann, 232
Million Dollar Baby (2005), 155
Minarich, Megan, 43, 45
Missing (1982), 133
Mitry, Jean, 127, 128
Modern Times (1936), 53, 54
Monet, Claude, 15, 16
"Monster, The" (1898), 203
Monster (2003), 70, 72, 73, 74, 112
Moonlight (2016), 74
Morgue, The (1992–1993), 100, 111
Morlan, Don, 216
Morris, Gouverneur, 239
Mort du Cerf, La/Death of a Stag (1951), 202, 217
Most Dangerous Game, The (1932), 184–5
Motherless Brooklyn (2019), 239
Move On (1903), 48
Mule, The (2018), 201–2
Munch, Edvard, 34, 69
Murder, Inc. (1960), 178
Murder, Inc., and the Moral Life (2016), 177
Musser, Charles, 48, 141
Muybridge, Eadweard, 35

Nadal-Melsió, Sara, 47, 48
Naishuller, Ilya, 239, 240
Naked City, The (1948), 164
Naked Jungle, The (1954), 198
Naked Kiss, The (1964), 89–91
Nana (1880), 84, 98
Naremore, James, 130
Naturalist, The (1878), 16
Nauman, Bruce, 249, 254
Newton, Joy, 64
Newyorkitis (1901), 80

Nichols, George, 34, 36, 37, 38, 39
Nietzsche, Friedrich, 156
Nobody (2021), 239–40
Nochlin, Linda, 125
Noé, Gaspar, 13, 123, 124
Nomadland (2020), 9, 11, 70
North, Michael, 213
Norton, Edward, 171, 239
Nutty Professor, The (1996), 143

O'Brien, Sarah, 114
Odell, Colin, 220
Oedipus Rex (c. 429 BCE), 1
Oil! (1927), 63
On the Waterfront (1954), 31
O'Neill, Eugene, 233
"Open Boat, The" (1897), 180
Open City (1945), 58
Or (My Treasure) (2004), 88–9
Origin of Species, The (1859), 19, 155–6, 160
Ossessione/Obsession (1943), 129
O'Sullivan, Tim, 153
Oswald's Collapse (1920), 34
"Out, Out" (1916), 63
Oval Portrait, The (1842), 84
Oz (1997–2003), 7

Pabst, G. W., 85
Panelkapcsolat/Prefab People, The (1982), 57
Papanikolas, Zeese, 99
Papillon (1973), 207
Paris Secret des Annés 30, Le/Secret Paris of the 30s, The (1976), 99
Park, Eun-Jee, 71
Parker, Alan, 218
Parker, James, 218
Parks, Gordon, 194
Pasolini, Pier Paolo, 89, 90
Pathology (2008), 133–4
Paths of Glory (1957), 65, 199
Patterson, Annie Ring, 249
Pay Day (1922), 212–13
Penalty, The (1913), 239
Penalty, The (1920), 150, 239
People of the Abyss (1903), 118

Pernick, Martin, 146, 147, 149
Perry, Frank, 16, 17
Petla/Noose, The (1958), 25
Philadelphia (1993), 231
Phillips, Julie, 154
Phillips, Todd, 1, 228, 229, 230, 231, 236, 237, 239, 241, 243, 244, 245, 249, 251
Phu, Thy, 205
Picard, Max, 243, 245
Pick, Daniel, 20, 250
Pinter, Harold, 158
Pixote: A Lei do Mais Fraco (1981), 193–4
Planet of the Apes (1968), 164
Poe, Edgar Allan, 84, 112, 158, 187
Poetics, The (c. 335 BCE), 214
Poetics of Space, The (1957), 157, 234
Porter, Edwin S., 48, 141, 142
Postman Always Rings Twice, The (1936), 129, 130
Postman Always Rings Twice, The (1946), 130
POW (2003), 109
Powers, Steve, 190
Pradziad, Maciej, 165
Pratt, William W., 24
Praunheim, Rosa von, 94
Precious (2009), 234
Prestuplenie i nakazanie/Crime and Punishment (1970), 162
Pretty Baby (1978), 97–8
Pribisic, Milan, 139
Prince, Stephen, 182
Princesa (2004), 94–5
Promesse, La/Promise, The (1996), 59
Prozess, Der/Trial, The (1925), 70
Psycho (1960), 157
Pulp Fiction (1994), 157
Pyaasa/Thirsty One, The (1957), 25–6, 27

Quatre Cents Coups, Les/400 Blows, The (1959), 89

Radford, Benjamin, 229
Raging Bull (1980), 30, 32, 178, 233

Rao, Kiran, 52
Rapfogel, Jared, 57
Ray, Nicholas, 30
Realism and Popular Cinema (2000), 8
Rechy, John, 94, 244
Refn, Nicolas Winding, 178
Regeneration (1915), 82
Regester, Charlene, 234
Rehlin, Gunnar, 121
Reinarz, Jonathan, 160
Reinhardt, Max, 34
"Relation of the Poet to Daydreaming, The" (1908), 29
Renoir, Jean, 20, 21, 22, 23
Reisz, Karel, 53, 55, 56
Reles, Abe, 177, 178, 179, 190
Repas de bébé/Baby's Meal, A (1895), 44, 138
Répas en Famille/Family Meal, The (1897), 138
repas frugal, Le/Frugal Meal, The (1894), 139
Requiem for a Dream (2000), 89, 245
Requiem for a Heavyweight (1962), 31
Ressler, Scott, 164
Restivo, Angelo, 130
Revenant, The (2015), 112
Revenants, Les/Ghosts (1890), 34
Rêves de poussière/Dreams of Dust (2006), 66
Rhodes, Gary D., 165, 208
Richebé, Roger, 91
Rich, Matty, 118, 153
Richard Jewell (2019), 232
Richardson, Tony, 250
Rider, The (2017), 9, 10, 11
Riker, David, 18, 57-8
Robertson, John S., 36, 166, 167, 168
Rogers, Anna Backman, 68, 69, 70
Rogers, James Allen, 146
Roman experimental, Le/Experimental Novel, The (1880), 3
Rose, James, 113, 144
Rosen, Philip, 170
Rosenberg, Stuart, 178
Rosetta (1999), 70-1
Roskam, Michaël R., 30

Rossellini, Roberto, 58
Rough Sea at Dover (1895), 15, 16
Rousseau, Henri, 181
Rulfo, Carlos, 59, 60
Rundskop/Bullhead (2011), 30
Russell, Ken, 171
Ruttmann, Walter, 147, 148

Salgues, Laurent, 66
sang des bêtes, Le/Blood of the Beasts (1948), 115
Sangre Negra/Native Son (1951), 203-4
Sarno, Joseph, 89, 90
Sartre, Jean-Paul, 240
Saturday Night and Sunday Morning (1961), 53, 55, 56
Saturday Night Fever (1977), 154
Saved (1965), 153
Scarlet Street (1945), 85
Schaffner, Franklin J., 164, 207
Scherer, Hermann, 231
Schlesinger, John, 93
Schoedsack, Ernest B., 169, 184
Schlüpmann, Heidi, 86
Schölermann, Marc, 133
Schrader, Paul, 185
Schroeder, Barbet, 178
Schumacher, Joel, 240
Schütze, Martin, 34
Schwartz, Vanessa R., 126, 132
Scientific American (1876), 228
Scorsese, Martin, 32, 49, 122, 157, 178, 230, 233, 236, 241, 242, 245, 253
Scott, Ellen, 204
Scott, Ridley, 108
Sears Roebuck Catalogue (1897), 79
Seine a Courbevoie, La (1885-1886), 128
Seine at La Grande Jatte, La (1888), 128
Self-Portrait (1924-1926), 231
Sellaisena kuin sinä halusit/Way You Wanted Me, The (1944), 87-8
Seltzer, Mark, 8, 126, 240
Sembène, Ousmane, 18, 50, 51, 52
Senate Intelligence Committee Report on Torture, The (2014), 189-90

Serling, Rod, 176
Serrano, Andres, 37, 100, 111
Set-Up, The (1949), 31
Seul contra tous/I Stand Alone (1998), 123–4
Seurat, Georges, 128, 215
Shadyac, Tom, 143
Sheep Run, Chicago Stockyards (1897), 113
Shen nu/Goddess, The (1934), 86
Sherwood, Robert E., 82, 103
Shizukanaru kettô/Quiet Duel, The (1949), 37–9
Short, Elizabeth, 133
Sin in the Suburbs (1964), 89–90
Sinclair, Upton, 63, 109, 197
Sipe, Daniel, 247
Sitney, P. Adam, 9
Six, Tom, 157
Sjöström, Victor, 85, 229, 239
Slesar, Henry, 240
Small Time Crooks (2000), 157
Smil, Vaclav, 110, 116
Smith, James Blair, 48
Smith, John D., 110
Soles, Carter, 111, 113
Something Good—Negro Kiss (1898), 205
Sommeil, Le/Sleep (1866), 101
Songs My Brothers Taught Me (2015), 10
Sontag, Susan, 98, 235
Sophocles, 1
Sopranos, The (1999–2007), 6, 7, 219
sortie de l'usine Lumière à Lyon, La/Workers Exiting the Factory (1895), 11, 43–4, 45, 46, 47
Soutine, Chaim, 220, 221
Springer, Jerry, 73
Stabile, Salvatore, 153
Stacey, Jackie, 33, 35
Stachka/Strike (1925), 13
Standing, Guy, 58
Strange Case of Dr. Jekyll and Mr. Hyde (1886), 117, 168, 175, 185
Stead, William Thomas, 80
Sternberg, Josef von, 206

Stevenson, Robert Louis, 117, 181, 168, 169, 171, 179, 185
Stiller, Ben, 217, 218
Stoddard, Lothrop, 146
Stone, Oliver, 132, 133
Stone, Phil, 37
Stormy Sea (1869), 15
Stormy Sea, A (1894), 15–16
Strada, La (1954), 58
Straight Out of Brooklyn (1991), 18, 153
Strasse, Berlin/Street, Berlin (1913), 147
Strasse mit rote Kokottel/Street with Red Streetwalker (1914), 147
Straus, Peter, 179
Street Scene: Hester Street (1905), 48
Strike, The (1886), 52
String of Pearls, The (1846–1847), 117
Stroheim, Erich von, 66, 188
Struggle, The (1931), 28
Struss, Karl, 208
Sullivan, J. W., 49
Superstar: The Karen Carpenter Story (1987), 231
Szabó, István, 149
Sweeney Todd (1928), 118
Sweeney Todd: The Demon Barber of Fleet Street (2007), 117, 118
Swimmer, The (1964), 16
Swimmer, The (1968), 16
Szenvedély/Passion (1998), 129

Tabakman, Haim, 120, 121
Tagebuch einer Verlorenen/Diary of a Lost Girl (1929), 85–6
Talbot, Eugene S., 33
Tancock, Leonard, 3
Tang, Pao-Chen, 46
Tangerine (2015), 95–6
Tank Cleaner (2021), 17–18
Tarantino, Quentin, 157
Tarr, Béla, 57
Taubin, Amy, 157–8
Taxi Driver (1976), 49, 230, 245
Taylor, B. F., 55
Taylor, Don, 186, 187
Téchiné, André, 93, 94
Ten Nights in a Bar-Room (1858), 24

Ten Nights in a Bar-Room (1926), 24–5
Tenderloin at Night (1899), 81
Terre, La (1887), 2
Terre, La (1921), 2, 4, 5, 6
Texas Chain Saw Massacre, The (1974), 111–12, 113, 114
Théâtre-Libre, 34, 108, 122
There Will Be Blood (2007), 63
Thérèse Raquin (1867), 124, 125, 129, 131
Thérèse Raquin (1953), 127
Thérèse Raquin (1980), 127–8, 132
Thomson, Richard, 139
"The Three Stooges", 215, 216, 217
Tilak, Raj, 170, 176
Titicut Follies (1967), 198
Toilers of the Sea (1873), 183
Tom, Patricia Vettel, 191
Tracey, Grant, 90
Trank, Josh, 39
Three Trout from the Loue River (1873), 131
Treasure Island (1883), 179
Trinkaus, Erik, 10
Trout, The (c. 1872), 131
Truffaut, François, 89
Turturro, John, 92
Twilight Zone, The (1959–1964), 176
2001: A Space Odyssey (1968), 64
Tzara, Tristan, 212

Uchida, Tomu, 102–3
Ulmer, Edgar G., 37
Umberto D. (1952), 11
Under the Brooklyn Bridge (1953), 15
Unforgiven (1992), 97, 99

Vallée, Jean-Marc, 231
Valle-Inclan, Ramon del, 108, 109
Verrufenen, Die/Slums of Berlin, The (1925), 201
Viegas, Susana, 44, 67
View from the Bridge, A (1955), 56
Vigderman, Patricia, 139, 140
Visconti, Luchino, 129, 130
Violent Playground, The (1958), 152–3
Vivre sa vie/My Life to Live (1962), 83–4

Voight, Jon, 93
Vu du Pont/View from the Bridge, A (1962), 56–7

Wagner, Keith B., 46
Wakeford, Edward, 6
Walk on the Wild Side (1962), 97
Walkowitz, Judith R., 80
Walravens, M., 114
Walsh, Raoul, 82, 245, 246
Wanda (1971), 68–70
War of the Worlds, The (1898), 99
Warhol, Andy, 95
Waterboarding Thrill Ride (2008), 190
Waterloo Bridge (1930), 82
Watts, George Frederic, 82
Weber, Die/Weavers, The (1892), 52
Weegee, 41, 194
Welcome to Fear City (1975), 236
Wells, H. G., 99, 179, 180, 183, 186, 187, 193, 197
West, Walter, 118
Wexman, Virginia Wright, 169
Whale, The (2022), 233
Whalen, Robert Weldon, 177
Wharton, Leopold, 146
Wharton, Theodore, 146
What Did Jack Do? (2017), 161, 163, 164, 165
What Drink Did (1909), 28, 41
What Ever Happened to Baby Jane? (1962), 26
White, Charles, 58
White, Frederick, 229
White, James H., 79, 81, 107, 113
White Heat (1949), 245–6
Whitman, Walt, 122
Who Killed Teddy Bear? (1965), 244
Whole Dam Family and the Dam Dog, The (1905), 141–2
Wideman, John Edgar, 154
Wiene, Robert, 232, 244
Wilder, Billy, 26
Williams, Raymond, 18, 40
Winner, Michael, 236
Wire, The (2002–2008), 7, 153
Wise, Robert, 31, 72

Wiseman, Frederick, 115, 116, 198
Witken, Joel-Peter, 111
Working Girls (1987), 101
World Trade Center (2006), 132–3
Worsley, Wallace, 150, 239
Wraich, Parvinder Singh, 17, 18
Wrestler, The (2008), 30–1, 32–3
Wright, Richard, 204, 205
Wrong Man, The (1956), 206
Wuornos, Aileen, 70, 72, 73, 74, 75, 112

Yan, Mo, 109
Yau, Herman, 118
Yedaya, Keren, 88
Yonggang, Wu, 86–7

Yôtô monogatari: hana no Yoshiwara hyakunin-giri/Hero of the Red-Light District (1960), 102–3
Young, Robert M., 129

Zecca, Ferdinand, 62, 63, 66
Zelnik, Friedrich, 52–3
Zemeckis, Robert, 186
Zhang, Chengyuan, 230
Zhao, Chloé, 9, 10, 11
Zin li Fik/Much Loved (2015), 83
Zola, Émile, 2, 3, 4, 5, 8, 18, 19, 20, 21, 52, 61, 62, 68, 73, 84, 98, 124, 125, 127, 128, 129, 131, 141, 169, 179, 185, 204, 214, 215, 238, 246, 247

EU representative:
Easy Access System Europe
Mustamäe tee 50, 10621 Tallinn, Estonia
Gpsr.requests@easproject.com